ECONOMIC ARITHMETIC

ECONOMIC
ARITHMETIC

BY

ROBIN MARRIS

FELLOW OF KING'S COLLEGE, CAMBRIDGE

LONDON
MACMILLAN & CO LTD
NEW YORK · ST MARTIN'S PRESS
1958

MACMILLAN AND COMPANY LIMITED
London Bombay Calcutta Madras Melbourne

THE MACMILLAN COMPANY OF CANADA LIMITED
Toronto

ST MARTIN'S PRESS INC
New York

PRINTED IN GREAT BRITAIN

To

MY MOTHER AND FATHER

FOREWORD AND ACKNOWLEDGEMENTS

THIS is intended primarily as a text book for students of economics who have already received some elementary introduction to economic theory and to the institutional branches of applied economics. Much of the book employs no form of mathematical symbolism whatsoever. Elsewhere, algebraical symbols and equations of a simple type are used where the exposition requires them, but the mathematical technique should with minor exceptions be quite within the grasp of the reader whose experience does not reach beyond the Ordinary level of algebra and arithmetic in the General Certificate, provided only that he does not allow himself to be intimidated by the mere appearance of x's and y's.

The level of exposition is aimed at second-year Honours students, in Part I, rising gradually to reach, in Part III, a level more appropriate to third-year students.

As this is a text book, such originality as is claimed lies in methods of presentation of arguments rather than in arguments themselves. Hence detailed acknowledgement is not offered specifically to all the various authors of the standard theories and concepts described. Exceptions lie in Part III, particularly in the Appendix to Chapter 8, the parts of Chapter 9 which depend on this Appendix and in some of Chapter 10. These sections are thought to develop certain original ideas. Here I should acknowledge the stimulus of the writings of Mr. J. L. Nicholson of the Central Statistical Office, in particular his contribution to 'Studies in Official Statistics No. 1',† which first started me on the ideas developed in the Appendix to Chapter 8, and his article 'National Income at Factor Cost or Market Prices' (*Economic Journal*, June 1955) which, although I do not agree with all of it, nevertheless influenced me considerably in Chapter 10. Mr. Nicholson did me the honour of reading the

† See Bibliography to Chapter 2.

vii

proofs of Part III, but he is of course in no way to be associated with errors—either of substance or of detail—which remain.

I also wish to acknowledge most kind and thorough assistance from Mr. C. T. Saunders, Deputy Director of the Central Statistical Office, who read the whole of Chapters 1 to 4 and provided comments which removed a number of errors in this area.

Summer 1957   R. L. M.

CONTENTS

PART I: ANATOMY

PART II: A SELECTION OF INSTRUMENTS

LIST OF ILLUSTRATIONS

DIAGRAMS

CHARTS

LIST OF TABLES

xii

INTRODUCTION

THE arithmetic of economics is a blend of rather distinct ingredients. If economics is a science it is certainly a statistical science, but in a considerably wider sense than is ordinarily understood by the natural scientist and mathematician. It is true that the mathematical techniques of the general statistician represent for the social scientist a useful substitute for controlled experiment, and it is true that on occasion the natural scientist himself employs these techniques in similar experimental situations to those which are typical of social science. But the similarities are deceptive. The natural scientist will employ statistical techniques when he is unable to control only, say, one or two of a number of relevant experimental variables: he regards 'statistics' as a synonym for the application of Probability theory to the problem of drawing valid inferences from moderately unreliable data. The natural scientist is nearly always able to control at least a substantial proportion of the total number of variables influencing his data, and nearly always he is able to obtain some independent experimental check (either positive or negative) on his conclusions. Where he is not, he is usually in trouble (as may be witnessed for example in the history of the attempt to determine the connection between cigarette addiction and lung cancer).

The social scientist, by contrast, is not only typically unable to control *any* of his variables but is also entirely dependent on statistical data for a basic description of his subject matter and what is happening to it. The subject 'economics' is concerned with the economic system, or national economy, in an entirely general sense. Therefore in the same way in which the medical scientist has need of a general anatomical picture of the human body as a whole, so the economist requires a description of the whole economic system, or at least of the part which he happens to be studying. The statistical form is almost the only conceivable quantitative form in which such a description could be given. The economic system could of course be described in purely qualitative terms, but a qualitative description which could never be 'quantified' would in this case be of little value. The position of the economist is thus entirely different from that of the human anatomist. The latter may state, for example, 'The human body consists of a trunk, to which are attached five major projections—two arms, two legs and a head.' This conveys meaning if typical measurements are appended or alternatively if a drawing or photograph is provided. The economist is denied the alternative: his only 'photograph' must consist of a further statistical description. Of course, in his search for knowledge about the economic body politic the economist may go out into the streets and make use of his eyes and ears. But by this means he can only obtain what is almost literally a worm's-eye view. To change the analogy, he is then examining the economy as a medical man examining the human body with a microscope. If the economist wishes to reduce the magnification and increase the scope of his lens, he must employ the method of statistical summary. From the nature of the case no alternative exists.

In consequence, many of the problems of economic arithmetic are problems of numerical arrangement and presentation, problems involved in converting statistical data into a coherent anatomical description. The solutions of these problems often involve substantial intellectual difficulty, even though their application requires little beyond fourth-form mathematics. This is particularly the case with economic index numbers, where to obtain the economic rationalisation of the simple algebraical formulae commonly used for computing index numbers of prices and of real incomes involves a considerable investigation into fundamental theory. Another outstanding example, of course, is to be found in the field of statistics relating to the 'National Dividend' or National Income.

Thus 'economic arithmetic' is a considerably wider subject than 'economic statistics', unless the latter expression is interpreted rather broadly. The object of this book is to assist the student with the broader subject and in particular to help him integrate his study of economic theory, on the one hand, with his study of the techniques by which the theory is applied, on the other. In the several excellent standard text books of statistical technique which are available to economics' students today, the basic mathematical groundwork which must be covered is sufficiently extensive that the theoretical economic background is necessarily, in these books, only sketched in lightly. The present book, while by no means carrying the integration of economic theory with statistical practice as far as would ideally be desirable, is believed nevertheless to go further in this respect. But by contrast with previous works, the present book deals with standard statistical techniques only selectively. In particular, the Frequency Distribution, which forms the fundamental basis of mathematical statistics, appears here mainly in the form of a shadow (albeit an 'essential' one) in the background. Means, Variances and Standard Deviations, instead of appearing first in the list of *dramatis personae*, as is usual, enter more casually later in the play, and only as required.

The plan of the book is to take first the basic problems of an anatomical nature, i.e. the problems arising from the need for a general statistical picture of the economic system; we then consider a selection of surgical instruments, i.e. a selection of orthodox 'statistical' analytical devices; finally we concentrate on the peculiar problems of theory and practice involved in the construction and interpretation of economic index numbers.

Part I, therefore, is entitled 'Anatomy' and contains *inter alia* an extended description of British official statistics of National Income and Expenditure.

Part II is entitled 'A Selection of Instruments' and concentrates mainly on the intellectual foundations of Regression Analysis and Time-Series analysis.

Part III deals with index numbers, taking first their formal algebraical properties, second their relation to the theory of economic value and finally their application to the measurement of 'real' National Product.

PART I

ANATOMY

CHAPTER ONE

BASIC PROBLEMS OF THE ECONOMIC ANATOMIST

The Economic Skeleton and its Statistical Flesh

We wish to construct a general statistical description of the national economy. Where to start? An economic system, considered as a set of statistical facts, is at once vast, detailed and yet conceptually nebulous. The national economy may be thought of as a system of circulating flows of quantities of real goods and services (in particular of labour services) together with a number of ponds, pools and puddles—stocks of commodities or other physical assets. Alternatively, any economy which has developed beyond the most primitive stages may be represented as a system of circulating flows of money, most of the flows of money being matched by corresponding flows of goods and services in the opposite direction.

A 'flow' in the sense used here is a rate over time, for example a rate of production measured in tons per annum. A money-flow divided by the corresponding quantity-flow states the average price ruling for transactions in a particular commodity or service during the year in question; for example the total receipts of producers for sales of commodity x during year z (the money-flow), divided by the total tonnage of x sold (the quantity-flow), is the average price of x ruling during z. Because of the critical rôle of prices in economic theory, statistics of prices are obviously essential components of the system. In theory, if we are given complete statistics of both quantity-flows and money-flows, all the prices are known, but in practice it is often necessary to collect statistics of prices directly, for instance if full information about the quantities is not available. Since the prices of commodities vary considerably from day to day and even from transaction to transaction, according to the higgling of the market, statistics of prices should always, in principle, refer

3

to an average price-level over a stated period of time. Where they do not, i.e. where they refer to the level of prices at a particular moment of time, such as a particular day during the month, it is important to remember that, unless this 'spot price' for the middle of a period happens to deviate very little from the average price for the period, multiplication of the spot price by the quantity-flow will not yield the correct statistic of the corresponding money-flow for the period—seemingly an obvious trap, but it has taken victims.

The upshot is that whether we are thinking of quantities of stuff, of sums of money, or of levels of prices, we may use the same analogy—that of a system of connected pipes and tanks—as a basis for a general statistical picture of the economy. Further, the specific pattern of the imaginary system will be basically similar whether we are thinking exclusively of the quantities or exclusively of money or of prices. The actual painting of the picture is done by collecting statistical data which measure the rates of flow past selected points in the imaginary pipes, the selection of the points to be made in such a way that the totality of measurements effectively describes all of the important economic characteristics of the system. The measurements will be of three types—rates of flow of quantities of goods and services, rates of flow of money payments and average levels of prices.

However, although in principle the imaginary system of plumbing should be much the same whether we are talking of prices, of quantities or of money, in practice it is not convenient to employ the same diagrammatic representation for the exposition of each case. Diagram I (see the end of the book), which is about flows of stuff in quantitative terms, is therefore a little different from Diagram II of Chapter 3 which describes the National Income Statistics. But these differences are allowed largely in order to assist in the exposition, and each diagram could, with adjustment, be resolved into the terms of the other.

Diagram I relates to flows of quantities of economic things— finished commodities, intermediate or semi-finished goods, raw materials, labour, and useful services such as distribution or transport. For convenience, this particular representation ignores the question of measuring the levels of the contents of the tanks:

stocks of fixed capital (buildings and equipment) and stocks of raw materials and partly finished work are ignored. (Adequate statistics of stocks of goods and money are, however, of great importance to the economist.) The fat boxes represent industries or groups of industries. The long thin boxes at the top and bottom of the diagram represent sources or destinations of the various types of goods and of labour. The 'pipes' and their contents represent some of the more important flows of goods and labour, each pipe of course summarising a huge number of individual component flows. The relative sizes of the boxes to other boxes, and of the pipes to other pipes, indicate in a sense the approximate relative quantitative importance of each box or sector in the national economy. However, the sense in which these relativities are valid is a particular one. As already stated, the pipes are summaries, they represent aggregates of many smaller flows. But when we are dealing with quantities only, i.e. when we are prohibited from using the monetary unit of account, there is no obviously meaningful way of adding together quantities (tons, therms, gallons, etc.) of commodities and services of widely varying types. In this diagram, the method used is to reduce everything into terms of labour: the sizes of the boxes indicate the relative quantities of man-power employed in each sector or industry, of the pipes the relative quantities of man-years of services (in the top half of the diagram) or an estimate of the amount of labour time embodied in the various flows of goods and services (in the bottom half); imports are assumed to contain British labour in proportion to the labour embodied in the exports which go to pay for them. (The sizes of the thin boxes of course do not conform because the thin boxes refer only to sources and destinations.) Readers who are familiar with theories of economic value will appreciate that the use of labour units in defining the sizes of the fat boxes and the pipes is not very satisfactory. Although measurements in terms of labour time do have some intrinsic interest, we know nevertheless that the average amount of economic value corresponding to one man-year of labour is by no means a constant throughout the system. The device is used in Diagram I mainly because we are not yet ready to use the monetary method of measurement.

Diagram I therefore only gives us a rough indication of the relative importance of industries and flows. As a matter of fact even were the diagram scaled in proportion to economic values, there would remain an important sense in which the relative significance of the various individual industries in the national economy would not be properly indicated. A quite small industry may be of considerable importance simply because it supplies many other industries with some essential product. Industries are very much dependent upon one another, and a proportion of the output of any one industry or firm will normally consist of partly finished goods, or partly worked materials, which are sold to another industry for further work and processing before being sold to final consumers. The industrial sector itself, therefore, is a labyrinth of interconnecting pipes or flows, and the flows by no means run all in one direction.† The predominant movement is from primary industry to secondary, from secondary to tertiary, and thence to final consumers, but there are many important back-eddies: the steel industry depends on coal, but coal production in turn depends on adequate supplies of steel pit-props. Diagram I indicates some of the major interconnections within manufacturing industry, but only in a purely illustrative fashion. The arrows are not a comprehensive statement of the facts. The interconnections between manufacturing industries and primary industries such as Fuel and Power, are, in particular, drastically simplified.

What statistical readings should we take in order to realise the picture implied in the diagram? A complete statistical description would presumably tell us the quantities (and later the values) of everything bought and exchanged by every person resident in the country during the year; in other words every tiny sub-flow summarised in Diagram I would be separately treated. But the national economy consists of some twenty-three million people producing some thousands of different commodities in some hundreds of thousands of industrial establishments or other places of work, not to mention housewives. A truly complete statistical description would therefore be hopelessly detailed, impossible to collect, im-

† For some of the statistical consequences, see Chapter 3, pp. 43–4, and Chapter 10, pp. 332 *et seq.*

possible to analyse, and furthermore, would be entirely inappropriate to the conditions in a modern society where the essence of economic life is the production and consumption of commodities by social organisation in clearly identifiable groups—the firm, the household, the government department. Sweeping summarisation is therefore essential. How, and how much, to summarise data is one of the most important of all the many judgments required in statistical work.

In Diagram I, the top oblong box depicts the supply of labour, that is, the total population *less* those not offering themselves for work. The simplest and most summary statistical reading which could be taken at this point would be one single figure, i.e. the total numbers in the Working Population at a given date, say in June 1953 when this figure was 23·373 millions; but such a figure (or 'statistic'), by itself is not useful for very much. To answer most of the interesting questions, for instance why the Working Population was then greater by 79,000 than in June the year before, we must go into the matter further. We can first look to see if there were demographic factors at work, such as for example an increase in the excess of the annual supply of new young workers over the annual number of people retiring from work, due perhaps to some change in the age-structure of the total population. Demographic detail is collected and published by the *Registrar General of Births and Deaths* and may also be found in the *Annual Abstract of Statistics*, Section 2. However, in the year in question in our example, there seems to be evidence that a rather different type of factor was involved: in 1952 there occurred something of an economic recession, which happened to be largely concentrated in industries employing an above-average proportion of women workers; unemployment among women workers rose, work for women was more difficult to find and a certain number may for this reason have decided to remain at home rather than go to the bother of seeking work. The effect of this behaviour would be to offset the normal demographic increase in the female working population and thus to reduce the statistic labelled 'working population, female'. The phenomenon occurs because a high proportion of married women do not have to work but only do so to supplement income when they feel economic conditions are sufficiently attractive (e.g. when there is work available near home and at convenient hours).

The foregoing is only a hypothesis; some support for it, but *not* proof (proof there can never be in this subject) is provided in the following example of elementary statistical analysis:

TABLE 1. *Changes in Unemployment and*
Working Population, 1951–1953

	Unemployment per cent.		Change in Working Population			
			Change, thousands		Change, per cent.	
	Spring 1952	Spring 1953	June 1951–June 1952	June 1952–June 1953	June 1951–June 1952	June 1952–June 1953
Men[1] -	$1\frac{1}{2}$	$1\frac{1}{2}$–2	+73	+19	+·46	+·12
Women[2]	3	$1\frac{1}{2}$–2	−7	+60	−·10	+·80
Total -	2	$1\frac{1}{2}$–2	+66	+79	+·28	+·34

[1] Percentages relate to total male working population at base date.
[2] Percentages relate to total female working population at base date.
Source: Monthly Digest of Statistics (Great Britain).

The increase of 79,000 in the total working population from 1952 to 1953 was much the same as the increase from 1951 to 1952, and the casual observer, who had not analysed the matter in terms of sex, might have thought that in both years this increase represented the normal demographic trends. In fact we can now see that the similarity between the two changes was largely coincidental. From 1951 to 1952 men increased substantially while women fell (probably because of relatively high unemployment in 1952, see the table); from 1952 to 1953 men rose rather moderately while women rose by an abnormally large amount, probably because the normal demographic increase was supplemented by recovery from the effects of economic recession in 1952.

The example illustrates not only that in order to answer the interesting questions we need information relating to the working population at a number of successive dates and also a comprehensive statistical description of the social characteristics of the working population; the example illustrates another point of considerable general importance. As economists, making use of statistics, we would frequently like to distinguish between things which are 'Supply' and things which are 'Demand'. In practice this is very difficult to do, because the price mechanism within the economy tends to eliminate such discrepancies as may arise between the quantities of goods and services supplied and the quantities demanded. Statistically all we can observe therefore is the level at which the balance was struck, i.e. we observe the result of the interaction of two groups of forces. We cannot tell by simple statistical inspection how much the forces of Supply and how much the forces of Demand each contributed to the final result. However, in the case of male labour, the elasticity of supply is presumably high, indeed probably almost infinite, below the point where most able-bodied men are employed; and obviously above that point the elasticity must be near to zero. This means that the statistical total of the male working population does not in fact represent a bad measure of the quantity-supply of male labour, since within wide limits the statistical total is little affected by demand. But, as we have seen, when we come to female labour we get into difficulty: the statistical size of the female working population is by no means independent of factors on the demand side. However, it is nevertheless conventional practice in this country and most others to regard the recorded Working Population as representing a measurement of the total *supply* of labour, on the one hand, and then to regard the statistics relating to Employment, discussed below, as representing quantities of labour *demanded* on the other.

So we are agreed that we should make statistical measurements of the Working Population in such a way as to provide demographic and other similar information. Looking at the diagram, the obvious next step is to analyse how the supply of labour is used. How much goes into each of the broad streams which run down from the top of the diagram:—Manufacturing, Agriculture, Building, Fuel and services? An analysis along these lines is provided by the *Ministry of Labour and National Service* in the first tables of the labour sections of the *Monthly Digest of Statistics* and of the *Annual Abstract of Statistics*. These figures incude not only manual workers and clerical workers, but all other manpower and womanpower gainfully employed in the sectors indicated, i.e. they also include self-employed persons working in connection with the industry, employers, managers and the like. Having obtained statistics relating to these large streams, we may proceed to a further subdivision according to the individual industries within the Manufacturing sector, within the Fuel and Power group and so on. Some fifteen to twenty tables in the *Monthly Digest* and/or the *Annual Abstract of Statistics*, as well as even more detailed tables in the *Ministry of Labour Gazette*, can provide us with such information, although in the latter case, the data published relate to employees only.

If we agree, as we surely must, to the principle of an industrial analysis of employment, we immediately come up against a difficulty. How are we to reconcile this method of summary classification (of Demand) with the social and demographic classification (of Supply) agreed to previously? We could of course combine the two, so that for every industry in the country we should present a table along the following lines:

Industry ....

Date ....

Total employment..................

of which,

      males ....

      females......................

Age distribution

males,

      aged 15–19 ....

           20–24 ....

           25–29 ....

    and so on

females,

      aged 15–19 ....

           20–24 ....

           25–29 ....

    and so on

Unemployment among workers usually employed in this industry ....

To present such a table as this, every year, for every one of the industries normally separately specified in British economic statistics would evidently involve a huge quantity of print: the tables concerning employment in the *Annual Abstract of Statistics*, which now take up about three-and-a-half pages of that document, already contain about fifteen hundred separate figures; in order to accommodate additional information such as suggested above they would have to contain over fifteen thousand. And there is no particular reason for stopping with the age-distribution; many other social details such as marital status, for instance, would be just as relevant. We must draw the line somewhere. Nevertheless some of the more detailed information would be intrinsically most valuable, for instance to an industrialist interested in the future of the labour supply to his industry. The compromise which is reached in British statistics is to provide in the *Annual Abstract*, the *Monthly Digest* and the *Ministry of Labour Gazette*, annual or monthly figures (as the case may be) of employment in the various industries divided only as between males and females. However in particular industries, such as for example coal mining, whose supply of labour has become a matter of particular national concern, more detailed information about recruitment, wastage and so on is provided elsewhere under the general heading of statistics relating to the coal industry. Furthermore in the periodic *Census of Population*, carried out by the Registrar General, information is collected which should, in principle, allow almost any kind of detailed demographic analysis—by industries, by ages, by sex, by marital status, by area of residence, and so on.

We can now move further into the diagram. We have discussed statistical measurements of the labour used by British industries in the process of producing current output. But labour is not the only thing needed by industry in order to produce output; quite apart from capital, other essential 'inputs' are as already mentioned, raw materials or semi-finished goods. There are also vital commercial services which may be performed by one industry for another, such as transport or advertising. These other inputs must come either from other British industries or from abroad. This is worth repeating. All other inputs, apart from imports, are directly or indirectly the product of British labour and capital and, to the extent that imports are paid for by exports made with British labour and capital, so are imports themselves. Essentially therefore, the inputs merely characterise the interdependence of the industrial system, which has already been mentioned.†

Basically, in any very summary treatment of the economy, we can boil everything down to labour at one end and output at the other (since capital is also embodied labour). But in fact for the analysis of a large number of important problems, particularly problems of economic policy, information about the flow through the inter-connecting pipes between industries within the system is frequently valuable and often essential. In particular it is clearly essential to possess detailed information about imports. The diagram shows the flow of imports from overseas; statistics relating to imports (and to exports) are collected and published by the *Board of Trade*. Food imports are shown for simplicity as flowing straight to the consumer: in real life of course many agricultural products, both imported and home produced, pass through the manufacturing sector for processing. With these statistics of imports we again come up against a difficulty of classification: the economist specialising in the theory and practice of foreign trade will require in his statistics an analysis of the countries from which the imports came, just as much as an analysis of the industries to which they went. (In addition, there is here a more serious conflict of criteria for classification—the conflict between a classification by commodities as against a classification by consuming industries—which also arises in later sections of the diagram and whose discussion, therefore, will be taken below.) As it happens, detailed statistical information about both imports and exports is available in the various publications of the Board of Trade and in all the important cases a two-way classification (by countries and by commodities) is also available: however, in the summary data reproduced in the *Monthly Digest of Statistics* and the *Annual Abstract of Statistics*, tables are available showing a classification by countries *or* by commodities, but not by both at the same time.

Other statistical measurements of inputs are in this country

† P. 6 above.

rather scanty. Although a certain amount of valuable information is available in periodic or once-and-for-all form such as in the reports of the Census of Production for the years 1935 and 1948, far too little appears in regular statistical publications. Coal consumption is analysed in the *Monthly Digest* according to a list of some eight major industries only; for electricity consumption there is no regularly available industrial analysis whatsoever; and for most of the important raw materials, while the total consumption of the material is often known, consumption according to consuming industries is not. And practically nothing is regularly published about the consumption of intermediate manufactured products. Finally there is still, at the time of writing, a serious dearth of information about *stocks* at all stages of the industrial process.

When we come to statistics of production or output, i.e. to the measurements to be made in the lower part of Diagram I, we are much better served, at least so far as the output of primary and secondary industry is concerned. In these fields the range of information is today very considerable and for details the reader is referred to the bibliography to Chapter 2 below.† The final output of the 'service' trades is inevitably difficult to assess in quantitative statistical form, both in theory and in practice, but nevertheless some useful information is available—in the National Income Blue Book—on that subject also.‡

In drawing this contrast between the adequacy of the information available about outputs and the inadequacy of information about non-labour inputs, one point must be kept clear: statistics of *total* production are as comprehensive for 'intermediate' goods as for final goods, which latter are normally defined as goods sold to the 'final' consumer, i.e. for any use except current production of some other economic commodity within the United Kingdom. Thus we do in fact have a part of the information necessary to build up a picture of the interconnections within the industrial system, we have the totals of output of intermediate goods; but we do not have details of how these totals were divided as between the user industries; in other words we do not know the distribution of

† Especially the Appendix of item 7 (Carter and Roy).
‡ See Chapter 10, below.

inputs. In terms of the diagram, while we have regular information for example as to the total output of the steel industry (aggregate of the output flows in the region of the point marked a_1), of the basic textile industries (see point marked a_3) and even of large parts of the chemicals industry (point a_2), we are much less well provided with data as to what proportion of the total tonnage of steel produced is consumed, say, by the ship-building industry (b_1) in contrast to the other metal using industries—road and rail vehicles, engineering and etc. The same can be said of chemicals consumption in textile finishing (b_2) and, in turn, of cloth consumption in the clothing trade (b_3).

The Problem of Industrial Classification

With the impressive volume of statistics of output the problem of classification reaches a climax. The obvious practical way in which to describe in statistical terms the various flows past the output ends of the system is in terms of the various different kinds of commodities produced—tons of steel of different types, yards of cloth of different types, numbers of radio sets, TV sets, motor cars, and so on. The single car or chassis, the pair of shoes, the ton of metal seem obvious basic units of measurement. But, and it is a very big but indeed, most 'industries' produce many different commodities. And so (in manufacturing industry) do most firms within industries. We cannot therefore get round the difficulty simply by defining industries in terms of the commodities they produce; this would mean classing most firms in several different industries at once. And since it is not generally possible to distinguish between the different parts of the labour employed in a firm as engaged on the production of the firm's various products (many of which will truly be joint products), a commodity classification of industries would destroy the basis of our classification for the analysis of the demand for, and use, of labour.

An 'industry' as economists think of it in the Marshallian tradition is an institution. It is a group of firms who are seen as belonging to one industry because they share a number of common characteristics and something of a common outlook; the nature of the characteristics shared may vary from case to case and an identical list of commodity-types produced is by no means essential. Some similarity in the technical processes and hence in the character of the inputs (many different commodities may be made by a given type of process) is however usually regarded as more or less of an essential feature. Thus, to use some long but helpful words, the crux of the problem we are up against is that the firms in what is accepted as an 'industry' will generally tend to employ fairly homogeneous inputs, while producing a relatively heterogeneous group of outputs.

One thing to do is adopt the compromise which we have already met in the case of the clash between a social and industrial classification of the working population. This would mean employing one type of classification for inputs and another for outputs: inputs would be classified on an industrial basis, outputs on a commodity basis. And that of course is what often has to be done: most of the statistical series of output in the detailed tables of the *Monthly Digest of Statistics* refer to the production of individual commodities rather than to the output of individual industries. The compromise is not a happy one. It denies the asking of many of the most interesting questions, in particular questions about the relation between changes in output and changes in input—questions which are of crucial interest to economists. For, evidently, if employment, for example, is classified according to one kind of definition of industries and output according to another, no measurement of the productivity of labour (output per head) is possible. Thus even though new and important information is often gained, something is always lost if it is necessary to change the method of classification as flows of goods and services move through the industrial process. Therefore, wherever examples of necessary re-classification crop up in Diagram I, they have been indicated by passing the flow through a special-shaped box labelled 're-classification'. Further examples (after leaving the output measurement points) are a re-classification of the goods flowing from producer to household consumer according to the type of consumer need they are expected to satisfy, and a re-classification of investment-goods production according to the industries where the investment is to be made as against the industries in which the goods were produced. Thus the

c

output of the textile industries, previously divided into 'Wool Cloth', 'Cotton Cloth', 'Rayon Cloth' and so on, is now divided into 'Men's Wear', 'Women's Wear', 'Children's Wear' and 'Household Textiles', while perhaps more than half a dozen industries go to supply the well-known final group named 'Private Motoring'. Supplies of long term investment goods—buildings, plant and equipment—can in fact be divided in at least three ways, each intrinsically significant in the proper context. They may be divided according to the type of buying institution (private persons, public companies, the government), according to the type of commodity (vehicles, machinery of different types, works and buildings), or, as already suggested, according to the industry in which the investment is occurring.† The case of exports and imports has already been mentioned. Finally we see that the consuming sector itself, the aggregate of households, is none other than our old friend the total population analysed in a different way yet again.

Fortunately there do exist means for measuring changes in quantities of outputs and changes in quantities of corresponding inputs on a comparable basis. One of these is to identify and measure changes in quantities produced of all the commodities normally made by one industry (define the industry how you will), then to combine these into some sort of average and finally to compare the average with the change in the relevant quantity of input. But there are serious theoretical difficulties involved in constructing such averages; and it is with these and cognate matters that the whole of Part III of this book is essentially concerned. However, assuming for the moment that the difficulties can at least to some extent be overcome, we must remark here that it is also essential that the basic compartment of the measurement system, the industry, is defined, or rather delineated, on a standard basis throughout. It is perfectly possible for widely differing but equally tenable views to coexist as to whether a particular firm belongs to Industry A or to Industry B, or whether a particular product is characteristic of Industry B or Industry C, or whether the characteristic products of Industry D are commodities P, Q, R or all three. In any standard

† All three are available in the National Income Blue Book; see Chapter 4, p. 86 below.

system, some arbitrary decisions on these points must be made. What is absolutely hopeless is if different persons responsible for the collection of statistics at different points in the system are allowed to suit their own convenience or predilection in the border-line cases; for the border-line alas is in fact a broad penumbra. If a firm is classed in one industry for purposes of measuring fuel consumption, in another for the compilation of employment statistics as collected by the Ministry of Labour, and yet another by the Census of Production Office of the Board of Trade (the basic authority for statistics of output) and perhaps in yet again another by the Registrar General, obviously no comparable series for the industries involved can be produced ever: the egg has been scrambled far too early. But up to fairly recently British economic statistics did in fact suffer greatly from just that defect and recognition of the weakness led to the establishment soon after World War II of an inter-departmental committee, which eventually agreed on a form of *Standard Industrial Classification*; this is now fairly widely used and is known for short as the *SIC*.† The Censuses of Production and of Population, and the statistics of Employment and Working Population are now definitely based upon the standard classification; foreign trade statistics, and a number of minor offenders are not. (Foreign trade statistics are based on a standard international classification which is a classification of the commodity type.) The principles of the British Standard Industrial Classification are as follows:

(1) Industries are descriptively defined largely according to the nature of the industrial process which goes on in them. Thus 'Order III' in the SIC, for example, which covers the production of such widely varying commodities as wine-glasses and sanitary earthenware, is defined as an industrial group named 'Treatment of Non-metalliferous Mining Products'.

(2) For each industry, as above defined, there is also defined a list of what are regarded as the characteristic products or commodities of the industry. These are technically known as Principal

† Published as a pamphlet, *The Standard Industrial Classification*, by H.M. Stationery Office.

Products. Every known product is one of the Principal Products of some industry, but none is the Principal Product of more than one. The firms (or, more precisely, the industrial establishments)† in an industry will not, of course, necessarily produce exclusively the Principal Products of their own industry, they may engage in subsidiary production of Principal Products of other industries; which means that the total output of the Principal Products of any one industry is not necessarily to be found in that industry. This last inevitable fact of nature creates obvious complications, but fortunately it is also an empirical fact that as we increase the degree of subdivision within the classification (for example by sub-dividing 'Cotton' into 'Cotton Spinning', 'Doubling' and 'Cotton Weaving'), the 'process' method of classification and the commodity method of classification begin to come closer together. Specialisation in the production of a particular commodity seems nearly always to involve, as might be expected, some significant degree of technical specialisation as well.

(3) Every separate establishment in the country should, in principle, always be classified to the same industry, whatsoever the purpose of the statistics being collected.‡ The basis of classification of establishments is that the establishment should belong to the industry of whose Principal Products the establishment's output forms a larger proportion of its total output (measured in money)

† Generally speaking, where a single firm owns or controls more than one industrial establishment, each establishment is treated as a separate statistical unit, and may be classed in a different industry. The rule is not followed universally, however, and the point should be watched wherever it is likely to influence results significantly. See also note following.

‡ It has been pointed out however that since several establishments are often controlled by one *business enterprise*, the effect of this criterion is to preclude the collection of statistics of *profits* on the standardised basis. The difficulty is a very real one, as it may well happen that the several establishments of a single company are properly classifiable to several industries. The solution would seem to be that where necessary the total profits of a firm should be attributed on some approximate basis to the establishments wherein the profits appeared to have been earned: most firms make some such attribution in their internal accounting in any case. Alternatively, it may in the long run be necessary to develop two parallel sets of national statistics, one based on a classification of firms and one on a classification of establishments, together with a reconciliation based on the method just suggested. The first classification would be used for analysis of financial problems, the second for analysis of technical problems (productivity measurement and so on) and the third for 'mixed' problems.

than does its output of the Principal Products of any other industry. Obviously this must involve some rather arbitrary placings for some establishments, and may even involve establishments being classed in industries which the management would not recognise. But with these border-line cases, any allocation to a particular industry based on a process definition is bound to be arbitrary, and the prime objective is consistency. In any comparison of changes in output with changes in input, the really important thing is to ensure that we are comparing the output and the input of the same set of industrial establishments.

The standard classification of establishments is not so consistently followed in official and other published statistics as are the other two features of the SIC. A published table may be stated to be drawn up 'according to the SIC', but this may mean no more than that standard descriptive definition of industries has been used; the treatment of border-line establishments may be quite unstandard: the moral is that the point, and other possible causes of non-comparability, must always be investigated before statistics from one source are combined with statistics taken from another.

Summary

The main groups of problems which initially confront the would-be anatomist of economic systems have been seen to divide into (1) those connected with the original definition of concepts— of a skeleton on which to hang the statistical flesh, (2) the provision of the flesh itself and (3) problems of classification and re-classification. We have of course done no more than provide an introduction to the solutions.

CHAPTER TWO

SOURCES OF ECONOMIC STATISTICS IN THE U.K.

It is not the purpose of this book to provide an exhaustive description of the sources of the statistics such as we have been generally discussing in Chapter 1. In that respect the British reader is now comparatively well-served, for apart from other works referred to in the bibliography given below,† the general reader has recently benefited considerably by the publication of Prof. Ely Devons' *Introduction to British Economic Statistics*,‡ a substantial book which provides comprehensive yet concise accounts over practically the whole of the field. The present chapter is concerned mainly with a small number of selected matters connected with the use and abuse of statistical sources which are thought to require special emphasis: for a comprehensive index of the economic series regularly published in this country at the time of writing, the reader is referred to the excellent book by Prof. C. F. Carter and Mr. A. D. Roy which is also cited in the bibliography.

The collection of statistical 'raw data' is something which the individual economist, without suppplementary resources of money, manpower and, most important, authority, can only rarely undertake himself. The collection of economic statistics nearly always involves the addressing of intimate questions to a large number of private firms, households or government organisations: these institutions must either agree to provide information from their existing records or to open special records for the purpose. In any event a good deal of form-filling is bound to be involved. Unfortunately, many British business men, unlike their foreign (and particularly American) colleagues, are distinctly hostile to statistical investiga-

† P. 29.
‡ See Bibliography, item 6.

tions: they appear to regard the keeping of statistical records as an arduous and unnecessary labour, and they seem uninterested in the statistical results relating to their own industry. Some large firms are more statistically minded, but dislike passing on information to outside parties.†

Hence the collection of economic statistics is difficult and expensive. Economic statistics are not for example like some of those statistics relating to experiments in genetics which may be collected entirely within the confines of a battery of rabbit hutches. Only an organisation which has compulsory powers or considerable moral authority can have much hope of success, that is to say either the Government or some body like a trade association. However, established economic research institutions, such as the *Institute of Statistics* at Oxford, the *Department of Applied Economics* at Cambridge or the *National Institute of Social and Economic Research* in London may often succeed in particular cases, especially in the type of investigation involving voluntary interviews with householders or selected firms.

The Government and Economic Statistics

In point of fact an overwhelming proportion of the total of available economic statistics in this country is collected, summarised and published by the government. But until recently the

---

† There are notable exceptions in a few progressive firms, but unfortunately this is a matter in which the saying about one swallow was never more apposite. Part of the difficulty is that in a country where state intervention in private industry is fairly considerable, firms fear that evidence given on statistical returns may be used against them, although this is to some extent a rationalisation of a generally hostile psychological attitude. The government administration is itself very much to blame, on the one hand pursuing an exaggeratedly timid policy in its approach and on the other exacerbating resistance by addressing numerous independent statistical enquiries to the same firms (in consequence of the decentralised administrative arrangements described below). Ideally, every firm in the country should be required to render one, and only one, statistical return say each month, or each quarter, wherein was to be entered on a standardised basis everything the government needed from it. To ask this, however, is to bleat in the wilderness; in the meantime considerably more could be done by way of education and consultation to enable government officials and managements to appreciate better each other's problems and points of view: attempts should be made to show business men the value and uses of the statistics which are collected and to show officials just what are and are not the enquiries which create the most difficulty.

government tended to collect economic statistics mainly as a by-product of administrative activity. The government would be given by Parliament some statutory task, such as the collection of a tax on motor cars, and, as a result, there would become available statistics of Licences Current and New Registrations of Road Vehicles. Similarly Income Tax returns have long been used as a source of National Income data. At a later stage of development the government found that the efficient performance of certain administrative functions itself required that certain statistics be collected; for example it is not possible to administer a scheme of food rationing without statistics of actual food consumption and supplies.

In the past, therefore, the government could often be accused of having taken a dangerously narrow view, and of lacking interest in important statistics for which no immediate administrative need could be seen. Thus, during the war, because coal was rationed, statistics showing the industrial distribution of stocks and consumption of coal were perforce collected by the appropriate department. But soon after the war rationing was temporarily abandoned, and with the rationing scheme went most of the detailed statistics which had previously been collected. The consequences were disastrous; for the lack of adequately detailed statistics was a major factor in the severity of the historic fuel crisis of 1947. There were of course exceptions. That is there were important cases where the government, usually by Act of Parliament, did in fact collect economic statistics as it were for their own sake†, and in the years following the 1939–1945 War things have changed very much. The government now collects and publishes a considerable quantity of economic statistics for economics' sake, both in periodic censuses of Production and Distribution and in more frequent statistical series. The government also publishes extremely important 'processed' statistics, which term may be applied to the results of computations upon (and rearrangements of) basic data originating in a large number of different places, with results of particular interest to applied economists: major examples are the

† For example, the Census of Production, governed by legislation, was originally initiated from a general interest in the industrial structure of the national economy.

Index of Industrial Production and the statistics of National Income and Expenditure. Nevertheless despite the enormously increased emphasis on statistics for their own sake, the government statisticians who carry out this work of 'processing' still seem much dependent upon raw data which was originally collected for quite other purposes and is therefore not very suitable for the job in hand.

The pattern of organisation of official statistics still follows the pattern of administrative responsibility for economic affairs. There is not in this country, as there is in some, a single government statistics-collecting agency. The so-called 'Central' Statistical Office is essentially a co-ordinating, not a collecting, body. Statistics of labour are collected by the Ministry of Labour, of production by the Board of Trade and so on. Newcomers to the subject often therefore find it extremely difficult to know where to begin to look for this or that type of statistical information, although the difficulty is much alleviated by the existence of two vital publications of the Central Statistical Office already extensively referred to— the *Monthly Digest of Statistics* and the *Annual Abstract of Statistics*. These two publications gather together and reproduce in reasonable, but necessarily lesser, detail, a large proportion of the statistical material collected by the various separate government departments. The *Monthly Digest* contains summaries of statistical series which are normally available on a monthly or quarterly basis; it is published during the last week of each month and brings many of the series up-to-date to the end of the preceding month; other series are brought up to as late a date as is possible at the time of publication. For most of the series the *Digest* shows back figures, monthly or quarterly as the case may be, for the past year or two, and also, for comparison, monthly or quarterly averages for about half a dozen past post-war years and usually a few pre-war years as well. The *Annual Abstract* reproduces most of the statistics contained in the *Digest*, but on an annual basis only (usually giving a complete annual series over a period of about ten years, together with at least one pre-war year for comparison) and also contains a number of important additional series which only become available, or are only worth while publishing, on an annual basis. Altogether the scope of the *Abstract* is much wider than that of the *Digest* since the latter is largely concerned with economic statistics only, while the former contains quantities of material relating to social conditions, education and so on. The reader will obtain a far better idea of the nature and scope of both these publications from even a cursory examination of actual copies than he can possibly obtain from text-book reading: and at least one number of the *Abstract* (which usually appears in the early autumn) and two or three carefully selected numbers of the *Digest* are essential workshop implements of any applied economist in the U.K. In other countries there are usually publications fulfilling similar rôles.

The *Digest* and the *Abstract* are what are known as secondary sources, that is are sources which reproduce (and probably summarise) statistical data which is primarily published elsewhere. Secondary sources vary considerably in quality; official secondary sources such as these digests and abstracts have the same degree of reliability and authority as the primary sources to which they refer, but others, such as magazines, periodicals, newspapers and privately published books may contain serious errors of presentation and even sometimes plain errors of arithmetic. Such secondary sources must only be used with great care and wherever it is at all possible the original source should at least be verified. (All other considerations apart, sloppy use of secondary sources is particularly liable to lead to serious public embarrassment.)

For many day-to-day purposes the average economist in this country will find all he wants in the *Digest* and the *Abstract*. But as soon as he starts to go into any matter thoroughly, for instance to carry out a modest piece of economic research on a definite special subject, he will almost certainly need to refer to the various original departmental sources, published and sometimes unpublished. He may also need to look at material published by Trade Associations and other non-public bodies. Obviously first clues in the detective hunt which necessarily follows are the footnotes to the summary material in the *Abstract* and the *Digest*, which always indicate the original source. Further, at the back of the *Annual Abstract of Statistics* for the year 1954 onwards there is provided a list of Departments and published sources. However, his task will be much easier if the detective is already reasonably familiar with the official pattern of administrative responsibility for economic policy and economic statistics. For the departmental organisation of economic policy is not based on economic theory, or even economic practice. It is largely the result of the accidents of legislative and administrative history. Thus the monthly *Index of Retail Prices* is compiled and published by the Ministry of Labour because the original idea of such an index was to help measure changes in the real wages and hence of the standard of living of the labouring classes, which latter was the official concern of the Ministry of Labour. Indeed, up to very recently the index itself did not purport to measure anything but changes in the cost of living for the 'working classes' and was inaccurate as a measure of changes in retail prices in general to any extent that the cost of living for 'non-working class' consumers moved differently.† The Ministry's standing in this matter was reinforced by the widespread introduction of sliding-scale clauses, based on the Ministry's index, into collective bargaining agreements. Statistics of wholesale prices, on the other hand, are collected by the Board of Trade because such statistics are in some way connected with 'trade', i.e. with business rather than directly with consumer welfare. Some government economic departments are responsible for policy towards a particular sector of industry; they may be thought of as 'vertical' departments. Others, 'horizontal' departments, deal with matters such as labour or foreign trade, which cut across all or a large part of the industrial landscape. Others represent a mixture of both principles operating together, while yet others deal not so much with a particular group of industries as with a particular group of final commodities (such as Housing, or, from 1939–1954, Food). A most delightful *mélange* is to be found in the *Board of Trade*, which department, in the economic field, is virtually a Ministry of Everything Else. (The Board is concerned, *inter alia*, with Imports, Exports, the Long Term Efficiency of British Industry, Consumer Goods and Retail Trade, Statistics of Trade (i.e. of output), Weights and Measures, Company Law Administration, Bankruptcy Law Administration and Monopolies.) It was originally intended at this point to provide a detailed description of the overall Whitehall administrative struc-

† For a theoretical discussion, see Chapter 9 pp. 263 and 272 *et seq.*

ture, for the guidance of readers, at the time of writing. But substantial changes in the structure have occurred so frequently that it is feared that anything which could be written down would become out of date too rapidly and too deceptively to be justifiable. The reader is reluctantly left therefore to the summary published annually at the back of the *Annual Abstract*, and to his own researches.

The Central Statistical Office

As already mentioned, the whole of the large decentralised statistical apparatus of the government is co-ordinated by a central statistical office (attached to the Treasury),† and the following paragraphs summarise briefly the work and functions of this office which is known for short as the CSO. The CSO is a fairly small, highly geared body; because it collects no statistics itself most of the staff are engaged on intellectual functions, for example the compilation of existing index numbers or the National-Income data, and on the development of new ideas along these lines. In addition the Director and staff are very much concerned with general statistical policy, co-ordination and hence much committee work. Apart from a modest computing and clerical section, the majority of the staff are university-trained professional statisticians and a large proportion are also trained in economics. In addition to their own publications, mentioned below, their work has substantially influenced the nature and standard of British economic statistics as a whole, in ways ranging from the minor but valuable matter of typography, to the organisation of the committee which established the Standard Industrial Classification. Apart from the *Monthly Digest* and *Annual Abstract*, by far the most important of the office's own publications are the *Index of Industrial Production* (which appears in the *Digest*) and the so-called National Income Blue Book

† At the time of writing the attachment is somewhat remote, at least in the purely administrative sense. The CSO is located in the Cabinet Office (office of the Cabinet Secretariat) which in turn is a substantially independent sub-Department of the Treasury. Treasury, CSO and Cabinet Secretariat are all housed in the same building, but the Treasury does not exert day to day control over these sub-departments. In consequence the CSO appears to be *sui generis* among Whitehall organisations.

—the precise title is *National Income and Expenditure*—which appears annually. The latter is probably the most substantial document of its type available to economists anywhere in the world today and will occupy us through two full chapters, Chapters 3 and 4, in the remainder of Part I of this book, below.

It is fair to add that notwithstanding the achievements described, the CSO has come in for a good deal of criticism on the ground that it has been insufficiently effective in dragging from government departments and industry certain types of data which are rather difficult by nature to obtain, but yet which are essential to the successful conduct of central economic policy. The criticism reached a climax when Mr. Harold Macmillan, as Chancellor of the Exchequer, remarked to the House of Commons† that in attempting to do his job with the statistics available to him he felt somewhat in the position of a traveller looking up trains in last year's Bradshaw. It is understood that the reverberations of the remark continued for some time within the Whitehall corridors, and that an attempt is to be made to provide, for example, estimates of National Income and Expenditure quarterly‡ as well as annually.

Other Official Publications

As already indicated the organisation of statistics collection being decentralised, the primary sources of most of the important statistical series are the various departmental statistical publications. There are indeed no less than thirty periodical statistical publications relating to Great Britain or England and Wales (or the United Kingdom as a whole) and more than a dozen relating to Northern Ireland and Scotland. The two most widely used of these official primary sources are the *Ministry of Labour Gazette* (monthly) and the *Board of Trade Journal* (weekly) which publish as soon as available all the primary data for which their sponsoring departments are responsible (see above). Both of these periodicals at the time of writing maintain a relatively old-fashioned typography and format, and are much more tiring and laborious to use than the secondary publications of the CSO. On the other hand, being more

† In the Budget Speech of April 1956.
‡ These have now appeared (January 1957).

cheaply printed, they are less expensive. Unlike the CSO publications, they contain editorial articles commenting on the statistics displayed; unfortunately these commentaries are usually so cautiously drafted and so narrow in scope as to be of limited value to the economist.†

It is essential for the user of any statistics which he has not gathered himself that he has a good idea of how the data were derived and of how the published summary results were computed. Only in this way can he be sure that the data are capable of being put to the use which is intended. Some official published statistics are necessarily based on estimates or for some other reason have a greater or lesser margin of error (all economic statistics contain some error), and it may be dangerous to attribute economic significance to small variations in such series. In other cases even larger variations may be the result of technical factors connected with the method of the construction of the statistics and of equally little economic significance. Some of the estimates are based on assumptions about the stability of certain economic or technical relationships: it is no use therefore, employing such series to test the hypothesis that the relation in question is in fact stable, however useful the series may be for other purposes.

It has been widely felt that published descriptions of the methods of compilation, etc. employed in the different official statistics have in this country been seriously inadequate.‡ However, major improvements have recently occurred, particularly in the cases for which the CSO is itself directly responsible. But unfortunately many of the other government departments continue to lag behind in this matter and the list of publications cited in the bibliography below is somewhat deceptive in superficial appearance. There are yawning gaps in the coverage and, as the list itself indicates, the work appears to move in fits and starts, and the publication programme is unsystematic. The truth is that in the day-to-day work of a government statistician, the preparation of publications such as these is given a low priority, so that a really substantial volume (e.g. the recent excellent account by the CSO of the Sources and

---

† See Carter and Roy *op. cit.*, pp. 130–1.
‡ See Carter and Roy, *loc. cit.*

Methods of the National Income Statistics) may take a number of years as well as the expenditure of much overtime to complete.

SELECT BIBLIOGRAPHY TO CHAPTER 2

Official Accounts of Official Statistics

(all published by H.M. Stationery Office on behalf of the sponsoring Department).

1. *Government Statistical Services*, pamphlet, 1953 (Treasury).
2. *Guides to Official Sources* (series of pamphlets sponsored by the Inter-departmental Committee on Economic Research—the 'North Committee'):
    (i) *Labour Statistics*, 1950,
    (ii) *Census Reports of Great Britain 1801–1939*, 1951,
    (iii) *Local Government Statistics*, 1953.
3. *Studies in Official Statistics* (series of pamphlets sponsored by the CSO):
    (i) *No. 1 The Interim Index of Industrial Production*,
    (ii) *No. 2 The Index of Industrial Production*.
4. *National Income Statistics: Sources and Methods*, book, 1956 (CSO), pp. 380, price 25/–.
5. *Report on Proposals for a New Index of Retail Prices*, pamphlet, 1956 (Ministry of Labour).

Private Works

6. E. Devons, *An Introduction to British Economic Statistics*, Cambridge University Press, 1956, pp. 250, price 22/6.
7. C. F. Carter and A. D. Roy, *British Economic Statistics*, Cambridge University Press (for National Institute for Economic and Social Research), 1954, pp. 190.
8. M. G. Kendall (ed.) *The Sources and Nature of the Statistics of the United Kingdom*, Oliver and Boyd (for Royal Statistical Society); Vol. 1, 1952, pp. 350, price 21/–; Vol. 2, 1957, pp. 340, price 30/–.

CHAPTER THREE

THE NATIONAL INCOME
BLUE BOOK (I): THE SUMMARY TABLES

THE present and the following chapter are concerned with the body
of statistical estimates prepared annually by the Central Statistical
Office, which are known by the generic expression 'The National
Income Statistics'. These data provide a range of information which
goes far beyond the broad totals of aggregate national income, product and expenditure as such, and they represent a most advanced
stage of development in the construction of the generalised statistical picture of the economic system which we first discussed in
Chapter 1. In Chapter 1, it will be remembered, we employed a
diagram which was thought of as representing circulating flows of
goods and labour services measured in their ordinary quantitative
units; the National Income Statistics by contrast describe the system in terms of the corresponding flows of money values received
in payment, moving in the opposite direction. What the Central
Statistical Office does is to convert a mass of detailed statistical
data about quantities and values of goods produced and consumed,
work done and income received, into estimates of the corresponding totals of money payments and receipts; and to summarise the
whole† in a single publication. The estimates are published

† The presentation is based on the conceptual framework known generally to
modern economists as that of Social Accounting, and it is assumed that the
student has received at least some introduction to this subject. The literature is
large, but a selection from the following selection would be sufficient for the
present purpose:

J. R. Hicks, *The Social Framework*, Oxford, 1952 (2nd ed.).
J. E. Meade and J. R. N. Stone, *National Income and Expenditure* (London
1944) but use 4th edition, Cambridge 1956.
H. C. Edey and A. T. Peacock, *National Income and Social Accounting*, Lon-
don 1954.
R. Ruggles, *An Introduction to National Income and National Income Analysis*,
New York, 1949.

annually† in a blue-covered book entitled *National Income and Expenditure*. The book consists almost entirely of statistical tables and for prose relief contains only brief notes defining central concepts and describing revisions made since the last issue: the full description of the principles and practices followed must be sought in the book, *Sources and Methods*, already referred to in the select bibliography to Chapter 2.‡ *National Income and Expenditure* is not strictly a Blue Book in the Parliamentary sense, since it is not a Command Paper; it is in effect a non-Parliamentary publication of the Treasury, but it is nevertheless widely referred to as 'The National Income Blue Book', and it is with the National Income Blue Book and its contents that we are here concerned.

We shall conduct our discussion with the aid of another diagram, Diagram II (which follows Diagram I at the end of the book) representing the main economic flows measured in terms of money, arranged in a form consistent with the present structure of the official national income statistics and depicting roughly the relative sizes of the flows as they were in the United Kingdom in the middle-nineteen fifties. In what follows, the official publication will be referred to for short as the 'Blue Book' and Diagram II simply as 'the diagram'. The Blue Book, at the time of writing, consists of about sixty statistical tables divided into ten main chapters or sections; and it seems unlikely that the general features of this basic structure will drastically be changed for some time. The first chapter, consisting of about ten tables, contains the so-called Summary Tables: these are really the guts of the document, although the detailed data in the following chapters (of the Blue Book) are of enormous importance and value. However, we are for the moment concerned only with these Summary Tables and the system depicted in the Diagram is essentially the system they represent: the rest of the Blue Book is the concern of Chapter 4 below.

Following the general ideas of social accounting, the Summary Tables of the Blue Book present the important national economic

† Quarterly data are now also available (1957) and will appear periodically in the *Monthly Digest*.

‡ See p. 29 above, item 4.

D

aggregates (flows) in a set of self-balancing 'National Accounts' and at the time of writing the tables are ten, as follows:

Reference used below:	Title in the Blue Book	Pages where discussed below:
1.	'National income and expenditure'	36, 50, 60
2.	'Personal income and expenditure'	51–3
3.	'Corporate income appropriation account'	54
4.	'Revenue account of Central Government including National Insurance Funds'	57–9
5.	'Current account of Local Authorities'	,,
6.	'Combined capital account of the United Kingdom'	55–7, 58, 63
7.	'Transactions with the rest of the world'	59–65
8.	'Shares in gross national product'	—
9.	'Gross national product by industry'	43, 44, 45–9
10.	'Gross national product by category of expenditure at factor cost'	—

Since from time to time minor changes may occur in the order and general arrangement of the tables as set out in the Blue Book, all references below to the tables (by use of ordinal expressions 'the first table', 'the second table' and so on) are to the above list, not to the table of contents of any particular issue of the Blue Book. However, since this is a subject in which discussion of parts is not easily separated from that of whole system, it would be most inconvenient to deal with the tables, and the concepts they represent, in any rigid, table-by-table, order—hence the baby index above.

Principles of Diagram II

Flows of money in the economy largely correspond to flows of goods and productive services by means of transactions in the market (but of course run in the opposite direction). However, there are some flows of money which are not matched by any transfers of goods or supply of services, for instance payments of National Insurance benefits, of interest on the National Debt, and pensions—all so-called 'transfer payments'. (The payment of wages, of course, is considered to be matched by a corresponding flow of labour service and that of profits by the service of providing capital and 'entrepreneurship'.)

There are also cases where flows of goods and services exist which are not matched by flows of money, for instance the cases of wages paid in kind and of the labour of housewives in the home: the labour of housewives is conventionally excluded from the national income statistics and from any assessment of the total national product, but where wages for ordinary industrial labour are paid in kind when they might in slightly different circumstances just as well have been paid in cash, an estimate is made of the cash value of the goods handed over (e.g. of the value of the concessionary coal granted to miners) and included in the statistics of the actual national wages bill. Also, in British statistics, the food, uniforms and accommodation provided for the armed forces is conventionally regarded as a form of payment in kind and an estimate of its value is included in the national total of incomes.

A rather different kind of exception to the rule that flows of money are always matched by corresponding flows of goods and vice versa, is the case where money is transferred as a loan or as a repayment of a loan. In some contemporary terminology, financial transactions of this type, 'on capital account', are covered by a general expression 'money flows', of which income flows form only a part, and a deeper discussion of the relation between such money flows and income flows may be found in Peacock and Edey: in their terminology, our diagram depicts income flows (or, more strictly 'value flows') only.†

In the diagram, flows of money in our more limited sense (see above) run from sector to sector in 'pipes', the widths of the pipes being roughly proportionate to the sizes of the flows during the middle 1950's.‡ The pipes and the entities represented by the boxes must be thought of as being 'full' of imaginary liquid, therefore each box is emptying at the same rate at which it is filling. Therefore the aggregate width of all the inlet pipes into any box equals that of all the outlet pipes. This is the same principle as that of the

† Peacock and Edey *op. cit.*, pp. 16–17, but read the whole chapter and possibly some of the later chapters where relevant.

‡ Also the *areas* of the boxes are roughly proportional to the total inflow (=outflow) into the sector or account represented (see text below).

self-balancing tables of the Blue Book; in the diagram therefore, unlike the case of Diagram I, each sector appears only once. National Income accounts are set out, literally, as accounts, with the debits on the right-hand side and the credits on the left,† so arranged that the total of both sides is equal; any 'surplus' or 'deficit' of credits over debits being added to one side or the other as a balancing item. Thus for example the second table of the Blue Book (Personal Income and Expenditure) corresponds to the Households Sector of the diagram. In the diagram, the inlet pipes roughly correspond to the left-hand side of the second table and the outlet pipes to the right-hand side: the difference between total personal income and expenditure including direct taxes, i.e. total 'personal' or household saving, is shown in the Blue Book as an 'expenditure', in order to make the table balance.

The diagram is both more summary and more symbolic in its treatment than was in general Diagram I. The basic division of sectors is now into 'Households', 'The Market Sector' and 'The Government Sector'. The Households Sector represents the population of households functioning as both consumers of goods and suppliers of labour. The 'Market Sector' means the whole of the 'productive' sector of the economy whose output consists of tangible goods and services sold for money in the open market. The Market Sector thus includes the nationalised industries. The Government Sector, by contrast, covers all those general services of local and central government and the National Insurance funds which although regarded as useful economic services are not in fact sold on the open market but instead are provided out of taxation in pre-determined quantities according to public policy. The Government Sector box also depicts other governmental transactions, such as the organisation of the income transfers already mentioned. National economic transactions with the outside world are represented by a single box labelled 'Overseas' and it is assumed that all sales of goods and services to residents of foreign countries are done by the Market Sector, sales of exports, visible and invisible, being represented by a flow of money *from* the 'Overseas' box to the

† In recent issues of the Blue Book the 'right-hand' side of a table is often printed *underneath* the 'left hand' side in order to save space.

Market Sector box. The Market Sector itself is depicted in a much more simplified manner than in Diagram I, no subsectors such as 'Manufacturing', 'Agriculture' or 'Transport and Distribution' being separately distinguished and the existence of interconnections between industries both within and without manufacturing industry being represented purely formally.

There are two boxes in the diagram, 'Company Appropriation Accounts' and 'Saving and Investment' which represent, not concrete sectors in the national economy, but certain abstract economic activities or decision-taking processes identified by contemporary theory: they are activities which must be distinguished from production and consumption, but which are in fact undertaken by individuals or corporate bodies drawn from the concrete sectors. This mixture of the concrete and the abstract in the meaning of the boxes in the diagram is awkward but unavoidable. The full meaning of the two 'abstract' boxes will appear later: 'Company Appropriation Accounts' is in effect an aggregation of the accounts of all the nation's joint stock companies and public corporations; 'Saving' includes the current saving of households, companies, public corporations and the government; 'Investment' is all current expenditure on productive plant and equipment, industrial and commercial vehicles and new buildings, for use or installation in the United Kingdom.†

The Important Aggregates

Much of the value of the national income data lies in the systematic presentation of individual money flows which are of considerable interest for their own sake: thus the estimate of personal (household) saving, seen with the estimate of personal consumption expenditure and taxation (second table of the Blue Book— outlet end of Households Sector in the diagram) is essential to any application of Keynesian general equilibrium theory. But in addition it is possible so to arrange things that, in the language of the diagram, certain groups of pipes are brought together for the measurement of their aggregate width. These aggregates are of

---

† Excludes repair work but includes conversions and extensions and new building to replace demolished buildings.

critical importance in welfare economics, in the study of the trade cycle and for economic planning both short term and long term, and it was for their estimation that the data were originally collated. The Summary Tables of the Blue Book are built round the aggregates and in this chapter therefore we shall discuss each (but not in turn). Specifically, we shall distinguish,

    (i) Gross National Product.
   (ii) National Income and Depreciation.
  (iii) Total Domestic Expenditure.
  (iv) Total Personal Income and Outlay.

All of these, except the first, are marked on the diagram. The first, as the reader will already know, is the central concept of the whole system with which we are here concerned, but it cannot be marked on the diagram for reasons which will later be obvious.

The Market Sector and the Government Sector

Consider first the two 'Production' sectors of the economy depicted in the diagram—the Market Sector and the Government Sector. Both engage in the activity of hiring factors of production and setting them to work in the creation of 'final' goods and services, that is to say of economic commodities which are considered to be 'finished'—i.e. to require no further economic transformation before they serve their ultimate economic purpose (the latter of course may be either the purpose of immediate consumption or that of service as a capital instrument; investment goods are by convention regarded as 'final' goods even though their purpose is to serve over a period of years in the production of consumer goods). These final commodities are 'sold' to the 'final' buyers either by means of an ordinary market transaction or, in the case of the Government Sector, through the medium of taxation. The total of their sales, i.e. the total value of their production, would in a closed economy be identical with the total expenditure of national residents on final goods themselves and this total is the aggregate which we name *Total Domestic Expenditure at Market Prices* (see diagram measurement no. 1 and first table of the Blue Book). Looking at the matter the other way round we see the total expenditure as flowing into the two productive sectors, through them (or around and about inside them), and finally from them as income payments to factors of production. The bulk of the payments to factors takes the form of payments to households, since the bulk is payments for the services of labour. Hence the broad river of final expenditure reappears as the income of households, and in turn becomes available for financing current expenditure by households: the river has returned to its own source, generating a perpetual circulation. However, if we look only at the 'main stream' of this circuit—the stream of consumer-goods expenditure which itself generates consumer-goods expenditure through the medium of the national wages bill—we observe there are a number of apparent leakages from it, leakages into profits, into personal savings, public savings (the government budget surplus) and foreign trade. Eventually all these leakages must find their way back into the circulation, and they must not alter their aggregate magnitude in so doing, otherwise the system would empty or burst (in the real economy there would be inflation or deflation until the situation was rectified†). However, in what follows we shall at first concentrate on the main stream, and then consider in turn the subsidiary circuits of apparent leakages.

Total Domestic Expenditure at Market Prices

We must break into the circle somewhere. Let us do it at the point where income becomes expenditure. Total Domestic Expenditure, as we have seen, is the nation's total expenditure on final goods of all kinds.‡ It divides into a market-sector-produced part and a government-sector-produced part, and the former divides in turn into consumer goods and investment goods.

The large pipe running down the centre of the diagram represents the flow of personal (i.e. household) expenditure on market-sector-produced consumer goods: this part of the measurement is quite straightforward, the goods are simply valued at the prices (after tax) at which they are sold in the shops. Expenditure on in-

† This is a convenient but loose statement of the analogy. In the Keynesian system, the process of adjustment is conceived as instantaneous.

‡ The aggregate should not be confused with 'Gross National Expenditure, see p. 59 below.

vestment goods would also involve no difficulties if all such goods were 'fixed', i.e. consisted of plant, equipment, vehicles and buildings. Unfortunately however, another form of investment must also be taken into account—a form which is separately indicated in the Blue Book table but not in the diagram—that is investment in the accumulation of inventories; stocks of raw materials and intermediate goods, finished goods awaiting delivery to consumers, work-in-progress in factories. Goods and services diverted from the national production into inventory accumulation must be thought of as a form of final expenditure whatever commodity-form they take: they are 'bought' by final buyers (investors) and put in the cupboard, as it were, against consumption needs in a subsequent year. Nevertheless, the item is awkward to handle in our conceptual system, for a number of reasons. In the first place it may be either negative or positive, inventories may on balance be reduced during the year, as happened in 1946 and in 1950, and it is not easy to depict a negative flow in the diagram. Second, any type of goods may be included, whereas with other components of final expenditure, the type of good is usually specific to the nature of the component.† Finally, there is a considerable poser in connection with the method of valuation. For clearly it is only the value of the change in tangible or 'physical' stocks of goods or work in progress which properly enter into Domestic Expenditure: if the value of the stock which existed at the beginning of the year changes simply on account of a change in the value of money during the year, there is no pre-emption from the national production: total domestic expenditure on fixed investment goods and consumption goods (in a closed economy) will in this situation be exactly equal to total national production. But unfortunately the conventional practices of business accounting do not allow of the necessary distinction: the accounts simply show the difference between the value of stocks held at the beginning of the accounting period and at the end, and they therefore mix together the effects of changes in physical stocks

† The most obvious exception is the case of private motor cars, which are counted as consumer goods if sold to a private purchaser, but as investment goods if sold for business use only (e.g. to commercial travellers). Another is coal, part of which is sold direct to final consumers for domestic heating and part to industry as intermediate input.

at given prices with those of changes in the value of given stocks due to changing prices; they tell the 'change in the value of' stocks, but not the 'value of the change in' stocks. All the raw data concerning profits in the Blue Book are derived, directly or indirectly, from companies' tax returns, and the definition of 'profit' adopted for tax purposes is the definition adopted by accounting convention and therefore includes 'inventory' profits or 'stock appreciation' as well as the value of the change in stocks. The compilers of the Blue Book are therefore forced to undertake a special adjustment in order to arrive at the figure for the value of the change in stocks alone as shown in the table: further details of the calculation involved are given in the table entitled 'Capital formation in stocks and work in progress' to be found in the tenth chapter of the Blue Book. The foregoing are some of the many reasons why no attempt has been made to depict inventory changes in the diagram.

In the diagram we see the measurement of Total Domestic Expenditure at Market Prices traversing the wide consumer-goods pipe and also the 'Gross Home Investment'† pipe. To complete the measurement of Domestic Expenditure it is therefore but only necessary to include additionally the value of the final output of the Government Sector. Here we come up against another serious problem of valuation. For since the government's output is not sold on a market of any kind, free or restricted, there would appear to exist no objective criterion for its monetary valuation:‡ we therefore adopt the convention that since the government is a non-profit-making body, the products must be regarded as being 'sold' at cost. Now the costs of production of government services consist partly of the wages and salaries paid to civil servants, doctors, school teachers and to the military forces, and partly of the costs of goods, such as armaments, food, uniforms, paper, red tape, and office equipment, purchased from private firms in the Market

---

† The investment is 'Gross' because it includes all types of investment goods, whether they are required for replacement of previously existing plant or whether for the creation of new capacity; and it is 'Home' because the aggregate includes only investment goods purchased for installation in the domestic territory. (In the Blue Book, the expression 'Gross Capital Formation' has now been adopted—Summer 1957.)

‡ There is a fuller discussion of this question in Chapter 10 below.

Sector. The total value of domestic 'expenditure' on government products is therefore presented in the diagram as the sum of two groups of items, the first group representing a flow of expenditure direct to households in the form of wages and salaries (soldiers and sailors being somewhat artificially regarded as belonging to 'households' in this context) while the second group passes initially into, and then through, the Market Sector and thus finds its way into the main stream by the same route as personal expenditure on consumer goods. Hence, in the diagram, the measurement of TDE will be seen to run across two separate outflow pipes from the Government Sector—the 'Goods' pipe on the one hand and the 'Wages and Salaries' pipe literally on the other. In the Blue Book table, however, no such distinction is made, and the item is presented as a single figure for all 'Public Authorities' current expenditure on goods and services'. ('Current' to exclude capital expenditure, see below,† and 'goods and services' to indicate the exclusion of transfer payments, see above‡). In effect, the Blue Book is here treating the Government Sector not so much as a producer but rather as a special type of consumer, itself responsible for the generation of a proportion of domestic expenditure partly by purchase from the Market Sector in the manner of a household and partly by hiring labour from households which would otherwise be available to the Market Sector for ordinary productive purposes. This is a perfectly valid way of looking at the matter, so also is the one we have offered above. In truth, the Government Sector is *sui generis*, a mixture of producer and consumer, validly treatable as either according to context.

From Expenditure at Market Prices to Expenditure at Factor Cost

If we now follow downstream the river of total expenditure we have been discussing—which is in effect a river of money flowing into retail shops and other distributive organisations including manufacturers' own sales offices—we find that a significant proportion of the initial flow never reaches the pocket of the producer or distributor at all. For to the extent that the government partly

† p. 58.   ‡ p. 32.

finances its operations by means of 'indirect' taxes, or 'Taxes on Expenditure' in Blue Book terminology, part of the expenditure is siphoned-off by the tax collector, as indicated in the diagram. However, since the government also pays out *subsidies* on certain commodities, i.e. injects an addition to the flow of receipts reaching producers over and above the money provided by final buyers, the width of the relevant pipe in the diagram is shown proportional to the total of indirect taxes *net*, i.e. to the total value of revenue from the taxes less that of expenditure on the subsidies (in the Blue Book the two items are shown separately). The total of domestic expenditure after attenuation by net indirect taxes is known as Total Domestic Expenditure at Factor Cost (measurement no. 2 in the diagram), because the goods and services are now being valued at what they would have cost the buyer if unit-rewards paid to factors of production had remained the same but indirect taxes had been abolished. Total Domestic Expenditure at Factor Cost is not given separately in the first table of the Blue Book, but may be computed from information given in a later table, the tenth, entitled 'Gross National Product by Categories of Expenditure, at Factor Cost'.

Indirect taxes have not only the practical effect of interfering with the flow of expenditure from consumer to producer, but also the theoretical effect of creating ambiguity in the interpretation of our original concept of Domestic Expenditure at Market Prices. For suppose we lived in a closed economy in which Total Domestic Expenditure at *Factor Cost* was fixed (full employment, constant output per man and fixed rates of money wages and profit margins). Suppose then the government suddenly decided to reduce indirect taxation sharply and increase direct taxation by the same amount. The increase in direct taxation must reduce the retained income of households and hence their expenditure and hence Total Domestic Expenditure at Market Prices. But expenditure at factor cost would remain, as postulated, unaltered because the reduction of the initial flow of consumer expenditure at market prices would be exactly offset by the reduction in the amount of government siphoning-off into net indirect taxes. Two countries might be identical in respect of wage-rates, profit rates, physical production and currency, so that TDE at factor cost was the same in each, yet they might differ in TDE at market prices simply because the government of one showed a greater predilection for indirect taxes than the government of the other, or vice versa.

The problem, however, is less serious than might at first appear. For although it is true that the two countries postulated would differ (bogusly) in the *money* value of TDE at market prices, the general level of final prices in the one would be higher than in the other, in such a way that the *real* value (see Part III) of the two aggregates would be the same. If relative *ad valorem* tax rates were the same on corresponding commodities (i.e. if the pattern of taxation were the same) in the two countries, there would be no real economic difference between them, and from this point of view the distinction between TDE at market prices and TDE at factor cost would be unimportant. If the tax rates differed, the difference between the countries would be a difference in the pattern of market prices in relation to the pattern of factor costs. We deal with the matter further in Chapter 10† and in the meantime the only essential point is that it is the aggregate of TDE at factor cost which passes into the next stage of the circulation in our flow-diagram.

Approaching the Gross National Product: the Productive Contribution of the Market Sector

By far the greater part of the flow of Domestic Expenditure at Factor Cost passes into the Market Sector and thus provides the effective demand which activates the national production. In a closed economy such as we are at present assuming, domestic production and domestic expenditure (at factor cost) must be identical, they merely represent different ways of composing and measuring the same aggregate. But as we follow the river into the interior of the Market Sector we become more and more interested in its industrial composition in contrast to the end-use composition such as we have so far been considering.‡ In other words we should like to see the aggregate broken down on an industry-by-

---

† Pp.. 327
‡ See Chapter 7, pp. 14–16 above for a fuller discussion of the difference.

industry basis: as we already know, many industries produce both consumer goods and investment goods and many produce no final goods whatsoever but instead make their contribution to the national effort by specialising in the production of vital intermediate goods. Thus we now wish to compute the country's 'Gross National Product'. But in saying this we must be quite clear what we mean. It must be emphasised that we are not looking for an aggregate which differs in total (in a closed economy) from Total Domestic Expenditure—the total value of the national production of final goods: we are merely seeking to divide the same aggregate in a different way. We must therefore be careful to avoid double counting.

As we have already seen, most of the 'GNP' is produced in the Market Sector (in capitalist economies and collectivist economies likewise), or, in the language of the Blue Book, is created by 'Production and Trade' (see ninth Summary Table). But in order to measure the total contribution of Production and Trade to the total national production we need, in terms of the diagram, to measure the net *through* flow in the sector. Evidently the flow of expenditure *into* the sector must make first impact on the industries which are mainly vendors of final goods. But after this the flow becomes subdivided, large parts being passed on by the final industries to various industries producing intermediate and primary products required for the production of final goods, and then again to other industries in payment for products needed to make these products, and so on. In consequence, if the whole inflow into each industry within the sector were crudely totalled without adjustment, parts of the throughflow of the sector would be counted many times over, i.e. at each time of passage through an intermediate industry: the amount of the duplication would depend on the degree of vertical disintegration within industry and the fineness of the industrial classification adopted. In order therefore to obtain a correct measurement of the *net* throughflow of the sector (inflow = net throughflow = outflow = the sector's total contribution to the national production of final goods) all inter-industry payments, however the industries have been defined, which represent nothing more than transactions within the sector must by some means be taken out of the calculation. The usual solution adopted is to measure only the so-called 'net output' of the several industries, that is to take the value of their gross output (sales, plus value of inventory increase) *less* all payments made to other industries within the sector for goods and services needed to produce that output.

This method is followed in the Blue Book, and the ninth Summary Table provides an analysis of the net contribution of the Market Sector, thus defined, broken down into separate industrial contributions under the broader headings of the Standard Industrial Classification.

A Digression on 'Gross' and 'Net'

The use of the expressions 'gross' and 'net' predicated to the word 'output' in contemporary language in the sense just described, leads to confusion with another conventional distinction —that between the 'Gross' and the 'Net' National Product, or Expenditure. When these adjectives are predicated to the national product, income or expenditure as a whole, in contrast to the product of individual firms or industries, they signify the distinction between the product (or income) before or after deducting the value of the flow of resources necessary to maintain *capital* intact: Net National Product is the Gross National Product less depreciation, it is thus the sum available to the nation for consumption, defence or *adding* to the stock of wealth. (An estimate of the Net National Product—described simply as the 'National Income'—is given at the bottom of the first table of the Blue Book and is discussed below on page 50, but it is not depicted in the diagram.) By contrast when the adjective 'net' is predicated to the output of a single industry or firm, it signifies the firm's *net* contribution to the *gross* national product, i.e. the firm's total output, free of duplication, but before making a deduction for depreciation of capital. However, for every rule there is the exception, and the 'gross' profits of an individual firm or industry represent, not the profits free of duplication in some sense or another, but the profits before making any deduction for depreciation and taxation. Also 'net income from abroad', discussed in the section immediately following, means no more than gross (property) income received from foreigners less gross property income paid to foreigners.

The Gross National Product: oddments

The Gross National Product as a conception of welfare economics represents the total value of the flow of economically useful goods and services created by labour or capital (factors of production) either resident within the national boundary or owned by national residents respectively. The aggregate largely consists therefore of the contributions of the Market Sector and of the Government Sector valued in the ways we have been investigating. But there are a certain number of 'awkward' items which clearly require inclusion on the welfare criteria, but which are not easily identifiable as products of either of these two sectors. The items concerned, although relatively small, cannot be ignored. (85 per cent of the total product is in the U.K. provided by the Market Sector, about 10† per cent by the Government Sector and the remaining 5 per cent by these awkward items.) None are separately depicted in the diagram, but in the ninth table of the Blue Book the reader will find them all. They are:

   (i) Domestic services.
  (ii) Services to private non-profit making bodies.
 (iii) Residual error.
 (iv) Ownership of dwellings.
  (v) Net income from abroad.

We shall discuss these in turn. But before so doing we should warn the reader of another adjustment which he will observe in the ninth table, the figure for so-called 'stock appreciation'. We have seen that that part of the change in the value of stocks which is attributable solely to changes in the price-level at which existing stocks are valued by business accountants must not be included in National Product and Expenditure. If the net output of the individual industries included in the ninth table were appropriately valued, all would be well. Unfortunately, the value of each industry's net output is in practice obtained from the income side

† The figure refers to wages, salaries and Forces' pay only.

(see section following), i.e. as an aggregate of the profits and wages accruing to the factors of production in the industry concerned. But 'profits' as computed by accountants and returned to the Inland Revenue, conventionally include 'inventory profits', i.e. the net gain (or loss) in the value of the company's assets attributable to any net rise in the price-level at which stocks are valued. It is impossible to disentangle these inventory profits from the data relating to the individual industries, and the compilers of the Blue Book are therefore driven to an overall adjustment, computed by other methods, at the bottom of the table. To the extent therefore that changes in price levels must affect different industries' inventory valuations differently, the pattern of industrial contributions as given in the ninth table is distorted.

The labour of *domestic servants* is a productive service supplied and consumed entirely within the Households Sector itself, that is by one part of the sector to another. But the value of the service must evidently form part of the GNP since it evidently contributes directly to the nation's standard of living† and could as well be thought of as a product of the Market Sector, a service sold for cash. In the diagram, domestic service is in fact treated as a product of the Market Sector, but the Blue Book refuses to regard it as part of 'production and trade' on the grounds that, as in the Government Sector, the value of the output (i.e. of the work done by domestic servants) has arbitrarily to be assumed equal to the value of the input (i.e. to the wages in cash and kind of the servants). No other method of valuation is available. The same holds for non-profit making institutions generally. Thus charitable organisations such as Dr. Barnardo's Homes, or Oxford and Cambridge colleges provide services which evidently contribute directly to the national standard of living and often supplement similar services provided by the state; but the value of charitable services can only be included in the national production by reference to the cash cost of the labour services performed for the institutions by their employees.

The '*Residual error*' is a technical adjustment for an explana-

† One says 'evidently', although the distinction between the services of a maid or paid cook and those of the unpaid housewife is to many people obscure.

tion of which the reader is best advised to refer to the official description.†

The remaining items '*ownership of dwellings*' and '*net income from abroad*' present more difficulty. They have it in common that they represent the value of a return on part of the past accumulated stock of national capital, rather than the value of the product of current labour. 'Net income from abroad' is the profits and interest paid by resident persons and companies in foreign countries, to resident persons and companies in the U.K., *less* the total of similar payments made by U.K. residents to abroad. In common parlance the item would therefore seem better thought of as part of the 'national income' rather than the 'national production', but in technical jargon this cannot be: the Gross National Income has the special meaning of 'gross national product measured from the income side' (see below, p. 50). Thus we have here a vivid example of the application of the well-known principle of social accounting that 'national production' should include not only the current value of the nation's labour, but also the current flow of product or income from the nation's capital. The profits of companies in the Market Sector included in the GNP in a manner already discussed, themselves of course include an element of return on capital, either as interest and dividends or as undistributed net profits: these may be thought of as representing the value of the flow of utility-creating service from the national stock of industrial capital held in the Market Sector, corresponding to the overseas capital assets which produce 'income from abroad'. The item 'ownership of dwellings' performs the same function in relation to the national stock of dwelling houses and flats. This item as included in the Blue Book may be thought of as the 'gross profits'‡ of landlords of dwelling houses—total rentals, less current maintenance costs and rates, plus the imputed rent on owner-occupied dwellings.§ The item is intended to indicate the value of the flow of utility annually accruing from the

† 'Sources and Methods', (*op. cit.* p. 29 above).
‡ See penultimate sentence of 'A digression on "Gross" and "Net",' p. 44 above.
§ I.e. what the gross profit would be if the owner let the property instead of living in it.

E

stock of dwellings, thus avoiding the absurdities which would arise if no such item were included.† (The corresponding item in Total Domestic Expenditure is 'consumers expenditure' on housing, the only difference between the two being of course that in the final-expenditure version landlords' outgoings are not deducted; i.e. this industry's output is included 'gross' rather than 'net'.‡) However, the inclusion of rent in this manner is not by any means a happy solution of the difficulty. Much of rental represents a true economic rent or 'surplus' and might well be regarded by some economic philosophers as a mere transfer of income between persons, validly excludable from the Gross National Product for much the same reasons as applied to transfers effected by the government. The method of valuation (of the flow of utility from housing) followed in the Blue Book is evidently rather arbitrary because rent control in the post-war period and the general stickiness of free market rentals in inflationary or deflationary conditions divorces the value of the actual product from its current demand price: when rent control is abolished the money value of the GNP will rise, but the total quantity of housing available may well remain unaltered.

As already indicated neither 'net income from abroad' nor 'ownership of dwellings' are depicted in the diagram in order to avoid over-burdening that tortured object further. If they were, the first would appear as a form of two-way flow running from the 'overseas' sector through the diagram until it could be taken parallel to the main flows so as to enter into the measurement of National Income and Depreciation.§ Rents of dwellings would also

† Otherwise, for example, a country which achieved a 20 per cent increase in the stock of houses and a consequent rise in standard of living would be shown in the statistics as having experienced no increase in GNP whatsoever.

‡ In Gross National Product we include each industry's total output net; in Total Domestic Expenditure we include (i.e. in a closed economy) each industry's final output gross. See again 'A digression on "Gross" and "Net"',' p. 44 above.

§ It would then divide into three branches, one running direct to 'households' (direct interest and dividend payments to British holders of foreign bonds and stock) one into the Appropriation Accounts of Companies (profits of U.K. companies operating abroad, *less* similar profits and dividends paid abroad) and one into the Government box (representing the difference between interest paid and interest received from inter-government loans such as in the case of the North American Debt).

start out as a single pipe, (running in this case from the Households Sector), entering into the measurement Total Domestic Expenditure as well as that of National Income, and then by some means dividing into three branches in a similar manner to income from abroad.† In the Blue Book, both 'net income from abroad' and 'ownership of dwellings' are given, as already stated, in the ninth summary table. Gross National Product less income from abroad is termed *Gross Domestic Product* (see also first table, right hand side): the latter is a concept which we shall find useful in Chapter 6 below and elsewhere.

Rents of land and buildings other than dwellings are also of course included in the Gross National Product, but do not appear as a separate item. If rent for a factory is paid by one firm to another, it is treated as a cost of production of the paying firm of the same type as the cost of raw materials, i.e. as an 'input' from another industry which must be deducted from the assessment of net output. In the ninth table of the Blue Book such rent is therefore credited to the value of output, free of duplication, of the industry in which the owner firm operates. That industry will in many cases be the industry of 'Insurance, banking and finance, (including real estate)'.

From National Product to National Income

We now know why the measurement of Gross National Product, from the production side, cannot be represented on the diagram: the 'netting out' of the contributions of the various industries would be impossible to depict, at least at all conveniently. We pass therefore to consideration of the Market Sector's *outflow*—identical of course with inflow and 'throughflow' (GNP). The aggregate represents in effect the total of incomes paid to factors of production in the Market Sector in reward for their productive activities. For, evidently, the net flow of money into the various

---

† (i) Returning directly back to the Households Sector (rents paid to small non-incorporated landlords and the imputed rents of owner-occupied dwellings); (ii) into the Appropriation Accounts of companies (rents paid to real estate companies and large incorporated single landlords such as the Dukes of Westminster, who operate as Belgrave Estates Ltd.); (iii) to the Government Sector (rents of Local Authority houses).

industries, the sum of which makes up the total net throughflow of the sector and is therefore identical with the sector's contribution to the GNP, must constitute the amounts available to these industries (or firms) for rewarding the factors of production working in them—labour or capital respectively. The 'net output' of the firm or industry is the gross value of sales (assuming no inventory changes) less payments to other industries for required intermediate products, i.e. is the cash sum left within the industry as a result of the year's productive activity. The sum is first required to pay wages and salaries, and the residue is gross profits, the latter being defined as the total 'factor reward' of capital. Hence, as already stated, the total outflow from the Market Sector, being the sum of the (different) net outputs of the industries and firms within it, represents the total of production income arising in the sector —the total of its wages, salaries and profits. The flow can be seen pouring out at the top right-hand corner of the box. With the addition of production incomes, (wages, salaries and Forces pay) arising in the Government Sector and also strictly of the income associated with the 'awkward' items in GNP not shown in the diagram, this river now represents the sum of all incomes arising from 'productive' activity by residents of the U.K. It is known as *National Income and Depreciation* (measurement no. 3 in the diagram), and obvious interest attaches to its analysis according to the different types of income payment; wages, salaries and profits. This decomposition represents yet another way of looking at the same central aggregate and is to be found on the right-hand side of the first table of the Blue Book.† National Income and Depreciation is

† In the 1957 edition of the Blue Book, which unfortunately was published rather late in the year—too late to alter the printed diagram—the expression 'National Income and Depreciation' was dropped. The aggregate of profits, rents and income from employment (less stock appreciation plus income from abroad) is now properly given the same name as the aggregate of the left hand side of the table (Gross National Product) thus re-emphasising that the analysis consists essentially in dividing the same basic concept in different ways. In the Blue Book, the expression 'National Income' is now reserved for the Net National Product, i.e. the Gross National Product less capital consumption, estimates for which latter became available for the first time in 1956. In this connection, two points arise;

    (i) The correct economic principles on which capital consumption should be assessed are the subject of some controversy, but it is important to remember that the resulting ambiguity relates to the estimate of the net concept

identical with Gross National Product and, in a closed economy, with Total Domestic Expenditure. We have thus completed consideration of the three classical methods of building up the National Product; from the expenditure side, from the production side and from the income side.

From National Income to Personal Income (Household Income)

The greater part of the national income flows directly into households in the form of wages and salaries and can be seen so doing in the diagram: the rest is diverted into Company Appropriation Accounts as gross profits; but a part of the latter returns almost immediately in the form of distributed profits, that is as interest on bonds and as dividends on stocks and shares. Thus we are beginning to be able to build up the receipts side of the accounts of households as depicted in the second table of the Blue Book. However, before the aggregate is complete we must of course include not only the wages and salaries paid by the government but also transfer payments (social security benefits and the like), these being payments by the government to the Households Sector which have been excluded, for reasons already explained, from the national total of production incomes but which of course must now be accounted for in arriving at the total of Personal Income. In the diagram these transfer payments are seen flowing direct from the government into the Households Sector via a separate pipe, but they are not treated in quite the same manner in the Blue Book (although they ought to be). For it will be remembered that the definition of transfer payments includes interest on the

only, leaving the status of the 'gross' data unaffected: for many purposes the latter are sufficient.
(ii) In principle it should be possible to provide a decomposition of the National Income by types of income, similar to that of the Gross National Product—the only difference would be that profits of all kinds would be presented net of depreciation (see above 'A Digression on Gross and Net'). In practice, however, the principles on which the national income statisticians estimate capital consumption are not quite the same as, and are theoretically superior to, the principles employed by business accountants in computing depreciation. Hence 'net profits' as shown by the Blue Book would not be the same as the total of the net profits recorded in the accounts of companies and taken as the basis of taxation. (See also p. 87 below.)

National Debt, but in the Blue Book such interest is lumped together with 'Rent, Dividends and Interest' generally, i.e. is lumped together with certain types of 'production' incomes. (National insurance benefits and other current transfer payments from public authorities are, however, given separately.) Transfer payments from the government to households may be thought of as paid for by taxation levied directly and indirectly on households. But the taxes earmarked for this purpose cannot of course be separately identified either in real life or in the diagram. The reader may appreciate nevertheless that these transfer payments represent a form of closed loop; the money is taken up from households in taxation at one moment and fed back to (other) households at the next.

With the addition of transfer incomes the total of Personal Income is nearly complete. (See measurement no. 4 in the diagram). But the reader who has glanced either at diagram or tables will have noticed a distinction which we have not so far discussed, the distinction between 'wages and salaries from employment' and 'income from profitable self-employment', by which latter is meant the gross trading profits of farmers, small unincorporated businesses and professional persons (see Blue Book table). 'Profits', whoever earns them, are not wages, but the accounting processes which occur in the minds of small business men are not such that a valid distinction can be drawn between profits 'distributed' and 'undistributed' as is made in the appropriation accounts of companies. Therefore it is necessary to show the whole of the gross profits of these persons as a form of simple Personal Income, analagous to, but distinct from, wages and salaries. The effect is that when small unincorporated businesses 'plough back' their profits, such savings are included subsequently in the national total of Personal Saving, and furthermore since the gross trading profits of unincorporated businesses perforce include their inventory profits, the total of Personal Saving includes these also.†
Finally we note the item 'Employers' Contributions'‡; these are

† The Blue Book offers a rough estimate of the amount of inventory profits so included in a later table entitled 'Capital formation in stocks and work in progress, by sectors'.

‡ In the table only: in the diagram the item is included with wages.

employers' contributions to pension funds, injury funds and to the National Insurance Funds, the benefits of all of which ultimately accrue to the employee, hence the payments are regarded as a supplement of wages. However, as we shall see, the National Insurance contributions of employers only enter the account immediately to leave it again, for all contributions, by employee, employer and self-employed are included as an item of outlay on the other side of the account.†

With details of income filled in we may tiptoe to the other side of the account. There is really very little to this. What is not taken in taxes is either spent or saved. What is spent is spent, by definition, on consumer goods, and pours down the central pipe of the diagram. We must notice however two small points in connection with the assessment of taxation. In the first place of course only 'direct' taxes are included at this point, and of them only taxes on income; taxes of a capital nature, that is to say inheritance taxes and capital levies are omitted since they are considered more likely to be paid out of the capital assets of households, rather than out of their current income. In the second place we must note the item 'additions to tax reserves' which is shown in the Blue Book but not in the diagram and whose meaning will be explained at the same time as a similar item in the companies account below.

The total width of the exit pipes from the Households Sector, consisting of consumer goods expenditure, tax payments of one kind and another and personal saving, is the same as the total width of the entry pipes. So also in the Blue Book table; in the table the total of income before tax is identically equal with the total of 'Expenditure' (the latter including saving). Thus our 'main stream' circuit is complete and it is time to examine the subsidiary circuits, or 'leakages'.

Leakages (1): Profits

The leakage circuits we must consider are:

† Employers' contributions to pension funds appear (implicitly) on the other side of the account as Personal Saving. Employers' contributions to National Insurance could alternatively be treated as indirect taxes on production in general but this is now contrary to international standard practice.

(i) Company Profits,
(ii) Saving and Investment,
(iii) Taxes,
(iv) Foreign Trade.

We shall take these in turn, commencing with company profits. In the diagram, the companies' gross profits are seen running from the Market Sector into Company Appropriation Accounts, a box whose meaning has already briefly been described in the introductory description. The box represents the process of decision-taking by which the companies' financial directors allocate the profits to the various important financial purposes. The first charge on gross profits is capital depreciation, and the depreciation allowances are usually set aside in a special fund. However, the sums so set aside by no means necessarily match up, either micro-economically or macro-economically, with the amounts actually spent on replacement of worn-out or obsolescent equipment during the year in question. Therefore there is no guarantee at this stage that the all depreciation allowances of the year will find their way back into the stream of national expenditure for the year. At this stage therefore depreciation allowances must be regarded as a form of national saving, on a par with any other form of saving. Depreciation allowances are one form of company saving, sums placed to general reserve are another. In the diagram both forms are shown as a single pipe running directly into the 'Saving' box, which is to be discussed later. In the Blue Book the treatment is much the same, except that 'saving' in the form of inventory profits is perforce included as well. (The Blue Book table is *Corporate Income Appropriation Account*; it includes transactions of public corporations, so does the box in the diagram.) The other main outlet from the box under discussion (apart from distributed profits which as we have already seen flow straight back to the Households Sector) is company taxation of one kind and another, i.e. in the U.K., company income tax and distributed profits tax. This flows directly to the government and will be included in the discussion of the taxation leakage. Thus, as far as profits are concerned, we can explain how they return to the circuit if we can explain how the three *remaining* leakages are accounted for, as follows.†

Leakages (2): Saving and Investment

We have depicted both company saving and personal saving (ignoring for the moment public authorities' saving and the implicit contribution to national saving represented by the balance of payments) as flowing into a single box marked 'Saving' but immediately flowing out of the other side of the same box, now labelled 'Investment'. The latter represents actual expenditure by business men on investment goods and is shown as contributing to total national final expenditure as such. But, investment expenditure in the real world depends on business decisions, on expectations of future profit and so forth, and does not depend directly on the amount of saving that happens to be going on in households and in corporate appropriation accounts. Why then are Saving and Investment shown in the diagram as automatically being equal? The answer is of course that the diagram and the Blue Book table represent *ex post* situations. They depict realised results only. They do not purport to describe what people and companies were originally planning to save and invest. They show what was actually saved and invested at an equilibrium level of income (for themselves and for the nation) which was eventually arrived at through macro-economic processes of adjustment. Readers with some knowledge of Keynsian general equilibrium theory will be familiar with the proposition that when the concepts of Saving and Investment are defined as in this system, realised saving from all sources must in the event equal actual total investment expenditure. If this were not so, some goods would be missing from the system or some expenditure 'lost'. In the language of the diagram it would imply that liquid would literally be leaking from the pipes (or seeping into them). In real life it would mean that

† The discerning reader will have noticed in the Blue Book an item on the receipts side of the Appropriation Account labelled 'non-trading income'. These are receipts by companies of various forms of transfer income, such as national debt interest, which must be included for completeness in the same manner as with the corresponding item in the households account. For details see 'Sources and Methods' *op. cit.*, (p. 29 above).

the nation's expenditure would be insufficient to buy the whole of the national product; a situation which cannot persist without something giving way. 'Something', in the now almost universally accepted theory, is the value and/or volume of the national product itself: entrepreneurs finding demand either deficient or excessive, reduce production and prices and dismiss workers, or raise prices and/or production respectively. The consequent changes in incomes and general prosperity induce changes in savings on the one hand and investment expenditure on the other so as to bring the system into equilibrium at some new, higher, or lower, level of economic activity and income. Hence, in the diagram, because it is an *ex post* diagram, the flow into the savings box is shown as identically equal to the flow out from the investment box. But the two parts of the combined box are divided by a dotted line as a reminder that there is no necessary equality between *decisions* of savers and *decisions* of investors, except as an indirect result of the process of getting the whole system into equilibrium. As already stated, this process consists in adjustments in the total level of income (and expenditure): the diagram and the Blue Book tables depict only one, equilibrium, level of income.

The saving and investment box in the diagram corresponds fairly straightforwardly with the sixth table of the Blue Book— Combined Capital Account of the U.K. (The account is 'combined' because it includes the saving and investment of a number of separate sectors.) In the account, the various forms of saving are 'receipts' and the various forms of investment are 'payments'. Inventory profits are deducted from saving as a separate adjustment, so that investment in stocks is 'real' investment only. There are, however, one or two items, such as saving of public authorities and net investment abroad which cannot be considered until we deal with the taxation and foreign trade leakages. The only remaining item calling for separate comment here therefore is 'additions to tax reserves'. It is frequently the case both with households and companies that the amount of money handed over to the government as tax payments during the year differs significantly from the amount of tax liability accruing on income earned during the year, because taxes are frequently paid some time in arrears, and many important taxes, of course, are levied on the income of past, rather than current, years. However, the receipts and expenditure accounts of the government are constructed on a cash basis only, so that the excess or deficit of persons' or companies' accruals of tax liabilities over actual payments would appear to represent a leakage in the full sense of the word. In effect therefore these increases in tax reserves represent a contribution to the national saving of the year; they are thought of as being put on one side by the holder against the eventual liability to pay tax in a future year, and they cannot be spent by the government during the current year. In order that the system be in equilibrium in the sense described previously it is necessary therefore that increases in tax reserves be matched indirectly by some form of investment expenditure. They are therefore quite properly treated as savings, and the individual components for households and companies will be found alongside the corresponding savings entries in the Personal Income and Expenditure account and in the Corporate Appropriation account respectively.

Leakages (3): Taxation

The position of the taxation leakages is simpler in principle but more complicated in practice. For as we have already seen the government inserts its scoop not only into personal income and into the accounts of companies, but also between consumer and producer by levying indirect taxes at the point where the national income is spent. If the government always spent on current goods and services or current transfer payments no more and no less than it received in taxation, and if it undertook no capital expenditure, there would be no difficulty. It is easy to see that in that case all the money taken in taxation would find its way back into the circuit either as the government's own expenditure on goods, or as government payments into household income in the manner we have already discussed. Personal expenditure from personal income is lower than it would be were it not for taxation; on the other hand personal income is itself higher on account of government payments from the proceeds of taxation. However, the government does not in fact always balance its budget and the government also undertakes capital expenditure. The current account of the government corresponding to the 'Government Sector' box in the diagram, may be found in the Blue Book as two tables, one relating to Central and the other to Local government; but they can easily be combined in the more summary form used in the diagram. In neither of these tables is there any indication of capital expenditure and it is a regular convention in national-income statistics to include government capital expenditure (on housing, schools, hospitals, roads and so on) with private sector capital expenditure in a single 'Combined' capital account, as already mentioned. The total of investment expenditure flowing out of the investment box in the diagram, therefore, includes capital expenditure by government as well as by private firms and public corporations; in the 'Combined Capital Account' (of the Blue Book) 'Gross Fixed Capital Formation at Home' includes government capital expenditure likewise. Therefore, unless the government in its current-account operations, as depicted in the Government Sector box, makes some contribution to the national total of savings, the savings of the Market Sector have to be sufficient to cover the investment expenditure both of the private sector itself and that of the government. In effect the government makes such contribution to savings, if any, by running a 'current-account budget surplus', that is to say, its total receipts from taxation and so on are made to exceed its total *current* (i.e. non-capital) expenditure on wages, salaries and goods, transfers and so on. If the current-account budget surplus is exactly equal to government investment expenditure, government savings are equal to government investment and the government's operations are entirely neutral to the general balance of saving and investment in the economy at large (except of course to any extent that the taxation required to raise the surplus has the indirect effect of reducing private saving). If the current-account surplus is less than government investment, a corresponding discrepancy in the opposite direction must be found between private saving and investment (and incidentally the government must be engaged in printing money or other form of financial borrowing from the public). Alternatively, if the surplus is greater than the investment, the government is assisting in the savings balance for private investment, and must be retiring debt or otherwise lending to the public.

It is of course possible for the government to run, not a surplus on current account, but a deficit, thus reducing the national total of savings: therefore the government's net contribution via its current surplus or deficit is depicted in the diagram by a pipe with a dotted line along one side, to indicate the possibility of a 'net' flow in either direction. In the 'Combined Capital Account' of the Blue Book, the surplus on current account of the central government defined in this way, is derived from the official revenue surplus of the public accounts by certain adjustments for capital taxes, etc., and the surplus of Local Authorities is shown separately.

We can now see how the total contribution of the Government Sector to the national income and expenditure circuit finally works out. The government 'leakage' is the current-account surplus. But this, combined with the saving of the private sector must in total equal national investment, the latter however includes not only private investment but also government investment itself.

Leakages (4): Foreign Trade

So far we have ignored foreign trade. A total of income ('the national income') generated by the production of the national product and identically equal to it, has found its way round the system to become a total of expenditure on final goods and services just sufficient to purchase the whole of the original product; 'leakages' into savings and taxation being compensated by investment expenditure on the one hand and government current expenditure on goods and services on the other respectively. In such a situation the total of the expenditure which purchases the national product, the national product measured from the expenditure end, 'i.e. the Gross National Expenditure' in the jargon, is exactly the same thing as the total Domestic Expenditure on final goods and services of all types by residents of the U.K. However, when foreign trade is introduced, the identity between the total expenditure of U.K. residents on goods and services of all kinds from all sources, and the total expenditure from all sources on the national product of U.K. residents disappears. Some of the product of the U.K. Market Sector is sold not to U.K. residents but to residents in foreign countries. Hence, although forming part of the U.K. Market Sector's total receipts, this part does not originate directly in the income and expenditure of the U.K. residents; it originates from the income and expenditure of foreigners. Furthermore, some of the goods and services manufactured and sold by the Market Sector both to U.K. residents and to foreigners were actually made from imports. Imports must be paid for and the sums so paid are not available for passing on to U.K. factors of production as part of the U.K. national income. They are in effect a deduction from U.K. income, another 'leakage' from the box. This situation evidently requires an adjustment of terminology.

If we want to measure national product from the expenditure end (rather than from the production side or the income end) we can do so by taking the total sales, *both* to British residents and to foreigners, *of* the British economy, and then deducting the value of imports used to manufacture the goods sold, that is to say, we take Total Domestic Expenditure plus U.K. exports minus U.K. imports. That is what is done on the left-hand side of the first table of the Blue Book and the result is entitled 'Gross National Expenditure'. (Evidently 'Gross National' and 'Total Domestic' expenditure will be identical in a closed economy, and they will be equal in an open economy in which the value of exports happens to be the same as that of imports.) The expression 'Gross National Expenditure' is not ideal for the purpose. For in an open economy we ought here to employ terminology which conveniently gives expression to a state of affairs where the nation is 'living beyond' or 'within' income as in the everyday usage, i.e. is running a balance-of-payments deficit or surplus. But we are provided with a concept of national expenditure which by definition cannot differ from what has been defined as National Income (or national product) and confusion arises because it is a natural reaction to interpret 'national' expenditure as meaning expenditure *of* the nation, i.e. as the aggregate which we know as Total Domestic Expenditure: the man in the street cannot be blamed for failing to appreciate that what is really meant by Gross National Expenditure is 'Gross National Product measured from the expenditure side': he does not expect expenditure to be something which is identically equal to income any more on the national plane than on the individual household plane.

In the diagram, payments and receipts for imports and exports respectively are shown as pipes running between the Overseas Sector and the Market Sector directly (all imports including food imports being thought of as passing through the Market Sector for working up and distribution),† and the total expenditure of the U.K. residents therefore represents the aggregate expenditure of the British nation on both home-produced goods and imports, or Total Domestic Expenditure, as already explained.

What is the effect on the equilibrium of the domestic income and expenditure, if the balance of external payments is not in balance and how is the situation depicted in the diagram and in the Blue Book? Suppose the sum of Total Domestic Expenditure is tending to exceed the Gross National Product, for example because firms in the Market Sector are trying to spend on new investment goods more in total than the sum of domestic savings which is forthcoming at the existing level of total GNP and with existing government fiscal policy. Something has to give way. We have seen that 'something' may be the level of domestic income itself. But in an open system with substantial foreign trade it is possible that at least part of the 'something' will also be the balance of overseas payments: instead of causing a rise in income and prices at home, the excess expenditure pouring into the Market Sector may be offset by a rise in imports and possibly also a fall in exports— the Market Sector in effect, gets from abroad part of the additional resources necessary to meet the additional demand from at home.‡ Thus general equilibrium is eventually achieved with a smaller

† Imports and exports include 'invisible trade' in services; this also is assumed (without involving over-much simplification) entirely to be paid for, or sold, respectively, in the Market Sector.

‡ If there is full employment of labour at home, the Market Sector may import consumer goods for resale to domestic consumers; if there is less than full employment at home the Market Sector will in all but the most self-sufficient economies require additional primary products from abroad to collaborate with domestic labour in increasing domestic production.

adjustment of domestic income than would otherwise have been necessary.

When the balance of external payments goes into deficit foreigners must become net lenders to U.K. residents (or U.K. gold reserves must be expended, which comes to much the same thing). In effect foreigners are 'not spending', i.e. they are saving part of the income they are deriving from the sale of goods to the U.K. This not-spending on the part of foreigners has exactly the same immediate effect as not-spending by domestic residents. It becomes part of the total compensation available to the U.K. for matching against the national total of investment expenditure: instead of resources being freed for investment by saving at home the resources are made available by obtaining goods without immediate payment from abroad. Thus a balance-of-payments deficit may be thought of as adding to the total of national saving, in which case the overall identity of saving and investment now takes the form:

Total Gross Home Investment ≡ Total Domestic Saving *plus*
Balance-of-Payments Deficit.

The balance-of-payments deficit (or surplus) is shown as pipe running from the Overseas Sector to the savings box and forming a net addition to (or deduction from) national saving. The qualifying sense in which the imaginary contents of this pipe can be regarded as a flow is exactly the same as in the case of other pipes running into the savings box (see page 55 above). The balance-of-payments pipe may also be thought of as a 'safety valve' not only in the economic sense of acting as a damper against internal inflation and deflation but also as providing for formal equality of receipts and expenditure from the Overseas box, i.e. equality of foreigners' saving and investment. The arrangement of the Overseas box in the diagram is the same in principle as in the seventh table in the Blue Book. However it should be noted that the table is arranged from the U.K. point of view, so the credits on the right-hand side are U.K. credits, i.e. the outflow (payments for U.K. exports) from the Overseas box in the diagram and vice versa.

The foregoing is not the only possible way of looking at the matter, although it is the only way which can conveniently be adopted in a fully articulated flow-diagram. In our arrangement, if the balance of payments should be in surplus, the 'safety valve' pipe is assumed to be functioning in reverse, i.e. the excess of U.K. current foreign receipts over expenditure is treated as a contribution by the U.K. to the savings of other countries and hence as a net deduction from the total of saving available to match domestic investment (i.e. a negative addition to domestic saving). But when the balance of payments is in surplus the U.K. is in effect investing abroad, i.e. is building up the national capital by acquiring foreign assets. The difference between this form of investment and domestic capital formation is only a modest difference in kind and one might as easily (and perhaps better) write the balancing equation as follows, and arrange the tables correspondingly:

$$\left.\begin{array}{c} \text{Total Home Investment} \\ plus \\ \text{Balance-of-Payments} \\ \text{Surplus (i.e. plus net} \\ \text{foreign investment)} \end{array}\right\} \equiv \begin{array}{l} \text{Total} \\ \text{Domestic} \\ \text{Saving} \end{array}$$

In other words instead of treating the surplus as a deduction from the credit side of the account it is put in as an addition to the debit side.

The alternative arrangement has much to recommend it even in circumstances when the balance of payments is in deficit, the deficit being treated as net 'disinvestment' abroad to be set off against the total of domestic investment in arriving at the national total of investment. The national total is then consistent with a definition of investment as the total increase in the national wealth. The arrangement is followed in the Blue Book Summary Tables, where the effects of overseas transactions are brought into the 'Combined Capital Account' for their contribution to the national balance of savings and investment, but could not be followed in the diagram without disturbing the whole of the rest of the dia-

F

grammatic arrangement and in particular the representation of the measurement of national expenditure.†‡

However the Blue Book itself is not able to follow the alternative arrangement without complications. It is forced in fact to put part of the current external balance on one side of the account (with appropriate algebraic signs) and part on the other. For the current-account balance of payments must be exactly offset by the total of corresponding international capital transactions which 'finance' it, but some such transactions very definitely do not represent net additions to, or deductions from, the national wealth: capital grants from foreign governments (such as Marshall Aid and so forth) and capital grants to foreign governments, which do not have to be repaid, evidently fall into this category. These items are much better thought of as additions to, or deductions from, the total of national savings. Accordingly in the Blue Book, the item 'investment abroad' on the right-hand side of the Combined Capital Account consists of the total net private or intergovernment lending from the U.K. to foreign countries plus the net increase or less the net decrease in that part of the national wealth which is held in the form of reserves of gold or foreign exchange.§ The arrangement of the Blue Book in the middle 1950's of course was much influenced by the prevailing tendencies of the period; the U.K. had usually been a net receiver of grants from foreign governments (mostly the United States) but at the same time there had usually been a net positive outflow of private investment funds from the U.K. to foreign countries (mainly in the sterling area); and the direction of changes in the gold and dollar reserves had

† The reader may best see the difficulty by attempting to work out for himself the modifications to the diagram which would be required. Basically the problem arises because the diagram follows a consistent treatment throughout (in order that the pipes may link) whereas the Blue Book Summary Tables are able to adopt the arrangement which is most appropriate to the particular aspect of the economic system each is intended to depict.

‡ Overseas transactions appear in the Summary Tables of the Blue Book in three separate places. First, in the first table as an element in the measurement of gross national product from the expenditure side; second, in the Combined Capital account as under discussion and third in the seventh table, Transactions with the Rest of the World.

§ It is very important to make this adjustment because it is quite common for net long-term lending by U.K. residents to abroad to have been financed by a reduction in U.K. foreign exchange reserves.

varied from year to year according to economic conditions and
government policy.

The Overseas box in the diagram is represented by the seventh
table in the Blue Book, (Transactions with the Rest of the World)
which is basically the same as the inflow and outflow table of our
box, but also gathers together a number of items of detail which
the diagram perforce ignores. Thus property income from abroad
here comes into its own (on both sides of the account) and 'invisible' trade is separately distinguished from visible. Also, 'genuine'
net investment abroad (i.e. the value of net additions to external
wealth, see above) is distinguished from the transfers.

Recapitulation

The above completes the discussion of the effects of foreign
trade and the balance of payments on the conceptual system of the
Summary Tables of the Blue Book, and thus largely also completes the discussion of the Summary Tables themselves. We will
therefore briefly recapitulate. At any one moment of time residents
of the U.K. are engaging in a certain total of expenditure on final
goods and services of all types from all sources. (Total Domestic
Expenditure at Market Prices.) As this expenditure passes 'over
the counter' the government levies indirect taxes and to some
extent grants offsetting subsidies, mostly but not entirely on consumer goods. (Diagram for simplicity shows net indirect taxes as
falling exclusively on consumer goods.) After tax most of the remainder of the TDE, now at 'factor cost', flows into the Market
Sector† and eventually becomes available for rewarding factors of
production in the sector. Some of the expenditure flow however,
will be passed on to foreigners as payment for imports and therefore will not become available for rewarding factors of production;
on the other hand the sector receives additional receipts, partly or
wholly offsetting this effect, from the sale of exports. The Total
Domestic Expenditure at factor cost need not equal the Gross
National Product (which latter is the total value of output of the
Market and Government Sectors) to the extent that current pay-

† But Total Expenditure also of course includes the government's own direct
expenditure on labour services; see diagram.

ments for imports of goods and services differ from current receipts from exports of same. If we think of the Gross National Product as 'the nation's income', the nation may be thought of as living within or beyond its income to the extent that the TDE is less or greater than the GNP respectively. The total amount available for rewarding the factors of production in the Market Sector, i.e. available to make up the sector's contribution to the total of the nation's production incomes, is therefore equivalent roughly to TDE *plus* export sales *less* import payments. This total of production incomes flowing from the Market Sector and joining with government 'productive' incomes and incomes arising from other elements in the GNP, together form the National Income and Depreciation as measured at position 3 in the diagram. The whole so far recapitulated may be seen set out in the first table of the Blue Book.

All the National Income becomes either Personal Income or undistributed income of companies. Most personal income returns immediately to form the major part of the TDE at market prices itself, i.e. becomes personal consumption expenditure; the rest is taken in taxation or saved. Most of what is taken in taxation is immediately put back by the government as the government's own direct contribution to the Domestic Expenditure, either in the form of purchases of goods or as purchases of labour services; the rest of the tax revenue is 'saved' by the government. Personal savings, company savings and government savings make up the total of the national savings which tend to reduce the national expenditure to below the national total of income. Domestic investment expenditure, on the other hand, has the opposite effect. In an open economy investment expenditure may in fact raise the gross expenditure of the nation by more, or by less, than the total of domestic saving reduces it. Such a discrepancy must be offset by a balance-of-payments deficit or surplus in the manner described: saving from all sources must equal domestic investment, or domestic saving must equal investment of all kinds.

CHAPTER FOUR

THE NATIONAL INCOME
BLUE BOOK (II): THE REST

At the time of writing the remaining chapters of the Blue Book, after the Summary Tables, are as follows:

Chapter 2. Output and Expenditure at Constant Prices.
3. Industrial Input and Output.
4. The Personal Sector.
5. Companies.
6. Public Corporations.
7. Central Government including National Insurance Funds.
8. Local Authorities.
9. Combined Public Authorities.
10. Capital Formation.

It is possible that in the course of time new chapters may be added or the above arrangement altered. In what follows references are to the chapters in their present order as printed.

Output and Expenditure at Constant Prices

In Chapter 3 above we discussed the Summary Tables of the Blue Book very much from the point of view of a single year, although the Blue Book of course gives figures for a run of years in nearly all its tables. Indeed, once we have established the framework of the system for drawing up and presenting the national accounts, perhaps the greatest interest in the whole corpus of data attaches to their *changes* over time. For example suppose that from one year to a later year we observe that the Gross National Product has risen substantially: does this mean the nation is 'better off' as a whole? Does it mean that the nation has become more efficient? The many qualifications and difficulties involved in such

interpretations are dealt with in elementary text-books and cannot
be extensively discussed here. However one particular qualification is especially important and relevant—that is the confusion of
the issue introduced by the possibility of changes in the general
level of prices.

The ninth Summary Table of the Blue Book (see p. 32 above)
may be thought of as a statement of how the multitude of goods
and services produced each year, measured in their ordinary
quantity units, may be converted through the 'measuring rod of
money' into aggregate money flows contributing to the Gross
National Product.† The tenth table does the same thing for the
quantities of goods and services which make up Final Expenditure. Now, in the Summary Tables, this conversion is done, in
principle, by valuing each quantity at its 'current' price, i.e. at the
average market price or factor cost ruling for the commodity in
question through the period to which the figures relate. In other
words, on the production side the data represent the actual cash
value of sales (plus inventory adjustment, see above) and on the
expenditure side the actual cash value of purchases (less indirect
taxes). If prices were always constant, then the only way the GNP
or any of its constituents could rise from one year to another
would be from a general increase in the quantities produced and
consumed (or invested)—more production in a physical sense,
more consumption in the sense of a higher 'real' standard of living.
But if during the period in which we are interested there happened
a rise in the general level of prices (i.e. any series of price increases
not offset by other decreases) it would be possible for the money
value of the Gross National Product, or one of its constituents,
to appear to rise statistically without any change in production,
consumption or investment whatsoever;—no increase in 'real' income, no increase in the standard of living or the physical volume
of investment. In fact, typically, the total observed change in GNP
will represent a mixture of the two extremes just described, it will
partly be due to changes in quantities of stuff produced and consumed, and partly to changes in prices.

† This underlines the essential distinction between Diagram I, Chapter 1, and
Diagram II, Chapter 3.

The second chapter of the Blue Book eliminates from the data all effect of changes in prices. The two main tables offered are much the same as the ninth and tenth summary tables *except* that they have been drawn up as if prices were constant—the aggregates depicted can only change from year to year as a result of changes in quantities. However, the techniques of construction involved, and the matters of principle raised, form a major separate subject in economic arithmetic, to which we have devoted a separate chapter (Chapter 10) in Part III. At this stage, therefore, we say no more.

Industrial Input and Output

The title 'Industrial Input and Output' is intended to provide a cover for tables which attempt to break down the 'single box' treatment of the Market and Government Sectors, as used in the Summary Tables (and in our diagram), into separate components. Inflows and outflows of these boxes are no longer left as single aggregates but are given separately for industries or groups of industries. Not only are data provided concerning flows from individual industries in the Market Sector to sectors outside, such as the Households Sector (payments of factor rewards), and vice versa (receipts from sales of consumer goods), but also concerning the intermediate payments between industries within the sector whose importance we have already mentioned in Chapter 1.† The Blue Book here attempts to tell us the sources of the monetary inflows into each industry (i.e. the destinations of the *sales* of the industry), source by source, as well as all the destinations of the outflow (factor rewards, intermediate product payments, etc.). The book is therefore attempting to make up some of the deficiency in data of this kind referred to previously,‡ and the results are of great importance for a wide number of general purposes in applied economics. Because of the difficulty in obtaining original data however, the Blue Book at the time of writing is unable to employ as detailed an industrial classification as could be wished.

The greater part of the results are displayed in two main tables supported by an annually increasing number of subsidiary tables. The first main table provides a breakdown of the amounts of the

† P. 6.   ‡ See p. 13 above.

various different types of factor rewards paid out by each broad industry group in the standard industrial classification, that is to say, each industry's total of factor payments is divided between wages, salaries and other incomes from employment (payments to households) on the one hand and gross trading profits (payments to corporate appropriation accounts) on the other. Thus in this table inter-industry payments within the sector are excluded. Factor payments arising from the production of government 'real' services are also included, divided into two parts—those which are substitutes for private services and contribute to the standard of living in a quite straightforward manner (public Health and Educational services) and those such as Defence and Administration which may be thought of as part of the necessary overheads of keeping the nation going. Also included are factor rewards arising from the various 'oddments' in the GNP,† other than income from abroad. The reader may verify for himself that the table must sum to (Gross) National Income and Depreciation less income from abroad (=Gross Domestic Product). Another way of looking at the table is to regard it simply as a more complicated version of the ninth summary table, with each industry's net contribution to the GNP broken down according to the type of factor reward into which it is subsequently divided. (Employers' contributions to National Insurance on behalf of their workers are treated as a subsidy to wages and included in the total of 'Incomes from employment' paid by each industry.)‡ Since the data are on an industry-by-industry basis total profits have to include inventory profits and the total of inventory profits ('stock appreciation') must therefore be deducted from the grand total before arriving at the GNI. Thus, in a year in which there are sharp differences in the price movements of materials used by different industries, the relevant contribution of each industry to the GNI will be distorted as in the case of the ninth summary table.§

The classification of industries used in this first table of the third chapter is perforce extremely broad; 'Manufacturing' is treated as a single entity. However in a subsidiary table the wages and salaries (but not other incomes from employment) of individual

† See pp. 45 *et seq.*, above.   ‡ See p. 52 above.   § See p. 45 above.

manufacturing industries are broken down according to the four-teen manufacturing Orders of the SIC. Further, in the later 'Com-panies' chapter of the Blue Book, trading profits of public and private companies in manufacturing industries are similarly analysed, leaving only Trading Surpluses of Public Corporations in manufacturing industry, profits of small manufacturing busi-nesses and Employers' Contributions needed to complete the picture for Manufacturing on an industry-by-industry basis.†
Unfortunately, so far, the missing data have not been provided.

The second main table of the chapter is a much more extensive enterprise—the so-called table of 'Inter-industry Relations' or 'Input-Output'. At the present time it is only possible to give the table for a single past year.‡ The object is nothing less than a systematic presentation of *all* flows between individual industries and all flows from final consumers to individual industries (pur-chases) and from individual industries to households (wages and salaries). The technique is to arrange the industries in a two-way table of intersecting rows and columns, each industry appearing twice, once in the rows and once in the columns. Each industry's payments *out* are given in its column, the payment being placed in the column against the row of the industry to which it is made; thus the *rows* show the industries' receipts and sales according to buyer. By this device the whole system of transactions between industries is conveniently set out on a single sheet.

However that is not the end of the matter. Transactions be-tween individual industries and other sectors (such as Households and Overseas) are brought into the picture by treating various types of final purchase or final buyer as specific entities in the system, giving a separate column for each of the main types of final sales—consumer goods ('Persons'), goods and services for the

---

† Nationalised industries in the manufacturing sector have never been very important except during 1951–1955 when the steel industry was nationalised; even then the total of surpluses involved was never more than about a £100 millions. Profits of small businesses in manufacturing cannot be further broken down but only amount to about three per cent of the total. Employers' contributions can easily be estimated from employment data.

‡ The year first chosen was 1950. The table relating to that year is available in Blue Books up to and including 1956, but did not appear in the edition for 1957. It is possible that a new table may be produced in 1958 or 1959.

government ('Public Authorities'), fixed-investment goods such as plant and buildings ('Gross Domestic Capital Formation, fixed'), goods put to the purpose of increasing stocks ('Gross Domestic Capital Formation, stocks') and Exports. Similarly there are rows for payments to Households, to Corporate Appropriation Accounts and to Overseas ('Income from Employment', 'Gross Profits' and 'Imports' respectively).

The 'Total Output' of each industry shown in the final column is thus the gross value of its total sales of final products plus its total sales of intermediate products, i.e. the industry's total output very much not free from duplication.† It is interesting to see how industry groups vary in the proportion in which their total output is composed of intermediate output on the one hand and final output on the other: thus the ratio, *intermediate* : *final* in Mining and Quarrying is 4 : 1, while at the other extreme in Building and Contracting it is 1 : 4.

The idea of constructing and analysing these so-called Input-Output tables was conceived by Professor Wassily Leontief of Harvard University, who published his first application in a pioneering study as long ago as 1941.‡ Since then the literature on the subject has multiplied apace,§ and the possibilities of the derived analytical techniques which Professor Leontief suggested have attracted widespread interest and have been much explored. The point is that by making certain assumptions about the stability of relationships depicted in the table it is possible to develop a model of the economic system which takes full account of industrial interdependence. For example, one of the subsidiary tables‖ in the chapter of the Blue Book which we are discussing attempts to

† But the values of sales between *firms*, within each sector are, of course, eliminated.

‡ W. Leontief *The Structure of the American Economy*, 1919–1929, Harvard, 1941.

§ A suggested reading programme:
    (i) Edey and Peacock (*op. cit.*, p. 30 above), Chapter 8.
    (ii) Leontief, *op. cit.*
    (iii) T. Barna 'The Interdependence of the British Economy', *Journal of the Royal Statistical Society*, Vol. CXV, 1952.
    (iv) A. A. Adams and I. G. Stewart 'Input-Output: an Application', *Economic Journal*, Sept. 1956.

‖ This table, also, did not appear in 1957.

estimate the total amount of intermediate output which is required from the several industrial sectors of the economy in order to produce £100 of *final* output from any given industrial sector itself. Thus the table shows that in order to obtain £100 of final output from the textile industries, we need ultimately (in addition to £38 worth of imports and £44 of textile workers' labour) some £2 of coal from the mining industry, so that the mills may be heated and powered; £3 worth of goods such as dyes and bleaches from the chemical industries, so that the cloth may be finished; £5 of engineering and metal products (including incidentally the steel needed for pit-props required to mine the £2 of coal) and so on. These calculations are based on the assumption that the proportions of input to output indicated for each industry in the main table are technical constants, but even with this simplifying assumption† an electronic computor is needed to solve the system of simultaneous equations which the sum involves. The utility of such data is self-evident. It should be noted however that in order to carry out some of the sophisticated applications which have been suggested in the literature, one must work with a main table containing a much finer classification of industries than at the time of writing it has been possible for the CSO to provide. This is not to say that the published table is not of great value in the provision of general economic information, but only that it is not suitable for what has come to be known professionally as an 'input output matrix'.

There are one or two catches in the published main table which the general reader should know about:

(i) The *Transport and Distributive Trades* are treated, following an obviously sensible current convention, as though they were agents selling or carrying their goods on commission, rather than as outright purchasers of the goods carried or distributed. The 'output' of Distribution is the gross distributive margin. The service of both Transport and Distribution is assumed to be rendered to the industry purchasing

---

† See Chapter 10, pp. 332 *et seq.*, below for some other statistical consequences if the assumption is invalid.

the commodity handled, not to the seller: thus Retail Distribution is a service rendered to household consumers. The estimates for this group of trades are in any case rather rough and are lumped together at the time of writing in the broad group; Transport, Distribution, Insurance and Finance.

(ii) In *'Other Industries'* is included 'Public Administration, Defence, Health and Education'. This 'real' productive part of government activity is here treated as an industry buying labour from the Households Sector and selling the final product (at cost, see p. 39 above) to the government (i.e. Public Authorities in the appropriate column).

(iii) *Indirect taxes* could be treated in a number of ways, since the flows at various points could be measured either with or without taxes. Here, net indirect taxes are shown as a row, i.e., as a kind of payment which some of the industries and other entities identified in the columns may have to make to the government. All indirect taxes are assumed to be paid, and all subsidies received, by the manufacturer selling the goods, except in the case of Purchase Tax and Customs Duties on imported finished consumer goods (both of which are shown as being paid by the final purchaser, i.e. by 'Persons').

Problems such as the foregoing are inevitably involved in the presentation of any kind of inter-industry transaction table, but the solutions found by the official statisticians may of course vary in future Blue Books.

The Personal Sector

The remaining chapters of the Blue Book each provide further detail about the transactions of specific entities (boxes) represented in the diagram, the fourth chapter doing so for the Households or 'Personal' Sector. Total 'Personal' income is here further analysed according to its distribution by ranges of income (i.e. as between rich and poor) and we are also shown the incidence of taxes upon income at different levels. Such tables, therefore, provide most important political and social information; from them for example general measures of the inequality of income can be derived. However there are a couple of significant snags about the tables as published, to wit:

(i) Income and income units are (perforce) defined as for tax purposes. Therefore the income of a husband and wife is counted as a single unit, but the incomes of other supplementary earners in the household are not. (However, incomes under £50 are excluded.) Thus Personal Income in the Blue Book is not really the same thing as household income. The total number of income units—26 million— exceeds the total Working Population, less working wives, by the number of retired pensioners, rentiers, etc.

(ii) All the personal income 'units' in the sense defined above are duly allocated to ranges of income, but in the process some of their income (about 15 per cent of the total before tax) is lost. Certain types of income which for one reason or another fall outside the scope of statistics (whose primary source is the tax administration) cannot be allocated.† It is not clear what distortion, if any is introduced into the picture of the national pattern of income distribution by these omissions.

The other major tables in the fourth chapter are tables providing a detailed analysis of the commodity make-up of personal consumption and expenditure. First, the expenditure as valued at current prices, is broken down into a total of some 45 separate commodity headings. Note that this is not an industrial classification but a classification according to type of consumer need satisfied: the industrial classification of consumer's expenditure was provided in the Input-Output table of the third chapter. Next come estimates of average price changes from year to year in each of the commodity classes identified, then estimates of the expenditure valued at constant prices, i.e. estimates of changes in the 'real' volume of expenditure (see Part III below). Finally estimates are given of the amounts of indirect taxes or subsidies falling on, or accruing to, the various commodity categories. The latter data are

† Employers' contributions to insurance, much income in kind, interest on national savings, incomes under £50 and so on. (For precise details see 'Sources and Methods', *op. cit.*, p. 29 above.)

evidently both interesting and useful: they show for example that in mid-twentieth century Britain expenditure on tobacco at factor cost is no more than 25 per cent of what it is at market prices, because of the heavy taxation, but that Purchase Tax and other indirect taxes falling on durable household goods account for little over 15 per cent of consumers' expenditure on these items.

Companies and Public Corporations

The next two chapters of the Blue Book represent a further analysis of the transactions of the 'Company Appropriation Accounts' box in the diagram, this being done separately for joint stock companies and public corporations (nationalised industries). The distinction is valuable, although for simplicity it was not made in the diagram, for in the case of nationalised industries the statutory requirement to publish full operating accounts provides data from which the CSO can construct a substantially fuller statistical picture than in the case of companies. For companies (fifth chapter) the essential starting point of the analysis has to be the Gross Trading Profits agreed for tax purposes with the Inland Revenue and these are simply shown as being appropriated to various purposes (Depreciation, Dividends, general reserves, etc.) exactly as in the diagram and in the Summary Tables of the Blue Book.† By contrast, for the public corporations the tables (sixth chapter) show precisely how the total trading surplus was arrived at; the Combined Operating Account of public corporations balances revenues from sales against costs of production of various types— payments to employees, purchases of materials, indirect taxes and etc. Further, the Appropriation Account is then itself, in a subsidiary table, broken down into an industrial classification.

Additionally, for public corporations the official statisticians are able to provide a complete capital account, both in aggregate and on an industrial classification, showing how the total investment expenditure of the corporations was financed (ploughed back trading surpluses, loans from the central government, net borrow-

---

† Except only that rather more detail is given as to the different types of out-payment—dividends on ordinary shares, dividends on preference shares, debenture interest, dividend reserves, general reserves and so on.

ings from the market, and etc.). For companies, no detailed capital account can be given at all, although in a later chapter of the Blue Book (see page 83 below) there is offered a general table of capital accounts which in effect provides a form of summary capital account for the Companies' Sector as a whole.

Miscellaneous points to note about the fifth and sixth chapters of the Blue Book are as follows:

(i) *Companies' Gross Trading Profits* are given by industry; these include inventory profits. Also for each industry a 'net' profit figure is shown at the time of writing, i.e. after deduction of depreciation allowances. The latter however are no more than the allowances permitted statutorily for income-tax assessment according to the state of the law in the year in question. The law regarding 'Initial Allowances' varied from year to year in the 1950's, and for this and other reasons the allowances are not an indicator of the cost of maintaining capital intact. For the latter it is necessary to refer to the Capital Formation chapter of the Blue Book, discussed below.

(ii) In the *Combined Operating Account of Public Corporations* there will be found an item, 'Sales to own Capital Account'. This represents the value of work done by the corporations' employees which is of a capital nature, for instance, work on sinking of new mine shafts done by employees of the Coal Board.

(iii) In the accounts of public corporations *Inventory Profits* are treated as a *deduction* from cost of production on the operating account; they are thus included in the total surplus on operating account which is carried into the receipts side of the capital account. Therefore on the payments side of the capital account both the physical increase in stocks and the 'inventory profit' must be shown as a liability; this is done by the inclusion of a single item the 'increase in the value of stocks'. There is however a table in the tenth chapter of the Blue Book where the item is separated into its real and inflationary elements.

Central Government and Local Authorities

The next three chapters provide additional detail about the Government Sector, Central Government and Local Authorities being taken separately in the seventh and eighth chapters respectively and in combined form in the ninth. In the seventh chapter we have first the 'revenue' or current account of the central government— on the left-hand side, receipts of revenue of all kinds according to eighteen different categories of taxation plus some other sources; on the right-hand side, a fairly broad classification of expenditure as between Current Goods and Services on the one hand and various classes of transfers on the other. This revenue account is not a true current account, because it includes all types of government revenue (and of expenditure) including taxes on capital—Death Duties, and so forth—which latter are best thought of not as paid out of the current accounts of households but rather as in the nature of lump-sum transfers of property from private owners to the government. Similarly, on the expenditure side, although expenditure on physical capital formation is properly excluded, there are included so-called 'Transfers to Capital Accounts'—war damage compensation, gratuities, capital grants to local authorities —lump-sum payments by the central government which are unlikely to be treated as income by the recipients, i.e. are likely to be put on one side rather than to be added to the stream of the recipients' expenditure. It will be remembered that because the revenue account of the central government is not a true current account it was necessary to adjust the Revenue Surplus when including it in the combined national saving and investment account.†

The revenue account shown in the seventh chapter of the Blue Book includes the current receipts and payments of the National Insurance Funds, insurance contributions appearing as a revenue like any other form of tax, and the various payments of benefit appearing as expenditure. The two accounts can however be distinguished if desired because a separate revenue account for the Insurance Funds is provided in a later table which gives considerably greater detail as to the sources of contributions and the various

† See p. 55 above.

classes of benefits paid. The advantage of the combined arrangement is that the current surplus of contributions over benefits paid
in the National Insurance schemes evidently makes a real contribution to current national saving and is thus automatically included.

The Central Government is also provided with a capital
account. This is a mixture of a 'real' account with a 'financial'
account and is thus concerned with money flows (in contrast to
income flows) in the more specific sense mentioned in the opening
paragraphs of Chapter 3. Thus the 'real' capital account of the
government (or for that matter, of any other individual sector)
might be written,

$$\text{Total Saving} \equiv \text{Total Investment} + \text{Sums available for net}$$
$$\text{lending to other sectors.}$$

In other words, as we have already observed, any difference
between the sector's own saving and own investment expenditure
must be matched by net lending to, or borrowing from, other
sectors. This tautology, however, must not be allowed to deceive
us into imagining that the lending and borrowing transactions can
always be regarded—from a causal point of view—as mere
residuals: the sector may be committed to a certain amount of
lending, and hence unable to undertake as much physical investment as might otherwise have been the case; conversely, the possibility of borrowing from the public may be an important factor in
deciding the government how much to save or to invest. In the
case of the central government the point is particularly important,
because central government financial transactions of a capital nature
outside 'real' saving and investment are necessarily many and
substantial. Hence the capital account is best expanded and
presented formally as follows;

$$\left.\begin{array}{l}\text{Total Saving} + \\ \text{Total Borrowing} + \\ \text{Other capital receipts}\end{array}\right\} \equiv \left\{\begin{array}{l}\text{Total Investment} + \\ \text{Total Lending} + \\ \text{Other capital payments}\end{array}\right.$$

In the Blue-Book capital account for the central government, the
reader will find total saving under the heading 'Surplus before
providing for depreciation and stock appreciation', and total

G

investment under various different headings on the right hand side
of the table relating to physical capital formation (stock appreciation is deducted by adding to the right hand side also). He will find
seven different types of borrowing—from overseas governments,
through National Savings, by increase in the Fiduciary Issue and
so on; and he will find at least six different types of lending, of
which one, quite logically, is 'increase in foreign reserves' (sterling,
in one form or another, must be given up in exchange for the gold
and foreign currency acquired). The reader will also find on both
sides of the account numerous types of capital transfers, of which
probably the most notable in the early 'fifties was the type labelled
'grants under the European Recovery Programme' (i.e. grants
under the Marshall Plan). In consequence of all these transactions it may be observed that although the real investment of the
central government is usually no more than of the order of about
£200 millions per annum (most Government-Sector investment is
done by Local Authorities) and the saving of the order of £500
millions, the total transactions of this capital account taken as a
whole may vary from as little as the bare £500 millions to anything
up to and even exceeding £1000 millions.

The eighth chapter provides the current and capital accounts for
Local Authorities. Receipts are analysed in some detail and include
current grants from the Central Government, i.e. regularly recur-
ring grants either in subsidy of the general local revenue or as
grants-in-aid against the provision of specific local services
(Education being by far the most important). The right-hand side
of the Current Account gives a fairly detailed analysis of expenditure according to the type of service—'Education', 'Child care',
'Roads', 'Sewers', etc.—provided. The account is a true current
account.

Capital grants and loans from the Central Government and proceeds of other borrowings (e.g. municipal loans floated on the
London market) are shown on the receipts side of the Local
Authorities capital account, together with the aggregate current
surplus of Local Authorities carried forward from the current
account (in some years of course some Local Authorities run
deficits but in the mid 'fifties these were usually offset by other

authorities' surpluses to the tune of £50–100 million or so per annum). The right-hand side of this capital account is a most important table containing all the 'real' capital investment expenditure of the authorities and representing in total some three-quarters of all fixed capital formation of the Government Sector; most of course is Housing.

Combined Public Authorities

Many aspects of Government-Sector transactions are best considered in combined form (as in the diagram), i.e. as the sum of Local Authority, Central Government and National Insurance Funds expenditures and receipts, excluding transactions *inter se*, taken together rather than separately. For many of the activities overlap, especially in the fields of Health, Education and child care. In this chapter of the Blue Book therefore a number of combined tables are given, the most important and interesting being a table running over some four pages in which Government Sector expenditure of all types, current and capital, 'goods and services' and transfers, is exhaustively analysed under some twenty-four separate functional headings. Thus if, for example, a reader were interested specifically in Education expenditure, he could read off in a single line the total amount spent on the current maintenance of all forms of public education (teachers' salaries, upkeep of schools, etc.), the total spent on capital development (construction of new schools, replacement of old ones) and the total value of educational grants to private persons in the form of state scholarships and county grants. When the table first appeared it represented a very considerable advance on the information which had been available earlier and it should, in the course of time, assist materially in improving the standard of public discussion of political and economic questions concerning the size and distribution of public expenditure. The table is relatively straightforward, the functional headings being arranged in rows, the various economic cross-classifications, in the columns. There is also a 'total' column which is itself further conveniently subdivided into the Central Government and Local Authority components. Only three further points require special comment:

(i) In the division of the total column into Central Government and Local Authority components, that part of any item of expenditure which although administered by Local Authorities is nevertheless financed by a specific grant from the Central Government is with some logic put into the Central Government column, leaving only the rate-borne part of the expenditure in the Local column. The total of grants to Local Authorities from the central Government which are not specific, i.e. not allocated to specific services, is shown as a separate 'functional' item at the end of the table, positive in the Central column, negative in the Local —the latter to avoid double counting, since expenditure from such grants is already in effect included, spread out over the whole of Local Authority expenditure generally.

(ii) 'Grants' does not include all kinds of transfer payments, since government debt interest is excluded: the figures for debt interest, however, are available in another table in the same chapter entitled 'Combined Current and Capital Account'.

(iii) In the case of Defence (on which current expenditure even as late as 1957 still represented nearly fifty per cent of the Combined Public Authorities' total current expenditure on goods and services), capital expenditure is defined rather narrowly. It excludes all expenditure on armaments, light or heavy. Armaments are treated as exclusively the subject of *current* expenditure, even when they represent such items as battleships or new military aerodromes. The capital expenditure shown in the table in the row 'Military Defence' covers only the minor items of military investment which can be regarded as direct substitutes for similar types of civil expenditure, for example investment in government ordinance factories or in permanent married quarters for the services. Atomic expenditure, capital and current, destructive and productive, is at the time of writing concealed in other headings.

Other useful tables in this chapter offer an analysis of goods and services expenditure as between wages and salaries on the one hand and other payments (mostly for goods) on the other; an analysis of housing subsidies; an analysis of net indirect taxes according to their incidence on consumer goods, government consumption, investment and exports respectively; and finally an analysis of all direct taxes according to the type of income, property and sector on which they fall. Thus total current direct taxes of some £3000 millions can be seen to be made up to the extent of two thirds of revenue from the Households Sector, with the remainder coming largely from companies. It is also interesting to observe that the contribution from the Households Sector is itself divided very roughly in the ratio of two thirds to one third as between, on the one hand, income taxes, which in the distributional sense are 'progressive' and, on the other hand, National Insurance Contributions, which being a form of poll tax are distributionally 'regressive', i.e. they take a larger proportion of small incomes than of large incomes. The foregoing is only a sample of the politico-economic information which can be derived from these tables.

Capital Formation

This chapter analyses in very considerable detail the various aspects of the investment and saving activity of the nation, both in fixed equipment and in inventories. Fixed investment is analysed by sector, by industry invested in, by type of asset bought, and at both current prices and constant prices; inventory investment is analysed by sector and by industry; savings are analysed by sector. The group of tables taken as a whole represents one of the most comprehensive and important bodies of economic data in the country, and their recent development has been impressive.

The first table at the time of writing breaks down the combined capital account of the nation into sectors: the table shows in effect just how the total investment activity of the country was financed. The left-hand side gives for five main sectors—households, companies, public corporations, central and local government—their gross savings including inventory profits, then adds or subtracts various kinds of capital transfers† and deducts inventory profits.

† Taxes on capital are considered as capital transfers between the government and other sectors, a receipt for the government column and a deduction for the

The total of each column, therefore, is the total of the finance available to the sector to be used either for actual expenditure on tangible investment goods or for the acquisition of financial assets (bank balances, securities and all other paper claims to wealth). On the right-hand side of the table, therefore, we have first the actual investment expenditure of each sector on physical assets—fixed capital formation and *volume* inventory increase. Then the difference between a sector's actual physical investment expenditure and the total of the sums of money becoming available to it for investment (total of left-hand side column) must amount to the sector's *net* acquisition of *financial* assets—i.e. net borrowing or net lending —and this difference is shown as the final balancing item in each left-hand side column.† (The net figure may, of course, represent the balancing of some very large and very different positive and negative items, for instance in the case of Companies, of substantial borrowing from the public by new issues of some companies more than offset by the increases in cash reserves, gilt-edged holdings and etc. of others.) In a closed economy, since any sum borrowed by one sector is a sum lent by another, these individual sector net totals would in aggregate cancel out, i.e. the row total of the item 'Net acquisition of financial assets' would be zero. But in an open economy this is by no means inevitable since some of the lending and borrowing may have been to or from persons, companies or governments abroad. Hence the row total works out, in effect, as the nation's total net investment abroad, the balance-of-payments surplus on current account (or deficit if negative) adjusted for capital grants and transfers so as to yield the total value of the nation's

other columns, therefore zero in the total column. Other capital transfers include both transfers between private sectors within the U.K. and net capital transfers from abroad: the former cancel out evidently so that the total column contains only the total of the latter.

† There is a complication here so complicated that the reader who wishes for precise instruction is advised to refer to 'Sources and Methods' (*op. cit.*, p. 29 above), p. 279. 'Savings' of Persons and Companies are defined after deducting the accruals of tax liability on the current year's income, but the saving of the government is reckoned after crediting only the taxes actually received in the year, which may be a very different figure. This is logical, but it involves the insertion of a dummy sector labelled 'Tax Reserves, etc.' in the column headings of the left-hand side of the table, and a countervailing row 'Net Borrowing from Tax Reserves' on the right-hand side. A similar problem arises in connection with changes in dividend reserves.

investment in physical assets overseas plus net increase in financial
assets.† The reader can verify for himself that the effect of the foregoing is that the grand total of the right-hand side of the table
must equal the grand total of the left-hand side, and that both
totals are equal to the national total of real investment at home plus
real and financial investment abroad. Therefore both are equal to
national saving.

The table described is evidently of critical interest, especially in
a period when the adequacy of the nation's real investment has been
questioned by many commentators. As an example of the information which can be derived, notice the following contrast between
the financial position of the Public Corporations and the Companies:

TABLE 2. *Data Abstracted from 'The Financing of Investment'*
(Blue Book)

Averages, 1954–1956   *£ millions*

	Companies	Public Corporations
Saving (free of inventory profits) -	1390	180
Capital Receipts (net) - - -	25	10
Total Finance Available - - -	1415	190
Less		
Capital Formation		
(*a*) Fixed - - - -	970	560
(*b*) Stocks - - - -	255	−10
Total Capital Formation - - -	1225	550
Adjustment[1] - - - - -	+110	−5
= Net Acquisition of Financial Assets	+300	−365

[1] Changes in tax reserves, etc. See text and footnote, p. 84.
Source: Blue Book 1957, rounded.

Thus the nationalised industries, which control about 25 per cent

† I.e. the increase in gold and dollar reserves, less the increase in foreign
sterling balances, plus net other lending to foreigners and etc.

of the total stock of fixed industrial capital,† have been doing about 40 per cent of the fixed investment. But they have been borrowing heavily for the purpose (as a matter of fact, it is known that their gross savings have been insufficient even to maintain capital intact, a disgraceful state of affairs largely attributable to their products being sold at prices which in the private sector would be described as 'below cost'). By contrast, the Companies, while almost certainly engaging in fixed capital formation at a slower rate than would be in the best long term national interest, have been saving more than they have been investing, accumulating financial assets steadily. In addition, they have also been able to finance from within their own resources a considerable accumulation of inventories.

In the remaining detailed tables of the chapter, which are largely self-explanatory, and do not contain serious snags, use is made of a basic division of types of investment goods into (1) Plant, (2) Vehicles and (3) Buildings. On the basis of this simple but adequately revealing division, data are provided for investment on an industry-by-industry basis according to all the main headings of the Standard Industrial Classification including 17 headings within manufacturing industry. The same is also available by *sectors*, Companies, Government . . . etc., with an extra division of the 'Buildings' category into Housing and Other. A further analysis of the different types of vehicles bought can be found in a separate table, but only for the nation as a whole, not for sectors or industries. *Net* investment, that is gross investment less capital consumption (see below) is available by sector and by type of asset, but not by industries, at the time of writing, nor in any two-way classification. Both gross investment and net are also given in constant prices but (at the time of writing) the industry, sector and asset analysis is less comprehensive than in the case of the estimates at current prices.

Net investment is gross investment less capital consumption. Capital consumption, by sector and by type of asset, is given separately in two tables which have only been published since 1956.

---

† Factories and other manufacturing plant, plus all fixed capital of Fuel and Power industries, the Railways and the plant of other Transport industries, but excluding roads, farms, capital of Distributive Trades and social capital.

The data are of considerable importance, although necessarily subject to a greater degree of conceptual ambiguity than most of the rest of the data in the book. They were first described in detail in the notes to the Blue Book of 1957, where it is explained that the measurement is based on the same type of principle as adopted by accountants in measuring depreciation: the use of an asset is regarded as being spread in an arbitrary way over a pre-determined life and the portion of the life which passes in a given year is taken to indicate the portion of the value of the asset which has been 'consumed' in the year. However, unlike many business accountants, the national income statisticians properly employ the *replacement* value of the asset, in contrast to its historical purchase cost, for the purposes of the calculation. Thus, net investment in 1956 at current prices is the total cost of investment goods delivered in 1956, valued at 1956 prices, less the consumption of capital from the existing stock (see above) valued at current, i.e. 1956, replacement prices. Net investment in 1956 at 1948 prices is gross investment in 1956 revalued at 1948 prices less capital consumption in 1956 revalued at 1948 replacement prices. The statistical method by which the estimates are arrived at is described in the notes already referred to and the description may be expected in due course to be incorporated into future editions of 'Sources and Methods'.†

The first publication, in 1956, of estimates of net, in contrast to gross, investment attracted considerable comment. For the estimates appeared to reveal the post-war investment record of the U.K. as having been remarkably poor. Net Fixed Investment as a ratio of Net National Income (at current prices), which was 8 per cent in 1938, was running at only from 5 to 6½ per cent in the years up to 1952, and did not exceed 1938 significantly until reaching 7½ per cent in 1953. The volume of net investment (i.e. the aggregate at constant prices) was also, in every year up to 1953, substantially below the 1938 level in absolute terms as well. (However, it is good to notice that in 1955 and 1956 the average level was now more of the order of 40 per cent *above* 1938.) A number of factors may be adduced to explain these results, of which the most obvious would

† *op. cit.*, bibliography to Chapter 2, p. 29 above.

be the deterioration in the terms of trade since before the war; the high level of defence expenditure after 1950 and the effects of post-war recovery in the years earlier; the increase in the cost of investment goods relatively to other goods due to the sharp decline in the relative efficiency of the building industry (which has the effect that in order to maintain a constant 'real' share of investment in the national income, the 'propensity to save' in monetary terms must be raised) and finally the inability, or unwillingness of the Companies Sector to make full use of the financial resources available to it for investment which we noted in discussion of an earlier table.† It would be unwise to speculate here as to reasons for the latter phenomenon; the least politically tinged explanation which has been put forward is a structural one, that is that the companies which were expansion-minded had been starved of finance by the difficulties of raising capital on the Stock Exchange, while the more cautious companies piled up financial reserves which by tradition are not lent to other companies, but invested in gilt-edged securities or held on deposit in banks. In order to investigate these problems more effectively, it would be necessary that authors of the 'Financing of Investment' table of the Blue Book found some way of analysing further the item 'Net Acquisition of Financial Assets'.

It may well be argued that 1938 was not a suitable year for comparison: although in that year the economy was in a condition of incipient recession, investment was almost certainly still running at a higher level than the average of say the slump-afflicted years of the earlier 'thirties. However, it is also well known that the post-war investment ratio in the U.K. has compared unfavourably with that of other countries. Yet, surprisingly enough, the rate of increase of production *per capita* has if anything been noticeably faster on average than before the war, and also does not seem (with the exception of the case of Western Germany) to compare so badly with the rates of increase in countries where investment is more flourishing. Part of the explanation, but only part, may be that the population of this country is increasing more slowly, and therefore less investment is needed for the 'widening',

† See Table 2, p. 85 above.

in contrast to the 'deepening', of the capital stock. We discuss this point further in an application of the techniques of time-series analysis at the end of Chapter 6.†

As to inventories, at the time of writing, only the increase in value, the combined total of the value of the 'real' (physical volume) increase plus inventory profits, is known on an industry-by-industry basis, the break-down eliminating inventory profits being available only by sectors. This however is an area where the statistics are rapidly developing and improvements in the published information are made yearly. The table of inventories also gives an extremely valuable column indicating the approximate total absolute value of stocks held (in contrast to the changes), industry-by-industry, at a given date.

†Pp. 138–40 below.

PART II

A SELECTION OF INSTRUMENTS

CHAPTER FIVE

SOME NOTES ON THE ELEMENTARY AIDS TO INSPECTION

In Part I we discussed the nature and sources of economic statistics. We now go on to discuss a selection of the analytical devices which are commonly used to assist the brain in drawing conclusions from them—or, in the analogy of the title, a selection of 'surgical instruments' for operating on the statistical corpus. By far the most elemental, and most essential, procedure for analysing statistical data is one which seems so obvious that it is easy to forget to mention, yet is nevertheless an expertise, or art in its own right. This, for want of a less pompous word, is the method of simple inspection. That is to say, the method of examining the data carefully ('with the naked eye' as it were), noting the movements of the important figures and of the corresponding movements of possibly related figures, performing perhaps a few mental calculations, and thus obtaining one's first impressions. Very often as much can be got out of a set of statistical tables by simple inspection as by any other method, and it is essential that data always be examined in this way before more sophisticated operations are attempted. 'The surgeon must examine his patient before he carves him up, otherwise he may remove the wrong organ'—the analogy is almost perfect, for over and again we see the inexperienced student performing elaborate computations designed to test some relatively far-fetched hypothesis when another simple explanation of the movements of the data is staring him in the face.

However, 'Inspection' is not entirely a simple matter. It is a technique which is much assisted by experience. The inexperienced person suddenly faced with a large table of numerical data will frequently suffer a kind of mental black-out; so much detailed information will appear in this unfamiliar form that eyes and brain will cry to abdicate their functions, and there will be a temptation to report that no general conclusions can be drawn from the data whatsoever. But the more experienced eye, on the other hand, will often, in a manner which to others appears uncanny, leap to some critical point in the table or otherwise notice something interesting.

'Feel', however, is not the only ingredient of success. There is also involved an important brand of know-how in the arrangement and presentation of statistics so that intelligent inspection of them is possible. In particular, there are a number of elementary arithmetical tricks—the computation of ratios, percentages, averages and so on—which can provide much assistance, and it is with these and some basic points concerning presentation that the present chapter is primarily concerned. Most elementary text-books deal with these matters; here we offer notes on points of particular importance in economics and on aspects or refinements of which text-books treat less commonly, or at any rate, less intensively.†

Statistical Tables

It is more or less impossible to inspect statistical data unless they are arranged in tabular form. The art of reading tables, and of tidily and effectively constructing tables, is an art which, like that of tying a tie, however mundane must become an essential routine. In many walks of life excessive concern with regularity and neatness may well represent a symptom of weakness at the higher intellectual level, but in statistical work failure to maintain a reasonable standard inevitably leads to unfortunate mistakes. One should always write out a table, even if it is merely a 'working sheet' to be used only for some intermediate computation and never intended for general display, as if one were liable at short notice to have to hand over the work for completion by a (reasonably technically qualified) outsider to whom little or no verbal explanation could be given. The majority of statistical mistakes occur not so much from small errors of computation, as from some major '*gaffe*', such as carrying

† A good compressed general text-book for the whole of this Part is Prof. Roy Allen's *Statistics for Economists*, Hutchinson's University Library, 1951 (Second Ed.), pp. 220.

the wrong line of figures from one table to another, adding the wrong two things together, misreading an important figure, and so on. Such mistakes are easy enough to make at the best of times, without the additional hazard of lack of system or untidiness in the tables. Thus for example if the distinction between component items and specific sub-totals is insufficiently emphasised in the tabular lay-out, sooner or later a sub-total will be added into a grand total along with its own components; or if the order of two items is different in one part of the table from their order in another, sooner or later they will be accidentally transposed and so on.

The best way to avoid mistakes is to adopt a routine style of basic tabular lay-out (to be varied of course according to the needs of particular cases) so that after a time one almost automatically avoids arrangements which are likely to induce mistakes and one can read one's own tables (and others drawn up in the same style) quickly and easily. At the present time there is developing a distinctive 'contemporary' style of tabular presentation which is already widely prevalent in the official statistical publications of English-speaking and many other countries and in the statistical publications of the United Nations. The notes which are offered later below have this style in mind.

There are three types of table—Source Tables (or 'reference' tables), Working Tables (or 'working sheets') and Summary Tables (or 'text tables'). The first provide original data usually in considerable quantity and detail, as a basic source of reference; such tables can never be very easy to read but they form the basis of all other tables. Working Tables or working sheets are, as the name implies, tabular arrangements of data used in the process of computation or rearrangement; a primitive example would be where figures relating to employment at two dates are to be expressed in a summary table as percentage increases: the first column of the working table would show employment in the different industries at the first date, the second column employment at the second date, the third column the differences between the entries in the first and the second columns and finally the fourth column would express the differences as percentages of the base figures in the first column. A more sophisticated example would be

H

in the kind of working sheet needed in Regression Analysis.† First the two series of data to be correlated are put in adjacent columns, then in the next two columns each item in each series must be expressed as deviations from a fixed central value and added up; then each of the deviations must be squared (two more columns) and added up; finally each pair of original deviations must be multiplied together and this set of products added up, making a total of seven columns in all—and this is only a beginning, in 'multiple' Regression Analysis many more columns are needed.

Summary Tables (in the drawing up of which there is more art than in all) are designed to set out a specific statistical finding, or set of related facts, that is, they are designed to tell a definite story and probably to emphasise some particular aspect of it. If the analyst has discovered for example that out of a large number of series found in a certain reference table, two are particularly significant and display closely related movements, he may select these two for presentation in a summary table, ignoring the rest. The objects of a summary table are therefore simplification and exposition, and there are a number of ways in which they may be achieved—by the omission of irrelevant data as just suggested; by the combination of detail e.g. combining the results for two relevantly connected industries such as cotton and wool; by the use of averages, ratios and percentages (see below); or merely by better arrangement, for example by putting series to be compared close together.

In the list of notes which now follows, those which apply to all three types of tables are taken first, and then follow notes which are specific to each type separately:

All Tables

(i) All should be balanced in shape, neither too short and fat nor too long and thin, as far as is possible.

(ii) All should possess:

    (*a*) A *title*, answering the questions, What? Where? Method of classification? and When?,

    (*b*) A *stub*—the left-hand column and its heading,

† See Chapter 7 below.

(c) A *caption*—the headings of the other columns of the Body (which is the name given to the statistical content of the table),

(d) A *source note*, explaining the source of the data, and possibly a *general* note explaining any important point about the construction of the figures, together with *footnotes*, as necessary, qualifying particular entries.†

(iii) In all tables there must be an indication of the units in which the data are given, either at the top right, below the title, or, where different units are used for different parts of the table, at the head of the columns. Where data are given in percentages, the base of the percentages (answering the question, percentage of what?) must always clearly be indicated except where it is self-evident.

(iv) Totals as a general rule should be put below their components and should be made to stand out clearly in some way, e.g. by ruling.

† These footnotes should be very carefully worded, giving all the *necessary* information with the minimum of ambiguity and the maximum of compression.

In Table 4 on page 104 below, the first two footnotes are reproduced exactly as they were worded in the official publication from which the figures are taken and they provide an excellent example of bad footnote wording; they are verbose and offer unnecessary information (such as that the cause of the adjustment in 1953 was the discovery of 'errors' made by colliery companies) and on occasion are misdirected (where they give the proportion of *output* by the Coal Board when what is relevant is the proportion of employment, which may be rather lower). Also phrases such as 'the adjustment resulted in a net increase of *x* wage earners', though reasonably clear in meaning are singularly unhappy in expression. Finally, to the uninitiated, the general meaning of the first note is by no means clear. The original table in the *Annual Abstract*, although an annual table, chooses to give the results in the form of weekly averages, so that total man-shifts worked per head in each year is shown divided by the number 52. In the case of employment, the figures shown for wage-earners on colliery books is the ordinary arithmetic average (total of the item divided by number of items) of the 52 weekly returns of workers on books made by all the collieries, thus providing a very accurate estimate of the average level of the item over the year. But in each weekly return the collieries also stated the number of workers who were completely missing for the whole week, thus providing the statistics for 'effective employment' in that week: what the figures shown in the second column of the table actually represent, therefore, are the averages of the 52 weekly effective-employment totals. This concept is a useful and understandable one, but as the footnote to the table is worded one might imagine that the column excluded all workers who were absent for the whole of any week during the year.

On the other hand footnotes such as these are very much better than footnotes which give too little information. Far too often the authors of notes are satisfied merely to indicate the existence of some discontinuity, for example, without giving the reader any quantitative indication of the order of its significance.

(v) Columns should always be separated by ruling, a triviality perhaps but in practice an enormous help to the eye. Rows, by contrast, should in general only be ruled off in special cases, e.g. to set off a total or to separate two distinct parts of a table. Light horizontal lines are sometimes also used in official secondary sources to indicate some minor discontinuity in a time series.

(vi) Always keep to a standard set of conventional signs. Those almost universally adopted at the present time are:

.. 'not available'

— 'negligible or zero'

Never leave an entry blank in lieu of either of these signs; a blank is to be interpreted as meaning that the item is omitted because it would be meaningless.

Reference Tables

(i) Always draw up these tables as if you yourself might some time have to spend several days extracting figures from them. Clear typography or manuscript (to reduce eyestrain) is essential, but also valuable and in some conflict with this desideratum is compactness: it is a great disadvantage to the user to have to keep turning over pages.

(ii) The order in which items are given should be simple and straightforward and there should certainly be no deliberate attempt at what is done in Summary Tables, i.e. allowing the order to depend on some current evaluation of the relative importance or relatedness of the different series. The test should be that a reader with no preconceived ideas about the data should be able to find any item he wants, not necessarily instantaneously, but with confidence and reasonable celerity.

Working Tables

(i) Keep them as self-explanatory as possible (e.g. number all columns, then some columns can merely be headed, e.g. 'Col. (1) + Col. (2)').

(ii) If the data have been adjusted in any way so that their derivation from the reference table is not immediately obvious, each such adjustment should be noted.

(iii) Always include the maximum number of intermediate stages in the calculation; they are valuable in checking errors. Always carry data from the reference table into the working sheets before performing any computations; never attempt to combine the process of extraction from the reference table with computation as one operation.

(iv) Try to arrange for automatic cross-checks.

Summary Tables

(i) Comparison of series is easier by adjacent columns than by adjacent rows. Also, individual figures within a series are more easily compared in the vertical rather than in the horizontal plane; as a general rule therefore always put time series in columns unless they contain only two or three entries.

(ii) Do not include very much more data than is necessary to make and to support the point at issue. But, be honest, give any material which seriously qualifies or even tends to contradict the conclusions suggested, and always offer a certain amount of background data, e.g. a few earlier years for comparison. A route map is useless unless details of some of the surrounding country are included. There is no greater scope for statistical dishonesty than in the drawing up of Summary Tables, therefore be as honest as you are constitutionally able. Specious statistical argument by means of misleading selection is constantly bringing the social sciences into disrepute and is clearly the origin of the adage 'You can prove anything by statistics'.

Rounding. In summary tables it is almost always essential to round the figures to a relatively modest number of digits in order to avoid confusing the eye. But rounding may also be useful both in reference tables and in working tables, in the former if the raw data are not in fact accurate to more than so many places of decimals and in the latter in order to avoid unnecessary labour in computation. But rounding has its own obvious dangers and must never be carried to a point where misleading or false impressions may be created.

In summary tables the extent of permissible rounding depends almost entirely on the nature of the economic interpretation intended. The official Index of Industrial Production for instance (which expresses the volume of industrial output each month as a percentage of the average monthly output of 1948) is published rounded to the nearest whole number. The procedure is entirely correct in this case because, apart from the question of whether the index is statistically accurate to within 1 per cent, small month-to-month movements of this magnitude are not of great economic significance. But suppose it were desired to combine the Index of Industrial Production, put on an annual basis, with Ministry of Labour employment data in order to obtain an index showing roughly the annual trend of production per man, as in the following example.†

TABLE 3. *Industrial Production Per Man Employed*, 1984–1986

Ratios, 1984 = 100

	(a) Industrial employment	(b) Industrial production	(c) Col. (a) rounded	(d) Col. (b) rounded	(e) Col. (d) ÷ Col. (c)
1984	100	100	100	100	100
1985	101·6	103·7	102	104	102
1986	102·4	106·8	102	107	105
		(f) Col. (b) ÷ Col. (a)	(g) Col. (f) rounded		
1984		100	100		
1985		102·1	102		
1986		104·3	104		

Source: Imaginary.

Between 1984 and 1985 the method used in column (e) accurately portrays the actual two per cent increase in output per man, but the apparent change between the two following years—from 102

---

† The example given in the text is constructed only for the purpose of illustrating the particular point under discussion: there are certain dangers involved in computing changes in productivity by the method assumed in this imaginary case, dangers which are fully described in Devons *op. cit.* (p.29 above), page 110 *et seq.* Prof. Devons could, however, be criticised for rather overwriting the negative side of his argument.

to 105—represents an exaggeration of nearly one per cent, an amount which is clearly significant in an economic variable whose normal annual trend in some countries may be no more than $1\frac{1}{2}$ per cent in all. Column (f) tells the true story (assuming the original data to be reasonably accurate) but suffers from the disadvantage of not being rounded and therefore cumbersome to inspect: the best procedure therefore is to publish a summary table showing three columns such as (c), (d) and (g), warning the reader in a footnote that because of the rounding the figures in the last column do not necessarily represent the precise quotient of the figures printed in the other two. Similarly, in a rounded table in which a number of items are *totalled* the total presented need not be the exact sum of the printed components, but instead may be the rounded result of adding the individual items in their unrounded condition. If a number of items making up a certain total are expressed as percentages of that total, the percentages may be rounded to one decimal place, or even to the nearest whole number, and will therefore not add precisely to 100 and can be printed as such. But never forget the footnote of warning, or endless correspondence with precise-minded readers will ensue. Because of the psychological objection to presenting tables which apparently do not 'add up' many statisticians will 'fiddle' one or two of the constituent items, thus preserving an appearance of precision but quite likely creating a misleading impression with regard to the movement of the items adjusted. This practice is understandable but it is usually undesirable, although there are cases, such as that of the National Income statistics,† where to display tables in which printed items do not add to printed totals is so hopelessly inconvenient as to be ruled out of the question.

Hence some notes on rounding:

(i) In Summary Tables avoid the type of error demonstrated in the discussion of Table 3 above.

(ii) In general, in Working Tables, round to some chosen number of significant figures, particularly in the case of multi-

† In the Blue Book, figures are always given to the nearest £1 million although most of the items are by no means accurate to the nearest £10 millions. All items add to totals. If they did not, the self-balancing tables would not balance and a whole host of miscellaneous difficulties would arise.

plication and subtraction. In other tables rounding to a chosen number of places of decimals (or to the nearest whole number or even to the nearest 10 or the nearest 100) is probably the best.

(iii) In Working Tables keep at least one more significant figure in the computation than is needed in the final answer.

(iv) Remember that the maximum absolute error in a sum or difference of a series of rounded figures is the sum of the maximum errors in the individual figures; in a product or quotient the maximum percentage error is the sum of the maximum percentage errors in the two figures.†

Graphs. As is well known, after the tabular form, one of the most convenient ways of inspecting statistical series is by the means of graphs or charts. In the case of time-series—statistical data representing movements of a single variable at successive periods of time —it is really extremely difficult to obtain the 'feel' of the historical development of the series without the aid of some form of graphical presentation, and if two time-series are to be compared in anything more than a superficial manner, a time graph of both of them plotted on the same diagram is almost essential; the method is also an essential preliminary to more sophisticated analysis and is particularly useful if it is suspected that two series follow each other with a time-lag. Patterns of association of the latter sort, where one of the curves regularly dips or rises a little ahead of the other, can be spotted far more easily on graphs than is usually possible on casual inspection of tables, and when they have been noticed by this means, more rigorous tests of the association, such as discussed in Chapter 7 below, can then be applied.

In a time chart the economic variables are without exception always plotted against the vertical scale and 'time' (i.e. the dates) along the horizontal scale; the plotting points which the continuous curve of the graph joins up are chosen intersections of the horizontal and the vertical scale and combine two pieces of information—the level of the observed variable and the date on which the observation was made. This is by far the commonest type of chart used in economic statistics, but it is by no means the only one.

† Please see Allen *op. cit.*, (p. 94 above) for a full discussion of this point.

An exhaustive discussion of different types of charts and graphs and other forms of visual presentation will be found in a well-known book by two American authors, Croxton and Cowden,† who also provide a list of rules and hints for the student. Many such rules are of course largely matters of commonsense and here we will content ourselves with emphasising only one point, that is the need to use care in the choice of the relationship between the horizontal and the vertical scale. There is obviously no one 'right' relationship, but clearly the combination of a large vertical scale with a comparatively small horizontal scale may create a subjective impression of violent fluctuation in a series which from an economic point of view has in fact been relatively stable. In deciding on the relationship between the scales one should ask oneself the question, 'What is the smallest percentage change in this series which I consider to be economically significant?' If the answer were say, 'one per cent in a year', then arrange the scales so that the equivalent of a one per cent change in a year will show up as a distinctly, but modestly, upward-sloping section of the graph.

Ratios and Percentages

Consider the table overleaf, which is in fact a simplified but otherwise an exact reproduction of a table in the *Annual Abstract*.‡

Table 4 is in fact a *reference* table, and except for the criticisms of the footnote drafting discussed above,§ it obeys the rules of good table construction. From it one may learn of the development of the various factors which determine the total output of deep-mined coal—labour supply (men and man hours) and labour productivity. Why for example did production fall from pre-war to post-war and why was the subsequent recovery only partial? However, with the different series written in different units and often moving in opposite directions, the answers to these questions, although obtainable in principle, cannot be obtained easily. Table 5 below

† E. Croxton and D. J. Cowden, 'Applied General Statistics', New York, 1946. This is still one of the most comprehensive introductory text-books on the market.

‡ *Annual Abstract of Statistics*, No. 91, 1954, table No. 144. The last column (of Table 4) however, which relates to saleable deep-mined coal, is derived from (*Abstract*), table no. 139.

§ P. 97.

TABLE 4. *Coal: Productivity*

Great Britain

Weekly Averages

	Number of wage earners		Average shifts worked per week per wage-earner on colliery books	Average output per man-shift worked	Total output
	On colliery books	Effective employment[1]			
	thousands	thousands	number of shifts	tons	mil. tons
1938	782	..	4·96	1·14	4·35
1943	708[2]	647	5·12[3]	1·03	3·72
1944	710	642	4·96	1·00	3·54
1945	709	629	4·73	1·00	3·35
1946	697[3]	626[3]	4·84[4]	1·03	3·46
1947	711	648	4·69	1·07	3·57
1948	724	661	4·70	1·11	3·78
1949	720	646	4·67	1·16	3·93
1950	697	626	4·72	1·19	3·92
1951	699	629	4·81	1·21	4·06
1952	716	647	4·78	1·19	4·10
1953	717	629	4·70	1·21	4·08

Source : Ministry of Fuel and Power.

[1] The term 'effective employment' is used to denote wage-earners who worked at least one shift or part of a shift during any given week and thus excludes those absent for the whole of any week from whatever cause. Comparable figures for 1938 are not available. The figures for 1953 relate only to mines operated by the National Coal Board, which account for 99 per cent of the output.

[2] The introduction of a revised form of return which defined 'wage-earners' more precisely brought to light errors by colliery companies in completing returns. This correction resulted in a net increase of about 1250 wage-earners in 1943.

[3] Revised on the basis of the number of wage-earners on colliery books shown in the first column. The figure for 1943 on the old basis was 5·24.

[4] Owing to the varying practice of collieries in recording men on colliery books a standard method of recording wage-earners was adopted as from the beginning of 1946. The effect of this was to reduce the number on colliery books by approximately 2,500. The effect of the change on the average number of shifts worked was very small.

therefore is a *summary* table. But in this particular summary table simplification is achieved not only by eliminating unnecessary intermediate years but also by the device of expressing the data as ratios of a common base year in percentage form: each element in each time-series is expressed as a percentage of the figure displayed by the series in the year 1938: thus the entry in the second row of the last column is $\dfrac{3\cdot54}{4\cdot35} \times 100$ ($=81$ rounded) taken from the reference table, or the entry in the bottom row of the penultimate column is $\dfrac{1\cdot21}{1\cdot14} \times 100$ ($=106$, rounded) and so on throughout the summary table (except where adjustments have been made for discontinuity, particularly in the case of the third column). The effect is to demonstrate clearly and simply the proportionate changes over time in the various elements in the reference table and also the relationship between them: thus in 1947 for example, the proportionate decline in output as compared with 1938 was greater than the proportionate decline in the labour force (numbers on books) because of a net deterioration in other

TABLE 5. *Factors Contributing to Changes in the Output of Coal, 1938–1953*

Ratios, 1938 = 100

	Wage-earners on colliery books	Proportion in effective employment[1]	Shifts worked per wage-earner effectively employed	Output per manshift	Total output
1938	100	100[2]	100	100	100
1944	91	99	104	88	81
1947	91	100	97	94	82
1950	89	99	97	105	90
1953	92	97	99	106	94

Source: Table 4 above.

Notes. The figures shown in the last column are not necessarily the exact products of the corresponding figures in the preceding columns because of rounding. All series are adjusted to correct for the various discontinuities indicated in the footnotes to the source table.

[1] 1947 = 100; that is, in each year the proportion of the wage-earners on colliery books who were in effective employment (see fn. 1 to Table 4 above, and also p. 106 below) has been expressed as a percentage of the 1947 proportion.

[2] Data for this series were not collected before the war. The figure is an estimate of the lower limit of the ratio which would have been observed had data been collected, provided that no men temporarily laid off for lack of demand had been counted as 'on colliery books'.

elements (efficiency?), but by 1953 this relationship had been reversed.

As a matter of fact, Table 5 does more than merely simplify the reference table, it rearranges the data in such a way as to bring out a point which the reference table conceals. In the reference table average Shifts Worked are expressed as per head of workers 'on colliery books', so that Total Output is the product of Workers on Books, average Shifts Worked (so defined) and average Output per Man-shift. On this basis a decline of some 5 per cent in average shifts worked per man was implied in 1953 as compared with 1938, and appeared as a major factor in the decline in total output over the same period. But on further investigation of data in the reference table it becomes clear that there were two distinct elements in this decline of shifts worked per head of wage-earners on colliery books, (1) a decline in the proportion of those recorded on the books who were actually on average at any one time in effective employment (as against being on holiday, paid or unpaid, seriously ill, or simply of whereabouts unknown†) and (2) a small decline in the average weekly number of hours put in by the typical collier when 'effectively' employed. Both changes were a consequence of full employment and a higher living standard, no doubt, but they have a rather different social and economic significance otherwise. The decline in the proportion of 'effective' to total employment probably largely reflected the increase in official holidays, while the much smaller decline in shifts worked per effective employee represented the taking of slightly more leisure during the normal working week. Table 5 shows that it is in fact possible to separate the two elements mentioned quite easily in the process of deriving the summary table from the reference table, putting shifts worked as *per capita* of effective employees and adding a new column for the effect of the change in holidays. In this new column the proportion of effective employment to total

† Unfortunately another defect of the footnotes to the original source table is that they do not indicate in exactly what circumstances a worker is struck off the books or whether these circumstances have been the same throughout the series. This is important because miners, owing to the nature of their work, often find it desirable to spend some months of the year in other employment above the ground, for example in casual agricultural employment.

employment, which is a kind of ratio or percentage, can itself be given in ratio form, in other words we present a series of ratios of a ratio. Thus taking in this case 1947 as a base (see footnote 2 of the summary table), if the 1947 percentage of effective employment to total employment was $\frac{648}{711} \times 100$ ($=91\cdot0$) which are the figures given in the reference table, and the 1953 proportion was say $\frac{629}{717}$ ($=87\cdot8$) then the 1953 figure in the second column of the summary table is $\frac{87\cdot8}{91\cdot0} \times 100$ [$\backsimeq97$]. The convenient effect of the arrangement (which should not be used unless there is some good reason†) is that the ratios in the final column of the table are the products (minus of course the requisite number of zeros) of all the preceding ratios along each row. Thus the build up of elements contributing to the final result is given completely, simply and clearly. Also, for small changes around the 100 mark, *changes* in the total are approximately the *sum* of the component changes. Thus the 6 per cent decline in the total output of deep-mined coal from 1938 to 1953— that is from an index-figure of 100 to an index-figure of 94—was made up from an 8 per cent decline in Workers on Books, plus a three per cent decline in the Effective Employment ratio, plus a one per cent decline in the normal working week, *less* a six per cent increase in labour productivity on the job. (The one per cent discrepancy in the summation is due to rounding.)

What emerges therefore, both interestingly and somewhat surprisingly, is that the major causes of the decline in coal output were the decline in the numbers of workers on the books and the increase in holidays (paid or unpaid). When in attendance in a normal week, the miner of 1953 put in much the same number of hours as the miner of 1938, if not more,‡ and his output per man-shift had modestly increased.

The discerning reader will perhaps have noticed an element of arbitrariness in the selection of 1938 as the base year for representing the pre-war period in the summary table. As it happens, 1938

† Because percentage changes in percentages are not *in themselves* particularly meaningful kinds of numbers.

‡ See fn. 2 to Table 5.

was in fact, for the heavy industries of Great Britain, a year of semi-slump; coal production in the previous, near-full-employment, year, 1937, had been some 5 per cent greater than in 1938, and Shifts Worked and Output per Manshift had also been higher in consequence. If 1937 were the base, the ratios in Table 5 would take on a somewhat different appearance. Yet, on the other hand, 1938 coal production was not unrepresentative of the average annual production of the late nineteen thirties taken as a whole and if, instead of a single year, the average say of the years 1935–1938 had been taken as the base, as is often done, (the heading is then '1935–1938 = 100'), the figures would in general be little different from those printed. This illustrates an essential point. The choice of date or period for the base must depend upon the nature of the economic question being posed; in this case the choice depends on whether we are asking 'How did post-war full-employment coal output and productivity compare with the typical output and productivity of the semi-slump years of the late 'thirties?' or alternatively, 'How did they compare with the pre-war output of the industry at its best?': the two questions are very different, but both are interesting.

Two small final points about the use of these ratios (which are frequently loosely referred to as 'index numbers', although strictly that expression should be reserved for a particular kind of ratio, the kind with which Part III of this book is chiefly concerned): remember that when the changes in the original data are large (e.g. the ratio comes out at say 70) a *one unit change* in the ratio will no longer be equivalent to a one per cent change in the data. If you have a series,

1938	100
1953	70
1954	67

the change indicated from 1938 to 1954 is, of course, 33 per cent, but 1954 shows a four per cent decline on 1953, not a three per cent decline. In order to avoid confusion it is customary to refer to a given absolute change in the *ratio* as a change of so many 'points' or so many 'index-points' while reserving the expression 'change, per cent' for cases where it strictly applies. Finally, when changes in the original data become very large, ratios in the form we have been discussing should not be used at all. It is of little value to state that the output of turnips in some locality is now 300 per cent of the output in a base year if all that this indicates is that production has risen from one ton to three tons.

Ratios in the form which we have just been discussing are something of a speciality of economists: much more widely known is the straightforward case when parts of some aggregate are expressed as percentages of the whole, thus:

TABLE 6. *Personal Expenditure on Consumers' Goods and Services in the United Kingdom* 1948 *and* 1953

	£ millions		Per cent of total	
	1948	1953	1948	1953
Food - -	2,262	3,549	26·9	32·1
All Other - -	6,146	7,527	73·1	68·0
Total- - -	8,408	11,076	100	100

Source: *National Income and Expenditure.*
Note. Percentages do not necessarily add to 100 because of rounding.

The increase, between 1948 and 1953, in the slice of our purses which is taken by expenditure on food was significant and was partly due directly to derationing (i.e. to increased quantitative consumption relative to consumption of things in general) and partly to increased relative prices of food.† This proposition can be put more precisely, for the percentage of expenditure on food in 1953 is given by the expression:

$$\text{Percentage in 1948} \times \frac{\text{Quantity of food in 1953}}{\text{Quantity of food in 1948}}$$

$$\div \frac{\text{Quantity of all goods in 1953}}{\text{Quantity of all goods in 1948}} \times \frac{\text{Prices of food 1953}}{\text{Prices of food 1948}}$$

$$\div \frac{\text{Average prices of all goods 1953}}{\text{Average prices of all goods 1948}}$$

the component ratios of this expression can all be computed from the Blue Book as follows:

$$26\cdot9(1\cdot10 \div 1\cdot05)(1\cdot43 \div 1\cdot25) = 26\cdot9 \times 1\cdot05 \times 1\cdot14 = 32\cdot1$$

† I.e. to a greater proportionate rise in food prices than in the prices of consumer goods in general.

Thus the fact that food prices rose by 14 per cent relatively to prices in general† emerges as the most important factor in the increase in the proportion of expenditure taken by food, rather than the fact of the 5 per cent relative rise in quantity: the effect of derationing was relatively unimportant except to the extent that derationing itself was indirectly responsible for much of the relative price rise. What we have done here in effect is an analysis based on a combination of both types of ratios; 1·10, 1·05, 1·43 and 1·25 are in principle no more than ratios or 'index numbers' of quantities and prices with the year 1948 = 100.

A table such as the right-hand side of Table 6, without its left-hand side, has the disadvantage that it suppresses the important information that *total* expenditure, on goods in general, rose during the period: in fact at first glance the table seems to suggest that expenditure on goods other than food actually fell, this of course is not true; the table shows only that expenditure on goods other than food fell *relatively* to that on food, i.e. rose less or fell more (in this case the former). Non-Food expenditure was a falling proportion of a rising total, food expenditure was a rising proportion of a rising total. But the method of presentation holds the 'total' artificially constant at 100 for both years. To avoid the difficulty one can express the two classes of expenditure in *both* years as percentages of total expenditure in the *first* year, as follows:

TABLE 7. *Consumers' Expenditure, 1948 and 1953*
Percentages of Total Expenditure in 1948

	1948	1953
Food - -	27	42
Other Goods -	73	89
Total - -	100	131

Source: Table 6.
Note. All ratios are rounded to the nearest whole number.

---

† 43 per cent as against 25 per cent, but remember that big changes in ratios cannot be compared by addition or subtraction; $\frac{1\cdot43}{1\cdot25} \neq 1\cdot18$.

The figure of 131, the total of the second column, is of course identical to $\frac{11,076}{8,408} \times 100$, i.e. is total consumers' expenditure in 1953 with 1948 = 100. The total is no longer held constant and a table of this sort is sometimes thought of as a compromise, giving at least part of the information which is available on the left-hand side of Table 6. However, in the absence of further mental arithmetic, this table now conceals the essentially interesting information of the decline in the relative share of expenditure on food. This is bound to be; no real compromise exists (short of showing both types of table side by side as in Table 6). Table 7 however does perhaps present the full information more concisely than is possible in any other way.

As a last word in the chapter, readers should be reminded that a set of ratios cannot be averaged unless each is 'weighted' (see Chapter VIII below) by the value of its own base.

CHAPTER SIX

INTERPRETATION OF ANNUAL
TIME-SERIES

In the Introduction we saw that the economist's unique dependence on statistics for the application of his science derived partly from his inability to make controlled economic experiments. One of the most important statistical substitutes for controlled experiment in the social sciences consists in attempting deductions from the purely historical development of past events: we observe the statistics relating to what actually happened in the past from year to year—in contrast to what would have happened had we, the economists, been effectively holding under control a large number of the basic causal forces—and we attempt to make allowances for the fact that we were not. We hope that if a sufficiently large number of historical occurrences is considered, the effects of lack of control in the experiment can be mitigated. The data are considered in the form of a series of observations of a single economic variable (or set of variables) over a number of consecutive years (or months or weeks as the case may be) and for this reason the method is known generally as the Analysis of Time-series; the method ranges in sophistication from elementary mental arithmetic to advanced mathematical analysis.

The method is inherently awkward, because it contains a major internal contradiction. It requires for its effective functioning that the number of observations be large, i.e. that the time-series analysed be reasonably long; but, because of the natural change-ability of human behaviour, if the period considered is long, the economic relationships under measurement may themselves vary during the experiment (hence for example the difficulties in attempting to predict post-war elasticities of demand for consumer goods from the behaviour of pre-war time-series). Be that as it may,

a major proportion of applied work in economics will always involve the examination of historical data covering periods of substantial length. Often indeed, from the nature of the case it is only
in that form that the figures can be given much meaning. For example, if one learnt—out of the blue, as it were—that the Gross
Domestic Product of the U.K. per head of population was in 1955
the figure of £335, one would hardly be able to say whether this
was a reasonable result to expect or not. However, with the additional
information that the £335 in 1955 compared with about £170 (adjusted for changes in the value of money) fifty years earlier, and
rather under £225, twenty-five years earlier, one could begin to
see that the achievement of 1955 represented the result of a not unreasonable amount of economic progress over the years; one would
now possess some perspective of judgement in the matter.

But with only a handful or so of back figures one cannot get very
far: one can obtain only rough conclusions and one is in danger of
making serious mistakes—perhaps 1955, 1905 or 1930 happened to
be very untypical years? (1930, after all, was the beginning of a
great slump.) For any comprehensive analysis it is essential, therefore, to work with a long consecutive series as e.g. in Table 8 below.

Suppose now we are interested in theories of economic development and/or theories of the trade cycle. What sort of questions
might we wish to pose of the data in Table 8? As a possible preliminary list of questions, let us take the following (realising of course
that even if we succeed in answering them to our satisfaction there
remains much else to be asked):

(1) Is the British economy a progressing economy, in the sense
that production *per capita* displays a long term tendency to
rise?

(2) How does the rate of economic progress since the 1914–1918
war compare with that achieved in the late-Victorian and
Edwardian times?

(3) Do these data provide evidence of a regular cycle of oscillations—i.e. a Trade Cycle—superimposed on the long term
tendency?

These questions will be used to illustrate the various methods of
analysis described throughout the rest of this chapter.

Table 8.   Real Domestic Product Per Head
United Kingdom 1870–1955

£ at 1955 prices

1870	122	1900	167	1930	214
1871	123	1901	162	1931	206
1872	120	1902	166	1932	208
1873	124	1903	162	1933	218
1874	124	1904	162	1934	234
1875	123	1905	169	1935	250
1876	126	1906	177	1936	260
1877	127	1907	177	1937	271
1878	128	1908	165	1938	..
1879	126	1909	171	1939	..
1880	128	1910	179	1940	..
1881	132	1911	182	1941	..
1882	135	1912	184	1942	..
1883	137	1913	184	1943	..
1884	135	1914	..	1944	..
1885	134	1915	..	1945	..
1886	139	1916	..	1946	268
1887	142	1917	..	1947	271
1888	150	1918	..	1948	282
1889	155	1919	..	1949	294
1890	154	1920	203	1950	304
1891	152	1921	174	1951	312
1892	150	1922	187	1952	304
1893	149	1923	187	1953	315
1894	154	1924	197	1954	328
1895	162	1925	195	1955	335
1896	164	1926	193	1956	338
1897	164	1927	214		
1898	169	1928	212		
1899	172	1929	224		

Note. The data relate, in principle, to the Gross Domestic Product of the present geographical area of the U.K. divided by total population of the area at the date stated, and valued at the level of prices estimated to have been ruling at the end of 1955 (which was some 2 per cent higher than the level ruling during 1955 on average).

Sources: The series has been constructed from information available in the sources listed below, but it should be made clear that although the series is thought to provide a reasonably faithful picture of the history of the national production during the period indicated, the standard of accuracy in the estimation is a standard appropriate to the expository purposes of this text-book and may in places fall short of the standard of an authoritative presentation. Responsibility for errors rests entirely with the author and cannot be blamed on any of the authorities cited; the figures taken from them have been subjected to numerous adjustments.

1870–1913; series given by Prest, *Economic Journal*, March 1948, adjusted to

The Concept of Secular Trend

Question (1), in the jargon of the subject becomes 'what, if any, is the long term, or *secular trend* of the series?' 'Trend' means merely any long-period movement relative to the length of the series, and could apply equally well to a series relating to, e.g. the twelve successive months of a single year: the operative word in the definition is 'relative'. But the predicate 'secular' definitely implies some type of change occurring persistently over many years: movements due to the trade cycle or, in a monthly series, seasonal fluctuation are distinctly excluded by this adjective. However economists frequently use the word 'trend' alone when they mean secular trend, provided the meaning is clear in the context.

The first essential preliminary to any analysis of a time-series is to plot the data on a chart and Chart 1a below is the time-chart for the data of Table 8.

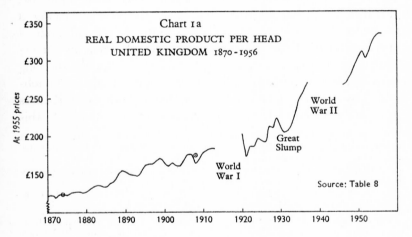

Our eyes immediately tell us that the answer to question (1) is in some general sense clearly affirmative: output *per capita* in the U.K. unmistakably snakes upwards across the page. But can we answer more precisely than by the vague statement of a visual impression? In other words, can we *measure* this trend?

(Notes to Table 8 continued on next page).

There are two intellectual approaches to the problem. The first considers the trend movement without any overt reference to whatever may be its underlying causes (such as technical progress and capital accumulation).† 'Trend' then becomes something inherent in the numerical behaviour of the series alone. The analyst does not say 'I believe this series to be rising in the long term at a certain rate because certain specific underlying causes are operating with that effect'; rather he says 'There seems to exist a group of residual forces, partly or wholly unknown and only partly understood, driving this series upwards (or downwards, as the case may be) in a rather regular way over time'. This latter might be termed the agnostic approach.

The evident weakness of the agnostic approach is that the trend of a given numerical time-series can only be defined in terms of the particular technique chosen to measure it; the concept measured is defined by the chosen method of measurement and nothing else. It is therefore rather arbitrary. The alternative way of looking at the matter is to take a definite view as to the nature and mode of operation of the basic causal economic factors. Thus, in our example, we should be stating that we wished to measure the long term effects of technical progress and capital formation unobscured by cyclical oscillations, wars, strikes and other disturbances to capacity working of the national economic resources. On this

eliminate Income from Abroad and adjusted also (with the aid of information privately supplied by Dr. Prest) to eliminate the influence of changes in the terms of trade (see Chapter 10, pp. 317 *et seq.*, below).

1913–1937; series constructed by the author, aided by the information given by Ridley, *Economica*, February 1955, and other sources.

1937–1956; Carter and Robson, *London and Cambridge Economic Bulletin* (in *Times Review of Industry*) December 1952, and Blue Book.

For a discussion of the principles of measurement of real national product, see Chapter 10. In Table 8 the estimates for 1937 to 1955 follow Blue Book principles and not the 'adjusted' principles referred to in Chapter 10, p. 316. The earlier data are altogether too rough for concern with finer points of principle, but there is some reason for believing that they may tend more toward an application of the 'adjusted' principle than of the Blue Book principle. It should also be noted that the methods followed give the whole series the character of a chain index; see Chapter 9, p. 276.

---

† By 'technical progress' here and below we mean the growth of technical knowledge, i.e. in theoretical language, the outward shifting of the production function; we exclude the effect of movements *along* the function.

basis there does indeed exist a 'right' way of measuring the trend; the method, whatever it is, which is appropriate to the actual mode of operation of these forces. In principle, therefore, the second approach is to be preferred. But in practice there is not all that much difference between the two; or rather, in practice the intellectually superior alternative can rarely be properly applied. This impediment arises from a combination of three ingredients which we usually find in the typical analytical situation. First, in most cases there will be at least one basic causal factor which is not capable of independent measurement, i.e. not capable of measurement except in terms of its own consequences. Thus in our example we may measure capital accumulation in terms of quantities of machines, buildings, etc. but not so, evidently, technical progress. (In effect we are forced to say that all movement of the series which we cannot explain in other ways must by definition be due to 'technical progress'.) Second, we do not, in fact, possess much independent evidence as to the likely mode of operation of the causal forces; we do not know whether they normally operate with constant or varying strength from year to year, or from decade to decade—perhaps we should expect them to be regularly accelerating, perhaps decelerating? Thirdly, it is probable that the cyclical forces and trend forces react upon one another; wars and slumps may well speed up or slow down technical progress and they obviously affect capital formation, and so on. Thus the situation of the observer may be likened to that of a man who, on a pitch-dark night, is watching the passage across his line of vision of a balloon which has been coated with phosphorescent paint: he believes this object to be attached by a string to the body of someone pedalling a bicycle at a constant speed up a moderate incline; but he can see neither bicycle, rider, string nor road. He would like to test this 'bicycle' hypothesis generally and in particular he would like to measure the gradient of the incline.

We will suppose that the balloon does appear to be moving generally both upwards and across, but its passage is by no means smooth; indeed there is a marked tendency to oscillation about whatever is the general line of flight; some movements seem entirely erratic. In short, if the path of the balloon were traced on a photogaphic plate exposed through the whole of the period of traverse, the developed negative would appear much as would that of a photostat copy of Chart 1a. The problem is that in this situation there are numerous plausible explanations of the balloon's observed behaviour, all of which are consistent with the general hypothesis to be tested; for example:

(i) The gradient of the road is not constant ('the forces of the technical progress are not constant').

(ii) There is blowing a gusty wind, whose gusts have a certain regularity; this causes the balloon to flap on the end of its string, while the string is being drawn independently upwards ('the trend and the oscillation are independent').

(iii) Some aerodynamic property of the balloon and the string causes the balloon to sheer up and down when, and only when, it is being drawn forward through the air ('trend and oscillation are connected, but it is the trend which causes the oscillation').

(iv) The effort of pedalling the bicycle uphill causes the rider to bob his shoulders; the string happens to be attached to his shoulders ('trend and oscillation are interconnected, but the causal relation consists in the oscillations being a necessary process in the generation of the trend and not merely a bi-product—therefore no oscillation, no trend').

All the above causal complexes would produce much the same picture on the photographic plate. In any other science the obvious next step would be to undertake some experiment analogous to switching on a searchlight: only in meteorology, in aerial reconnaissance in war and in the social sciences is the analyst so frequently left to continue by renewed contemplation of the original ambiguous evidence. These sciences are notoriously inaccurate in consequence. However, suppose for working purposes we *assume* both that the road exists and that its gradient is fairly constant. On that assumption we may be able to make some measurement and with this measurement apply some retrospective test of consistency (but we shall still be unsure as to quite what it is we have measured, and we shall be able to say little about causation). Specifically, let us assume:

(a) The gradient is precisely constant and so also the speed of the bicycle, i.e. the trend forces operate with absolutely constant effect, year in, year out.

(b) All (oscillatory) movements and other disturbances in the long period in some sense cancel out (this would tend to be the case in all situations (ii) to (iv) above).

The argument which follows does not depend on believing these assumptions literally to be true.

Straight-Line Trend

Assumption (a) implies that the trend would be 'linear'; i.e. that the inclined road, if we could see it, would be cutting across the landscape in a perfect straight line, a line which, were it not for disturbances, would be traced almost exactly by the balloon on the photographic film. Because the speed of the bicycle is constant, the forward movement each year would be constant (the time-scale on our chart being of course constant throughout the length of the horizontal axis) as also the upward movement, and the amount of this constant upward movement would approximately be equal to the total vertical rise from top to bottom of the road, divided by the horizontal distance traversed (number of years elapsed). This given vertical increment for a one-unit horizontal advance is the gradient of the road, the slope of the trend line, 'the trend rate of increase' of the series.

Assumption (b) would imply that the whole of the observed upward movement of the series from its beginning to its end could be attributed to the secular forces ('the whole of the vertical rise in the balloon was due to the incline in the road, and none to the wind, etc.'). Could the trend rate of increase in Chart 1a be assessed therefore simply by dividing the total increment from 1870 to 1913 (£62) by the number of years elapsed (43)† yielding a measured gradient of £1·44 per annum? In principle, yes, but only

† 1870–1913 inclusive is 44 years but because the data in effect represent rates of flow of production at a moment of time, (although expressed as £ per annum,) we must measure from point to point. Preferably we measure from mid-year to mid-year, but even if we do not we must at all costs avoid measuring from e.g. beginning—1870 to end—1913 when the actual data do not in fact relate to this period (as would be implied if we divided by 44 here).

if both the years 1870 and 1913 happened to be years of *zero disturbance* or, if not, were both disturbed in the same direction by the same amount. Otherwise, suppose 1913 had happened to be a year of sharp cyclical recession (as e.g. 1908 evidently was) the trend would be significantly understated by this method, and if 1913 had been at the peak of a boom as perhaps it was, vice versa. Similar arguments apply to 1870.

The difficulty can to some extent be got around by taking as the starting and the ending point of the calculation the average level of the series over the first five or ten years, (say), and that of the last five or ten years correspondingly. (The period should be fixed to coincide roughly with the length of any regular cycle which is suspected to be present.) This device will eliminate the effect of all disturbances which are self-cancelling within the chosen period and these may indeed represent good proportion of the total. Thus, in the example, the average level of *per capita* product for the years 1870 to 1879 (i.e. the sum of the results for all those years divided by 10) works out at £124, and the corresponding figure for the period 1904 to 1913 is £175. The total increment is thus £51, the relevant divisor is the time elapsed from the middle of the first period to the middle of the second, i.e. 34 years (the total number of years in the series less ten) so that the computed average annual increase by this method is 51/34 = £1·50: thus the cruder method did in fact understate the trend because although the year 1913 was reasonably normal, 1870 was a little high.

The two points, £124 at the end of 1874 and £175 at the end of 1908 are marked and circled in Chart 1a. In Chart 1b, which is otherwise the same, they are joined by a straight line. This is the linear trend-line implied in Assumption (a) above. Such a line provides a useful visual representation of the estimated trend since it joins all the levels of *per capita* production which would have been experienced had it not been for the disturbances and had Assumption (a) been precisely correct. The line shown has of course a slope, or gradient, of 1 : 1·5 (see above) and the fact that it passes beneath the actual result for 1870 but clean through the actual result for 1913 explains more precisely why the cruder method gave us an understatement of the probable trend. For we see that the result for 1870 was not actually higher numerically than the average of the next ten year period but it nevertheless appears high *when account is taken of the fact that it came earlier in time*, i.e. when account is taken of the probable existence of at least some upward trend. This is a point such as might easily be overlooked in a back-of-an envelope type of calculation and demonstrates the value of more formal analysis.

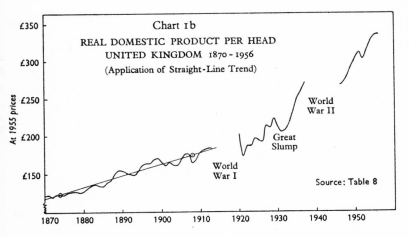

Chart 1b

REAL DOMESTIC PRODUCT PER HEAD
UNITED KINGDOM 1870 - 1956
(Application of Straight-Line Trend)

While the second of the methods just described is thus evidently an improvement on the first it still only eliminates the effect of disturbances which are self-cancelling within the ten years. There may be others. The concept of secular trend is perfectly consistent with the existence of disturbances capable of raising or depressing the average results for a whole ten-year period, or even longer; one such disturbance appears to have occurred for example in 1890–1900 and another, in the opposite direction, due to misguided economic policy in the nineteen-twenties. Hence we search for a more general solution.

Pause for Algebra

It is not possible to proceed further without the aid of a little elementary algebra; theoretically, everything could be described in words and with arithmetical examples, but in practice the prose

passages required would be excessive in length and no less awkward to comprehend. We will here explain the use of a few basic
symbols and formulae, and will illustrate their use. Others will be
introduced later as required.

Let n stand for the total number of elements in a time series, or
in a particular segment of a series which is under consideration.

[*Example:* The segment analysed in the preceding section was
from 1870 to 1913 inclusive, hence $n = 44$.]

Let the individual years in a series be identified by numbering
from 1 to n, 1 standing for the first year, 2 for the second and so on,
and n for the last.

[*Example:* 1 stands for 1870, 2 for 1871 and n ($=44$) for 1913.]

Let X stand generally for the number of any given year in the
series.

Let Y stand generally for the value of the variable described in
the series, and let the year be specified by suffix. Thus $Y_{(1)}$ stands
for the actual value in the first year, $Y_{(n)}$ the actual value in the last
year and $Y_{(X)}$ for the actual value in any given year.

[*Example:* $Y_{(1)}$ indicates Domestic Product per capita in 1870
(i.e. from Table 8 $Y_{(1)} = £122$); $Y_{(4)}$ is *per capita* product in
1873, (i.e. £124), etc.]

Let $Yc_{(X)}$ stand for the *theoretical* value of the series (in any given
year X) according to some trend line (see above), in contrast to the
actual value.

[*Example:* In Chart 1*b*, the actual value in 1890, i.e. $Y_{(21)}$ is £154;
the value according to the trend line drawn, i.e. $Yc_{(21)}$ is £147;
the year was disturbed by a trade cycle.]

Let $\overset{n}{\underset{1}{\Sigma}} Y$ indicate the sum of all the elements in the series, i.e.,

$$\overset{n}{\underset{1}{\Sigma}} Y = Y_{(1)} + Y_{(2)} + Y_{(3)} \ldots + Y_{(n)}$$

Then $\overset{X}{\underset{1}{\Sigma}} Y$ indicates the sum of all the elements from year 1 to year
X inclusive.

Now evidently $\dfrac{1}{n} \overset{n}{\underset{1}{\Sigma}} Y$ is the arithmetic mean (average) of all the
Y's in the series or part-series indicated. This operation of

averaging may be indicated more generally by placing a bar over the symbol to be averaged; thus given any set of numbers such as $Q_1, Q_2 \ldots Q_n$, then $\bar{Q} = \frac{1}{n} \sum_1^n Q$.   Thus

$$\bar{Y} = \frac{1}{n} \sum_1^n Y$$

The bar is only used when the whole of the series is to be averaged.†

Note that in the system described, the whole set of possible values of X, corresponding to the whole set of years in the series, form an arithmetical progression; hence,

$$\bar{X}\left(= \frac{1}{n} \sum_1^n X\right) = \frac{n}{2}$$

and indicates the mid-point of the series in time.

[*Example:* $\frac{n}{2} = \frac{44}{2} = 22$. $X = 22$, indicates the year 1891 which is the year *at the end of which* the period 1870–1913 is exactly divided in half; with an odd-numbered series, say, 1870–1912, $n/2$ comes out as $21\frac{1}{2}$, indicating that the series is divided in the *middle* of 1891, 21 being the X-number of the preceding year, 1890. This is admittedly awkward.]

The system can be illustrated in a formal description of the simple methods of trend fitting explained verbally in the previous section.

† In the particular example, the average of all the *per capita* products (Y's) from 1870 to 1913 will not be quite the same thing as the mean level of income *per capita* in the period, although it will probably be fairly close to it.

Let $O_{(X)}$ stand for total income (not *per capita*) in year X and let $P_{(X)}$ stand for the population in year X. Then, in the example,

$$Y_{(X)} = \frac{O_{(X)}}{P_{(X)}} \quad \text{and} \quad \bar{Y} = \frac{1}{n}\left\{\frac{O_{(1)}}{P_{(1)}} + \frac{O_{(2)}}{P_{(2)}} \ldots \frac{O_{(n)}}{P_n}\right\}$$

But the mean or average level of product *per capita* in ordinary parlance implies the average total product divided by the average level of population, during the period, i.e.

$$\frac{1}{n} \sum_1^n O \div \frac{1}{n} \sum_1^n P = \frac{O_{(1)} + O_{(2)} \ldots O_{(n)}}{P_{(1)} + P_{(2)} \ldots P_{(n)}}$$

This will not necessarily be the same as Y. The point must be watched when using data in this form. It can be shown that the extent of the divergence depends on the extent to which the years of higher output *per capita* tend also to be years of higher population; in the example this is the case since both population and productivity are rising over time.

Any straight line trend is described by an equation of the general form,

$$Yc_{(X)} = A + BX \qquad (1)$$

A and B are constants to be computed from the data in a manner to be specified. When this has been done the equation is merely a formula stating that the trend value of the series in any year, X, can be worked out simply by substituting the chosen value of X (i.e. the number of the chosen year) on the right-hand side of the equation, together with the values of A and B.

Thus the first method of trend fitting described in the preceding section (page 119) specifies in effect the following simple rules for determining A and B,

$$A = Y_{(1)} \qquad (2)$$
$$B = (Y_{(n)} - Y_{(1)})\frac{1}{n-1} \qquad (3)$$

Thus A is defined as the value of the series in the first year and B the average annual increase from the first year to the last. Hence equations (2) and (3) describe the method completely.

Before going further, the meaning of the constants A and B requires further discussion. B represents the measure of the *slope* of the trend line, i.e. the amount of increase on the vertical axis for one unit advance along the horizontal axis; in this case B is the estimated trend rate of increase of *per capita* income measured in pounds sterling per annum. As B measures the slope of the line, so A fixes its position, i.e. A tells us where the line starts. Any straight line on a graph is completely defined by two constants such as these and, given any pair of values for the constants, there is only one corresponding straight line. Hence when we have settled A and B we have settled our estimate of the trend.

The second method of trend fitting described in the preceding section (page 120) is also defined by three equations, as follows:

$$Yc_{(X)} = A + B\{X - \tfrac{1}{2}(K+1)\}\dagger \qquad (4)$$

K standing for the number of years at the beginning and end of the series over which it is decided to do the averaging (i.e. in the example, $K = 10$). A and B are now given by,

$$A = \frac{1}{K} \cdot \sum_{1}^{K} Y \qquad (5)$$

† $K + 1$, rather than K, is required to obtain the correct positioning.

$$B = \frac{1}{(n-K)} \cdot \left\{ 1/K \sum_{(n-K+1)}^{n} Y - A \right\} \qquad (6)$$

[*Example*†:

$$A = 1/10\,(Y_{(1)} + Y_{(2)} \ldots + Y_{(10)}) = \frac{122 + 123 + 120 \ldots + 126}{10}$$

$$= 124$$

$$B = 1/(44 - 10) \left\{ 1/10 \sum_{35}^{44} Y - 124 \right\}$$

$$= 1/35 \left\{ \frac{162 + 169 \ldots + 184}{10} - 124 \right\}$$

$$= 1\cdot50.$$

Equation (4) therefore becomes

$$Y_c = 124 + 1\cdot5\,(X - 5\tfrac{1}{2})$$

This is the 'trend equation' for Chart 1*b*. The trend value in 1890 is therefore given by

$$Y_c = 124 + 1\cdot5\,(21 - 5\tfrac{1}{2}) = 147$$

as already noted by inspection (122 fourth example).]

Again notice that the constants were determined by the following three things, and nothing else:

(i) the general method of trend fitting as given by the rules specified in equations 4–6,

(ii) the particular application of these rules as given by a choice of a particular value for K,

(iii) a selection from the actual data of the series.

This completes the basic description and illustration of the system of notation; it is more or less standard. We shall now use it to describe a more advanced method of trend fitting, the type of use for which it was designed.

The Method of Least Squares

The weaknesses of the methods of trend fitting described so far may be stated as follows: they would be capable of yielding false estimates even if applied to time-series where both Assumption (*a*) *and* Assumption (*b*) (on page 119 above) happened in fact to be perfectly valid. Assumption (*a*) said, in effect, 'The mode of operation of the trend forces is linear.' Assumption (*b*) said, 'The effect

† From the data of table 8.

of shocks and disturbances cancel out in the long run.' But the methods described do not consider shocks and disturbances in the long run, they eliminate only those which happen to cancel in a specified short- or medium-lengthed period such as ten years. There may well, as we have seen, be others.

In our next method therefore—the method of 'least squares'— we shall attempt to choose a trend line which while conforming to the assumption of linearity, also, when compared with the actual data over the whole length of the series, *most nearly* satisfies Assumption (*b*), i.e. most nearly eliminates shocks and disturbances in the long run. We search for the straight line which by implication sets the apparent effect of disturbances in some sense at a long run minimum. This is not as easy as it sounds. The effect of a disturbance in year X may be measured quantitatively by the amount by which the actual result for year X deviates from the theoretical result postulated by the trend line which is being considered. Name such deviation with the symbol, y^*, so that,

$$y^*_{(x)} \equiv Y_{(x)} - Yc_{(x)} \qquad (7)$$

It would seem then that given the data of the series all we have to do is to find values for A and B in a trend equation such that the sum $\sum_{1}^{n} y^*$ is at a minimum, i.e. is less than could be obtained with any alternative pair of values for A and B. Unfortunately it happens that, taken literally, the condition is nonsense.

Consider the infinity of straight lines which could be drawn on any given graph. In the case of all the reasonable ones—i.e. all the lines which pass through the data at all—some of the resulting y^*'s will be positive (i.e. $Y_{(x)} > Yc_{(x)}$) and some negative; if therefore *all* the deviations were algebraically added without alteration of sign there would be a considerable amount of self-cancelling, the pluses tending to offset the minuses. A line might indeed be found which over half the period in question passed a long way below the actual data, but yet yielded a very low value of $\sum y^*$, simply because over the other half of the period it passed a long way above the data. As it happens, *any* line which has the property of passing through the mid-year/mean-value point of the series—

i.e. the point where $Y = \bar{Y}$ and $X = \bar{X}$—will set Σy^* at zero; as, therefore, there exist in principle an infinite number of lines passing through this or any other point, including one running horizontally up and down the page, the criterion 'Σy^* at a minimum' is useless.

The usual solution to the conundrum is to *square* the deviations before aggregating them, i.e. to find and minimise not Σy^* but $\Sigma (y^*)^2$.

Since all squares are positive, self-cancelling is impossible and although by this method we are not minimising the 'aggregate deviation' in ordinary parlance, we are minimising something which is directly related to it; and the sum of a set of squared deviations is a concept which is fundamental to the greater part of general statistical theory.†

A squared deviation in our notation is $(y^*)^2$, therefore the quantity we are concerned to minimise is $\Sigma (y^*)^2$. For any given time-series, i.e. any given set of actual values of $Y_{(1)}, Y_{(2)} \ldots Y_{(x)} \ldots Y_{(n)}$, there is only one straight line, i.e. one unique pair of values for A and B in the linear estimating equation, which sets at an absolute minimum the sum $\overset{n}{\underset{1}{\Sigma}} (y^*)^2$. And it is possible to determine these unique values of A and B by simple computations upon the data without resort to trial and error. Standard texts give a number of variants of the basic method for doing this, from which the following is chosen as being simple to apply while still clearly displaying

† An alternative—little used because more cumbersome to apply—is to change the signs of the negative deviations before carrying out the aggregation. Actually, the usual method has a certain drawback, which this more cumbersome one avoids; the usual method attributes disproportionate importance to the larger deviations. However, the exaggeration takes a specific form, that of the direct Square Law, and can on certain assumptions be justified in probability theory. Roughly, the idea is that as deviations increase in magnitude, the likelihood of their representing the result of purely chance disturbances diminishes disproportionately. The existence of a small number of large deviations therefore represents a more serious criticism of any suggested trend line than that of a correspondingly larger number of small deviations: the line is therefore chosen so as to pay disproportionate attention to avoiding large y^*'s in relation to small ones. As a matter of fact, in the conditions surrounding many economic time-series problems, the assumptions of the probability theory involved here are not valid, in particular if the series is rather on the short side. If the least-squares criterion is employed to fit a trend line to a short economic time series, one single large disturbance, for example caused by a strike, may influence the computed result quite inordinately and from a theoretical point of view, quite irrationally.

K

the basic theoretical principle. We shall need some new concepts and symbols for them.

Define,

$$y_{(x)} \equiv Y_{(x)} - \overline{Y} \qquad (8)$$

$y_{(x)}$ therefore represents the amount by which the actual result in any given year deviates from the mean level of actual results over the whole period of the series. Similarly we can define,

$$yc_{(x)} \equiv Yc_{(x)} - \overline{Yc} \qquad (9)$$

$yc_{(x)}$ represents the extent to which the *trend value* in any given year deviates from the mean of all the trend values: and since the series of trend values form an arithmetical progression, this mean of all the trend values coincides with the trend value at the mid-point of the series, i.e.

$$yc_{(\overline{x})} = 0$$

The mid-point of the series is given by $\overline{X}$ (see above) so define

$$x \equiv X - \overline{X} \qquad (10)$$

x is thus the distance in time between year X and the mid-point of the series and can be used to modify the numbering system of the years so that they are numbered from the middle of the series, rather than the beginning. In this arrangement, if n is odd, we call the mid-year, year o, since for that year $X - \overline{X}$ is obviously zero; then the year after the mid-year becomes year $+1$, the year before it, year -1 and so on. If n is even, $\overline{X}$ is not a whole number, i.e. the mid-point falls between two years and the series will have to be enumerated $-2\frac{1}{2}$, $-1\frac{1}{2}$, $-\frac{1}{2}$, $+\frac{1}{2}$, $+1\frac{1}{2}$, $+2\frac{1}{2}$, etc. If speed is essential this last-mentioned inconvenience can be circumvented by dropping one year at the beginning or end of the series (as is done in the example Table 9 below); this is unlikely to make much difference to the result unless the year dropped is a year displaying unusually large disturbance. Then the first step in the computation of A and B for minimum $\Sigma(y^*)^2$ is to transform the series, by means of simple subtraction, from the set $Y_{(1)}$, $Y_{(2)}$ ... $Y_{(n)}$ into set of the corresponding y's and then to number these y's from the mid-point, i.e. number them with the system of x's. Thus the whole series now becomes a series such as,

$$\cdots y_{(-2)}, y_{(-1)}, y_{(0)}, y_{(+1)} \cdots y_{(x)} \cdots$$

Now, corresponding to the trend equation of the form

$$Yc_{(X)} = A + BX$$

relating to the untransformed data, there is an equation

$$yc_{(x)} = a + bx \tag{11}$$

But we know that when $x = 0$, $yc_{(x)} = 0$; hence $a = 0$ and (11) becomes

$$yc_{(x)} = bx \tag{12}$$

relating to the data in deviation form. It can easily be shown there is a simple relationship between the two forms so that if we know b in the second we soon know A *and* B in the first, actually

$$B = b \tag{13}$$
$$A = \overline{Y}_c - b\overline{X} \tag{14}$$

Hence our problem has become that of finding $\overline{Y}_c$ and b. This is actually simple, although proof of the method requires a couple of propositions in the differential calculus and should therefore be passed over by readers unfamiliar with the technique. As a preliminary, notice that the definitions imply

$$y_{(x)}^* = y_{(x)} - yc_{(x)} + \bar{y} \tag{15}$$

where $\bar{y} \equiv \overline{Y} - \overline{Y}c$, the difference between the mean of the data and the mean of any trend line which may be fitted. Now if we substitute (12) into (15) we get

$$y_{(x)}^* = y_{(x)} - bx + \bar{y} \tag{16}$$
$$\therefore (y_{(x)}^*)^2 = y_{(x)}^2 - 2bx \cdot y_{(x)} + b^2 x^2 + 2\bar{y} \cdot y_{(x)} - 2\bar{y}bx + \bar{y}^2 \tag{17}$$

and $\quad \Sigma (y_{(x)}^*)^2 = \Sigma y_{(x)}^2 - 2b \Sigma x \cdot y_{(x)} + b^2 \Sigma x^2 + 2\bar{y} \Sigma y_{(x)}$
$$- 2\bar{y}b \Sigma x + n\bar{y}^2 \tag{18}$$

Now, as is well known, the sum of a set of deviations from a mean must always be zero, i.e. in this case $\Sigma y = \Sigma x = 0$, hence

$$\Sigma (y_{(x)}^*)^2 = \Sigma y^2_{(x)} - 2b \Sigma x \cdot y_{(x)} + b^2 \Sigma x^2 + n\bar{y}^2 \tag{19}$$

(19) may be differentiated for a minimum with respect to b and $\bar{y}$, the condition being

$$\frac{\partial \Sigma (y_{(x)}^*)^2}{\partial b} = \frac{\partial \Sigma (y_{(x)}^*)^2}{\partial \bar{y}} = 0 \tag{20}$$

Differentiating accordingly we get

$$- 2 \sum x \cdot y_{(x)} + 2b \sum x^2 = 2n\bar{y} = 0 \qquad (21)$$

Hence

$$\bar{y} = 0 \quad \therefore Y = Yc \qquad (22)$$

and

$$b = \frac{\sum xy\dagger}{\sum x^2} \qquad (23)$$

In other words the line of 'best fit', the line which minimises the sum of the squares of the deviations from itself is fixed by the two conditions (1) that it has the same mean $\bar{Y}c$, as the mean of the data, $\bar{Y}$, (and that it pass through this mean at the mid-point of the series) and (2) that its slope be the ratio of the sum of the cross-products between the $y_{(x)}$'s and the corresponding x's themselves, to the sum of the squares of the x's. The latter is a formula which the practising statistician meets in one context or another every working day of his life; the use made here represents in effect a special application.

To recapitulate; we wish to find the constants A and B in a trend equation of the form

$$Yc_{(X)} = A + BX$$

The conditions are,

$$A = \bar{Y} - B\bar{X} \qquad (22a)$$
$$B = \sum xy / \sum x^2 \qquad (23a)$$

(The above is merely the result of combining equations (22) and (23) with (13) and (14).)

Hence the complete operating procedure may be summarised as follows:

(1) Plot the data on a chart in order to see whether the assumption of linear trend seems generally suitable.

(2) Find the mid-year ($\bar{X}$) of the series and number all the other years from it, calling these numbers x's.

(3) Add all the items (Y's) in the series and divide by the total number of elements in the series (n), thus obtaining the 'mean' or average of the series ($\bar{Y}$).

(4) Express all the items in the series as deviations from $\bar{Y}$, naming these deviations y's ($y_{(x)} = Y_{(x)} - \bar{Y}$).

† The top line is an abbreviation for $\sum x \cdot y_{(x)}$.

(5) Arrange the x's and y's in historical order in adjoining columns, multiply each y by its corresponding x, and obtain the total of these products ($\Sigma\, xy$).

(6) Square all the x's and sum the squares ($\Sigma\, x^2$).

(7) Find the required slope of the trend line from the formula $B = \Sigma\, xy / \Sigma\, x^2$.

(8) Position the line either by ensuring that it passes through the mid-year mean-value point of the series or by finding A in the formula given (equation 22a).

The working table for the computation, using the data of Table 8 would appear as follows:

TABLE 9. *Example of Working Table for Least-Squares Trend*

	(1)	(2)	(3)	(4)	(5)	(6)
Year	X	Y	x	y	xy	x^2
1870	1	122	− 21	− 28	+ 588	442
1871	2	123	− 20	− 27	+ 540	400
1872	3	120	− 19	− 30	+ 570	361
.	.	.	.	.	.	.
.	.	.	.	.	.	.
.	.	.	.	.	.	.
1890	21	154	− 1	+ 4	− 4	1
1891	22	152	0	+ 2	—	—
1892	23	150	+ 1	—	—	1
.	.	.	.	.	.	.
.	.	.	.	.	.	.
.	.	.	.	.	.	.
.	.	.	.	.	.	.
1911	42	182	+ 20	+ 32	+ 640	400
1912	43	184	+ 21	+ 34	+ 714	442
Totals		6443	—	—	+ 10140	6620

$\overline{X} = 22$ $\qquad\qquad$ $\overline{Y} = 6443/43 = 150$

$b = \dfrac{\Sigma\, xy}{\Sigma\, x^2} = \dfrac{10,140}{6,620} = 1\cdot 53$ $\quad$ $A = \overline{Y} - b\overline{X} = 150 - 1\cdot 53 \times 22 = 116$

The Short Method of Computation

If from the nature of the data the work of computing Y (step 3 above) seems likely to be unduly laborious in relation to the time available, there is a short-cut method which is sometimes recommended. This relies on the proposition already referred to that the sum of a set of deviations from a mean must be zero: if therefore instead of the true mean there is used an estimated or 'arbitrary' mean based on inspection rather than actual computation, the average extent to which the deviations taken from this arbitrary mean *do not* sum to zero measures the amount by which it is necessary to adjust the arbitrary mean itself in order to obtain the true mean. On this principle the formula for the true mean is then

$$\overline{Y} = \overline{Y}' + \Sigma y'/n \qquad (24)$$

where $\overline{Y}'$ is the arbitrary mean and y' is a deviation taken from the arbitrary mean instead of the true mean, i.e. $y'_{(x)} = Y_{(x)} - \overline{Y}'$. And conveniently it happens that provided the x's are not also measured from an arbitrary $\overline{X}'$ these arbitrary y's can be used unadjusted in the computation of the line of best fit, for it can be proved that

$$\Sigma xy' = \Sigma xy \qquad (25)$$

It is unlikely in time-series work that there would often be much saving in time from the employment of an arbitrary $\overline{X}'$.†

The Rate of Economic Growth in the U.K.

If the least-squares method is applied to the data of Table 8 for the period 1870 to 1913, B works out at 1·53 and A at 116. The reader will find that this positions a line on Chart 1b negligibly different from the line already drawn there. Thus in this particular case the cruder method yields a result very similar to that of the more sophisticated method, a conclusion which might have been expected from the superficial observation that of the periods 1870–1879 and 1904–1913 neither in fact appears to have been unduly economically buoyant or depressed. (Evidently the least-squares method is most likely to yield markedly different results

† For a fuller account of short methods of computation see standard textbooks, in particular Allen, *op. cit.*, sections 5.8 and 7.5.

from the cruder method in cases where the disturbances are large relatively to the total length of the series.†)

We are thus now in a position to provide a reasonably confident answer to the first of our original questions posed on page 113. Production *per capita* in the British economy does indeed appear to display a secular rising tendency, at a rate which in the period specifically studied—1870–1913—could be put at about £1 10s. od. per annum in money of 1955 purchasing power. Furthermore (turning to the second question posed) it also seems that despite the interruptions of two world wars and a severe slump, this trend has continued up to the present time and has in fact apparently accelerated: the trend line fitted to the pre-1914 data is flatter, and if projected forwards passes well below any which could reasonably be fitted to the subsequent data. However, may be perhaps we should expect some acceleration? For perhaps it is the *proportional* rather than the absolute rate of growth on which we should have been concentrating attention? In the late nineteenth century an annual increment of £1 10s. od. represented a proportional rise of about one per cent (the absolute level being around £150 *per capita*), but to-day this increment would represent only about one half of one per cent, on account of the doubling of the absolute level through economic growth in the interim. This point will now be considered.

Non-Linear Trends (especially Logarithmic)

The assumption that the fundamental forces causing the upward trend are operating with linear effect is not essential. It is possible to employ the least-squares criterion to fit curving trends, provided the nature of the curvature can be precisely specified mathematically. For instance the estimating equation

$$Y_c = A + BX + CX^2 \qquad (28)$$

† Thus the least-squares method which, as we have already seen, is inappropriate for application to very short series (fn. p. 127 above) may be unnecessary for very long ones: it is at its most useful for series of medium length such as of twenty or thirty years. In very short series the trend can only be estimated by subjective guess, based on direct visual examination of the Chart. In no circumstances should the first-and-last-year method be mechanically applied to very short series since with these series the disturbances are likely to be large in relation to the length of the series.

is that of a line whose slope is always changing; at any one point of time the slope is,

$$B + 2CX\dagger \tag{29}$$

which thus varies with X although the rate of change of the slope itself is constant at $2C.\ddagger$ This would possibly be appropriate to an economy whose production *per capita* were increasing at a constantly diminishing rate or vice versa. Methods of fitting such curves and other non-linear trends are well described by Croxton and Cowden.§

Generally, however in economic time-series, if the assumption of linearity in the trend is clearly unsatisfactory, it is best to give up this particular approach to the problem altogether: the whole concept (of trend) is so subjective that excessive mathematical refinement is undesirable. But there is one development from the simple assumption of arithmetical linearity which is of clear value and frequent validity in economic cases. As already suggested the characteristics of economic systems are such that one may well expect forces making for long term secular trend to operate with constant proportional (in contrast to constant arithmetic) effect, i.e. for example so as to cause national production *per capita* to rise by a constant percentage amount per annum, rather than a constant number of pounds and shillings per annum. Most people would probably agree that the meaning to be given to a concept of a 'constant rate of technical progress' would be that the proportional reduction in the number of man-hours required to do a certain job was the same, say, over 1900–1905 as over 1950–1955. Evidently on the kind of time-chart we have so far been using, a trend of this nature would appear not as a straight line but as a rising curve; since a one per cent increase will represent a larger number of shillings earlier in the series than later, on account of the rise in the base of the percentage (product *per capita*) in the meantime. Such curvature is an obvious disadvantage.

However it happens that if on the vertical axis there are measured not the actual Y's and Yc's, etc., but instead their *logarithms*, it

† The first differential of Yc with respect to X.
‡ Second differential.
§ *Op. cit.* (p. 103 above).

follows from the well-known properties of logarithms that data with a tendency to a constant proportional rate of increase will now tend to fall along a straight line. How this occurs can be seen quite simply, for what must be the form of the estimating equation for a trend representing constant proportional rate of growth?—none other than an old school friend, the compound interest formula:

$$Yc_{(X)} = A(1+r)^X \qquad (30)$$

where A is the level of the series at the starting period ('the principal' in schoolroom examples) r is the proportional annual increase due to trend (the 'rate of interest') and X is the number of years from the start. From the properties of logarithms this means that

$$\log Yc = \log A + X \log (1+r) \qquad (31)$$

in other words the graph of log Yc is a straight line with position-fixing constant $\log A$ and slope, $\log (1+r)$, i.e. $\log (1+r)$ has taken the place of B in the linear case.

If therefore it is suspected that the trend of a particular series is best represented by the assumption of 'log-linear' rather than linear, growth, all we need to do is to look up the logarithms of the actual Y's and plot them against a suitably chosen vertical scale, leaving the horizontal scale (the time scale) in the original units. On the vertical scale it is best to show both numbers and logs as in Chart $1c$ below. The transformed data are then plotted on the chart in the ordinary way and if inspection confirms the suggestion of log-linear growth, then a least-squares straight line can be fitted to the log Y's exactly as in the previous section it was fitted to the Y's. The B-term or slope so obtained is $\log (1+r)$ and its antilog, minus 1, gives the proportional annual rate of increase of Yc according to least-squares trend.

Logarithmic Growth in the U.K.

Chart $1c$ shows the same data as Chart $1a$, but on a logarithmic scale (strictly a *semi-logarithmic* scale, because only the vertical axis is logarithmic). The comparison is extremely interesting. Both the slope and amplitude of fluctuation of the pre-1918 curve are increased relatively to that of the later curves: a least-squares trend line (as shown) fitted to the period 1870–1913, projected forwards

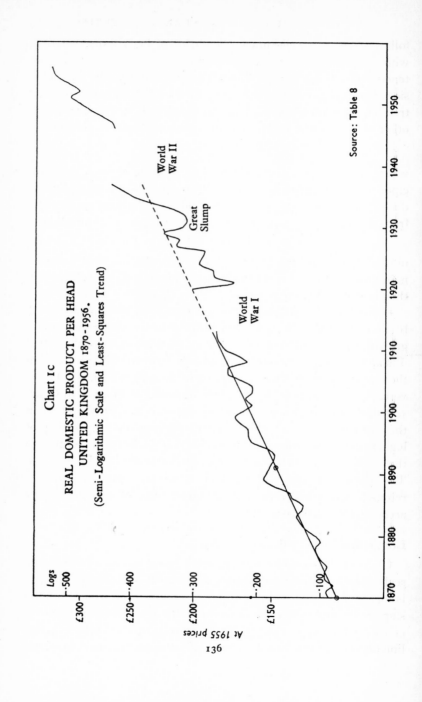

Chart IC

REAL DOMESTIC PRODUCT PER HEAD
UNITED KINGDOM 1870-1956.
(Semi-Logarithmic Scale and Least-Squares Trend)

World War II

Great Slump

World War I

Logs

·500
·400
·300
·200
·100

£300
£250
£200
£150

At 1955 prices

1870   1880   1890   1900   1910   1920   1930   1940   1950

Source: Table 8

fits distinctly more closely with the actual results of the subsequent years than is the case in Chart 1b (although still running about £50 or 15 per cent below the actual achievement for 1955). Any data displaying marked long-term upward trend which is nearly linear on a logarithmic scale will obviously be bent upwards on an arithmetic scale and vice versa; the amount of the bending will depend on the rate of growth itself, the more rapid the rate of growth the more severe the bending.

The least-squares trend line fitted to Chart 1c has a slope of ·0044, the antilog of which is 1·01, i.e. the line represents a constant proportionate rate of increase of 1 per cent per annum. This does appear to be the best way of describing the trend of British production *per capita* in the late nineteenth and early twentieth centuries. And it may reasonably be suggested that the general appearance of Chart 1c provides a good justification of the basic assumptions on which the trend-fitting operation was based; (linearity in the trend and long-period self-cancelling of disturbance).† The fitted line gives a good 'prediction' of the actual results in the later part of the period, and except for a general disturbance in the naughty 'nineties, seems well to describe the long period movement of the series generally. But we must be careful what we mean by prediction here; it is prediction with a strong element of hind-sight. Thus if the trend had been fitted on the basis of the data up to say the year 1899 only, the least-squares formula would have given a significantly steeper slope, and the line would have passed well above the actual results of the Edwardian era.

Since 1913 the interruptions due to wars make further comparison difficult; should wars be expected to halt, delay or speed up economic progress? However, it is clear that on any assumption about the effect of war which is at all reasonable, the record of the second twenty-five years of the twentieth century, contrary to general belief, compares rather favourably with that of the preceding half century‡ and it also appears that our recent experience of recovery

† See p. 119 above.
‡ This judgement is based on the assumption that in both wars some growth was permanently 'lost', on account of the retardation of capital accumulation. Hence, had it not been for a speeding up of the rate of growth after 1918, one would have expected the subsequent curve of the actual data to have passed *below*

after war was much superior to that after World War I. Although precise trend fitting is not appropriate when series are badly broken as after 1913 and 1939, inspection of Chart 1c suggests that one might reasonably put the typical rate of progress which can be expected in the twentieth century—when free of crippling wars and slumps—at two per cent per annum.† Compound interest at two per cent, if maintained uninterruptedly, doubles the principal every thirty-five years.

Logarithmic Growth and Economic Theory

It is important not to apply logarithms where they are not appropriate. If an economic rationalisation for their application cannot be found, be wary. Two examples of reasonably satisfactory rationalisation follow.

(a) Effects of Technical Progress and Capital Formation on Real Product per capita

Let us assume that technical progress and capital formation in

the trend line projected from the nineteenth century; instead, as already noted, by 1955 despite the occurrence of yet another war, the actual data lay above this line. Such arguments are necessarily subjective, and it could as easily be argued that at least during the 1914–1918 war, the result for 1920 suggests that underlying growth continued normally throughout.

† In the inter-war period the data give the appearance not so much of an economy dominated by a regular trade cycle (see pp. 141 *et seq.* below) as of an economy in a state of almost permanent slump or recession, punctuated only occasionally by lapses into full employment. Even in 1929, the British economy, unlike the American economy, seems hardly to have reached capacity. (This would explain the remarkable speed of the increase in production after 1934.) Trend fitting, in such a case, can hardly be attempted by the types of methods we have been discussing. One alternative is to select the years in which it is judged that the economy was working at or near to capacity, and then to estimate the rate of growth from peak to peak, ignoring the years between. The 'trend line' which results represents an estimate of the rate of growth of the capacity of the economy; it will lie above a trend line fitted, e.g., by least squares and will only bear the same slope if the average severity of slumps in relation to the selected peaks is the same throughout the total period of analysis. The rate of growth of 2 per cent per annum suggested in the text is based simply on a comparison of 1920 with 1937, ignoring the whole of the deplorable events of the 'twenties and 'thirties between. In other words the slope of a straight line joining the data of 1920 to that of 1937 on Chart 1c, is about double that of the slope of the trend line fitted to the nineteenth century. Hence we find that underlying the chronic unemployment in capacity which characterised the whole period, capacity itself continued to grow quite rapidly. (See further discussion below.)

fact go hand in hand, the one depending on education, which increases 'the stock of knowledge', the other on investment, which increases the stock of tangible capital. Then use the following symbols:

$O_{(X)}$ —the capacity level of total Real Net Domestic Product (*not per capita*), at time X.

$C_{(X)}$ —the stock of physical capital valued at constant prices, which will also be taken as an indicator of 'the stock of knowledge'.

$I_{(X)}$ —the amount spent on investment and on education in year X over and above the bare minimum necessary to keep the stock of capital and knowledge intact.

$s \equiv I_{(X)}/O_{(X)}$—the share of the national production devoted to education and investment.

$dC_{(X)}$ —the increase in the effective stock of capital and knowledge after the expenditure $I_{(X)}$ in year X has come to fruition.

$dO_{(X)}$ —the consequent increase in $O_{(X)}$.

r_P —excess of birth rate over death rate, i.e. annual proportional increase in population.

r_0 —annual proportional growth of product, which will be taken as approximately equal to $\dfrac{dO_{(X)}}{O_{(X)}}$.

r —annual proportional trend growth of real product *per capita*, i.e. the antilog (minus one) of a trend line of the type plotted in Chart 1c; it will be assumed that near enough $r = r_0 - r_P$.

Economic Assumptions

(i) $O_{(X)} = \gamma C_{(X)}$ for all values of $O_{(X)}$ and $C_{(X)}$

$\therefore \dfrac{dO_{(X)}}{dC_{(X)}} = \gamma$ where $\gamma = $ constant

—this is a restrictive assumption on the form of the relationship between the growth of output and the growth of material and intellectual capital; it conforms with commonsense but will of course only be valid if all resources of capital and labour are in use and if capital and knowledge do in fact maintain a uniform advance; otherwise γ will not be constant.†

(ii) $dC_{(x)} = I_{(x)}$ —the effective addition to the stock is the same as the amount spent,

It can easily be shown that on the above assumptions,

$$r = \gamma s - r_P \qquad (32)$$

Hence if, s and r_P are constant and independent of one another (no Malthus), so r will be constant; if they are not constant, equation (32) is a valid form for analysing the consequences of their variation. Hence the use of logarithmic estimates of trend is justified.

r_P in the late nineteenth century was about ·01 (population increasing at one per cent per annum); in the 'thirties and since, r_P has been about ·005. Thus part of the apparent increment in r (see above) can be explained by the fall in population growth. The remainder is probably explained by what amounts in effect to a rise in s. During the late nineteenth century the proportion of the national income devoted to accumulation was no less than today, but a large part of the effort was taken up with investment overseas, which latter of course, however desirable on other grounds, does little to further the growth of *domestic* product. Incidentally, s at the time of writing is about ·12, so that if the corresponding rate of growth (r) is ·02, as suggested, γ must be of the order of ·20. Also notice that the relatively low level of r_P today may itself account for the rather low level of s which has been prevailing in this country compared with some others: in the U.K. at the present time we can achieve the same r as in other countries, with a lower s‡.

† Readers familiar with contemporary theories of economic growth will realise that we have postulated a particular form of 'neutral' technical progress. At any one time only one technique of production is effectively known and employed in each industry, but from time to time new techniques are discovered and applied; these new techniques however, always combine increased mechanisation with technical progress in such a way that as they are introduced, although output per man increases, output per unit of real (physical) capital does not.

‡ See pp. 87–8 Chapter 4 above. A one point difference in the rate of population growth requires a $1/\gamma$ difference in s to maintain the same rate of growth of output *per capita*; thus the U.S., where population is increasing at one per cent compared with the U.K. half per cent, would need s equal to $14\frac{1}{2}$ per cent compared with the U.K. 12 per cent.

(b) Long Term Price Movements

Another clear case for the use of logarithms is in the analysis of long period price movements, or secular inflation. Apart from the rather obvious intuitive proposition that a £1 increase in the price of coal is a very different matter when the increase is from £6 to £7 per ton to when it is from £1 to £2, we can also show that a constant *absolute* inflationary impulse measured in real terms will have a constant proportionate effect on the price level. For example, if chronic inflation were due to a chronic tendency for investment demand—measured in terms of the man-hours needed to construct the new machines and factories—to run ahead of saving—measured in terms of the man-hours which would have been required to produce the goods which could have been bought with the money saved,—then, other things being equal, prices should rise at a constant percentage rate per annum.†

Oscillations

It now remains to discuss methods for tackling the third and final question: do the data provide evidence for the trade cycle? The analytical problem is here reversed: instead of interesting ourselves primarily in the secular trend of the data, we are concerned to find some method of eliminating the effects of the trend in order to concentrate attention on the movements which are left. In effect, we want to obtain a series something in the nature of a set of

$$y^*_{(1)}, \ y^*_{(2)}, \ y^*_{(3)}, \ \text{etc.}$$

One obvious method, which is sometimes used, is first to fit to the data a trend line of one of the types described above and then, for each year, i.e. for each X, compute the corresponding value of $y^*_{(X)}$ by simple subtraction of $Yc_{(X)}$ from $Y_{(X)}$. But this is unsatisfactory. For in originally defining the nature of the trend we also in effect defined the nature of these y^*'s, and we shall see that thus defined the y^*'s are not suitable for the purpose now in hand.

Assuming that we had fitted a linear trend line by the method of

† In this formal statement we ignore the effects of secular growth of aggregate real product.

least squares we can derive from the previous definitions the proposition

$$Y_{(X)} = Yc_{(X)} + y^*_{(X)} \tag{33}$$

that is to say, each actual Y in the series consists of the result expected according to trend plus the total effect of all disturbances, including any effect of a trade cycle. Let us write this out algebraically in a more general way, using for the trend term instead of $Yc_{(X)}$, an expression $T(X)$, which merely states that given X there exists some formula (function) which will specify the trend value for that year X. Similarly specify the effect of the trade cycle by an expression $C(X)$ which indicates that there exists some law of oscillation which will specify the amount by which the result for any given year ought to deviate from trend because of the trade cycle.† Then $D_{(X)}$ stands for 'disturbances'. Now this has changed the concept of a disturbance from that used previously: a disturbance is now any movement of Y which cannot be explained *either* by the trend hypothesis *or* by the hypothesis of the existence of a regular, systematic trade cycle. Note that in $T(X)$ and $C(X)$ the X is written on the same line, whereas in $D_{(X)}$ it remains a suffix. This is to indicate that the trend values and cyclical values depend systematically on X—the expressions state 'given X, we know $T(X)$ and $C(X)$'—but the disturbance, by definition does not; $D_{(X)}$ merely states 'the disturbance happening to occur in year X'.

We now consider further the nature of the disturbances as newly defined. $D_{(X)}$ for any X evidently consists of the total effect of the failure of any or all of the assumptions made in applying the concepts of linear trend and regular cycle. Reverting to the balloon-on-a-bicycle analogy of page 117 we see two distinct types of such failure: (1) the gradient of the road is not constant—technical progress wobbles, whole decades of relative stagnation being followed by decades of abnormal progress, etc., (2) the gusty wind (or whatever is the appropriate analogy) is far from regular in its effects; thus in

---

† The law might postulate a trade cycle of complete regularity, perfect symmetry and constant length; then, if the standard length were ten years and X were 33 (i.e. 1902 in the example), and if the first year of the first cycle had been 1870, then we are in the third year of the third cycle since the origin. The law might specify that in the third year of the cycle production should have risen to £2 *per capita* above trend; then the value of $C(X)$ for that year would be $+2$.

real life some trade cycles will be strong, others weak, some a little short, some distorted in shape, and so on. The economic hypothesis of the existence of structural features in the system making for a cyclical movement does not require that the result shall be *perfectly* regular; no economist would have the temerity to suggest such a thing. Thus $D_{(X)}$ may be further subdivided into say $Dt_{(X)}$ and $Dc_{(X)}$ representing deviations from linear behaviour in the trend forces and deviations from regularity in the cyclical forces respectively. Thus,

$$Y_{(X)} = \{T(X) + Dt_{(X)}\} + \{C(X) + Dc_{(X)}\} \qquad (34)$$

Now what is it we need to test the hypothesis that a reasonably regular trade cycle exists? It is a series consisting of the second bracket of the above expression, e.g. a series such as

$$Q_{(1)}, Q_{(2)} \cdots Q_{(X)} \cdots Q_{(n)}$$

where Q is defined as

$$Q_{(X)} \equiv C(X) + Dc_{(X)} \qquad (35)$$

With such a series one could try out a number of alternative forms of C (i.e. a number of specific hypotheses as to the length and amplitude of a characteristic cycle), subtracting each resulting $C(X)$ from each $Q_{(X)}$ and noting the general extent of the residual $Dc_{(X)}$'s which were left. If it were impossible to find a form of C which kept the $Dc_{(X)}$'s at a low level relatively to the total amount of movement to be explained, the general hypothesis of the existence of a regular trade cycle could be said to fail against the facts. Conversely, if the experiment were more successful, the hypothesis could be said to have found some support, although not, of course, absolute proof.

We can now see why the proposal suggested at the beginning of this section (analysis of a series consisting of the total deviations from a linear trend line) is unsuitable. For, in effect, that method would give a series not of Q's as defined above but say R's where

$$R_{(X)} = Y_{(X)} - T(X) = C(X) + Dc_{(X)} + Dt_{(X)} \qquad (36)$$

in other words the $Dt_{(X)}$ (deviations from linearity in the trend) would be mixed with the $Dc_{(X)}$ and there would be no objective way of separating them. The discovery of a large quantity of aggregate deviation after subtraction of some series of $C(X)$'s from the

L

$R_{(x)}$'s might mean either that the cycle hypothesis was bad, or the trend hypothesis, or both. The point can be seen fairly easily intuitively by a glance at Chart 1c; some apparent trade cycles fall largely below the trend line drawn and others largely above it (e.g. the one following 1887): but we discussed the matter more formally in order to provide a background for the explanation of the inwardness of the well-known, but less well understood, method of the Moving Average, which will be described in the following and final sections of this chapter.

The Moving Average

What is really wanted for the analysis of oscillations is a method of eliminating trend which by definition rules out the possibility of disturbances of the type Dt creeping back into the data after 'trend' has been eliminated. The $Dt_{(x)}$ it will be remembered were able to arise because we made a definite assumption about the nature of the trend, and because any such assumption is liable to periodic failure. If therefore we were to eliminate trend by some entirely agnostic device, involving no specific assumption about the trend's mode of operation whatsoever, **we** should have what is here wanted. And, since in this case we are not interested in the trend itself, but only in the cycle,† we have no need of such assumption or hypothesis, since it is not an assumption about trend which is under test. The measurement of trend is now only a means to an end, rather than an end in itself.

Whenever the assessment of trend is only a means to an end, either as in the case of trade-cycle analysis or for example the analysis of seasonal fluctuation (see any standard text-book), the method of the moving average is appropriate. The operation starts out in the same way as the second of all the methods for fitting trends so far here described (page 120) above); the actual values for the first so many years of the series being averaged, the average set against the mid-year of the period and taken as the first trend value. Then, however, the next trend value is obtained by dropping from the total the first year of the series, but including

---

† In the language of balloon-on-a-bicycle analogy, we are not interested in the road, but only in the curves of the balloon's bobbings.

the next value in the time series not so far included (with a ten-year moving average fitted to the national product data this would mean dropping the *per capita* income for 1870 and including instead the figure for 1881). This second trend value is deemed to relate to the year immediately following that assigned to the first trend value. The procedure is then repeated.†

Thus a moving average eliminates all oscillation which is self-cancelling within the chosen period. A perfectly regular and perfectly symmetrical trade cycle would be completely eliminated by a moving average of the same period as the (constant) length of the cycle; each successive advance of the average would take in a segment of the cycle equal in amplitude but opposite in direction to the segment dropped. Even if the cycle were not perfectly regular, i.e. even if some disturbances of the type Dc were in fact occurring, they would be largely, although not completely eliminated by the device, for in principle a moving average eliminates all oscillation regardless of amplitude; strong cycles and weak cycles are all taken, provided the exaggeration or weakness of the upswing is in each case matched by an equal distortion of the downswing.‡ Thus we can say that a moving average will eliminate from a series the greater part of the movement consisting of $(C(X) + Dc_{(X)})$. Conversely, if a moving-average trend series be subtracted from the original series from which it was computed we are left with a series of $C(X) + Dc_{(X)}$, i.e. a series of the type we are looking for. A ten-year moving-average trend line computed from part of the data of

† The technique for computing a moving average is so obvious as to need little elaboration; details are given in most standard texts. The only small snag is that a moving average for an even number of years strictly requires 'centering', i.e. in the example used in the text, the first ten-year average does not really correspond strictly to the year 1874 nor to 1875 but to part of each year, a point which was of no importance when fitting linear trend so long as the same procedure was followed at both ends. With a moving average the difficulty is evaded by interpolation, i.e. in effect, averages of pairs of moving averages are taken which will then be found to correspond to single whole years all along the line.

‡ Unfortunately this is only approximately true because part of the effect of a disturbance in the amplitude of any given cycle is thrown by the method into the results which will be obtained in the two adjacent cycles, although no disturbance may have occurred in them at all. The trend which may in truth be flat will appear to wobble. More serious difficulties arise when a disturbance occurs to the length of the cycle, for rather obvious reasons. Moving averages possess a number of awkward properties and have generated a substantial literature. See any standard text and in particular see Allen, *op. cit.*, sections 8.2, 8.3, and 8.7.

Table 8 is shown in Chart 1*d*. (The linear trend line of Chart 1*b* is also shown for comparison.) It will be seen that the actual data do appear to oscillate around it, but it cannot be said that they do so with great regularity. The economic system appears to possess certain oscillatory features but it is doubtful, if on the evidence since 1870, these can be glorified into a *regular* trade cycle.†

Comparison of Moving Average and Linear Trend

A moving-average trend line provides us with a series from which the $\{C(X) + Dc_{(x)}\}$ have been eliminated that is to say a series which in our previous formulation would have consisted of a series of sums $\{T(X) + Dt_{(x)}\}$. This series is here *defined* as representing the trend; in other words everything which is not cycle is trend, and what in the previous formulation would have been the trend value is lumped together with trend disturbances. A moving-average trend, not being wedded to any particular hypothesis about the nature of the trend can wobble as much as it wishes.‡ It thus provides a reasonably accurate historical description of the long term behaviour of the series. 'What' it may well be asked, 'is wrong with this; if the trend wobbles, this is something we want to know, why be tied to the hypothesis of linearity if the hypothesis is false?' There is much in this argument, and if all that is wanted is a historical description, a moving average should be used. But the agnostic nature of the moving-average result is both its strength and its weakness; in assuming nothing about the nature of the trend it leads to no conclusions about the nature of the trend, and anyone interested in economic growth, for example, who first fits a moving average to his data will soon find himself trying out some type of straight line over at least part of the series in order to test his pet theories. The comparison of British economic development in the nineteenth and twentieth centuries which we attempted above would have been impossible without the aid of linear analysis. The ideal arrangement is first to 'smooth' the data with a

† The evidence for regularity is rather stronger, however, if the whole of the nineteenth century is considered, rather than the last thirty years only.

‡Thus in 1*d*, the moving average lies below the linear trend from 1875 to 1885, along it from 1885 to 1890, then rises above it and finally dips below again at the turn of the century.

moving average and then to fit some specific form of trend line to the resulting smoothed series. Moving averages can also of course be made from the logarithms, in which case each computed average is

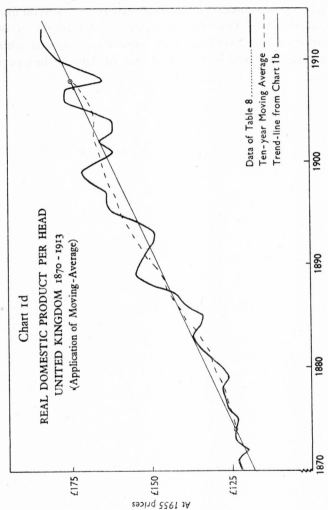

Chart 1d

REAL DOMESTIC PRODUCT PER HEAD
UNITED KINGDOM 1870 - 1913
(Application of Moving-Average)

Data of Table 8 ....
Ten-year Moving Average – – – –
Trend-line from Chart 1b

At 1955 prices

in effect the logarithm of the geometric means of the actual Y's for each ten years. This last procedure should be followed in trade-cycle analysis if the data, in addition to oscillations, also display marked secular trend (as is normally the case) and it is desired to observe the amplitude of fluctuation in *proportional* terms. On a semi-logarithmic chart, a constant proportional deviation from trend will show up as a constant vertical distance (between trend line and data) on the chart. Thus the apparently greater amplitude of the fluctuations in the later part of the period as compared with the earlier part, displayed in Charts 1*b* and 1*d*, largely disappears in Chart 1*c*.

CHAPTER SEVEN

THE INTERPRETATION OF ASSOCIATED MOVEMENTS IN ECONOMIC VARIABLES

IN the last chapter we discussed the analysis of a single time series. The analysis represented a first step in the investigation of the underlying causes of the data's behaviour. The types of operations demonstrated, however, related to a single economic variable only, and no attempt was made to find measurable evidence of links between the movements of the variable in question and of others with which economic theory might suggest it to be causally associated. If we want to attempt the latter sort of measurement, as inevitably we must as the investigation develops, we are taken into a further field of statistical method—a field which is larger both in the quantity and the quality of the ideas involved than the whole of the rest of the corpus of statistical theory taken together: the central techniques involved are commonly known as Regression Analysis. It would be quite out of keeping with the scope and objectives of the present book to attempt to provide in any sense a comprehensive description of this great body of theory and practice; the object of the chapter is to introduce the reader to the basic ideas from which the analysis proceeds, and to indicate the underlying difficulties and limitations.

The Black Box

Imagine a man facing a closed box, into which he cannot see but out of which project through holes a large number of moveable pistons. He believes these pistons to be connected together inside the box by a complicated mechanism of cogs and levers. This mechanism we will treat as an analogy for the economic system, in whole or in part. The positions of the pistons represent the levels of important economic variables, such as income, expenditure on different commodities, saving; production, wages, and prices. The cogs and levers represent the institutional and psychological factors—such as markets adjusting supply to demand, or households attempting to maximise satisfaction— by which the economic variables are thought to be connected. The man—our economic investigator—aspires to find some means for constructing an effective description of the invisible mechanism. (By 'effective' is meant a reasonably accurate description of how the pistons are likely to behave in given circumstances. Thus it is not required that the description be exactly the same as a blueprint made by a draftsman who could actually see inside the box.)

There are three distinct steps in any sensible procedure for such an investigation:

>Step   (i) Induction
>Step (ii) Deduction
>Step (iii) Experiment

Step (i) consists in setting up a hypothesis as to the general *type* of the mechanism, based perhaps on one or two tentative observations of the position and behaviour of the pistons under certain critical circumstances; step (ii) consists in proceeding to attempt to deduce by formal reasoning the detailed properties of a mechanism of the type postulated. If we were dealing with a natural science—if the box were a physical mechanism rather than an analogy for the economic system—the tests in the next and final step, step (iii), would consist of a series of planned manipulations of the pistons. Because of the immutability of natural laws, a relatively small number of relatively unambiguous experiments would quite likely be sufficient to settle the validity of the theory.† However, as we have already seen repeatedly, the case of the social sciences is very different: its characteristics, in terms of the present analogy are that,

(*a*) There is a great deal of 'play' in the mechanism, so much indeed that any given constellation of one group of the pistons will not by any means always be associated with pre-

---

† Notice, however, the essential interdependence of the steps; a set of random manipulations with no particular theory behind them would be of little value.

cisely the same constellation of the remainder, even when the basic linkages in the system are in essence unchanged.

(b) The basic linkages in the system are not in fact unchanging, but are developing biologically as it were, and not necessarily at an even pace over time.

(c) The investigator is not able to manipulate the pistons.

In short, the box is literally alive with gremlins.

All that the social scientist can do in substitution for the procedures which would normally be followed by a natural scientist at this stage is to attempt to observe *statistical tendencies*; for example a tendency that when piston A moves inwards, piston B usually appears to move outwards; and furthermore that a depression of x inches in A seems usually to yield an extrusion of about, say, bx inches in B (b being regarded as a 'constant') and that departures from this rule occur only moderately. (The last statement, we shall see can be put more precisely.) However, even if fairly strong and regular tendencies of such kind are noticeable, the theoretical position remains weak. For evidence of statistical association by no means implies evidence of direct causation in the sense that if an independent agent were to depress A one could be sure that B should be extruded. It might be the case that piston A is linked in the concealed mechanism to a third piston, C, which in turn is linked to B in such a way that although depression of C is normally likely to depress A and extrude B, depression of A by an independent agent is not—owing to the existence of some one-way-only characteristic in the link between C and A. Thus the observed *association* between the movements of A on the one hand and those of B on the other could entirely be due to movements of C;—a very different chain of causation, therefore, to what might have been supposed. Thus the famous association between cigarette addiction and the incidence of lung cancer might have been due (although in fact it was not) to an association of both things with residence in towns, so that prohibition of smoking would not have eliminated cancer since people would have gone on living in towns anyway. In that particular case, the explanation was eventually ruled out by the observation that smokers who lived in the country were almost as abnormally susceptible to the disease as the rest, but the fact did not rule out the possibility of some other, unknown, 'bogus' explanation of the basic association; one which, not having been thought of perhaps, could not be investigated through the statistics in the form in which they had been collected: for example there might have existed an undiscovered biological characteristic possessed by some humans but not by others which at the same time both caused the greater susceptibility to cancer and produced a greater tendency to addiction to tobacco. (In practice, enough is now known about cancer, smoking and the human organism for such explanation to appear highly improbable.)

Notice that the difficulty of deducing evidence of causation from evidence of association arises from the co-existence of all the factors in the situation, (a), (b) and (c) listed above. Thus if we could manipulate the pistons at will, instead of relying on observation of their own uncontrolled autonomous movement, we could quickly settle the question at issue simply by pushing A while keeping our hand on C. Alternatively, were it not for 'play', the situation creating the difficulty could not exist; if all smokers were certain to contract cancer after consuming a specific aggregate number of cigarettes, but *no-one* who had smoked less than this number was ever known to contract the disease, residence in towns as an explanation of the association would be quite ruled out, except in the improbable case that no country dwellers whatsoever were smokers. Finally, if there were not the likelihood of the system changing through time it would often be possible to overcome nearly all ambiguity by a sufficiently exhaustive series of statistical tests, i.e. observation of all the possible alternative constellations of positions of the levers, many times over. This is why statistical investigations of systems which are relatively unsusceptible to structural change tend to be more successful than statistical investigation of social systems.

Time Series versus Cross Section

The particular significance of the foregoing remarks in the context of the present chapter is that the elementary methods for analysis of statistical association are little more than devices for circumventing factors (a) and (c) in the list above. Only with the aid of the more advanced type of analysis is it possible to make a formal attack on factor (*b*).

There are however two rather distinct types of application of the methods which must be distinguished even at this elementary level. One is when regression analysis is performed on time-series data, the other when the method is applied to so-called 'cross-section' data. In the former case we may imagine that we consider a single example of the mechanical box, inhabited by gremlins so lively that the pistons are in constant, apparently autonomous movement, subject only to the restraints imposed by the nature of the linkages. The positions of the various pistons at successive moments of time (or their average positions over successive periods) are regularly noted, the resulting data forming in effect a collection of time-series, each series relating to the successive positions of one of the pistons: the co-varying behaviour of the several series is then used as evidence of association between *movements* of the pistons. This application was extremely popular in the early stages of development of applied economics, but is now recognised to be fraught with peculiar dangers; it should only be applied therefore in clear-cut cases and with especial care.

In the 'cross-section' approach we imagine the 'box' to represent not a whole system, but some single specifically delimited part, of which a reasonably large number of separate examples exist and are available for measurement. Thus, in effect, in place of a single box we have a number of similar boxes, or rather a number of boxes whose basic content we believe to be similar in the sense that the pistons, levers and cogs are linked in the same mechanical fashion, albeit perhaps with varying gearing. It is required, however, that the actual constellations of the pistons show significant variation from example to example. If the variation is adequate we can note down (collect statistics) the positions of the pistons in each case and we can hope that by analysing the resulting data we may be able to deduce the nature of the supposedly common basic mechanism. A typical example is the analysis of family budgets. Here, ideally, the total income and details of the entire expenditure of a large number of individual families are statistically summarised according to income and other characteristics such as occupation and family composition. Each family will show varying average expenditure on the different consumer goods, in particular for instance on food. We then try to see whether there is a reasonable regularity in the way average food expenditure per family varies with income and/or occupation or family composition, thus perhaps providing evidence of a definite 'income-elasticity' of demand for the commodity, food. The obvious danger of the cross-section method is that the assumption on which it is based—that the boxes contain a similar basic mechanism—may be incorrect, for example some families might ignore their income entirely in deciding how much to spend on food (as it happens, this is hardly possible, hence family budgets make good material for the application of the method). More serious perhaps is a more subtle kind of variation. We have already noted that variation in 'gearing', in contrast to variation in the basic linkage system, is in principle permissible, e.g. so long as income were a major determinant of food expenditure, it should not matter that the income elasticity of demand for food varies moderately as between individual families. This is because the statistical method can in principle arrange for the effects of individual idiosyncrasies to be cancelled out in the final measurement. But that will only be possible if the pattern of idiosyncrasies is random, rather than 'biased'. Thus suppose the boxes whose pistons happen to be in a particular position, also happen to be boxes with a tendency to some particular characteristic 'gearing'. The rich are different from the poor in other ways than in the possession of a larger income, particularly if they have been rich for some time; thus the demand for food by a rich family of long standing might be significantly lower than that of a hitherto poor family whose income had recently been raised up to the same level. An income-elasticity of demand for food estimated by comparing the income and food expenditure of the actual rich with that of the actual poor might considerably under-estimate the elasticity to be expected in the event that all families' incomes were raised sharply together (e.g. as a result of a cyclical rise in economic activity).

Nevertheless, despite such difficulties as just mentioned, regression analysis on cross-section data has been notably more successful than regression analysis of time-series, not so much because the difficulties in principle are less serious but rather because they are in practice more amenable to circumvention. In what follows we shall describe the basic principles of the method entirely in terms of an example drawn from imaginary cross-section data, although referring *en passant* to methods for avoiding the more elementary traps in the time-series application.

Elementary Principles of Regression Analysis

Suppose, in the year 3000, an archaeologist were digging in the ruins of the British metropolis and came upon a cache of part of the records of the Accounts Department of the present London Electricity Board, relating to one particular quarter in 1980. We will imagine that the records surviving gave only the total amount of electricity consumed in each house and the *total* amount of money due to the Board from the householder, no details being provided as to how the total was arrived at (i.e. no breakdown as between fixed charge, unit charge, charges for hire of equipment, etc.). Suppose that these data when statistically summarised appeared as in Table 10*a* below.

TABLE 10*a*. *Consumption of Electricity and Size of Electricity Bill in Ten London Households,   1st quarter* 1980
(First Example)

Case No.	Consumption (Units–kWh)	Payment due (Pence)
1	500	1,100
2	600	1,200
3	650	1,350
4	700	1,300
5	710	1,310
6	800	1,400
7	980	1,420
8	1,000	1,600
9	1,100	1,700
10	1,200	1,800

Note: For simplicity only a small number of cases are shown; in a typical real example a much larger number would be needed.

The problem which we set our archaeologist is the estimation of the *domestic electricity tariff* which had been in operation in London in 1980; and we will suppose that people were still employing regression analysis in such cases.

Inspection tells us immediately that the tariff could not have taken the form of a straight flat-rate charge per unit consumed, since the average cost per unit appears to vary from case to case, e.g. in case 10 it is 1,800/1,200, = 1·5d per unit, while in case 2 it is 1,200/600, = 2d. Nevertheless there is evidently some method in the system since with only one exception the larger consumers pay more than the smaller. In this simple example most of us could see the answer fairly quickly without the aid of complicated statistical methods, but we shall now apply the method of regression analysis by way of demonstration.

We first set up the hypothesis that the payment, Y, of each household is related by some definite law—the tariff—to the consumption X. We then plot the data on what is called a *scatter diagram*, as shown on Chart 2a.

Scales suitable to Y and X are set up on the vertical and horizontal axes respectively, and each case is plotted at the intersection of its Y-value with its X-value. Thus case 1 paid 1,100 pence having consumed 500 units, so the spot labelled '1' in the diagram lies at the exact intersection of the ordinates $Y = 1,100$ and $X = 500$, and so on.

The picture of this example as it emerges in Chart 2a is clearly extremely suggestive, since the plotted points appear to fall almost entirely along a single straight line. This would imply that there was indeed a regular law relating the two variables, in other words that the same tariff applied to nearly all the households. Furthermore, the law is linear, i.e. the tariff is apparently of the form,

$$Y_c = \alpha + \beta X \tag{1}$$

where α represents a fixed quarterly charge which must be paid however much is consumed so long as the consumer remains connected, and β is the unit charge. (Following Chapter 6, we write Yc for the value of Y postulated by the law, in contrast to the value actually observed; the two only being the same in cases where

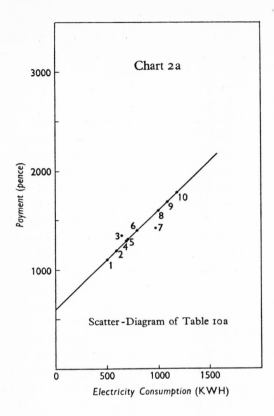

Chart 2a

Scatter-Diagram of Table 10a

the law in question 'works' perfectly.) By drawing a line through the points, we find it cuts the Y-axis at 600, but has a slope of unity: α is 600 and β is one. Hence the equation of the line is specifically,

$$Y_c = 600 + X$$

The tariff expressed in words therefore would be:

Fixed Charge   50/- per quarter
Unit Charge   1d per unit

(If the unit charge were instead of 1d, say $\frac{1}{2}$d, β in the formula would be $\frac{1}{2}$, and the equation would be $Y = 600 + \frac{1}{2}X$.) So far, so good. But what about cases 3 and 7? In these cases the formula fails to 'work' as indicated by the fact that the two plotting points concerned do not fall on the line. In case 3, the consumer was paying

157

a supplement for the hire of equipment and in case 7 there had been a clerical error. Perhaps further investigation of the ruins would reveal documents which would establish these explanations, perhaps not. But even if not, it matters little, since the evidence of the other points is so overwhelming as to create a virtual certainty that we have obtained the right answer for the normal case. However, our example is a highly unrealistic one. As we know from our earlier discussion, in a social-science example characteristically every single point plotted will probably show some degree of individual idiosyncrasy; to change the analogy, 'clerical errors' in the application of social laws are the rule rather than the exception. Furthermore, in the social sciences it is often the case that there exists no practicable further line of investigation which might help explain away the variations; no process analogous to digging among the ruins can easily explain why one individual is possessed of a higher demand-curve for food than another; some people are greedier than others and that is that.† Even with our apparently innocuous example of the electricity bills, in reality the fixed charge is assessed by the Electricity Board separately for each house so as to vary directly with the floor area. Hence unless the investigator could also discover—perhaps in the ruins of the Rating Authority offices—independent information of the floor-area in each case, he would be in difficulty. Instead of falling almost exactly along a straight line, his plotting points would be scattered, as for example in Chart 2b below. (Hence the appellation 'scatter diagram'.) The less the scatter the closer can be said to be the association between the variables under analysis; conversely in the extreme case in which there is no objective association whatsoever the points will literally be scattered all over the chart.

The imaginary data from which Chart 2b is constructed are given in Table 10b. The picture which emerges results simply from assuming that the electricity tariff was basically similar to that of the first example, except only that there was a varying fixed charge

† This is a slight over-statement. We can and should search for objective social factors, such as number of children in the family, which may influence family 'tastes'—and it is arguable that applied economics has to date devoted insufficient resources to the investigation of the sociology of its subject matter, generally.

due to varying floor area in each house. This example will now be used to demonstrate the application of regression analysis, although by the standards of many typical examples in social science the amount of scatter depicted is relatively small.

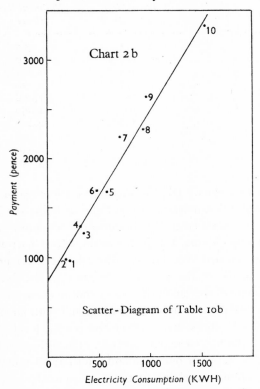

Chart 2 b

Scatter - Diagram of Table 10b

No single line fits the points precisely, yet the points display a visual *tendency* to lie along a straight line. This could be taken as evidence of some underlying law of association, disturbed by idiosyncrasies in individual cases. Can we choose a formula for a line which may be regarded as the 'best' representation of the underlying law, i.e. which passes through the scattered points, following their general path and keeping the scatter about itself at as low a level as possible? The reader will see at once that the problem is similar intellectually to that of estimating linear trend in time series.

M

TABLE 10*b*. *Consumption of Electricity and Size of Electricity*
Bill in Ten London Households, 1st quarter 1980
(*Second Example*)

Case No.	Consumption (Units–kWh)	Payment due (Pence)
1	215	965
2	180	980
3	355	1,255
4	320	1,320
5	580	1,680
6	490	1,690
7	720	2,220
8	950	2,300
9	980	2,630
10	1,550	3,350

In the first electricity tariff example, the investigator chose his
estimate simply by ignoring cases 3 and 7 as being obvious aber-
rations. He was justified in this because the remaining points lay
precisely on a single line. But in the example of Chart 2*b* no such
procedure is justified. We know, although the investigator does
not, that the cause of the scatter is variation in the fixed charge;
the best estimate of the tariff, therefore, should consist of a correct
value for the β-term, the unit charge, together with an estimate of
the α-term which represents, in effect, the average level of the fixed
charge for all the houses taken together. Hence there is no reason
to discriminate between one case and another; all must be taken
into consideration in arriving at the final estimate except in the
special case where there is independent evidence of, e.g. clerical
error. It must be assumed that all disturbances, whatever their
cause, in some sense or other cancel out. Hence one is driven
through exactly the same process of reasoning which lead us to the
least-squares principle for fitting a linear trend in Chapter 6. We
seek the line passing through the scattered plotting points which in
some sense sets the aggregate deviation of the points from itself at a
minimum, i.e. at a lower level than with any other possible straight
line. But as we saw in Chapter 6, to minimise the aggregate arithmetic deviation, allowing pluses and minuses to cancel, is virtually

meaningless and we operate instead therefore on the aggregate of the squares of the deviations. Again, by the same arguments as those of Chapter 6, we note that this method has the effect of paying disproportionately greater attention to the avoidance of large deviations than of small ones, in accordance with the square law.†

The formulae and procedures for fitting the line, i.e. for choosing the values of the parameters α and β, are exactly analogous to those given previously for fitting a least-squares trend, except that here we have on the X-axis, in place of the discrete variable, time, the continuous determining variable of the problem in question; in this example, units of electricity consumed. However, if short-cut methods of computation are being used, it will now be desirable to take an arbitrary mean for X as well as for Y, since X is now a continuous variable. The ordinary formula for β is therefore,

$$\beta = \Sigma xy / \Sigma x^2 \qquad (2)$$

where x and y are deviations taken from the computed true arithmetic means of X and Y respectively; and the short-cut form is,

$$\beta = \frac{\Sigma x'y' - \Sigma x' . \Sigma y'}{\Sigma x'^2 - \dfrac{1}{N}\left(\Sigma x'\right)^2} \qquad (3)$$

x' and y' being the deviations from the corresponding arbitrary means. The constant α is given by,

$$\alpha = \overline{Y} - \beta \overline{X} \qquad (4)$$

in the same manner as in Chapter 6. ($\overline{Y}$ and $\overline{X}$ being estimated from the arbitrary $\overline{Y}'$ and $\overline{X}'$ in the manner of equation (24) in that chapter). These formulae applied to the data of Chart 2b below, give the line of best fit as drawn therein: the slope is 1·70 and the value of the α-term, 760 pence. Hence the complete investigation of the estimating equation of best fit is,

$$Y_c = 1\cdot70X + 760.$$

The method was first developed in application to experiments in genetics, and by historical accident therefore, the straight line of

† See Chapter 6, p. 127.

best fit in a scatter diagram has come to be known as a *regression line*, and its slope β, as the *regression coefficient*.

How may the above result be interpreted? More specifically;

(1) Can we now believe with reasonable confidence that X and Y (consumption and payment) were objectively associated?

(2) Are we necessarily justified in assuming that the relationship was directly causal and that the electricity tariff ruling at the time was as apparently indicated, viz. a unit charge of about $1\frac{3}{4}$d together with a fixed charge which, although varying from house to house, worked out on average at about 760 pence, or 63 shillings (cf. 1d and 50/- in the first example)?

The fairly obvious thought which lies behind question (1) is that it would always be possible to find a line of 'best' fit which reduced the scatter to a minimum, but the minimum might still represent a very substantial amount of scatter nevertheless. If so, the result would have little meaning beyond reaffirming a visual impression that the variables were not, in fact, much associated: if the plotting points are scattered all over the diagram, the parameters of the line of 'least bad' fit are of little interest to us. We can reverse this argument: the degree of association between two variables can be measured by reference to the level to which the line of best fit succeeds in reducing the scatter. Thus when in common speech one hears that two variables are 'closely correlated' all that it means is that if the analysis which has been described were applied to their data, the scatter remaining about the regression line would be expected to be relatively small.

The Correlation Coefficient

In fact it is possible to devise systems of 'marking' to indicate the extent to which any two variables are correlated in the above sense. We require a system which is easily understood, comparable as between different examples (i.e. that the marks should always be awarded out of 100, so to speak) and which is so designed that assessment of the marks does not involve unduly elaborate computations. The *'product-moment correlation coefficient'* or *'coefficient of linear correlation'*, or colloquially, *'the correlation coefficient,'* which we shall now describe is a numerical measure which fulfils these requirements, and is the one which is the most widely used.

At first sight the obvious numerical indicator of the quality of fit achieved by a regression line would simply be the magnitude of the aggregate residual squared deviation, $\Sigma (y^*)^2$; for this would be a direct measure of the extent to which the actual values of Y deviate from the values 'expected' from the hypothesis that Y is determined by X according to the chosen equation. (It would of course constitute an inverse system of marking—the worse the correlation the higher the marks awarded.) But this method would not be satisfactory because the marks would not be comparable between examples: although $\Sigma (y^*)^2$ must evidently be zero in the case of a perfect result and positive and rising with the degree of disassociation in less-than-perfect results, its upper limit (the mark representing complete disassociation) will vary from example to example. Thus employment of $\Sigma (y^*)^2$ as an inverse measure of correlation would be rather as if each competitor in a horse jumping competition were made to take his horse over a different number of jumps, but the prizes were nevertheless awarded to the rider who accumulated the smallest aggregate of penalties.

However, it can be demonstrated that the upper limit of $\Sigma (y^*)^2$ is actually Σy^2. Now Σy^2 (already encountered in Chapter 6) is the aggregate of the squared deviations of the observed Y's about their own mean; it is a quantity which, when divided through by the number of cases in the example (say, N), is known as the *variance* of Y and may be used as a general measure of the extent to which the data of a variable are scattered about their mean. (For comparative purposes the square root is usually taken, the formula $\sqrt{\dfrac{\Sigma y^2}{N}}$ representing the famous *standard deviation*, almost universally designated by the symbol σ and employed as a general measure of dispersion).† The proof that the upper limit of $\Sigma (y^*)^2$ is Σy^2 is as follows: evidently,

$$y^* = y - \beta x \tag{5}$$

† The variance of a variable, say, Y is usually signified as VARY, thus
$$\text{VAR}Y = \frac{\Sigma(Y - \bar{Y})^2}{N}.$$

if β is to be estimated by the method of least squares, (5) can be written,

$$y^* = y - x \cdot \frac{\Sigma\, xy}{\Sigma\, x^2} \tag{6}$$

This may be squared, expanded and aggregated, yielding,

$$\Sigma\,(y^*)^2 = \Sigma\,y^2 - \frac{(\Sigma\, xy)^2}{\Sigma\, x^2} \tag{7}$$

The significance of the last equation can be appreciated by further considering the properties of the expression $\Sigma\, xy$, the top line in the formula for the regression coefficient. $\Sigma\, xy$ is the sum of the cross-products of the corresponding deviations of X and Y from their own means, and when divided by the total number of items in the example, N, is known as the *co-variance*† of X and Y. Co-variance is the central construct of regression analysis and all statistical theory cognate. For, some of the deviations included will usually be positive (X exceeding $\overline{X}$ or Y exceeding $\overline{Y}$) and others negative, hence the cross products also will be of varying sign. But unless there is a tendency either for positive x's to be associated with positive y's and negative x's with negative y's—i.e. for high values of X itself to be associated with high values of Y and vice versa—or unless there is a tendency for negative x's systematically to be associated with positive y's and vice versa, cases where the cross product is positive will tend on balance to cancel out against cases where it is negative: if X and Y are completely without connection $\Sigma\, xy$ can only differ from zero by chance, and the likelihood of this happening will diminish the larger the number of cases in the example. That is to say if X and Y represented for example the successive numbers coming up at two separate tables in a Casino, it would be extremely surprising (or extremely suspicious) if in the results from a full year's working the computed value of $\Sigma\, xy$ differed noticeably from zero.

Now, if in equation (7) $\Sigma\, xy$ is zero, then $\Sigma\,(y^*)^2$ must equal $\Sigma\, y^2$, which in effect is the proposition we wished to prove: when the variables are completely disassociated in the sense that $\Sigma\, xy$ is zero, $\Sigma\,(y^*)^2$ has reached its maximum possible value at a level

† The co-variance of a pair of variables, X and Y is usually signified by cov_{XY}.

which is equal to a measure of dispersion—Σy^2—of Y itself. Thus the observed magnitude of $\Sigma (y^*)^2$ in any particular case depends not only on the degree of association or disassociation in the movements of the two variables, as measured by Σxy, but also on the dispersion of Y, a proposition which is also understandable intuitively by imagining the difference to be expected in the aggregate amount of scatter round the line of 'least bad' fit in the scatter diagrams of two examples of disassociated variables; first an example in which the vertical spread of the plotting points was large and then one in which this spread was comparatively small (representing examples of large and small dispersion of Y respectively). The dispersion of Y depends on the underlying nature of the data and must evidently vary from example to example: in the human animal for example, body weight varies more from individual to individual than does body height. Thus it might well happen that of two examples under consideration, although the underlying degree of association between the variables considered was much the same, the computed value of $\Sigma (y^*)^2$ in one would turn out to be significantly different from its value in the other simply because the dispersion of Y in the two examples happened significantly to differ. Therefore any standardised measure of association—i.e. measure in which the marks are always out of 100—must be made relative to the computed variance of Y in each case. Further, it would be convenient to avoid having to employ an inverse measure, i.e. it would be better to employ an indicator which was higher the higher the degree of association, rather than vice versa. Hence the formula which is almost universally used proceeds by first subtracting the observed $\Sigma (y^*)^2$ from its theoretical maximum, Σy^2, and then expressing the result in proportional terms, i.e. as a ratio of Σy^2 itself. The precise formula is

$$r = \sqrt{\frac{\Sigma y^2 - \Sigma (y^*)^2}{\Sigma y^2}} \qquad (8)$$

the symbol r being known as *the coefficient of linear correlation*, or *the product-moment correlation coefficient*, or the *zero-order correlation coefficient*; for short simply 'the correlation coefficient', this last abbreviation being permissible in any context where there is no danger of confusion with other measures of correlation. The square root is taken in order to eliminate the possible distorting effects of the original squaring in the deviations.

Another interpretation of equation (8) may be of help. The magnitude of any deviation, y, of Y from its own mean, $\bar{Y}$, can be divided into two parts, a part which would exist even if Y lay exactly on the regression line and an additional part (either positive or negative) which is left 'unexplained' by the line; this additional part, in effect, is y^*; the explained part is y_c: hence

$$y = y_c + y^* \tag{9}$$

$$y^2 = y_c^2 + y^{*2} + 2y_c y^*$$
$$= y_c^2 + y^{*2} + 2(y_c y - y_c^2) \tag{10}$$

Now,

$$y_c = \beta x, \text{ hence (10) implies,}$$
$$\Sigma y^2 = \Sigma y_c^2 + \Sigma (y^*)^2 + 2(\beta \Sigma xy - \beta^2 \Sigma x^2) \tag{11}$$

The reader may verify that if the regression line has been estimated so that $\beta = \Sigma xy / \Sigma x^2$, the bracketted expression at the end of equation (11) turns out to be zero, so that in the circumstances when $\Sigma (y^*)^2$ is at a minimum we know also that,

$$\Sigma y^2 = \Sigma y_c^2 + \Sigma (y^*)^2 \tag{12}$$

Divide both sides by N and equation (12) states that the total variance of Y can be partitioned into the variance explained by the law of association postulated by the regression line, and a remainder which cannot. Substitute (12) into (8) and we get,

$$r = \sqrt{\frac{\Sigma y_c^2}{\Sigma y^2}} \tag{13}$$

The correlation coefficient is thus defined as the ratio of the 'explained' variance to the total variance. When the regression line explains the whole of the variance—i.e. the fit is perfect—the two variances are identical and r reaches an upper limit of unity, indicating 100 per cent correlation. The less successful the hypothesis, the greater the unexplained variance relatively to the total variance, and hence the smaller is r. This is also evident in equation (8) for a perfect fit means that there are no unexplained deviations and $\Sigma (y^*)^2$ is zero, hence top and bottom line of the fraction are equal. In a case of complete disassociation, r falls to precisely zero, for in such a case we know that $\Sigma (y^*)^2 = \Sigma y^2$. Thus we have successfully defined the standardised marking system for which we are seeking, all the marks which can be awarded lying between o and unity, i.e. between zero and 100 per cent. However, if the line whose slope is represented by β is not a true regression line, but has been fitted visually without ensuring that it is providing best fit, although a version of r may still be em-ployed, the equivalence between the formulae of equations (11) and (8) breaks down, and r loses its limiting properties.

In equations (11) and (8) r is a square root, and hence of in-determinate sign. But it is conventional to give r a positive sign when the association is a direct one (i.e. when positive deviations of Y are associated with positive deviations of X and negative deviations of Y with negative deviations of X so that the sign of β is positive) and a negative sign when it is indirect—the latter being described as a 'negative correlation'. We may deter-mine the sign of r and also conveniently describe the operations required for its computation by yet another presentation of the formulae for r; for (13) may evidently be written,†

$$r = \sqrt{\frac{\beta^2 \Sigma x^2}{\Sigma y^2}} = \beta \cdot \frac{\sqrt{\Sigma x^2}}{\sqrt{\Sigma y^2}} \qquad (14)$$

If β has been estimated by the method of least squares, (14) with a little manipulation becomes,

$$r = \frac{\Sigma xy}{\sqrt{\Sigma x^2} \sqrt{. \ \Sigma y^2}} \qquad (15)$$

Thus r in effect is the *co-variance* of X and Y divided by the pro-duct of their respective standard deviations. The sign of r is thus given by the sign of the co-variance, and the only computation re-quired additional to the computations necessary to obtain the re-gression coefficient is the computation of Σy^2. Equations (14) and (15) also demonstrate the close connection between the regression coefficient and the correlation coefficient; each converts to the other merely by multiplication by a ratio of the variances (see

† $y_c = \beta x$, $\therefore y_c{}^2 = \beta^2 x^2$, $\therefore \Sigma y_c{}^2 = \beta^2 \Sigma x^2$

equation (14)). Thus if the correlation is perfect, the regression coefficient is equal to the variance of Y divided by the variance of X (if these variances are equal we have a case in which all the plotting points on the scatter diagram fall along the 45° line from the origin); if the correlation is zero the regression coefficient is zero and the line of 'least bad' fit is a horizontal straight line crossing the diagram at the level of $\overline{Y}$.

Statistical Significance of Results

The reader may now verify for himself that if r is computed for the data of Table 10b, its value works out at just ·97. This would be considered a high value of r, as they go, since it means that nearly 95 per cent of the variance of Y has been 'explained' by the equation fitted (i.e. $r^2 = ·94$, see equation 8). Correlation coefficients of ·8 and over are usually considered satisfactory. Values of less than, say, ·6 are not usually regarded as very significant since they are quite likely to arise by chance, although the precise assessment of significance must vary with the circumstances of each example;—number of cases (N), magnitude of the variances, and so on. Obviously if the number of cases in the example is small (e.g. less than 20) the possibility of a purely chance result is much increased. There is a definite technique by which the 'statistical significance'—i.e. unlikelihood of having arisen by chance—of a correlation coefficient may on certain (rather limiting) assumptions be precisely numerically established, but the methods involved are not elementary. However, even with a sample of only ten cases, a correlation coefficient as high as ·97 would probably work out to be rather significant in the above sense: with a sample of 30 cases say, a result as high as this would almost certainly be significant in all typical examples. This would not be the case if r were to work out at, say, ·75, because *ceteris paribus* significance increases rapidly as the measured value of r approaches unity. If the more precise methods for computing significance were used, the conclusion would be given in the form of a statement to the effect that if instead of only ten electricity bills, a very large number indeed had been taken, so many that the possibility of a chance result were virtually eliminated, the odds would have been as high as twenty to one against the 'true' value of r thus measured lying more than, say, 5 per cent on either side away from the original estimate (i.e. in this example outside the range $\cdot 97 \pm \cdot 049$). Now, evidently, if there is a margin of error in r, there must be a corresponding margin of error in the estimates of the regression coefficient β, and also in the constant α, since all are algebraically linked. Thus for example, if a five per cent revision of r were necessary as a result of a revision of the co-variance (but with unchanged variances of both Y and X) β would also evidently have to be revised by five per cent in the same direction (see (14)); in the example worked, the corresponding revision of α would then work out at about 50d. Estimates of regression coefficients are therefore sometimes printed with estimates of the 'standard error' in small type beneath, meaning that in the absence of bias the chances are about twenty to one against the computed value of β lying outside the range of plus or minus twice the standard error from the 'true' value.

Assuming that the results obtained in the example of the ten electricity bills can in fact be regarded as significant, albeit subject to a certain margin of error due to chance, we can proceed to tackle the second question posed on page 162, the question it will be remembered whose answer is critical to the validity of the whole operation. The results to date may be summarised as:

TABLE 11. *Regression of Household Electricity Bill on Household Electricity Consumption*
(*Data of Table 10b*)

Symbols: X = electricity consumption of household, kWh per quarter;
Y = electricity bill of household, pence per quarter;

Regression coefficient of Y on X,	1·70
Correlation coefficient,	·97
Mean Values of X and Y,	$\overline{X} = 635$, $\overline{Y} = 1840$
Hence, estimating equation,	$Y_c = 760 + 1\cdot70X$

Bogus Results

We may recapitulate the problem by asking whether we may safely conclude that the above results mean that the electricity tariff in operation in 1960 involved a fixed charge of about 67/– per quarter, plus or minus about 2/–, and a unit charge of around $1\frac{3}{4}$d, either or both figures being subject for one reason or another to a certain amount of individual variation between households as evinced by the fact that r, though high, is less than unity. Put in this form the temptation to answer the question with a confident affirmative is obviously extremely strong. Nevertheless, as it happens, the proper answer is a categorical 'no'. For the data of the example were deliberately constructed in a manner designed to belie this simple interpretation and thus to demonstrate the inherent difficulties of our method. The figures for consumption of electricity and of fixed charge supposed to have been payable in each household were not invented arbitrarily, but were determined by reference to an assumed third factor, household income, according to a set of simple and reasonable economic assumptions. Each household from case 1 to case 10 was first allocated an imaginary income and its electricity consumption and electricity bill were then assumed to be determined in the following manner:†

† In mathematical language the assumptions made in constructing the example may be specified precisely as follows (for symbols, see below):

(a) The tariff

$$Y_i = A_i + BX_i$$
$$A_i = CZ_i$$
$$\therefore \quad Y_i = BX_i + CZ_i \tag{i}$$

—equation (i) representing the complete specification of the tariff, i.e. mathematical statement of the verbal information which would be given by the Electricity Board to an enquirer.

(b) Behaviour equation for family demand for house-space

$$Z_i = \gamma_i M_i \tag{ii}$$

(c) Behaviour equation for household demand for electricity

$$\frac{X_i}{Z_i} = \Delta_i M_i \tag{iii}$$

Now combine (ii) and (iii) so that Z_i is expressed as a function of X_i

$$Z_i = \sqrt{\frac{\gamma_i}{\Delta_i}} \cdot \sqrt{X_i} \tag{iv}$$

Write (iv) in abbreviated form,

$$Z_i = \lambda_i \sqrt{X_i} \tag{v}$$

Substitute (v) into (i),

$$Y_i = BX_i + C\lambda_i \cdot \sqrt{X_i} \tag{vi}$$

Definitions of Symbols

Y_i; electricity bill of the ith (i.e. any given) household, in pence,

(1) The larger the income, the larger the house occupied, hence the larger the floor area and the larger the fixed charge assessed by the Electricity Board according to the usual rates.

(2) In general, the larger the income the larger the electricity consumption *per square foot of floor area*, i.e. richer people not only lived in larger houses but they tended to keep them warmer and brighter and to use more electrical appliances.

(3) The economic laws of behaviour in which tendencies (1) and (2) could be more formally expressed were of an extremely

A_i; fixed charge payable by the ith household,
B; unit charge, common to all households, in pence per unit consumed,
X_i; consumption of ith household, in kWh,
Z_i; floor area of the ith household, in hundreds of square feet,
C; constant used by the Electricity Board in computing fixed charge from assessed floor area,
M_i; income of the ith household, in suitable units of money,
γ_i; social parameter of consumer demand equation for house-space,
Δ_i; social parameter of consumer demand equation for electricity.

$$\lambda_i = \sqrt{\frac{\gamma_i}{\Delta_i}}$$

Application

Equation (vi) was assumed to govern the electricity bill of any given household and thus to represent the basic form of the law of association between Y and X; hence the regression measured in Chart 2b represented in effect a poor linear approximation to this evidently non-linear relationship. Scatter was assumed to be caused by the existence of a modest amount of individual variation, as between households, in the value of λ, as follows:

TABLE 11. *Values of* λ

Case	Assumed value of λ
1	1·025
2	1·191
3	·955
4	1·120
5	·907
6	1·085
7	1·119
8	·875
9	1·052
10	·915

The above were metaphorically drawn out of a hat, as it were, except only that they were arranged to have the property of averaging approximately to unity. A household with a high value of λ would be a family which chose to occupy a house abnormally large for their income, or one which chose to keep their house abnormally cold and ill-lit for their income (or had a strong preference for gas or solid fuel heating and cooking) or both, and vice versa.

simple type (see footnote) but there was a certain amount of
individual variation in their application; some housewives
were assumed to prefer gas to electricity for many purposes
irrespective of their income, some houses to have solid fuel
central heating; some rich people (e.g. the English aristo-
cracy, if any were included in the sample) liked to keep their
large houses rather cold even though they could afford not to;
and so on.

(4) The Electricity Board's actual tariff, in contrast to what has
so far been supposed, was in fact;

Fixed Charge—5od for every 100 square feet of assessed
floor space,

Unit Charge —1d per unit.

The combined effect of the application of the foregoing assumptions in the manner described in the footnote is what is seen in
Chart 2b. The effect of assumption (1) is that houses with above-
average consumption have also above-average floor area and above-
average fixed charge, hence pulling the plotting points in the scatter
diagram upwards to positions systematically above where they
would be expected to lie on the basis of unit charge only. This raises
the regression coefficient of Y on X and distorts the apparent 'unit
charge'. Assumption (1) in the absence of (2) would tend to produce
a scatter diagram in which the path of the plotting points was a
straight line radiating from the origin, so that the measured value
of the constant α in the regression analysis would be zero: families
with near-zero incomes would live in very small houses and hence
be assessed to a near-zero fixed charge. The addition of assumption
(2) has the effect of inducing a curving path to the plotting points,
rising rapidly from the origin, then gradually flattening and finally
tending to linearity in the higher stages (i.e. at high levels of consumption and income) as payment on account of unit charge becomes so great as to swamp the effect of the fixed charge. Since for
obvious reasons our sample did not contain any households with
very low incomes, the most curving part of the path was not visible
on the scatter diagram and a bogus impression of approximate
linearity was created (if non-linearity had been apparent, the in-

vestigator might have been expected to smell a rat), and an excellent fit was obtained with a linear regression line which bore no relation to the actual tariff whatsoever. The apparent 'fixed charge' of 760d where this line intersected the Y-axis was economically meaningless, representing not the typical or average fixed charge of all the houses in the sample but in fact about that of the two smallest. Thus we have obtained entirely deceptive results in what appeared to be a straightforward example, yet an example constructed from assumptions which are typical of social reality. How may such disasters be avoided? The answer in general is that the investigator must have a definite, and more important, a reasonably correct idea of the nature of the system which is governing his data before he can interpret his results; in this example he would have had to have known not only the principles on which the fixed charge was computed but also to have had sense enough to see that this meant that the charge was itself likely to be correlated (via the third factor, income) with electricity consumption. How specifically he might apply such knowledge will be considered briefly below.

Bogus Results with Time Series

In the meantime we must glance at the ways in which similar or worse dangers arise in the application of regression analysis to time-series data. In such examples, X and Y will represent time series of the determining and the dependent variables respectively, the value of Y in any given year being plotted against the value of X in that year or in some cases the previous year (if the relationship is thought to work with a lag). If this is done, there is one particularly obvious way in which bogus correlation can arise through the intervention of a 'third factor': they may both be variables correlated with the passage of time itself. In other words they may both be possessed of secular trend, both, e.g. growing secularly through the process of economic development yet without any direct causal connection between them existing whatsoever. In the later years of the series both X and Y will tend to show values above their respective average levels over the period as a whole, and in the earlier years, below-average values conversely. *Ergo* the covariance of X and Y will be high—in the case quoted, positive—ergo they will appear to be correlated. Yet X and Y may be causally quite unconnected so that a computed regression coefficient will then represent no more than the ratio of their linear-trend slopes (see Chapter 6).

An ingenious device is commonly used to overcome the foregoing difficulty. Instead of correlating the values of X and Y as given in the original time series, we correlate the *first differences* of the two variables, that is to say their year-to-year changes. At any given point in the series, the *change* in the value of Y from the preceding year to the given year is plotted on the scatter diagram against the change in X over the same period (or in the case of a lagged relationship, specified earlier period). A substantial co-variance in the first differences and hence substantial correlation coefficient will only materialise if above-average *changes* in X are associated with above-average changes in Y and/or vice versa; and this certainly cannot occur just because both series are possessed of a secular trend: the method is therefore much akin to a process of eliminating trend before correlating the two series, but is definitely both simpler and superior to such. Notice, however, that a successful result with the first-difference method by no means establishes the causal validity of the apparent relationship observed; it merely eliminates one rather common cause of invalidity. Notice also that absence of correlation in the first differences does not completely destroy the possibility of a causal connection. X and Y might in fact be causally connected in a 'long-period' manner; X might be possessed of an autonomous trend which was *causing* the trend in Y. Suppose then the trend in X was linear and constant in magnitude over the whole period and suppose both X and Y were also subject to short period disturbances which were not causally connected. Then there would be no correlation in the first differences, despite the underlying long-period causal connection between the absolute values of X and Y. In truth, if two variables are suspected to be causally connected in this manner, with the trend in the one as the possible cause of the trend in the other, there is almost no way in which the hypothesis can be tested by regression analysis.

The regression coefficient calculated by the first difference method corresponds in a simple way to that which would be obtained by the ordinary method. In the ordinary method the regression coefficient represents an estimate of the parameter β in the following system,

$$Y = \alpha + \beta X; \quad dY/dX = \beta$$

In the first-difference method we have an estimating equation,

$dY/dt = \alpha' + \beta' \cdot dX/dt; \; dY/dX = \beta'$, where dt is a unit of time.

Hence β' is in principle the same parameter as β, but is estimated by a different method (i.e. from the covariance of dY and dX in contrast to that of Y and X). The parameter α' in the first-difference method, however, has a special and useful significance of its own. It represents the constant element, if any, in the annual change in the determined variable, in other words that part of its representative change which appears to be independent of the determining variable. α' thus can be taken as an estimate of the residual trend in Y which would be expected to continue in the absence of change in X. If α' turns out to be significantly non-zero, we might form the tentative conclusion that Y is only partly dependent on X, being also influenced by autonomous trend forces of its own.

Multiple Regression Analysis

It cannot be over-emphasised that even when applied to first differences, regression analysis of time-series data still remains more than capable of producing 'bogus' or at least extremely misleading results in the same general manner as described in the cross-section example above. Some, but not all, of these general difficulties can effectively be attacked by proceeding from the 'simple' analysis described in this chapter to what is known as 'multiple-regression' analysis. Multiple Regression Analysis is an extensive development of the whole method, far-reaching in importance and capable of considerable theoretical and practical refinement. In practice a very large part of what has come to be known as 'Econometrics'—the advanced mathematical/statistical branch of applied economics—involves the use of the multiple regression method and indeed, the simple, two-variable version of

N

regression analysis we have described here is more properly seen as but a step towards the larger goal. Needless to say we can in this book do little more here than sketch the nature of the goal, and can say practically nothing of the details of the methods which are used to reach it.

In multiple regression analysis the objective is to identify and take account of, not just one of the factors influencing our dependent variable, Y, but all of them, or rather all which are important. All are then included on the right-hand side of the estimating equation, each with a parameter (to be estimated) indicating how its movements are likely to contribute to movements of Y. The idea can only be visualised geometrically in terms of a multi-dimensional scatter diagram; algebraically the general form of the estimating equation is something like,

$$Y_c = \beta_1 X_1 + \beta_2 X_2 + \beta_3 X_3 \ldots, \text{ etc.} \qquad (16)$$

Y_c might represent the national demand for tea (in tons per annum, say), X_1, the price of tea, X_2, the price of coffee and X_3 the money national income. In principle there is no limit to the number of determining variables which may be inserted, in practice for various reasons four or five are the maximum. The regression co-efficients, β_1, β_2, β_3, etc. are estimated through a logical development of the least-squares principle: the procedures, which are described in a voluminous literature, attempt to provide a unique *combination* of 'best' estimates of the multiple coefficients such that if the combination chosen be applied to the data, the sum of the squared deviations of the actual values of Y from the computed values of Y_c—i.e. the values postulated by the proposed estimating equation—is reduced to a lower level than would be the case with any other combination. A *multiple correlation* coefficient, usually designated R, can then be computed to measure the success of the operation in a similar manner to the computation of r in the simple case. R is the square root of the ratio to the total variance of Y to the variance which can be explained by the 'multiple' regression equation. It is to be noted that the bringing in of additional variables will always improve the fit, i.e. reduce the 'unexplained' variance of Y; otherwise they would not be brought in. Hence typical values of R are substantially higher than of r, and usually R needs to be rather high to be statistically significant in the sense discussed earlier.

By the use of multiple regression analysis it may sometimes be possible to reduce some of the problems of 'third factor' correlation such as have been described, but the requirements for the successful application of the method are nevertheless rather severe. In the first place the investigator must possess some definite, and reasonably sensible, pre-conceived idea of what the multiple determining factors in the case really are: e.g. in our electricity example he would have had to know that the fixed charge was assessed on floor area, or at least that it was assessed on some factor which was likely to be correlated with income. Secondly the factors themselves must be capable of quantitative measurement or at least of some form of numerical expression—vague qualitative forces such as for example 'the climate of business opinion', cannot very well be measured numerically despite the fact that they may be of real causal importance. Thirdly, reliable quantitative data concerning all the factors must be available: in the electricity example the investigator would have needed to find information as to the floor area of each of the houses in his sample, which could be matched up with each entry in the records of the Accounts Department, case for case. Thus, in the example, assuming the necessary information was in fact available, the estimating equation would be written,

$$Y_c = \beta_1 X_1 + \beta_2 X_2 \qquad (17)$$

X_1 now standing for consumption and X_2 for floor area. But there is one final, and critical, condition for the derivation of reasonably easily interpretable results from a multiple regression exercise, that is that the multiple variables should not themselves be much intercorrelated. If they are, i.e. if for some reason large values of X_1 are to be associated with large values of X_2, bias may be introduced into the estimates and ambiguity into the interpretation. For the estimate of β_2 will be supposed to indicate how Y changes if X_2 changes while X_1 remains constant; but if, in the observed data, X_1 never does remain constant and instead moves regularly in association with X_2, β_2 as defined cannot validly be estimated. Fortunately, the difficulty is not overwhelming unless the correlation coefficient of the association between X_1 and X_2 is fairly substantial: if it is small, there may be enough independent variations of X_1 and X_2 to allow of reasonably valid estimates of their respective coefficients, but the estimates will still be liable to some bias. In the example above, the correlation between the two determining variables is known to be likely to be high, since larger houses are inhabited by richer people and require more electricity. Hence multiple regression analysis will by no means necessarily overcome all the difficulties inherent in the type of economic assumptions from which the example was constructed.

However, it sometimes happens that in the kind of case just described, the difficulty can be overcome by a simple manipulation of the form of the estimating equation. Thus if we divide (17) through by X_2, we get

$$\frac{Y_c}{X_2} = \beta_1 \frac{X_1}{X_2} + \beta_2 \tag{18}$$

This form of the relationship makes the payment *per square foot of floor area* dependent in a simple linear manner on the consumption per square foot. If therefore the original data are converted on to a per-square-foot basis, and the regression of payment per square foot on consumption per square foot is calculated in the normal way, valid estimates of both β_1 and β_2 will become available. β_1 and β_2 are the basic components of the tariff in operation, i.e. the information which we imagined the investigator to have set out to obtain, and should in principle be the same for all households. If they vary, they should do so only through 'clerical error' or some similar form of disturbance which can reasonably be assumed to be distributed randomly and without intercorrelation. However, it is obvious that the application of transformations of this sort is limited to a relatively small proportion of examples; more typical is the example of the demand for tea suggested at (16) above; there it might quite well happen that the movements of the various price and income series inserted as determining variables were all intercorrelated in some complicated cyclical fashion the effects of which no amount of re-arrangement could entirely eliminate.

An Ambiguity

The catalogue of major problems and ambiguities in the application of regression analysis is not yet complete. We must now explain yet another difficulty which applies to all forms of the method so far discussed. It will be remembered that in the second electricity example we saw an analogy to the characteristic situation of applications of statistical analysis to the social sciences—the apparently simple relationship between two variables was in fact merely one manifestation of a complicated system of additional relationships involving both the observed factors themselves and several others (such as floor area and income). Now it is not difficult to see that the logical effect of such a situation is that there can be no real basis for distinguishing one of the observed variables as determining and the other as determined. They could just as well be put the other way about. We could just as well have said that the electricity consumption was dependent on the electricity bill as vice versa, for the bill depended partly on the fixed charge, which depended on floor area, which itself was a major factor determining consumption (even ignoring the complication introduced by the further dependence on income). Hence the regression analysis could just as reasonably have been conducted by computing the regression of X on Y as of Y on X: the computed regression coefficient would then have been given by $\Sigma xy / \Sigma y^2$ instead of $\Sigma xy / \Sigma x^2$. The significance of the proposition can be seen when it is realised that if such reversal in fact is carried out, the new computed regression coefficient will normally not be, as might have been thought, the exact reciprocal of the coefficient obtained in the first instance, but something slightly different. For in the language of the scatter diagram, in the first instance the deviations which were squared and set at a minimum were the vertical deviations of the actual Y's from those postulated by the regression line, whereas in the inverse case the quantity minimised is the sum of the squares of the *horizontal* deviations of the *actual* X's from the X's postulated by the regression line. The two computations can only give the same result (in reciprocal) in the case of a perfect correlation; in all other cases they will give different results, the difference increasing in magnitude the smaller the correlation coefficient (the latter of course is the same whichever way the regression is taken). From the basic formulae for regression coefficient and correlation coefficient we can see that the relation between the regression of any given variable Y on another, X and the corresponding regression of X on Y is given by,

$$\frac{\Sigma\,xy}{\Sigma\,x^2} \div \frac{\Sigma\,y^2}{\Sigma\,xy} = \frac{(\Sigma\,xy)^2}{\Sigma\,x^2\,.\,\Sigma\,y^2} \tag{19}$$

If we write β_{yx} for the regression coefficient of Y on X and β_{xy} for the reciprocal of the regression coefficient of X on Y (19) becomes:

$$\beta_{yx} = \beta_{xy}\,.\,r^2 \tag{20}$$

Hence β_{yx} can only be equal to β_{xy} if r is unity.† By the same token, the difference between β_{yx} and β_{xy} will not be large unless the correlation coefficient is small. But it is clearly important that all statements of results should specify whether they relate to the regression of one variable on the other or vice versa.

Simultaneous Equations

A method of avoiding the last discussed difficulty and at the same time in principle eliminating the bias caused by interdependence in the multiple variables of a typical regression system (see page 177 above) is known as the method of Simultaneous Equations. In this rather sophisticated procedure the analyst attempts to construct a 'model' of all the whole system of interdependent relationships which he believes to be governing his data. (In the electricity tariff example this would mean attempting to specify all three basic equations of fn. page 170.) Then, by manipulation of the equations in the model, followed by a form of regression analysis conducted on all the variables together, it is sometimes possible to estimate the parameters of the entire system. The estimates are made simultaneously, in the mathematical sense of the word, so as to take full account of the interdependence. The ambiguity in distinguishing between determined and determining variables and the bias in the measurements obtained by the ordinary method can by this means be avoided. The method of simultaneous equations however has its own drawbacks and its employ-

† Equation 20 provides yet another form of the formula for r; $r = \sqrt{\beta_{yx}/\beta_{xy}}$.

ment is the subject of a certain amount of controversy: some distinguished theorists assert that the disadvantages are greater than the advantages and certainly some of the results obtained have in practice been surprisingly little different from those obtained by the ordinary 'single-equation' method as described.

Application to Logarithms

Our catalogue of dangers is complete, a full one would fill many chapters. We conclude this chapter by noting for the reader that on economic data regression analysis is frequently most usefully applied to the logarithms, in contrast to the original numbers; an obvious extension of the use of logarithms described at the end of Chapter 6. In the time-series case, it will be remembered, we plotted the logarithms of Y against the numbers of X, X in this case representing the passage of time, and we thus obtained an estimate of the proportionate rate of change of Y per absolute unit of time, X. But in the more general case we may just as well wish to convert both Y and X into logarithms, thus estimating in the regression analysis the proportionate change in Y to be expected from a given proportionate change in X. It follows from the mathematical properties of logarithms that the slope of the path of the plotting points in a double-logarithmic scatter-diagram (i.e. diagram where both original series have been converted into logarithms) represents the 'elasticity' of the relationship at that point. Hence the appearance of a strong linear correlation in the logarithms of two variables suggests that the relationship between the variables is of a constant-elasticity type: for example if family consumption of tea were related to family income in this way we could say there seemed to be no tendency for the income elasticity of demand for tea to alter as income rose, the proportionate increase in consumption of tea bearing a constant ratio to the proportionate increase in income which caused it, all the way up the curve—obviously a most unlikely result in practice.

We end by reiterating that the chapter was intended to represent a guide to, rather than a map of, its subject matter.

PART III

ECONOMIC INDEX NUMBERS

CHAPTER EIGHT

FORMAL PROPERTIES OF ECONOMIC INDEX NUMBERS

Introductory: The Purpose of Index Numbers

IN Chapters 2 and 3 we discussed the economist's methods of building up a general statistical picture of the national economy, and we saw how the picture could be constructed from measurements of circulating flows of goods and money. The discussion there, however, was conducted largely in static terms; the picture described related to a particular moment of time, or to a relatively short period such as a single year. But economists, as we have already seen, are also much interested in changes in the picture, i.e. in movements in the sizes of the aggregates measured. And more often than not, this interest derives from an interest in the corresponding changes, if any, in the 'economic welfare' of the society concerned or of its economy's capacity to produce welfare. Index numbers are essentially devices for converting information about changes in flows of goods or money into some sort of measure of changes in welfare or, more strictly, in 'real income',† and real income-producing capacity.

The need for special devices arises because the economic welfare of an individual or group of individuals is believed to depend on the physical quantities of the goods and services they consume (or could consume given the purchasing power at their disposal). And since we produce and consume a wide variety of different goods and services, all of very varying psychological importance, welfare must depend in a complicated and only very partly specifiable way on the size of each separate quantity of the various commodities consumed or produced. If we knew the entire 'utility

† For a discussion of the distinction between welfare and real income see p. 238, Chapter 9.

function' or 'preference system' of all individuals we should be able to say how much a particular person's (economic) welfare had increased as a result of a given change in the list of quantities of goods received. But we do not. At first sight, therefore, we do not possess the information which is necessary to evaluate, say, a one-ton increase in the production of coal coupled with another of one hundredweight in the production of crucifixes, i.e. we do not know how much relative importance should be given to two such different changes in assessing the consequent total change in welfare or real income. 'However', says economic theory, 'men purchase goods with limited money incomes, a rational man will try and make the best of his income, *ergo* the amount of money (the price) which men are prepared to pay for one ton of coal, or one crucifix, should provide a pretty good indication of the relative valuation placed upon these two quantities in the psychological preference system which lies hidden in the buyer's mind. Let us therefore give weight to the various observed changes in quantities in accordance with the observed pattern of market prices of the collection of commodities concerned.' This reasoning, although fraught with many logical difficulties, is nevertheless capable of considerable constructive application. If prices never changed, the suggestion would come to the same thing as comparing the change in the size of the total money flow involved; each tonnage increase of a commodity would be multiplied by the (constant) price per ton (or per crucifix as the case might be) of that commodity and the resulting sum of the thus 'weighted' changes would of course be the net increase in the total money value of the whole collection; this, expressed as a ratio of the initial money value could be taken to indicate the increase in welfare.† But prices unfortunately do change, not only in relation to one another but also in their general level: as everyone knows it is quite possible for monetary inflation to have the effect of raising the money value of the National Product without any increase whatsoever in the total quantities of goods and services nationally produced or consumed. The mone-

---

† If we are considering a group of individuals, welfare depends on the distribution of income, as well as on the total: we shall discuss this point in Chapter 9 (pp. 272 *et seq.*).

tary measuring rod, apparently so useful, transpires to be most un-constant. Money itself changes in value, therefore the change in the size of a total money flow, examined *solo*, is of little use as an indication of the change in the economic welfare arising from the flow of goods and services to which it corresponds.

Index numbers, then, are largely devices for mitigating deceptions caused by changes in the value of money. They usually either attempt to measure the change in the value of money directly (*a price index*) with the idea that the measure computed can then be used to adjust observed changes in particular aggregate money flows so as to eliminate the bogus inflationary element, or they tackle the problem by assessing the aggregate effect of all the observed changes in quantities in some way which keeps the effects of changes in prices out of the picture from the outset (*a volume index*). Both methods in fact come to much the same thing and, as will be seen, the simplest formula for a price index is but a mirror image of that for a volume index. In addition however, price index numbers are of considerable intrinsic interest as measures of the rate of inflation itself.

The basic reasoning behind a volume index, which also applies in effect (although, in a sense, in reverse) to a price index, derives from the proposition that in order to decide the appropriate contribution or 'weight' of a unit of a given commodity in the conspectus of economic welfare, it is really only necessary to decide the contribution *relatively* to that of other commodities. We are looking for a pattern of relative marginal utilities, not absolute ones. And this pattern may be taken as being indicated by the pattern of relative money prices: the importance or 'weight' of one ton of coal is indicated not so much by the simple price in pounds sterling per ton, but in the relation of that price to prices in general.

Of course, the pattern of relative prices no more in practice remains stable than does the general level of prices: the operation of the laws of supply and demand, which includes in effect the operation of consumers' preferences, requires a constant adjustment of the relationships between prices as part of the normal working of the economic system. Thus the user of the index-number technique is faced with a choice as to whether his weighting system should be based on the pattern of prices (and hence presumed 'marginal utilities') obtaining just before the change with which he is concerned, just after, or at some point in between. This choice raises issues of principle which are extensively discussed in Chapter 9.

It follows from the foregoing introductory remarks that the construction of an economic index number involves two intellectual stages: (first) in the principles of construction of any 'weighted' aggregate, i.e. aggregate in which the individual items summed are not given equal importance in determining the result and (second) the particular implication of using weights derived from the theory of economic value; the present chapter is particularly concerned with the first stage, Chapter 9 with the second.

The phrase 'index number' has also been used in the sense of 'indicator', that is to say a measure based on a regularly selected *sample* of price or quantity movements which are taken as representative of the movements of some major economic aggregate of which they form part, and of which a comprehensive statistical measurement would be difficult or impossible for practical reasons. A large proportion of the regularly computed and published index numbers possess this feature as well as the theoretical feature described above. The function is an important and useful one, but the problems of selection and weighting involved are adequately discussed in existing literature† and will not, therefore, be pursued here.

Plan of the Rest of Part III

In the rest of this Part we pursue almost exclusively the central theoretical problem, that of the employment of index numbers to pull down the veil of money. The present chapter is concerned with the formal, or algebraical properties of two basic formulae in common use. Chapter 9 attempts to connect these properties with the theory of economic value and to the specific problem of defining and measuring changes in an individual family's real income. Finally, in Chapter 10 we investigate in some detail the problems of measuring 'real' changes in National Product, and National Expenditure, as a whole.

† See in particular *The Measurement of Production Movements*, by C. F. Carter, W. B. Reddaway, and J. R. N. Stone, Cambridge 1950.

The treatment which follows in the rest of Chapter 8 is divided into two parts, main text and appendix. In the main text we develop the various propositions loosely and descriptively, using practical examples all along and avoiding proofs. In the appendix we give more formal expression to the arguments and prove our points by means of algebra. This separation is necessary because in some cases the algebraical manipulations involved, although by no means formidable, are sufficiently extended that if they were included in the main text readers might lose the thread of general arguments. But it is by no means intended that the appendix should be skipped, even by the most unmathematically minded reader. The two parts of the chapter are thought to be complementary, intended to be studied side by side, each assisting the comprehension of the other. The algebra is, if anything, simpler than that of Chapters 6 and 7, although it is assumed that the theoretical content of these chapters has been reasonably successfully absorbed.

Simple Weighted Averages

Now consider the following data:

TABLE 12. *United Kingdom Textile Industries Percentage of Females in Total Employees*

	June 1955
(1) Cotton - -	66
(2) Wool and Worsted	56
(3) Rayon and Nylon -	44
(4) Hosiery - -	72
(5) Textile Finishing -	34
(6) All Other Textiles	57

The table demonstrates that there is significant variation in the proportion of females employed, ranging from as low as only one third female in Finishing (where there is much heavy, man's work) to as high as 72 per cent in Hosiery, where the knitting machinery is almost entirely operated by women and girls. Thus it is not true that all the textile industries are predominantly run with lady workers, but it does appear, as expected, that female labour is more important in these industries than is normal in U.K. manufacturing: the overall proportion of lady employees in manufacturing industry as a whole, according to the Ministry of Labour, is just on 33 per cent, whereas for the industrial group covered by Table 12 it appears to be . . . what?

Now, although we can say that the answer to that question is evidently a figure greater than the national manufacturing average of 33 per cent (because each individual percentage in the textile industries is shown as being greater), we cannot, from the information given in Table 12 alone, compute the precise extent of the difference. We certainly cannot compute the overall percentage for textiles as a simple arithmetic average of the set of ratios given in the table. For the percentages given in the table represent a set of ratios such as,

$$x_i = \frac{Z_i}{Y_i}$$

where x_i is the ratio for any given textile industry, Z_i the number of female employees and Y_i the total number of employees of both sexes, in that industry. (In the table, x_i is given multiplied by a hundred.) Now the overall ratio for which we are seeking is evidently given by $\Sigma Z_i / \Sigma Y_i$, i.e. it is the ratio of the total number of females in the whole group to the total number of employees of both sexes in the whole group. But if we were to take a common or garden arithmetical average of the x_i, simply adding them all up and dividing by the total number of industries, six, we should arrive at $\dfrac{\Sigma Z_i / Y_i}{6}$, which, as we have seen elsewhere† is not the same thing at all.

However, notice that, since

$$Z_i = Y_i x_i,$$

it must be that, $$\frac{\Sigma Z_i}{\Sigma Y_i} = \frac{\Sigma Y_i x_i}{\Sigma Y_i}$$

In other words, we could get what we were after if we knew the size of Y_i (total employment of both sexes) for each industry and if we then multiplied the ratio x_i for each industry by its correspond-

† Chapter VI, p. 123.

ing Y_i, summed these products and divided the result by the aggregate of all the Y_i, that is by aggregate employment in the whole textile group. This is the operation known as the construction of a *weighted average* of the x_i; we would be taking a weighted average of the x's using the Y's as the 'weights', for we would be constructing an average in which each x is given varying importance or weight in accordance with the magnitude of its corresponding Y.

Following the notation explained in the Appendix, we describe the operation generally by the 'operator' symbol $\mathbf{W}$; thus in general a weighted average of any set of values, X_1, X_2, ..., X_i, ..., X_n, using a corresponding set of weights, Y_1, Y_2, ..., Y_i, ..., Y_n, will be indicated by $\mathbf{W}_Y(X)$, thus

$$\mathbf{W}_Y(X) = \frac{\Sigma\, Y_i X_i}{\Sigma\, Y_i}$$

As explained in the appendix, weights may very conveniently be expressed as ratios of their own aggregate, thus define

$$y_i = \frac{Y_i}{\Sigma\, Y_i} \quad (Note\ \Sigma\, y_i = 1)$$

in which case we can describe the operation as,

$$\mathbf{W}_Y(X) = \Sigma\, y_i X_i$$

This last expression demonstrates an important point. It is only the *relative* weights which matter in a weighted average: if all the Y_i change in the same proportion, i.e. so as to leave all the y_i unchanged, the average is unaffected. The weight given to the cotton industry in the example depends on the industry's share in the provision of total textile employment; the absolute numbers employed are unimportant except as they affect this share.

The weights expressed as percentage ratios (i.e. as $y_i \times 100$) for the example above are in Table 13 below. The reader may confirm that he has understood the operation by verifying that with the above weights and the data of Table 12, $\mathbf{W}_Y(X)$, (where X_i is the proportion of females in the ith textile industry and Y_i the industry's total employment of workers of both sexes) works out at just under 58 per cent.

o

TABLE 13. *United Kingdom Textile Industries*
Total Employees of Both Sexes, June 1955

	Per cent of Group Total
(1) Cotton - -	$28\frac{1}{2}$
(2) Wool and Worsted	$21\frac{1}{2}$
(3) Rayon and Nylon -	$9\frac{1}{2}$
(4) Hosiery - -	13
(5) Textile Finishing -	$9\frac{1}{2}$
(6) All Other Textiles -	18
Total above - -	100

The crude average of the unweighted ratios, as a matter of fact, works out at 55 per cent and would thus understate the correct result by three percentage points. An error of this relatively small magnitude would not matter much if we were merely wishing to confirm the impression that the textile industries employ substantially more female labour than in typical national industries, but might matter seriously if for some reason we wished to know the difference between the textile result and the national result precisely. Much of the difference between the weighted and the unweighted average for textiles is due to the fact that Textile Finishing, which has a particularly high proportion of men, is the smallest total employer, i.e. has a smaller weight in the weighted than in the unweighted average (one can conceive of an 'unweighted' average as a special case of a weighted average in which all the weights are the same). The difference would have been greater had not the effect of the case of Textile Finishing been partly offset by that of Hosiery, which has also a small weight, having a particularly high proportion of ladies, as already noted. In general, if there is no systematic association between the sizes of the Y_i's and the sizes of the corresponding X_i's, a weighted average may not show such great divergence from the unweighted average of the same set of data, because cases in which the effect of the weighting pulls in one direction will tend by the laws of chance to be offset by cases where the effect pulls in the opposite direction. (See Appendix, p. 205).

Index Numbers

The principles involved in the example we have just worked through in the last section were so simple as to be almost trivial: the weights were dictated entirely by the arithmetical nature of the problem in hand; we were unscrambling an egg which had been artificially scrambled to demonstrate the exercise. But this of course will not always be so; weights may be determined arbitrarily for some special purpose, or, more likely, they will be selected according to an economic principle which arises out of the inherent economic, in contrast to purely mathematical, nature of the matter under analysis. This is the case with economic index numbers.

Index numbers represent in fact a special form of weighted average, or to be more precise a special type of comparison of pairs of weighted averages, evolved for a particular purpose.† However, the formal principle of an index number (for definition see Appendix, p. 209 *et seq.*) is applicable over a wider field than that of welfare economics proper and in the following exposition we shall first demonstrate this basic principle by reference to a 'technological' example outside the strict welfare field, and then show the application to the measurement of real income, changes in the value of money, etc., subsequently.

Consider the following ratios:

TABLE 14. *Consumption of Solid Fuel, Gas and Electricity in Private Households*

Ratios for 1953, 1938 = 100

(1) Coal, direct sales,[1]	72
(2) Electricity, - -	295
(3) Gas, - - -	147

[1] Coke, wood and minor solid fuels are excluded for greater simplicity.

To be quite explicit we will define algebraically what each of the above ratios precisely represents: let us, following the notation more fully explained in the Appendix (sec. 2), label them x_1, x_2, x_3; the ratios for coal, electricity and gas respectively. Then

$$x_1 = \frac{X_{11}}{X_{10}} \quad \text{and} \quad x_2 = \frac{X_{21}}{X_{20}} \quad \text{and} \quad x_3 = \frac{X_{31}}{X_{30}}$$

† See p. 187 above.

where

X_{11} = direct sales of coal to private households, in tons, 1953;
X_{10} = ditto, 1938;
X_{21} = household consumption of electricity, in kilowatt hours, 1953;
X_{20} = ditto, 1938;
X_{31} = household consumption of gas, in therms, 1953;
X_{30} = ditto, 1938.

Suppose now for the sake of argument we say that we wish to compute some sort of general measure which would enable us to compare total household consumption of all three forms of energy in 1953 with that in 1938. It appears that we need a weighted average of the above ratios such as might tell us the 'average' ratio of consumption in 1953 to that in 1938. But what weights should we use? There is no system of weights obviously dictated by the arithmetical nature of the problem as so far stated; and the weights we use now must depend on the result of a further enquiry into the real nature of the economic question we are trying to answer in computing such a measure. The most likely question would be that concerning the changes in consumer welfare flowing from the changes in their consumption of energy, as already indicated: but this is not the only possible one; we might, for example, be wanting to measure the change in the total demand, direct and indirect, placed by the domestic consumer on the nation's coal supplies (i.e. allowing for the coal used in the production of his domestic gas and electricity, as well as direct sales),as part of an assessment of postwar national fuel policy.

Suppose in fact this question about coal economy were the one we were interested in. We would examine Table 14 and we would notice that between 1938 and 1953 the direct retail sales of coal fell substantially (to be precise, by 28 per cent) but that the indirect domestic consumption of coal in the form of electricity and gas on the other hand had changed considerably in the opposite direction. Some contemporary commentators as a matter of fact were suggesting that the increase in indirect forms of consumption had been so great as to offset the fall in direct sales, and that the total load,

direct and indirect, placed on the nation's coal supplies had if anything increased between 1938 and 1953. It was suggested that the
policy of restricting consumption by rationing solid fuel direct
supplies had been vitiated by the absence of restrictions on the
other two outlets for energy. We could verify this assertion by constructing a weighted average of the ratios in the table, weighting in
accordance with the *relative quantities of coal* consumed in 1938 in
direct sales, in power stations and in gasworks for the production
of domestic electricity and gas, respectively. The figures were
(ignore the 1953 column for the time being):

TABLE 15. *Coal Consumed, 1938 and 1953*

	Mil Tons		Per cent of Total	
	$1938^{(1)}$	1953	$1938^{(2)}$	1953
(1) Direct Sales - -	52	37	78	58
(2) Production of Domestic Electricity -	5	12	7	19
(3) Production of Domestic Gas - - - -	10	15	15	23
	67	64	100	100

[1] In the notation developed in the Appendix, this column corresponds to C_{i0}.

[2] This column corresponds to $\left(\dfrac{C_{i0}}{\Sigma C_{i0}} \times 100\right)$ i.e. to $c_{i0} \times 100$.

The weighted average is then obtained by the usual arithmetical
operations as follows:

TABLE 16. *Working Table for Construction of
Weighted Average of Ratios from
Table 14, with weights from Table 15*

	$x_{i_1/0}$	c_{i0}	$x_{i_1/0} \cdot c_{i0}$
(1) Direct Sales -	·72	·78	·56
(2) Electricity -	2·95	·07	·21
(3) Gas - -	1·47	·15	·22
		1·00	·99

$\mathbf{W}_{c_0}(x)$ is thus 99, indicating a negligible overall decline of one per cent and thus some support for the commentators' criticisms.

The weighted average $\mathbf{W}_{c_0}(x)$ is a typical *index number* and it is a subtler construct than might at first appear. For as is explained more fully in the Appendix (sec. 7a), the basic algebra of the operation we have just carried out is,

$$\mathbf{W}_{c0}(x) = \frac{\Sigma \ Y_{i0}X_{i1}}{\Sigma \ Y_{i0}X_{i0}}$$

where Y_{i0} is defined as,

$$Y_{i0} = C_{i0}/X_{i0}$$

We show in the appendix that the operation amounts in effect to the comparison of *two* weighted averages, one of the values X_{10}, X_{20}, X_{30} and the other of X_{11}, X_{21}, X_{31}, using as weights Y_{10}, Y_{20}, Y_{30} in both cases. These weights, the Y's, evidently represent (in the present example) the average quantities of coal which were required in 1938 to manufacture and deliver a ton of domestic coal, a kilowatt-hour of domestic electricity or a therm of domestic gas, as the case might be, respectively. These particular weights, therefore, were determined by the technical conditions reigning in the electricity and gas supply industries in 1938.

The operation of constructing an index number will be described (see Appendix, p. 209 *et seq.*) by a special operator, $\mathbf{I}$, so that

$$\mathbf{I}_{Y_0}(X_{1/0}) = \mathbf{W}_{c0}(x) = \frac{\Sigma \ Y_{i0}X_{i1}}{\Sigma \ Y_{i0}X_{i0}}$$

The suffix to $\mathbf{I}$ indicates the nature of the weights, that to X the period over which the comparison is to be made. What is the significance of this operation? Why do we do it? We were trying to analyse the effects of household consumption of various forms of energy—expressed as consumption of certain quantities of kWh's of electricity, therms of gas, etc.—on the total national consumption of the basic energy-source, coal: we needed, therefore, to take account of the appropriate *conversion ratios*, of how much coal for example was consumed on average in power stations in order to manufacture each kWh of electricity. Hence our use of a system of weights such as the Y's as defined above. We took the statistics concerning total consumption expressed in units, therms, etc., in 1938, we then weighted them by the corresponding conversion ratios, the Y's, and we compared these data with the data for 1953 (by which time electricity consumption in kWh's, for example, had increased enormously), similarly weighted, and hence arrived at our index number of the change in the total 'coal-equivalent' consumption of energy in private households.

But here we reach a critical point in the argument. The discerning reader will already have noticed that we were making a very big assumption in using the same set of conversion ratios as weights to apply to the year 1953 as well as 1938. Y_1, the weight for direct sales, must of course have remained constant at unity by definition, but there is no reason to believe that the technical conditions which determine Y_2 and Y_3 remained unchanged, especially over a period as long as 17 years. Indeed it is a well-known fact that the average efficiency of conversion in the electricity industry, in particular, has been increasing very rapidly as more and more new power stations embodying modern improvements in design have come into operation. To the extent that such changes have occurred, the index $\mathbf{I}_{Y_0}(X_{1/0})$ as computed in this example will be significantly in error if it is intended as a measure of what it has so far been suggested to be, i.e. the *total* change in direct and indirect household consumption, from all causes. A glance at the 1953 data in Table 15 shows the actual error to have been indeed significant since total coal-equivalent consumption, far from remaining virtually constant, fell by some 3 million tons. It would therefore appear that we ought to obtain information as to the extent of the technical changes which actually occurred, as expressed in data giving revised values of the Y's appropriate to the year 1953; these would be labelled, Y_{11}, Y_{21}, Y_{31} respectively. We should then compute our 'index' as $\Sigma\, Y_{i1}X_{i1}/\Sigma\, Y_{i0}X_{i0}$ and this would appear to give us the answer we want. Why then, do we not do so?

In the first place of course it might be that we are unable to obtain the information necessary to compute these revised values of the conversion-ratios. In the second place, if we were able to obtain this information we should already in effect be in possession of all that we needed, without going through the rigmarole of computing an 'index number'. For $Y_{i1} = C_{i1}/X_{i1}$ and, therefore, requires for its computation that we already know C_{i1}. But if we knew all the C_{i1}'s, i.e. the amounts of coal consumed in the various processes in 1953 corresponding to the information given in Table 15 for 1938, we should know the total consumed in 1953 ($\Sigma\, C_{i1}$), and hence should already know $\Sigma\, C_{i1}/\Sigma\, C_{i0}$ (the ratio of total coal-equivalent domestic consumption in 1953 to that in 1938), i.e. the thing we were trying to measure. No; the real reason for the use of formulae such as

$$\Sigma\, Y_{i0}X_{i1}/\Sigma\, Y_{i0}X_{i0}$$

in contrast to

$$\Sigma\, Y_{i1}X_{i1}/Y_{i0}X_{i0} \quad (= \Sigma\, C_{i1}/\Sigma\, C_{i0})$$

is much deeper: they enable us to throw a new and interesting light upon the problem in economic policy which we are studying.

The clue lies in something which has already been said: that as a matter of observable fact the average conversion efficiency of the industries which make electricity and gas from coal was increasing over the period in question. For if such changes have occurred the fact is bound to confuse the issue which we set out to discuss, i.e. whether the government's fuel-conservation policy had not been defeated by consumer adjustments between rationed and unrationed brands of domestic energy. We have so far been attempting to judge the question by whether or not the total domestic coal-equivalent consumption of energy had or had not increased. But we now see that this total change must be divided into two parts, that part which was in fact due to changes in household energy consumption and that part (working in the opposite direction) which was due to changes in the conversion efficiency of production. If the whole of the total change were predominantly due to the one part, rather than the other, the implications as regards the success of fuel-conservation policy would be very different: it would hardly be possible to claim a 'success' for the rationing policy on account of a stable total of coal-equivalent consumption if all that this meant was that a substantial potential saving of coal due to improved conversion efficiency in the electricity supply industry had been entirely used up in increased household consumption of energy. It is of the greatest interest therefore to be able to separate out statistically the two constituent parts of the change in such a total: we can then see separately the 'coal-equivalent' of the change in household energy consumption on the one hand and a measure of the average or overall change in conversion efficiency itself on the other, both expressed in ratio form; the latter ratio of course being of considerable intrinsic interest as a direct indicator of the rate of technological progress in the supply industries.

Formulae of the type we have been discussing are in fact expressly designed to make just such a separation. Suppose we were in possession of complete information about all the Y's and X's for both the years 1938 and 1953. Then $\mathbf{I}_{Y_0}(X_{1/0})$, which uses only the weights for 1938 and ignores those for 1953, tells us *what would have been the change in total coal-equivalent consumption had no changes in conversion efficiency occurred.* Conversely we could compute,

$$\mathbf{I}_{X_0}(Y_{1/0}) = \frac{\sum X_{i0} Y_{i1}}{\sum X_{i0} Y_{i0}}$$

as a measure of what would have happened had the changes in conversion efficiency occurred as they did, but household energy consumption of all types had remained constant. This latter would constitute a direct measure of the change in average conversion efficiency. Thus we have the analytical separation required, and it is this which constitutes the essential feature of a true index number. Ratios such as $\sum X_{i1} Y_{i1} / \sum X_{i0} Y_{i0} (= \sum C_{i1} / \sum C_{i0})$ referred to above are not true index numbers in this sense, since they combine inextricably the effects of changes in both components, X's and Y's, in the final result: when applied in welfare measurements for example, they combine the effects of changes in real income with changes in the value of money.

However, the analytical solution which is provided by index-number formulae such as $\mathbf{I}_{Y_0}(X_{1/0})$ and $\mathbf{I}_{X_0}(Y_{1/0})$ is unfortunately itself by no means free of ambiguity. Notice, as further discussed in the Appendix (sec. 8) that

$$\mathbf{I}_{X_0}(Y_{1/0}) \cdot \mathbf{I}_{Y_0}(X_{1/0}) \neq \frac{\sum C_{i1}}{\sum C_{i0}}$$

The product of the average change in conversion efficiency with average increase in energy consumption (when both averages are based on 1938 weights) does not return us to the number we first thought of, i.e. the ratio we were trying to partition, the ratio of 1953 to 1938 total direct and indirect household coal consumption. Actually, if we divide $\Sigma C_{i1}/\Sigma C_{i0}$ by say the index of energy consumption, $\mathbf{I}_{Y0}(X_{1/0})$, we arrive (see Appendix) at the following:

$$\frac{\Sigma X_{i1}Y_{i1}}{\Sigma X_{i0}Y_{i0}} \div \frac{\Sigma Y_{i0}X_{i1}}{\Sigma Y_{i0}X_{i0}} = \frac{\Sigma X_{i1}Y_{i1}}{\Sigma X_{i1}Y_{i0}}$$

This is an (inverse) index number of conversion efficiency, but it is not $\mathbf{I}_{X_0}(Y_{1/0})$; it is in effect $\mathbf{I}_{X_1}(Y_{1/0})$, that is to say it is an index of the Y's using the X_1's, not the X_0's, as weights: it indicates what would have been the difference between total consumption of coal in 1953 and 1938 on the assumption that household energy consumption remained constant at the 1953 level and pattern, in contrast to the 1938 level and pattern assumed in the measure $\mathbf{I}_{X0}(Y_{1/0})$. Similarly we could compute,

$$\mathbf{I}_{Y_1}(X_{1/0}) = \frac{\Sigma Y_{i1}X_{i1}}{\Sigma Y_{i1}X_{i0}} \qquad \textit{(For an example, see Table 17 below)}$$

which would measure the average change in household energy consumption on the assumption that conversion efficiencies were fixed at their 1953 level and pattern. This, if multiplied by the original $\mathbf{I}_{X_0}(Y_{1/0})$ index of conversion efficiency would get us back to $\Sigma C_{i1}/\Sigma C_{i0}$. Thus for both our partition measures we have a choice of 'base weighted' and 'current weighted'† variety; the two varieties will by no means necessarily always give the same answer and it is necessary to 'cross' the two in order to multiply back to 'the number we first thought of'. Hence, as already stated, the partitioning involves a major ambiguity.

Notice that when the 'weights' are given in the composite form as in both example tables (i.e. where we weight the *ratios*, x_i, with 'weights' in the composite form $C_{i1} = X_{i1}Y_{i1}$, rather than separating the computation into all the components of $\Sigma Y_{i1}X_{i1}/\Sigma Y_{i1}X_{i0}$)

† See Appendix, sec. 7c for discussion of a confusion to which this conventional terminology is liable to give rise.

it is necessary with the 'Y_1-weighted' index to obtain the answer by the apparently roundabout method of summing the products of the weights against the *reciprocals* of the x's and then taking the reciprocal of this result. Otherwise, as shown in the Appendix at pp. 211–13, we get nonsense.

TABLE 17. *Working Table for the Computation of Current-Weighted Index of Household Energy Consumption*

	$\dfrac{1}{x_{i1/0}}$	c_{i1}	$\dfrac{1}{x_{i1/0}}c_{i1}$	
(1)	1·39	·58	·81	$I_{Y_1}(X_{1/0}) = \dfrac{1}{1 \cdot 03} \times 100 = 97$
(2)	·34	·19	·06	
(3)	·68	·23	·16	
Total		1·00	1·03	

$I_{Y_1}(X_{1/0})$ thus works out at 97, a difference of two points from $I_{Y_0}(X_{1/0})$ and the reader may verify for himself that the corresponding measures of conversion-efficiency, $I_{X_0}(Y_{1/0})$ and $I_{X_1}(Y_{1/0})$ work out at approximately 99 and 96 respectively.† The main reason for the differences in this particular case is that the industry achieving the greatest increase in its conversion-efficiency, electricity, also saw the greatest increase in sales of its product to domestic consumers; hence the value of the particular x_i, x_2, which made the greatest contribution to the general increase received a smaller weight in $I_{Y_1}(X_{1/0})$ than in $I_{Y_0}(X_{1/0})$, hence $I_{Y_1}(X_{1/0})$ was bound to be the smaller since it was so to speak 'handicapped' by comparison: for further discussion see Appendix, page 217 *et seq.*

There is no obvious way of saying whether either type of index, such as either $I_{Y_0}(X_{1/0})$ or $I_{Y_1}(X_{1/0})$ is a 'better' measure than the other. Both are usually no more than approximations to what is basically wanted; later, in Chapter 9, we shall show that in the typical application to the measurement of economic welfare, the one measure tends to come out too low while the other is too high.

† Indicating improvements in average conversion efficiency of one per cent and four per cent respectively.

CHAPTER EIGHT

ALGEBRAICAL APPENDIX

1. Notation

WE commence with the development of a general notation for the construction and indication of weighted averages and index numbers. This notation involves the use of a number of suffixes and subscripts, etc., which nearly always throughout this appendix will for the sake of clarity be given in full, but in day-to-day usage subscripts can frequently be omitted if there is little possibility of confusion resulting.

Suppose there be a certain collection of variables (e.g. the prices of a certain set of commodities), identified by numbers 1 to N,

$$1, 2, \ldots, i, \ldots, N$$

Now let,

$$X_1, X_2, \ldots, X_i, \ldots, X_n$$

stand for the quantitative magnitude of each variable (e.g. the actual money price of each commodity), X_i being the general expression for 'the value of any given variable, say, the ith'.

A *specific* set of values of the variables, at, e.g., a certain time or in a certain place, is indicated by,

$$X_{10}, X_{20}, \ldots, X_{i0}, \ldots, X_{n0}$$

'o' being the number generally assigned in the literature to some base period from which an index-number comparison is to be made. Other specific sets of values of X at other (usually later) times or in other (usually overseas) places, may be indicated generally by the use of X_{i1}, X_{i2} or $X_{i3} \ldots$, etc.

Thus the complete specification for all possible values of X is,

$$X_{10}, X_{20}, \ldots, X_{i0}, \ldots, X_{n0}$$
$$X_{11}, X_{21}, \ldots, X_{i1}, \ldots, X_{n1}$$
$$X_{12}, X_{22}, \ldots, X_{i2}, \ldots, X_{n2}$$
$$\text{etc.} \quad \text{etc.} \quad \text{etc.} \quad \text{etc.}$$

The first suffix to X, i.e. the column-suffix, always specifies the variable whose magnitude is in question, the second suffix, the row-suffix, the set of which the specified magnitude is a member.†
The foregoing may be recapitulated verbally as follows:

X_{i0} ... 'the value of a given variable, in a specific collection of variables, in some specified *set* of values of the whole collection' (commonly the value of a given variable in some chosen base time-period).

X_{i1} ... 'the value of the *same* given variable in another set of values of the collection' (commonly a set taken at a later period of time).

We next indicate a system of *weights* to be applied to the above values in the operations to be described. A set of weights to be applied to a set of variables will be indicated by

$$Y_1, Y_2, ..., Y_i, ..., Y_n$$

A specific set of weights, and alternative sets, will be indicated in a similar manner as in the case of the X's,

$$Y_{10}, Y_{20}, ..., Y_{i0}, ..., Y_{n0}$$
$$Y_{11}, Y_{21}, ..., Y_{i1}, ..., Y_{n1}$$
$$Y_{12}, Y_{22}, ..., Y_{i2}, ..., Y_{n2}$$
$$\text{etc. etc. etc. etc.}$$

The significance of the alternative sets of weights is as follows. Suppose we have an example where the weights are not arbitrary but are chosen by some rational rule, e.g. that the weight given to the price of a particular commodity in a cost-of-living index shall depend directly on the quantity of that commodity bought by the typical consumer. Then Y_{i0} might represent the quantity bought of any given commodity in some base period 'o' and Y_{i1} the quantity bought of the same commodity in some later period: either of course might be used to weight X_{i1}, depending on the type of index.

† It would have been more logical to employ a symmetrical system for the enumeration of both rows and columns, numbering rows from 1 through i to n, as the columns. But it has become so common in the literature to use 'o' for 'any given set' and '1' to indicate 'some other given set', that we have followed this usage.

2. Values and Weights as Ratios

The values and the weights, i.e. the X's and the Y's, are frequently expressed as some form of ratio, in particular X_{i1} may be expressed as a ratio of X_{i0} and Y_{i0} as a ratio of the sum of all the weights in its set, i.e. of ΣY_{i0}. An X or Y as a ratio will be indicated by the use of the lower case with if necessary a suffix to indicate the base of the ratio (with one exception in what follows all such suffixes are always included). Thus

$$x_{i1/0} = \frac{X_{i1}}{X_{i0}} \quad \text{or} \quad y_{i1/0} = \frac{Y_{i1}}{Y_{i0}}$$

$$x_{i0} = \frac{X_{i0}}{\Sigma X_{i0}} \quad \text{or} \quad y_{i0} = \frac{Y_{i0}}{\Sigma Y_{i0}}$$

Note therefore the general rule that

$$\Sigma x_{i0} = \Sigma y_{i0} = 1 \tag{2.1}$$

3. Ordinary Unweighted Averages or Arithmetic Means

The ordinary unweighted average of the set of values

$$X_{10}, \ldots, X_{i0}, \ldots, X_{n0},$$

is to be indicated by $\overline{X}_0$, thus

$$\overline{X}_0 = \sum_{i=1}^{i=n} X_{i0}/n \tag{3.1}$$

$\sum_{i=1}^{i=n}$ indicates summation 'over all i from 1 to n', i.e. for all the variables in the collection. In all that follows $\sum_{i=1}^{i=n}$ will be printed plain Σ.

4. Simple Weighted Averages

An (arithmetic) weighted average of a set of values is constructed by multiplying each value by its assigned weight, summing the resulting products and dividing the resulting sum by the sum of the weights. This operation will be indicated by the operator, $\mathbf{W}$, with suffix as necessary to indicate the nature of the weighting system to be used. Thus a weighted average of a set of X's, using as weights a certain set of Y's will be indicated by $\mathbf{W}_Y(X)$. Thus,

$$\mathbf{W}_{Y_0}(X_0) = \Sigma \, Y_{i0}X_{i0}/\Sigma \, Y_{i0} = \sum \frac{Y_{i0}}{\Sigma \, Y_{i0}} \cdot X_{i0} = \Sigma \, y_{i0}X_{i0} \qquad (4.1)$$

From the last line of the above development emerges our first important (if rather obvious) theorem: $\mathbf{W}_{Y_0}(X_0)$ will change, *if, and only* if *either* some X_{i0} changes *or* some y_{i0} changes, (or both). Changes in the Y_{i0} which leave all the y_{i0} unchanged, i.e. uniform proportionate changes in all the Y_i together, do not affect the weighted average.

5. Difference between Weighted Average and Unweighted Average

$$\text{Now,} \quad \Sigma \, y_{i0}X_{i0} = \Sigma \, \{\bar{X}_0 + (X_{i0} - \bar{X}_0)\} y_{i0} \qquad (5.1)$$
$$= \bar{X}_0 + N.\text{cov}_{X_0 y_0} \qquad (5.2)$$
$$= \bar{X}_0 + N r_{X_0 y_0} \cdot \sigma_{X_0} \sigma_{y_0} \qquad (5.3)$$
$$= \bar{X}_0 + N \beta_{X_0/y_0} \cdot \sigma_{y_0}^2 \qquad (5.4)$$

(For explanation of these symbols, see Chapter 7.)

Thus we see that, given N, the difference between an unweighted average and a weighted average of the same set of values depends on the *covariance* of the magnitude of the values themselves with the magnitude of their own weights. The size of the difference thus depends (see Chapter 7) on the existence of *correlation* between the magnitudes of the weights and the variables and, given this correlation coefficient, on the dispersion of the weights and of the values respectively. Alternatively, the difference can be said to depend on the size of the *regression coefficient* in the association (if any) between the weights and the values. Such association may arise by chance and yet be sufficient to yield a significant difference between the weighted and unweighted averages since a fairly small value of the correlation coefficient can yet be consistent with a fairly large absolute magnitude of the covariance if the weights are sufficiently dispersed (i.e. if σ_{y_0} is sufficiently large). Nevertheless, really substantial differences between weighted and unweighted averages of the same set of values are unlikely unless there is some causal connection, direct or indirect, leading to a substantial magnitude to the correlation coefficient between the weights and the values. If such causal connection exists, the greater the sensitivity of the relationship and the greater the dispersion of the weights (i.e. the extent to which they differ from one another as indicated by their variance), the greater the difference between the two measures. Thus there will be no difference between a weighted and unweighted average of the same set of variables in any of the following circumstances:

(1) There is zero correlation between weights and values, $(r_{x_0 y_0} = 0)$.
(2) All the weights are the same, $(\sigma_{y_0} = 0)$.
(3) All the values are the same, $(\sigma_{x_0} = 0)$.

The above formalises the argument of p. 192 in the main text of the chapter above.

6. Weighted Variances, Covariances and Etc.

The concept of weighting can also be applied to the tools of regression analysis—variances, co-variances, regression co-efficients and, etc.—which were first discussed in their ordinary form in Chapter 7. Weighting can be of great importance in regression analysis, since it is by no means always desirable to pay equal attention to the positions of all the plotting points in a scatter diagram; some may be obviously more important than others. In explaining this we must first accommodate ourselves to a change in notation from that used in the exposition of unweighted regression analysis in Chapter 7. In that chapter, the values of a certain dependent variable, Y, were correlated with the *corresponding values* of a certain determining (or thought-to-be-determining) variable, X; the correspondence arising from the fact that the paired values set against each other on the scatter diagram were possessed of some other common characteristic, such as that they related to the same year in a time series, or the same household in a family expenditure survey. In the present chapter, however, we have appropriated the letter Y to the concept of a weight and in weighted regression analysis the weights are to be applied to the corresponding *pairs* of values, i.e. in effect to positions of the plotting points in the scatter diagram. We are trying to find the line of best fit through the plotting points taking more account of the positions of some points (i.e. those to which it has been decided to attach the larger weights) than of others. For instance, it will be recollected from Chapter 7 that in our imaginary attempt to assess the electricity tariff ruling in the year 1960 we took data relating to a sample of households and plotted the recorded electricity consumption of each household against its recorded electricity bill in respect of that consumption. However, it might be the case that the data with which we were working related not to the consumption and expenditure of individual households, but to the average consumption and average electricity bill of a number of *groups* of households, the data having been summarised into that form for convenience or some other reason. Now suppose the groups of households were not all of equal size, some groups containing a substantially larger number of households than others, and that this was known to us together with the actual number of households (but not the consumption and electricity bill data for the individual households) in each group. Then we would obviously want to weight our regression analysis so as to give more importance to the results for the larger groups than the smaller, otherwise our estimates of regression coefficient, correlation coefficient, etc. might be significantly different from those which would have been obtained had we been able to work with the 'unscrambled' data.†

We can no longer employ the letter Y to indicate one of a pair of variables to be correlated, since it is to be used as the symbol for the weights to be attached to the pair: we can continue to use X for the determining variable, but we have to use another letter, e.g., Z for the determined variable. The effect of this is more far-reaching than might at first be appreciated. We have now to consider in place of the simple set of economic variables, 1, 2 ... i ... N (such as the prices of different commodities) with which we set out at the beginning of this appendix, a set of economic *categories* or 'boxes' which may contain more than one variable of distinct economic type. Thus the set of categories 1, 2, ..., i, ..., N might be the set of groups of households in the electricity-tariff example, a set of commodities themselves. In the first case we would distinguish

† Although, for reasons analogous to those given in discussing the difference between a weighted and unweighted average (see above) the estimates will not *necessarily* differ and quite specific conditions are required to be present to make them differ substantially.

P

two variables in each category (electricity consumption and electricity bill) and in the second case we might distinguish the various measures of the market situation of each commodity, e.g. we might wish to correlate the price level of each commodity against the quantity of it being bought. The effect is to modify our notation as follows:

X_i ... 'the value of a certain (thought-to-be) determining variable in a certain given category, viz. the ith category;'

Z_i ... 'the value of another variable, thought to be determined by X_i, in the same category;'

Y_i ... 'the weight to be attached in the regression analysis to any magnitude arising in the ith category, either of the variable X or of Z.'

In a weighted regression analysis, the deviations of either X_i or Z_i are taken from the *weighted* means of X and Z respectively, using Y_i as weights in both cases, and in computing variances, co-variances, etc., the squared deviations and cross-products thus obtained are again weighted by Y_i before being aggregated. The full range of formulae are as follows:

(6.1) *Weighted Variance* $= \mathbf{W}_Y(\mathrm{VAR}_X) = \Sigma Y_i \{X_i - \mathbf{W}_Y(X)\}^2 / \Sigma Y_i$

(6.2) *Weighted Standard Deviation* $= \mathbf{W}_Y(\sigma_X) = \sqrt{\mathbf{W}_Y(\mathrm{VAR}_X)}$

(6.3) *Weighted Co-variance* $= \mathbf{W}_Y(\mathrm{COV}_{XZ})$
$$= \Sigma Y_i \{X_i - \mathbf{W}_Y(X)\} \{Z_i - \mathbf{W}_Y(Z)\} / \Sigma Y$$

(6.4) *Weighted Regression Coefficient* $= \mathbf{W}_Y(\beta_{Z/X})$
$$= \frac{\mathbf{W}_Y(\mathrm{COV}_{XZ})}{\mathbf{W}_Y(\mathrm{VAR}_X)}$$

(6.5) *Weighted Correlation Coefficient* $= \mathbf{W}_Y(r_{ZX})$
$$= \frac{\mathbf{W}_Y(\mathrm{COV}_{XZ})}{\mathbf{W}_Y(\sigma_X) \cdot \mathbf{W}_Y(\sigma_Z)}$$

The additional suffixes 0, 1, 2, ..., etc. may of course be used in the same manner as previously to indicate alternative sets of values of the same variables in the same categories. Thus in the electricity tariff example, the Y_i might represent, instead of the number of families in each group, the aggregate amount of their income at some period or other; Y_{i1} would then be income measured, say, in the current quarter and Y_{i0} income in some earlier quarter. Then it might be desired to test the hypothesis that the bills were paid two quarters in arrears, i.e. that the bill for a given quarter related to consumption in the quarter ending three months earlier; then consumption in the earlier quarter of a given group of families, the ith group, would be X_{i0}, say, and their group average electricity bill paid this quarter, Z_{i1}; Z_{i0}, then to be correlated with X_{i0} in a weighted regression analysis with, e.g., Y_{i0} as weights.

The foregoing modifications of the notation are only necessary in relation to weighted regression analysis.

(7a) Economic Index Numbers

An economic index number is usually thought of as a weighted average of a set of *changes* in a set of *variables*, e.g. prices or quantities, whose average absolute level cannot be given economic significance. This interpretation, however, can be rather deceptive. If we consider first principles we see the index number as representing, in effect, a ratio between *two* weighted averages of two different sets of values of the *same* set of variables, using the *same* set of weights for both. For example, the volume index of direct and indirect domestic coal consumption, demonstrated on page 233, in effect compares two weighted averages of the quantities sold of three specified commodities (coal, gas and electricity) in 1938 and 1953 respectively, using in both years the 1938 prices of these commodities as weights. Thus an economic index number is typically represented by $\mathbf{W}_{Y_0}(X_1)/\mathbf{W}_{Y_0}(X_0)$, the common weights here being of the set, '0'; or the index may be $\mathbf{W}_{Y_1}(X_1)/\mathbf{W}_{Y_1}(X_0)$, where the common weights are of another set, '1'. The construction of such an index number from any two sets of values of X, with a given set of weights Y, will be indicated by the operator $\mathbf{I}$, with appropriate suffixes as follows:

$$\mathbf{I}_{Y_0}(X_{1/0}) = \frac{\mathbf{W}_{Y_0}(X_1)}{\mathbf{W}_{Y_0}(X_0)} \tag{7.1}$$

and

$$\mathbf{I}_{Y_1}(X_{1/0}) = \frac{\mathbf{W}_{Y_1}(X_1)}{\mathbf{W}_{Y_1}(X_0)} \tag{7.2}$$

or the reciprocal case,

$$\mathbf{I}_{Y_0}(X_{0/1}) = \frac{\mathbf{W}_{Y_0}(X_0)}{\mathbf{W}_{Y_0}(X_1)} \text{ etc.} \tag{7.3}$$

It is evident from the description already given of the operation, **W**, that the foregoing implies that

$$\mathbf{I}_{Y_0}(X_{1/0}) = \frac{\Sigma \, Y_{i0}X_{i1}}{\Sigma \, Y_{i0}} \div \frac{\Sigma \, Y_{i0}X_{i0}}{\Sigma \, Y_{i0}} = \frac{\Sigma \, Y_{i0}X_{i1}}{\Sigma \, Y_{i0}X_{i0}} \qquad (7.4)$$

The complete expression describing the operation of constructing the index, **I**, is thus quite simple; the original sums of the weights, $\Sigma \, Y_{i0}$, to which little economic meaning can be attached, having disappeared by cancelling. This is of considerable convenience to economists, and the index number formulae are often in fact written in the open form of expressions such as $\dfrac{\Sigma \, Y_{i0}X_{i1}}{\Sigma \, Y_{i0}X_{i0}}$ above. It may be asked why, this being the case, there is any need to introduce a new operator symbol. The answer is that, although a formula such as $\dfrac{\Sigma \, Y_{i0}X_{i1}}{\Sigma \, Y_{i0}X_{i0}}$ is quite simple, it is not very evocative; a moment's hesitation is usually necessary before appreciating exactly what type of index is described; which are the weights and which the variable being weighted, and so on. The notation we suggest, though less streamlined, is thought more effectively to speak for itself, as it were, but the student who disagrees is of course free to employ the 'open' notation as often as it suits him.

There is an important alternative method of describing the computation of an index. Notice that:

$$\frac{\Sigma \, Y_{i0}X_{i1}}{\Sigma \, Y_{i0}X_{i0}} \quad \text{could be arranged as} \quad \frac{\Sigma \, Y_{i0}X_{i0} \cdot X_{i1}/X_{i0}}{\Sigma \, Y_{i0}X_{i0}}$$

Hence

$$\mathbf{I}_{Y_0}(X_{1/0}) = \frac{\Sigma \, Y_{i0}X_{i0}x_{i1/0}}{\Sigma \, Y_{i0}X_{i0}} \qquad (7.6)$$

Now this last expression is in effect itself a sort of weighted average, a weighted average of the $x_{i1/0}$ using as weights the products $(Y_{i0}X_{i0})$. Suppose then we define a 'composite' weight, C_{i0}, such that $C_{i0} = Y_{i0}X_{i0}$ or $C_{i1} = Y_{i1}X_{i1}$ and

$$c_{i0} = \frac{Y_{i0}X_{i0}}{\Sigma \, X_{i0}Y_{i0}} \quad \text{or} \quad c_{i1} = \frac{Y_{i1}X_{i1}}{\Sigma \, Y_{i1}X_{i1}}$$

then,

$$\mathbf{I}_{Y_0}(X_{1/0}) = \sum c_{i0} x_{i1/0} = \mathbf{W}_{c_0}(x_{1/0}) \qquad (7.7)$$

This is the operation which is carried out in Table 16 of the main text. The convenience and simplicity of the arrangement is obvious. Index numbers are commonly computed in the manner which this description of the operation implies and, indeed, the information relating to weights and variables is often regularly available only in the form of a set of weights c_1, c_2, c_3, ..., c_i, ..., c_n and values to be weighted x_1, x_2, x_3, ..., x_i, ..., x_n respectively. The published 'weights' of official index numbers such as the Index of Retail Prices or the Index of Industrial Production nearly always consist of a set of ratios such as the c's, usually expressed not 'per cent' but 'per thousand'. Indeed, the ordinary user of the data would derive little benefit if the weights were given in any other form. Nevertheless, as we shall see, the description, $\mathbf{I}_{Y_0}(X_{1/0}) = \mathbf{W}_{c_0}(x_{1/0})$, provides considerable opportunity for deception and error.

(7b) Two Common Errors

There are in fact two common errors which arise out of the use of the form $\mathbf{W}_{c_0}(x_{1/0})$, to describe the construction of an index number, both relating to the question of alternative weights. First, notice that if we face a number of sets of values of the X's, i.e. sets 0, 1, 2, ..., etc., as specified in our introductory notation, together with a corresponding number of sets of weights, of the type Y, then there is a definite relation between the complete specification of the Y's and X's and that of the corresponding 'weights' written in the form of C. It must be, by definition, that each $C_{i1} = C_{i0} \cdot x_{i1/0} \cdot y_{i1/0}$. For C_{i1}, being the product of X_{i1} and Y_{i1} (see above), by definition must be equivalent to the original C_{i0} times the ratio of X_{i1} to X_{i0} and of Y_{i1} to Y_{i0}. We must therefore be very careful in what we do if we wish to substitute 'set 1' weights for the original 'set 0' weights; if we do this when using weights in the composite, i.e. C-form we must remember that the changes in C_i from C_{i0} to C_{i1} are not independent of changes in the values to be weighted. Students and others who neglect the point are sometimes to be found describing the operation of constructing an index with 'year 1' weights in contrast to 'year o' weights as

$$\mathbf{I}_{Y_1}(X_{1/0}) = \mathbf{W}_{c_1}(x_{1/0}) \quad (\textit{false})$$

However, if we multiply this out we see that it means,

$$\Sigma\, c_{i1} x_{i1/0} = \frac{\Sigma\, C_{i1} x_{i1/0}}{\Sigma\, C_{i1}} = \frac{\Sigma\, Y_{i1} X_{i1} X_{i1}/X_{i0}}{\Sigma\, Y_{i1} X_{i1}} = \frac{\Sigma\, Y_{i1} X_{i1}^2/X_{i0}}{\Sigma\, Y_{i1} X_{i1}}$$

which, is (a) not the index intended, viz. $\Sigma\, Y_{i1} X_{i1}/\Sigma\, Y_{i1} X_{i0}$, and (b) nonsense. The only way to obtain $\mathbf{I}_{Y_1}(X_{1/0})$ from a set of weights of the form C_{i1} when the problem is set up so that in fact each $C_{i1} = C_{i0} x_{i1/0} y_{i1/0}$, is by means of the proposition,

$$\mathbf{I}_{Y_1}(X_{1/0}) = \frac{\Sigma\, Y_{i1} X_{i1}}{\Sigma\, Y_{i1} X_{i1} \cdot X_{i0}/X_{i1}} = \frac{\Sigma\, C_{i1}}{\Sigma\, C_{i1} x_{i0/1}} = \frac{1}{\mathbf{W}_{c_1}(x_{0/1})} \qquad (7.8)$$

In other words $\mathbf{I}_{Y_1}(X_{1/0})$ must be obtained as the *reciprocal* of a c-weighted average of the *reciprocals* of the $x_{i1/0}$, and in no other way, so long as C-type composite weights are used.

The second error is a little more subtle. We know from the original formulation that for $\mathbf{I}_{Y_1}(X_{1/0})$ to differ from $\mathbf{I}_{Y_0}(X_{1/0})$ it is required that there be some difference in the relative pattern of the Y_{i1} from that of the Y_{i0}; if all the relative weights in both sets are the same, i.e. all $y_{i1} = y_{i0}$, the 'o-weighted' and '1-weighted' indexes will be identical. If however the indexes are being constructed by an operation such as (7.7) and (7.8) above, and if there is some difference in some y_{i1} from some y_{i0} then this will be reflected in an appropriate change in the corresponding C_i from C_{i0} to C_{i1}, via the connection already indicated. However, changes in the y_i are evidently not the only cause of differences between c_{i1} and c_{i0}; these must also change from changes in the X_i, i.e. from the fact that not every x_{i1} equals its corresponding x_{i0}. Now these latter changes in the C_i are of course purely mechanical and do not reflect any change in the basic weighting system of the index; unless some y_{i1} does not equal some y_{i0}, $\mathbf{I}_{Y_0}(X_{1/0})$ remains identical to $\mathbf{I}_{Y_1}(X_{1/0})$. Yet superficial contemplation of the problem in terms of the formula (7.8), sometimes leads people to refer to *any* change in the C_i as representing a change in the weighting system of the index, even though it be a change entirely attributable to changes in the X's themselves:

they forget the composite character of the 'weights' to which they are referring and they forget that $1/\mathbf{W}_{C_1}(x_{0/1})$ means

$$\Sigma\, Y_{i1}X_{i1}\,/\,\Sigma\, Y_{i1}X_{i1}\frac{X_{i0}}{X_{i1}},$$

a formula in which the values of the X_{i1}'s, while of course affecting the top line, have no effect on the bottom line nor hence on the magnitude of the *difference* if any between the two indexes $\mathbf{I}_{Y_1}(X_{1/0})$ and $\mathbf{I}_{Y_0}(X_{1/0})$. It must therefore be appreciated that to refer to a set of magnitudes of the type of the C's as defined above as the 'weights' of an index represents a deceptive, if common, usage.

To some readers the foregoing warnings may have seemed unnecessary. Nevertheless, the first of the two errors referred to has been perpetrated by as many as 20 per cent of the candidates answering one question in an examination, while the second has not infrequently been implicit in published government explanations concerning the revision of an official index number. In cases where serious danger of confusion still exists it may be desirable to drop the 'C-notation' altogether and write out the description rather more fully, e.g.

$$\mathbf{I}_{Y_0}(X_{1/0}) = \mathbf{W}_{X_0Y_0}(x_{1/0}) \tag{7.9}$$

(7c) Comparability of Index Numbers

It is common to refer to index numbers such as $\mathbf{I}_{Y_0}(X_{1/0})$ as 'base-weighted' and those such as $\mathbf{I}_{Y_1}(X_{1/0})$ as 'current-weighted'. The use of this terminology can occasionally lead to confusion. Index numbers are more often than not given as time-series, e.g.,

year	index
0	100
1	$\mathbf{I}_{Y_0}(X_{1/0})$
2	$\mathbf{I}_{Y_0}(X_{2/0})$
3	$\mathbf{I}_{Y_0}(X_{3/0})$

might represent the successive annual values of a base-weighted index with weights of year 0. In this case there is no confusion. But if a 'current-weighted' index is to be given in a similar manner we have to decide whether the adjective 'current' means 'current in the year of publication' or whether it means 'contemporary' in the historical sense, i.e. meaning that the weights to be used in year 1 were $Y_{11}, Y_{21}, ..., Y_{i1}, ..., Y_{n1}$ and in year 2, $Y_{12}, Y_{22}, ..., Y_{i2}, ..., Y_{n2}$ and, etc. In the former case, for a time-series published in year 2, we would give,

year	index
0	100
1	$\mathbf{I}_{Y_2}(X_{1/0})$
2	$\mathbf{I}_{Y_2}(X_{2/0})$

then, when the series came to be revised for publication in the following year, we would have to revise the entire series and give,

year	index
0	100
1	$\mathbf{I}_{Y_3}(X_{1/0})$
2	$\mathbf{I}_{Y_3}(X_{2/0})$
3	$\mathbf{I}_{Y_3}(X_{3/0})$

That is strictly the correct procedure, laborious as it is. However, if we took the second of the interpretations of 'current', we should simply give a series such as,

year	index
0	100
1	$\mathbf{I}_{Y_1}(X_{1/0})$
2	$\mathbf{I}_{Y_2}(X_{2/0})$
3	$\mathbf{I}_{Y_3}(X_{3/0})$

and add to it year by year without any back revision. Now in such a series, a true index number comparison can only be made directly between each separate year and the base year: comparisons between pairs of years subsequent to the base year are not strictly valid. For example, if $\mathbf{I}_{Y_1}(X_{1/0}) = 102$ and $\mathbf{I}_{Y_2}(X_{2/0}) = 104$, one can correctly state that the index of prices rose by 2 per cent from year 0 to year 1 and by 4 per cent from year 0 to year 2, but one cannot then strictly go on to say that the index rose by 2 per cent from year 1 to year 2. For the comparison between $\mathbf{I}_{Y_1}$ and $\mathbf{I}_{Y_2}$ is not a true index number comparison as the two numbers do not have the same weighting system. The comparison does not therefore obey the criterion of achieving a complete separation of the effects of changes in weights and changes in values to be weighted: no doubt most of the 2 per cent difference between I_{Y_1} and I_{Y_2} given may have been due to changes in prices (the X's), but some nevertheless may have been due to a change in the pattern of the Y's, i.e. in some of the y_i's. In many cases the error will be small for reasons which are apparent from the analysis of the effect of changing the weights of an index number given in section 9 below, but the point should be watched nevertheless. The trap is commonly set, accidentally as it were, when a base-weighted index of a set of X's is used to 'deflate', i.e. is divided into, a series such as,

$$
\begin{array}{l}
100 \\
\Sigma\, C_{i1}/\Sigma\, C_{i0} \\
\Sigma\, C_{i2}/\Sigma\, C_{i0} \qquad \text{where } C_i = X_i Y_i \\
\Sigma\, C_{i3}/\Sigma\, C_{i0}
\end{array}
$$

in order to obtain a series of X-weighted index numbers of the Y's (see section 8 below). From what we know already this must produce a non-comparable 'current-weighted' series of the type just discussed. Some official index numbers of foreign trade have been known to be published in this manner.

8. Reversal of Roles of Weights and Values to be Weighted

Not infrequently, having commenced an analysis by weighting a set of values of a set of economic variables of a certain specific type, designated as a set of X's, with a set of weights representing in effect the values of a set of economic variables of another specific type, designated as a set of Y's, we later wish to construct an average of the Y-type variables (originally used as weights), now using the values of the original X-type variables as weights. For example, we start by weighting a set of prices of a certain set of commodities by the corresponding quantities of each of the commodities sold on the market over a certain period, thus obtaining what was called a *price index*; then we construct an index in which the same set of prices is used as the weights for the quantities, the variable to be averaged, thereby obtaining a *volume index*. This procedure is very simply indicated in our notation:

As $\qquad \mathbf{W}_{Y_0}(X_0) = \Sigma\, Y_{i0} X_{i0} / \Sigma\, Y_{i0},$

so $\qquad \mathbf{W}_{X_0}(Y_0) = \Sigma\, X_{i0} Y_{i0} / \Sigma\, X_{i0} \qquad\qquad (8.1)$

This reversal may then be applied to the index number operation:

As $\qquad \mathbf{I}_{Y_0}(X_{1/0}) = \dfrac{\mathbf{W}_{Y_0}(X_1)}{\mathbf{W}_{Y_0}(X_0)} = \dfrac{\Sigma\, Y_{i0} X_{i1}}{\Sigma\, Y_{i0} X_{i0}} = \mathbf{W}_{C_0}(x_{i1/0}),$

so $\qquad \mathbf{I}_{X_0}(Y_{1/0}) = \dfrac{\mathbf{W}_{X_0}(Y_1)}{\mathbf{W}_{X_0}(Y_0)} = \dfrac{\Sigma\, X_{i0} Y_{i1}}{\Sigma\, X_{i0} Y_{i0}} = \mathbf{W}_{C_0}(y_{i1/0}) \qquad (8.2)$

From the above follows an important property:

$$\mathbf{I}_{Y_0}(X_{1/0}) \cdot \mathbf{I}_{X_1}(Y_{1/0}) = \frac{\Sigma\, Y_{i0} X_{i1}}{\Sigma\, Y_{i0} X_{i0}} \cdot \frac{\Sigma\, X_{i1} Y_{i1}}{\Sigma\, X_{i1} Y_{i0}} = \frac{\Sigma\, C_{i1}}{\Sigma\, C_{i0}} \qquad (8.3)$$

The significance of (8.3) is that the ratio, $\Sigma\, C_{i1} / \Sigma\, C_{i0}$, which is not of course an index number (see text of chapter, p. 199), may, nevertheless, be of considerable significance in economic applications, since sums such as $\Sigma\, C_i\ (= \Sigma\, X_i Y_i)$ will often represent important economic aggregates. For instance if the X's are prices and the Y's are quantities (of commodities sold in some particular market), or vice versa, these aggregates represent the total money value of the sales or purchases of the whole set of the commodities over the period in question. $\Sigma\, C_{i1} / \Sigma\, C_{i0}$ thus represents the ratio of the aggregate value of sales in the market in situation '1' (e.g. some given time period) to the aggregate value of sales in situation '0' (e.g. some earlier time period). In some cases this ratio might be the ratio of the total money value of the National Expenditure in one period to its value in another, and so on. In the example worked in the chapter, X_i was the quantity of a particular type fuel or power used domestically, Y_i was the quantity of coal required to produce a unit of fuel or power of that type, and $C_i\ (= X_i Y_i)$ was therefore the total amount of coal used in producing that type of fuel or power. The ratio $\Sigma\, C_{i1} / \Sigma\, C_{i0}$ was the ratio of total coal used, directly or indirectly, for all types of domestic fuel and power in 1953, to the corresponding aggregate in 1938. We first constructed an index of domestic energy consumption $\mathbf{I}_{Y_0}(X_{1/0})$ and subsequently reversed rôles of weights and values to produce indexes of the change in average conversion efficiency, such as $\mathbf{I}_{X_0}(Y_{1/0})$.

It is important therefore to remember that in order to arrive back at the ratio of $\Sigma\,C_{i1}$ to $\Sigma\,C_{i0}$, we must multiply an Y-weighted index of X by an X-weighted index of Y and that,

$$\mathbf{I}_{Y_0}(X_{1/0}) \cdot \mathbf{I}_{X_0}(Y_{1/0}) \neq \Sigma\,C_{i1}/\Sigma\,C_{i0} \qquad (8.4)$$

9. Consequences of Changes in Weights

We have seen that unless some $y_{i1} \neq y_{i0}$,

$$\mathbf{W}_{Y_0}(X_0) = \mathbf{W}_{Y_1}(X_0) \quad \text{and} \quad \mathbf{I}_{Y_0}(X_{1/0}) = \mathbf{I}_{Y_1}(X_{1/0}).$$

But even if a large number of the y_{i1} differ from their corresponding y_{i0}, the two weighted averages will not necessarily differ. Some changes of weight will work in the direction of increasing the average and others of decreasing it, and the two types of effect may tend on balance to cancel out. The complete formal development of the difference between the two averages is as follows:

Write $(y_{i1} - y_{i0}) = \varDelta y_i$, then

$$\mathbf{W}_{Y_1}(X_0) - \mathbf{W}_{Y_0}(X_0) = \Sigma\,y_{i1}X_{i0} - \Sigma\,y_{i0}X_{i0} \qquad (9.1)$$
$$= \Sigma\,X_{i0}(y_{i1} - y_{i0})$$
$$= \Sigma\,X_{i0}\varDelta y_i \qquad (9.2)$$

Now $\Sigma\,y_{i0} = \Sigma\,y_{i1} = 1.$ Hence

$$\Sigma\,\varDelta y_i = 0$$
$$\therefore \qquad \Sigma X_{i0}\varDelta y_i = N.\,\mathrm{cov}_{X_0\varDelta y} \qquad (9.3)$$
$$\therefore \qquad \mathbf{W}_{Y_1}(X_0) - \mathbf{W}_{Y_0}(X_0) = N\,r_{X_0\varDelta y} \cdot \sigma_{X_0} \cdot \sigma_{\varDelta y} \qquad (9.4)$$
$$= N\,\beta_{\varDelta y/X_0} \cdot \sigma^2_{X_0} \qquad (9.5)$$

In other words the difference depends on the degree of statistical association between the magnitudes of the values to be weighted and those of the *changes in the weights* to be applied to them. Thus there will, e.g., be a large positive difference between a 'revised' average and its unrevised predecessors if the largest differences between the revised and unrevised weights tend for any reason systematically to be associated with the largest of the X's to be weighted. There will be little or no difference between the two averages if:

(i) The correlation coefficient (or regression coefficient) of the association between the magnitudes of the changes in weights and variables to be weighted is zero or small.

(ii) The changes in weights are all virtually the same $(\sigma_{\Delta y}=0)$.†

(iii) The magnitudes to be weighted are all virtually the same $(\sigma_{x_0}=0)$, in which case of course there would have been little difference between weighted and unweighted averages in the first place, (see above, p. 206).

The difference between two *index numbers* with common $x_{i1/0}$ but genuinely different weights, i.e. different y_i, involves a rather more complicated mathematical development, but the results are of considerable economic interest. For convenience we will express the magnitude which we are seeking to analyse in terms of the ratio ϕ, where

$$\phi \equiv \frac{\mathbf{I}_{Y_1}(X_{1/0}) - \mathbf{I}_{Y_0}(X_{1/0})}{\mathbf{I}_{Y_0}(X_{1/0})} \tag{9.6}$$

ϕ is thus the 'proportionate' gap between the two index numbers, the difference between them expressed as a ratio of one of them. This expresses our intuitive believe that *ceteris paribus* the absolute magnitude of the gap will increase with the absolute level of the indexes themselves: thus if conditions were in general such as to create a certain absolute difference, q, between a base-weighted and a current-weighted cost-of-living index, 1938 to 1960, we would expect q to be twice as large if prices in general (as measured, say, by the 1938-weighted index) had quadrupled between the two years as it would have been if they had only doubled. We then develop an analytical formula for ϕ as follows:

Notice $\quad X_{i1}Y_{i1}=X_{i0}Y_{i0}x_{i1/0}y_{i1/0}$

Therefore $\quad \mathbf{I}_{Y_1}(X_{1/0})=\dfrac{\Sigma X_{i0}Y_{i0}x_{i1/0}y_{i1/0}}{\Sigma X_{i0}Y_{i0}y_{i1/0}}$

But $\quad \Sigma X_{i0}Y_{i0}y_{i1/0}=\mathbf{W}_{C_0}(y_{i1/0}) \cdot \Sigma C_{i0}=\mathbf{I}_{X_0}(Y_{1/0}) \cdot \Sigma C_{i0}$
$$\text{(where } C_{i0}=X_{i0}Y_{i0})$$

Hence $\quad \mathbf{I}_{Y_1}(X_{1/0})=\dfrac{1}{\mathbf{I}_{X_0}(Y_{1/0})} \cdot \dfrac{\Sigma C_{i0}x_{i1/0}y_{i1/0}}{\Sigma C_{i0}} \tag{9.7}$

Combine (9.7) with (9.6) and we get

$$\phi=\frac{1}{\mathbf{I}_{Y_0}(X_{1/0})}\left\{\frac{1}{\mathbf{I}_{X_0}(Y_{1/0})} \cdot \frac{\Sigma C_{i0}x_{i1/0}y_{i1/0}}{\Sigma C_{i0}}-\mathbf{I}_{Y_0}(X_{1/0})\right\}$$

† The dispersion of a set of identical values must be zero, since all 'deviations' from the 'mean' are then zero.

$$=\frac{1}{\mathbf{I}_{Y_0}(X_{1/0})} \cdot \frac{1}{\mathbf{I}_{X_0}(Y_{1/0})} \left\{ \frac{\Sigma C_{i0} y_{i1/0} x_{i1/0}}{\Sigma C_{i0}} - \mathbf{I}_{Y_0}(X_{1/0}) \cdot \mathbf{I}_{X_0}(Y_{1/0}) \right\} \quad (9.8)$$

It can be shown (see fn. (†)) that the contents of the bracket are equivalent to the *C-weighted co-variance* of $x_{i1/0}$ and $y_{i1/0}$. This means that

$$\phi = \mathbf{W}_{C_0}(r_{x_{1/0}y_{1/0}}) \cdot \frac{\mathbf{W}_{C_0}(\sigma_{x1/0})}{\mathbf{I}_{Y_0}(X_{1/0})} \cdot \frac{\mathbf{W}_{C_0}(\sigma_{y_{1/0}})}{\mathbf{I}_{X_0}(Y_{1/0})} \quad (9.9)$$

Equation (9.9) although appearing complicated, is of exceptional interest. It states that the proportionate gap between two index numbers of the same set of $x_{i1/0}$ but with different weights is equal to the weighted correlation coefficient from a regression analysis of the $y_{i1/0}$ with the $x_{i1/0}$, multiplied by what are known as (weighted) *relative standard deviations* of $x_{i1/0}$ and $y_{i1/}$ respectively. This correlation coefficient measures the extent to which the economic variables showing above-average changes in their values from set 'o' to set '1' also tend to require consistently above-average revisions in the weights. The relative standard deviations are measures of *relative dispersion*, that is measures of dispersion which are adjusted to eliminate the effect—on the ordinary or 'absolute' standard deviation—of the general numerical scale of the data, and are thus more easily comparable between examples.‡

† Any co-variance such as the simple cov_{XY} can be shown to be equal to $\frac{\Sigma XY}{N} - \overline{X}\overline{Y}$, for

$$\text{cov}_{XY} = \frac{1}{N} \Sigma(X - \overline{X})(Y - \overline{Y}) = \frac{\Sigma XY}{N} - \overline{X}\frac{\Sigma Y}{N} - \overline{Y}\frac{\Sigma X}{N} + \overline{X} \cdot \overline{Y}$$

$$= \frac{\Sigma XY}{N} - \overline{X} \cdot \overline{Y} - \overline{Y} \cdot \overline{X} + \overline{X} \cdot \overline{Y} = \frac{\Sigma XY}{N} - \overline{X} \cdot \overline{Y}$$

Q. E. D.

This principle applies, by analogy, to the weighted case also.

‡ The relative standard deviation may most simply be explained by reference to properties of the simple unweighted variety. The standard deviation, it will be remembered, measures the dispersive tendency of a set of data by aggregating the squares of the deviations of each item of the data from their own mean or average value: the greater in general such deviations, either positive or negative, the more evidently must the data be scattered about their own mean and the greater the sum of the squares of the deviations. However, this ordinary standard deviation (square root of the sum of the squared deviations divided by the number of items) is not only affected by what might be regarded as the underlying dispersive tendency of the data but also by their general scale; *ceteris paribus* (including the underlying dispersive tendency) a set of data whose

Thus equation (9.9) describes the difference between two index numbers in terms which are absolutely general, clearly interpretable and independent of the size of either of the index numbers themselves. Its particular interest is due to the fact that substantial correlation between changes in weights and changes in values to be weighted will, in fact, often occur in typical examples from the normal working of elementary economic laws. This is explored further in the following section.

ϕ evidently can also be expressed in terms of the weighted *regression coefficient* of the y_i on the x_i; the higher the coefficient, *ceteris paribus*, the higher ϕ. Thus with a little manipulation (remembering that the regression coefficient in general, $\beta_{Y/X}$, is given by $\mathrm{cov}_{YX}/\mathrm{var}_X$) we can write the formula for ϕ as

$$\phi = \left\{ \frac{\mathbf{W}_{C_0}(\mathrm{var}_{x_{1/0}})}{\{\mathbf{I}_{Y_0}(X_{1/0})\}^2} \right\} \times \left\{ \mathbf{W}_{C_0}(\beta_{y/x}) \right\} \times \left\{ \frac{\mathbf{I}_{Y_0}(X_{1/0})}{\mathbf{I}_{X_0}(Y_{1/0})} \right\} \qquad (9.10)$$

average magnitude was, say, ten times as great as that of another set would be expected to show ten times the standard deviation. Suppose we wished to measure the dispersion of the daily milk consumption of the households in a street, e.g. as in the following simplified example:

(1) Household No.	(2) Consumption, (X), Pints	(3) $X - \bar{X}$	(4) $(X - \bar{X})^2$
1.	0	-2	4·00
2.	$\frac{1}{2}$	$-1\frac{1}{2}$	$2\frac{1}{4}$
3.	1	-1	1
4.	$3\frac{1}{2}$	$1\frac{1}{2}$	$2\frac{1}{4}$
5.	5	3	9
	10		$18\frac{1}{2}$

$$\bar{X} = 2 \qquad\qquad \sigma = \sqrt{\frac{18\frac{1}{2}}{5}} = 1\cdot9$$

We would then say that the dispersion of the milk consumption (i.e. its tendency to vary from family to family) could be measured by a standard deviation of 1·9 pints. However, suppose now that the value of each X in the above table was halved, e.g. because all families reduced their consumption by exactly that amount or perhaps because the measurement was now to be made in quarts instead of pints. The reader can verify for himself that the numerical value of the standard deviation would then be halved, even though nothing which we could intuitively recognise as a change in the degree of non-homogeneity of the families' milk-consumption habits had occurred whatsoever. The *relative* standard deviation, however, i.e. the standard deviation divided by the data's own mean, $\bar{X}$, would be quite unaffected by a change of the type described, for if all the individual X's had doubled, so would have $\bar{X}$. The relative standard deviation is therefore a measure of dispersion which facilitates comparisons between examples.

This is not quite so clear to interpret as (9.9), but may be rationalised as follows. The first bracket is the square of the relative standard deviation, and may be termed the *relative variance*, of x_{i0} and is in effect an alternative measure of relative dispersion which it happens to be convenient to employ here (it bears the same relationship to the relative standard deviation as the absolute variance bears to the absolute standard deviation, see above). We may imagine the sequence of events as commencing with an autonomous set of variations in X's, as expressed in the observed relative variance of $x_{i1/0}$. For one reason or another the Y_i are economically linked to the X_i so that the changes in the X_i set off a rather closely associated set of changes in the Y_i, generating a particular set of $y_{i1/0}$. This produces a substantial co-variance between the $x_{i1/0}$ and the $y_{i1/0}$ and thus causes the occurrence of a large value of ϕ. The sensitivity of the relationship between y_i and x_i is expressed in the regression coefficient, $\beta_{y/x}$, i.e. in the slope of the regression line between the two. The greater this sensitivity, the greater the magnitude of the $y_{i1/0}$ typically associated with a given $x_{i1/0}$, the greater the typical magnitude of the cross-products of the deviations of $x_{i1/0}$ and $y_{i1/0}$ from the respective means, hence the greater the co-variance and the greater ϕ. Finally, it is a feature of the basic mathematical relationship involved that in this arrangement ϕ will also be greater, *ceteris paribus*, the greater the average size of the $x_{i1/0}$ relatively to that of the $y_{i1/0}$, i.e. the greater $\mathbf{I}_{Y_0}(X_{1/0})/\mathbf{I}_{X_0}(Y_{1/0})$. An economic rationalisation of this last feature of the formula is given in the section immediately following.

10. Economic Applications of Section 9

As has already been noted, commonly in economic analysis, X_i and Y_i represent the prices and quantities respectively (or vice versa) of a collection of commodities produced and/or sold, while the suffixes 'o' and '1' represent alternative times or places (years or countries). If the X's represent prices and the Y's quantities, then we have,†

† This section to some extent overlaps with the following chapter, but is placed here for convenience in order to demonstrate the uses of the formulae. In Chapter 9 we use the more familiar specific notation, with P's standing for prices, and Q's for quantities, in place of the X's and Y's above, respectively.

1. $\mathbf{I}_{Y_0}(X_{1/0})$—*Laspeyres*' price index,
2. $\mathbf{I}_{Y_1}(X_{1/0})$—*Paasche's* price index,
3. $\mathbf{I}_{X_0}(Y_{1/0})$—Volume index on the Laspeyres principle,
4. $\mathbf{I}_{X_1}(Y_{1/0})$—Volume index on the Paasche principle.

ϕ can thus represent the difference between the results obtained with Paasche and Laspeyres principles and may relate either to the volume indexes or the price indexes. (However, notice that if the volume indexes are to be represented as 3 and 4, it is necessary in equations (9.9) and (9.10) to substitute y_i for x_i and $\overline{Y}$ for $\overline{X}$ and *vice versa*, etc., throughout.) Considerable gaps between Paasche and Laspeyres price and volume index numbers, as reflected in large values of ϕ, will result from association between changes in prices and changes in the quantities of the commodities sold. Such association can come either from the forces of Demand, or of Supply, or both. The commodities whose prices rise most will experience the smallest increases or the largest decreases in sales in accordance with the normal working of the laws of demand. On the supply side, commodities whose sales increase most will generally experience reductions in supply price, if economic conditions of 'decreasing supply price' prevail, i.e. supply curves are generally falling from left to right, and the opposite association will be displayed if supply curves are predominantly rising. The total result of the forces of demand and the various types of the forces of supply acting on the price and quantity changes of the commodities produced and sold in a particular market for which the two index numbers $\mathbf{I}_{Y_0}(X_{1/0})$ and $\mathbf{I}_{Y_1}(X_{1/0})$ have been computed will be reflected in a complicated way in the magnitude of the regression coefficient β_{yx} in equation (9.10). It is however possible to give illustrations of the formal working out of these theoretical effects provided we are prepared to accept some rather drastic simplifying assumptions.

Suppose we select an imaginary commodity, designated 'commodity c' forming one of our whole set $1 \ldots c \ldots i \ldots n$, which happens to possess the characteristic that it has experienced both price and quantity changes as between 'o' and '1' such that its $y_{c1/0}$ is of exactly the magnitude which would be predicted by the measured regression equation of the y_i upon x_i; i.e. if a scatter diagram of the y's and x's were constructed in the normal manner the plotting point for commodity c would fall exactly on the computed (weighted) regression line for that diagram. From the elementary properties of regression line and regression coefficient, we know that this definition of c implies:

$$\mathbf{W}_{C_0}(\beta_{y/x}) = \frac{y_{c1/0} - \mathbf{I}_{X_0}(Y_{1/0})}{x_{c1/0} - \mathbf{I}_{Y_0}(X_{1/0})} \tag{10.1}$$

If (10.1) is substituted into equation (9.10), we get,

$$\phi = \left\{ \frac{y_{c1/0} - \mathbf{I}_{X_0}(Y_{1/0})}{\mathbf{I}_{X_0}(Y_{1/0})} \right\} \left\{ \frac{\mathbf{I}_{Y_0}(X_{1/0})}{x_{c1/0} - \mathbf{I}_{Y_0}(X_{1/0})} \right\} \left\{ \frac{\mathbf{W}_{C_0}(\text{VAR}_{x1/0})}{\{\mathbf{I}_{Y_0}(X_{1/0})\}^2} \right\} \tag{10.2}$$

Let us write this in abbreviated form,

$$\phi = \epsilon_{y/x} \cdot \text{RV}_{x_{1/0}} \tag{10 3}$$

with ϵ standing for the contents of the first two brackets and RV for Relative Variance. The nature of $(\text{RV})_{x_{1/0}}$ has already been discussed in the preceding section, but what of ϵ? In fact,

$$\epsilon = \left(\frac{y_{c1/0}}{\mathbf{I}_{X_0}(Y_{1/0})} - 1 \right) \div \left(\frac{x_{c1/0}}{\mathbf{I}_{Y_0}(X_{1/0})} - 1 \right) \tag{10.4}$$

The second bracket of this, however, measures the proportionate change in the *relative price* of the commodity c, i.e. its price-change relative to that of commodities in general as estimated by the Laspeyres index, $\mathbf{I}_{Y_0}(X_{1/0})$. Similarly, the first bracket can be taken as a measure of the *relative* change in the quantity sold of c; it measures the extent to which sales of the commodity have increased or decreased their quantitative share of the market. (If the set $1 \ldots c \ldots i \ldots n$ included all the goods and services involved in the National Expenditure, then this bracket would measure the extent to which consumption of the commodity was increasing or decreasing relatively to real national expenditure.) *Hence ϵ expresses the ratio of the proportionate change in the relative quantity of c to the associated proportionate change in its relative price.* In other words ϵ is the 'best estimate'—as obtained in simple regression analysis—

Q

of the 'elasticity'† of the relationship between relative price and relative quantity, as exhibited by the set of commodities in question.

Thus we can now state the conditions for ϕ in an even more interesting form: given the original (assumed to be autonomous) variance in the prices, the greater the elasticity of the relationship between these 'relative' price changes and the (relative) quantity changes the greater will be ϕ, and vice versa. We now make our first simplifying assumption. Suppose ϕ measures the difference between a Paasche and a Laspeyres index of *retail prices*, then we will assume that forces from the side of demand (i.e. the effects of consumers adjusting their buying habits to changes in relative supply prices) are the only ones affecting the data; forces of supply, etc. being assumed independent (more precisely, all goods are sold under conditions of constant supply-price, i.e. all supply curves are horizontal straight lines, whose positions change, but whose slopes do not). On this assumption it can easily be seen that ϵ represents for commodity c the well-known concept of the *elasticity of substitution* as between c and commodities in general.‡ This elasticity of substitution will generally be negative in sign, hence on these assumptions ϕ will be negative and Paasche's index must work out lower than Laspeyres'. The foregoing assumes that changes in supply-prices are the only factors affecting demand, and that other factors, such as tastes and real income, are constant. Alternatively we assume here that if tastes or real incomes change, they do so in such a way as to leave the index numbers unaffected, which means that, e.g., the income effects are themselves uncorrelated with the price changes: if the income effects were for some reason, or by chance correlated, commoditywise, with the price changes, the effect would be similar to that of ϵ, but of course might work in the opposite direction. For extensive application, see Chapter 9 (pages 248 *et seq.*).

---

† To be precise we should note that this is an 'arc-elasticity' and not a true elasticity as would be measured by the logarithmic regression analysis suggested at the end of Chapter 7. The two measures will only differ significantly if the changes in price and quantity are rather large.

‡ The elasticity of substitution between two commodities is defined as the ratio of the proportionate change in the ratio of their quantities bought to that of the ratio of their prices.

Now, of course, ϕ only relates to the case of the commodity c or other commodities whose results happen to fall exactly on the regression line. But not all commodities will experience from the consumer the same elasticity of substitution; some have many close substitutes, others have not. Hence the results for the whole set of commodities will be scattered around the regression line and ϵ must be regarded as in some sense an estimate of the 'representative' elasticity only. However, it is a fair generalisation that, other things being ignored, the greater the magnitude of the representative elasticity of substitution between commodities, the greater will be ϕ. This will be found to link with the discussion of index number theory in terms of indifference curves in Chapter 9.

The alternative possible simplification is to assume that the forces of supply are the only ones affecting the data and that it is the forces of demand which do not exist. ϕ would then represent the best estimate from regression analysis of the representative elasticity of supply. This may be positive or negative, as we know (but cf. below), depending on the conditions of production and the nature of competition in the market. If conditions of increasing supply price generally prevail, ϵ will be of positive sign and hence the Paasche index greater than Laspeyres' (ϕ positive) and conversely in conditions of generally decreasing supply price. This application is more usefully thought of in relation to a volume index: suppose we write:

$$\phi' = \frac{\mathbf{I}_{X_1}(Y_{1/0}) - \mathbf{I}_{X_0}(Y_{1/0})}{\mathbf{I}_{X_0}(Y_{1/0})}$$

ϕ' thus measuring the difference between the Paasche-type index of volume and Laspeyres-type volume index in the same set of data of prices and quantities as was conceived to be used to compute ϕ. Then it is easy to appreciate that the appropriate formula for ϕ' can be obtained by reversing all the suffixes in the basic equations,

$$\phi' = \mathrm{RV}_{y_{1/0}} \cdot \mathbf{W}_{C_0}(\beta_{x/y}) \cdot \frac{\mathbf{I}_{X_0}(Y_{1/0})}{\mathbf{I}_{Y_0}(X_{1/0})} \cdot$$

Following the development of ϵ we now define ϵ':

$$\epsilon' = \mathbf{W}_{C_0}(\beta_{x/y}) \cdot \frac{\mathbf{I}_{X_0}(Y_{1/0})}{\mathbf{I}_{Y_0}(X_{1/0})}$$

$$\phi' = \epsilon' \cdot \mathrm{RV}_{y_{1/0}}.$$

Here the price changes are assumed to be causally dependent on the quantity changes, rather than the other way about, and the measure ϕ' is reciprocal to the elasticity-of-supply concept.

ϵ' indicates the proportionate change in relative price which is expected to follow from a given proportionate change in relative quantity sold. This formulation makes economic sense if we believe, for example, that market prices are largely cost-determined (i.e. the gross profit margin as a percentage of average prime costs is largely constant) and further that commodities are in general produced under conditions of long term decreasing cost, either on account of increasing returns to scale in the orthodox textbook sense or for some other reason such as suggested below. ϵ' would then represent the typical elasticity of the long term cost curve. This application is particularly relevant to the case of index numbers of industrial production, which are of course index numbers of volume.

Any reader who has absorbed the later part of Chapter 7 wherein were described the many traps in simple regression analysis will have no difficulty in appreciating the dangers of attempting to apply the foregoing ideas to an actual case. Actual data will be affected by both supply forces and by demand forces and they will also be disturbed by other factors such as autonomous changes in taste or changes in the pattern of demand caused by changes in real income. All these factors may cause scatter and, as already indicated, they may well also cause 'bias' of just the sorts of types described in the second example of Chapter 7. Only if there are special reasons for believing that little such bias exists in a particular case can the apparent value of ϵ or ϵ'† be taken as a genuine best estimate of the typical elasticities of substitution or of cost curves.

---

† ϕ and ϕ' can be measured by simple computation, so also the relative variances, hence the 'apparent' value of ϵ is $\phi/\mathrm{RV}_{x_{1/0}}$ and of ϵ', $\phi'/\mathrm{RV}_{y_{1/0}}$.

CHAPTER NINE

THE MEASUREMENT OF CHANGES IN FAMILY REAL INCOME

In the preceding chapter and its appendix we examined the basic algebraical properties of economic index numbers and we saw that they consist in essence of comparisons between two weighted aggregates using the same system of weights. The example we employed was a technical one not involving directly any consideration of economic welfare. In this chapter we shall consider how index numbers may be employed to 'measure', or indicate, changes in welfare and/or changes in the value of money in terms of welfare. We shall find eventually that economic welfare, 'utility', or 'satisfaction', is not a thing which is capable of direct measurement by index numbers as such, but rather that index numbers measure something—*real income*—with which we believe welfare to be closely connected: we shall explain how we understand the distinction between real income and welfare more fully below. The fundamental reason why we shall be unable to measure changes in welfare directly is that we shall accept the argument that utilities or 'states of satisfaction' are mental conditions which although capable of *ordinal* comparison cannot be numbered *cardinally*. Or at least we accept the 'ordinalist' argument as far as concerns the purposes of this book. As the reader will probably know, the matter is the subject of controversy, but what is quite clear is that cardinal measurements of utility are not possible without techniques which go well beyond our present terms of reference, i.e. cardinal measurements of utility certainly cannot be made with index numbers alone. To put the point in another way, index number theory contains quite enough 'problems' of its own, and we shall be happy enough if we can carry the student a little way towards a better understanding of these, without attempting

227

to solve at one time all the multifarious problems of utility theory as a whole.

Having said all the foregoing, we admit an exception. It is appreciated that the *language* of the so-called 'cardinalist' school of utility theory—the language of Utility, Marginal Utility, Total Satisfaction and the like—is often found initially both more evocative and more intelligible than the relatively astringent language of the ordinalist school (the language of Indifference Curves, Preferred Positions, Price-Possibility Lines, etc.) and for this reason we shall make some use of the cardinalist language in the introductory section which immediately follows; but we shall go on to develop the full treatment in terms of indifference curves over the rest of the chapter. We shall first simply pick up the example of domestic consumption of fuel and power, employed in the previous chapter, and see how we might construct an index number to measure the 'total change in consumer utility' associated with the changes in consumption which occurred; then, in the later sections (with the aid of the indifference curve diagram) we shall investigate the problems of measuring changes in consumer real income as a whole, i.e. taking account, in principle, of the whole range of a consumer's expenditure, in contrast to his expenditure on a single group of commodities only.

Throughout, we shall mean by a consumer, a 'family',† since the family is the ultimate unsplittable particle in economic society: individual members of families cannot be considered as free and independent agents in their consumption behaviour, any more than can babes in arms.

Elementary Index Numbers of Price and of Volume

If the total value of commodities purchased increases by 9 per cent between year 0 and year 1, how much is due merely to monetary inflation, i.e. to a rise in the general level of prices, and how much to a genuine 'net' increase in the quantities of goods which these purchases represent? We can use exactly the same technique to separate the two factors as was used in the Chapter 8 example to separate the effect of increased household consump-

† More precisely a family-household.

tion of energy from that of improvements in the conversion efficiency of the supply industries. The total money value of the commodities purchased in year o corresponds to the total of direct and indirect household coal consumption in year o, and similarly for year 1. The quantities of the commodities purchased, measured in their conventional units, in the present example, correspond exactly to the X's of the previous example, i.e. to the quantities purchased of the various forms of domestic energy measured in kWh, therms, etc. The *market prices* at which the commodities of the present example are presumed to have been purchased correspond to the Y's of the previous example, i.e. to the average coal-conversion efficiency ratios. When index numbers are used in this way we will use a special notation (which is indeed almost universal):

Q_{i0} = quantity purchased of the ith commodity, in some given year, year o, measured in units conventional to that commodity.

P_{i0} = money price at which the ith commodity was purchased in year o, expressed in units of currency per conventional unit of the commodity.

Also, Q_{i1}, Q_{i2}, etc. and P_{i1}, P_{i2}, etc.

Using this notation our problem appears as that of partitioning the total change in expenditure as expressed in the ratio

$$\Sigma P_{i1} Q_{i1} / \Sigma P_{i0} Q_{i0}$$

(which corresponds to $\Sigma C_{i1} / \Sigma C_{i0}$, i.e. $\Sigma Y_{i1} X_{i1} / \Sigma Y_{i0} X_{i0}$, in the previous example) into two parts: the part attributable to changes in the Q's and the part attributable to changes in the P's. The obvious index to use for the former measure is the one which corresponds to $\mathbf{I}_{Y_0}(X_{1/0})$ in the previous example, i.e.

$$\mathbf{I}_{P_0}(Q_{1/0}) = \frac{\Sigma P_{i0} Q_{i1}}{\Sigma P_{i0} Q_{i0}}$$

This measures what would have happened to consumer expenditure on the commodities in question if the quantities bought had changed as they in fact did, but the prices had remained fixed at the level and pattern of year o. This is known as a 'base-weighted volume index'. Similarly we can derive a 'current-weighted volume index',

$$\mathbf{I}_{P_1}(Q_{1/0}) = \frac{\Sigma\, P_{i1}Q_{i1}}{\Sigma\, P_{i1}Q_{i0}}$$

These formulae attempt to remove any inflationary element from the change in expenditure and thus represent rough and ready measures of the change in welfare thought to be associated with the observed changes in purchases (assuming for the sake of argument that purchases are identical with consumption). We can therefore assess the extent of the inflationary element itself in the same way as we measured the change in average conversion efficiency; we then arrive at a *price index*, or inverse index of the change in the value of money: the base-weighted version,

$$\mathbf{I}_{Q_0}(P_{1/0}) = \frac{\Sigma\, Q_{i0}P_{i1}}{\Sigma\, Q_{i0}P_{i0}}$$

and the current-weighted version,

$$\mathbf{I}_{Q_1}(P_{1/0}) = \frac{\Sigma\, Q_{i1}P_{i1}}{\Sigma\, Q_{i1}P_{i0}}$$

In both these indexes we are in effect comparing weighted averages of the prices, using quantities as weights. The base-weighted index is often known as *Laspeyres' index*, after its inventor—a nineteenth-century German professor—and the second as *Paasche's index*. It is not always easy to remember which index is which and the best suggestion which the author can offer is to note that Paasche's index requires more work for its computation than Laspeyres'† and hence users of Laspeyres' index might be said to be *Lasy*.

We may look more closely into the economic significance of index numbers of price and of quantity if we follow the analogy with our example taken from the data of domestic energy consumption a little further. Suppose now we wished to assess, in some rough way, the change in aggregate consumer welfare (or 'utility' or 'satisfaction' or what have you) attributable to the complex of changes in the consumption of solid fuel, of electricity and of gas

† For reasons which are apparent in section 7c of the Appendix to Chapter 8 above.

recorded as occurring between 1938 and 1953 as already set out in Table 14 of Chapter 8. (Evidently, this is by no means the same thing as the change in total consumption in units of coal equivalence.) We appear to need to compare a weighted average of the utilities obtained from the tons, kWh and therms consumed in year 0 with a similar weighted average for year 1. We obviously cannot continue to use conversion-efficiency ratios as weights, since these bear no direct relation to consumer utility whatsoever. The consumer does not give a damn how much coal was required to manufacture the commodities he is buying, what interests him here, one would imagine, is the amount of *energy* obtainable from each unit, i.e. how much heat, light or power is obtained. One solution therefore might be to weight the quantities in accordance with the *calorific value* of each of the different types of energy unit, allowing perhaps for differences in the thermal efficiencies of the appliances which are typically used to burn the various forms of energy in the home.† This procedure would be a possible one, and indeed is one which has been followed by some analysts of the national fuel problem; 'utility' would then be treated as identical with the objective physical measure, 'calories', and we should be home. The obvious objection which the reader will see at once is that a solution of this type is only applicable over a relatively narrow range of economic commodities where the need which the commodities satisfy happens to be homogeneous, easily identifiable and physically measurable. Even in the present case, calories are not the only things a consumer wants from a source of energy. He (or more appropriately, she) is also very much interested in the kinds of the appliances required for domestic conversion, their convenience of operation, their appearance and the qualitative nature of the heat or light they transmit. Coal is dirty and heavy, but on the other hand electric fires give out a rather unattractive and dry form of heat (or so some people say) and so on. These other factors in the consumer calculation are intangibles, they cannot be measured directly by any simple physical criterion and they depend on each consumer's personal pattern of values: some people have a

---

† Thus a badly designed open grate may waste 80 per cent of the heat by sending it up the chimney, which is not the case with an electric fire.

'thing' about the desirability of an open grate, others particularly dislike coal dust and ash about their houses. And in truth, of course, all economic commodities contain a major element of intangible utility and in most (in contrast with the present example) this element is predominant. Except *in extremis*, we do not measure the value of a diet by the calories it provides alone, or that of a wine by its alcoholic content, and when we come to complicated consumer durable goods such as television sets and motor cars the problem is seen in its birthday suit. This, then, is the crux of the puzzle which is called Welfare Economics, and it is the crux of the 'problem' which faces the would-be constructor of index numbers of welfare. Not only is the utility embodied in typical economic commodities incapable of simple physical measurement, but even if it were, there would remain the impossibility of adding the different unitary measures together: the problem would disappear only if there existed only one economic commodity.

Economic theory therefore suggests an indirect method of assessing relative utilities. It is suggested that the *relative price* that the consumer is observed to be prepared to pay for each unit of each commodity reveals his relative valuation of the utility he obtains from such unit. If the pattern of relative utilities he was obtaining were at variance with the pattern of relative prices he was paying, he would if he had any sense, so the argument runs, adjust his pattern of purchases to bring the two into line by the operation of the law of diminishing marginal utility. (It has to be assumed, of course, that the prices used in the calculation relate to a market where supply and demand are in equilibrium, i.e. where there is no rationing or other permanent manifestation of excess demand, which was not in fact the case in the example.) Therefore it is argued, relative prices may validly be used as weights in the comparison we are seeking to make and we are thus provided with the theoretical justification for the use of index numbers such as $I_{P_0}(Q_{1/0})$ or $I_{P_1}(Q_{1/0})$, the base-weighted and current-weighted index numbers of volume respectively already described. The use of $I_{Q_0}(P_{1/0})$ or $I_{Q_1}(P_{1/0})$, i.e. comparisons of weighted averages of the prices using the quantities as weights then follows by simple converse. The reciprocals of the latter indexes then represent indexes of the value of money, in other words of a unit of money's command over utility.

However, we are still left with the difficulty that,

$$\frac{\Sigma P_{i1}Q_{i1}}{\Sigma P_{i0}Q_{i0}} = I_{P_0}(Q_{1/0}) \cdot I_{Q_1}(P_{1/0}) = I_{P_1}(Q_{1/0}) \cdot I_{Q_0}(P_{1/0})$$

and the ambiguity arising from the possibility of differences between the results from base-weighting and current-weighting raises very considerable theoretical problems indeed. The two types of volume index number are liable to give different results if the relative pattern of prices is different in year 1 from what it was in year 0 and, evidently, if the two types of volume index differ so must the two types of price index. If relative prices have changed, so must the relative pattern of consumer valuations of the commodities. (If relative prices have not changed, there is no 'problem' anyway.) For example, in the case of electricity whose consumption has risen and whose relative price has fallen, the relative marginal utility of a kWh must be presumed to have fallen. Thus we are faced with two alternative patterns of presumed marginal utilities which might be used to determine the weights of our index—two alternative patterns which may well yield different results, as follows:

TABLE 18. *Construction of Base- and Current-Weighted Volume Index Numbers of Household Fuel Consumption* 1938–1953

	ratios		£ millions			
	$q_{1/0}$	$q_{0/1}$	C_0	C_1	$C_0 \cdot q_{1/0}$	$C_1 \cdot q_{0/1}$
(1) Coal, Direct Sales	·72	1·39	111	189	80	263
(2) Electricity - -	2·95	·34	34	110	100	37
(3) Gas - - -	1·47	·68	35	106	52	72
			180	405	232	372

$$I_{P_0}(Q_{1/0}) = \tfrac{232}{180} = 1.29$$
$$I_{P_1}(Q_{1/0}) = \tfrac{405}{371} = 1.09$$

Notes.
(a) $q_{1/0}$ and $q_{0/1}$ are identical with $x_{1/0}$ and $x_{0/1}$ respectively, from Tables 16 and 17 in Chapter 8 (pp. 195 and 201).
(b) $C_0 = P_0 Q_0$, the quantity purchased in 1938 multiplied by the price per unit in 1938, i.e. total consumer expenditure on the item in 1938; C_1 is total consumer expenditure in 1953.

The reader will have little difficulty in appreciating that the considerable difference both in magnitude and direction between the base- and the current-weighted results above arises precisely because consumption rose most for the product (electricity) whose price rose least, and that furthermore this development is precisely what elementary economic theory would predict. (The price-change ratios can be obtained by computing C_1/C_0 and dividing by $q_{1/0}$.) In the appendix to Chapter 8 (section 9) it was shown that the magnitude of the difference between results obtained with Paasche-type, as against Laspeyres-type index numbers of volume (which is which in the above?) computed from the same set of data depends on:

(i) The extent to which the pattern of relative prices did in fact change during the period over which the comparison is made, that is on the dispersion of the absolute price changes about their own mean as measured by their variance.

(ii) The extent to which such changes in relative prices were *correlated*, commoditywise, with changes in the quantities purchased.

These conditions apply also to the case of price index numbers except that in this case, in condition (i) the words 'relative quantities' and 'quantity changes' are substituted for 'relative prices' and 'price changes' respectively. Correlations such as (ii), it was shown in the appendix (section 10), may arise either because consumers tend to buy relatively more of the commodities whose prices have relatively fallen, and vice versa—the demand-side effect—or because goods whose production has most expanded are most likely to achieve above-average reductions in productive efficiency—the supply-side effect—or both. Certainly both effects were probably present in the case of electricity in our example. The appendix further went on to show that the gap (between the results from the two types of index number) will be greater, *ceteris paribus*, the greater the typical magnitude of the elasticity of demand (or more strictly elasticity of substitution) for the commodities concerned, or the greater the sensitivity of the supply-side effect as measured in elasticity terms, i.e. the greater the proportionate reduction in

relative supply price typically associated with a given proportionate increment in relative output. Thus the difference we are discussing is itself the product of the normal working of economic
laws and represents a considerably more serious theoretical problem than a mere formal ambiguity. In fact, as we shall see, neither
the Paasche nor the Laspeyres indexes are normally likely to be
'right' against the criteria of the pure theory of welfare economics,
even accepting for the moment that some right index could ever be
said to exist.

First Steps in the Measurement of Real Income†

The theory which we shall now expound is held by some to be
highly speculative, or 'metaphysical', or tautological, according to
individual taste in epithets expressing scepticism; and there is much
force in many of the objections to it. Nevertheless experience has
shown that the student who has looked at the matter in the light of
this theory will gain a considerable insight into the general nature
of the problem we are discussing, without by any means experi-
encing the necessity of swallowing the whole of the theory itself.

In order to demonstrate the analysis diagrammatically, as in
Diagram III overleaf, it is necessary to postulate a highly simplified
example: we must assume the existence of only one consumer (thus
dodging entirely the question of the validity of interpersonal comparisons of utility) and we consider at first his reactions to a situation in which only one commodity changes its price, all other prices
remaining constant. However, we will assume that the commodity
in question is an important one in his total consumption, and that
its price rises very considerably, so that as far as this consumer is
concerned there occurs a significant deterioration in the value of
money (to him) as well as a significant disturbance to the pre-
existing pattern of relative prices.

On the horizontal axis of the graph we depict the amount of the
commodity which he buys in a given period, say one year, measured
in lb. avoirdupois. On the vertical axis we represent the money he

† Throughout the remainder of the book the student will find it of great
assistance if he or she has already received some introduction to the elementary
principles of indifference-curve analysis.

may spend on goods *other* than this commodity: since the prices of other commodities remain constant, changes in the amount of money spent on them are unambiguously analogous to changes in the quantity of them purchased were they regarded as a single commodity. His total income in the initial position we will put at £1,000 p.a. so that the maximum he can possibly spend on other goods (i.e. if he bought nothing of the subject commodity or if its

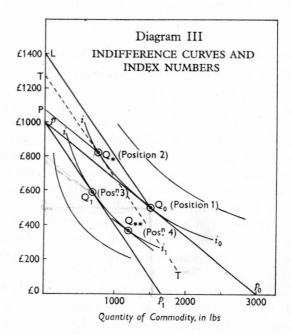

Diagram III

INDIFFERENCE CURVES AND
INDEX NUMBERS

Quantity of Commodity, in lbs

price were zero) is also £1,000 and this is indicated by a mark on the axis. The actual price of the commodity in the initial position we will put at 6/8d. per lb. so that if at the other extreme he were to spend all of his income on the commodity he would obtain 3,000 lbs. per annum.† A straight line joining the two points, £1,000 on the vertical axis and 3,000 lbs. on the horizontal, passes through all the points representing all the alternative combinations of lbs. of the subject commodity versus £'s spent on other commodities which

† No known domestic commodity is consumed in these quantities, but we have to exaggerate for the reasons already indicated.

are open to him so long as his income remains at £1,000 and the
price of the subject commodity at 6/8d. per lb. This line is labelled
pp_0 and is usually known as a price-possibility line.

Of the various possible combinations open to the consumer we
will assume that he chooses to take that represented by the point
marked *Position* 1, i.e. consuming 1,500 lbs. at a cost of £500,
leaving himself with £500 for other goods. The theory assumes
that this is the combination which he *prefers*, in some conscious
rational sense, over all others, and that he is reasonably fully conscious of the possibility of all others. It is also assumed that the
consumer is able to conceive of combinations which would in fact
satisfy him equally, i.e. which he would regard as putting him on
the same level of welfare; however these do not lie on the price-
possibility but on an *indifference curve*, ii_0 which throughout its
length lies to the right of the price-possibility line except just at
the point of the chosen combination, i.e. at position 1. The latter
follows from the logical properties of indifference curves as developed in the voluminous literature of the subject—in short from
the presumption that the consumer chooses his combination so as
to place himself on the indifference curve representing the highest
level of welfare obtainable: if the indifference curve on which he
put himself were actually at some point to cut the price-possibility
line there would in principle exist some other combination of purchases open to the consumer on a 'higher' curve, the curves representing an *ordering* of welfare levels. (A simple, if loose, way to
establish these propositions is to imagine the economic implications
of assuming anything else.)

If the price of this important commodity is now assumed to rise,
catastrophically for the consumer, by, say 75 per cent to 12s. per
lb., with an income of £1,000 he could now only buy at the most
1,666 lbs. the price-possibility line having shifted to pp_1. He can no
longer therefore attain as 'high' an indifference curve as before: he
is forced to make the best of a situation which we know from his
previous actions he regards as inferior, since when in situation 1
('year 0') he had the opportunity of choosing either the combination at position 1, or any of the positions to the left of it such as
positions on pp_1, he nevertheless chose position 1, thereby un-

ambiguously signalling or 'revealing' (in the language of the trade) his preference. He is therefore considered to have suffered a loss of welfare. If his money income has indeed remained constant, how may this loss of welfare be measured? We shall first consider the question by reversing it: the consumer's money income might not have remained constant—how much would his income have needed to rise so that he would have considered he had lost nothing? In the language of the indifference curve theory, therefore, we need to ascertain the money income which would be necessary to enable the consumer to remain somewhere on the same indifference curve, ii_0, as before, despite the change in price.

Welfare and Real Income

But before considering how the question posed at the end of the preceding paragraph may be answered it is necessary to pay some attention to the meaning of the expressions 'level of welfare' and 'loss of welfare' in the context. We have already suggested that 'Utility', 'Satisfaction' or 'Welfare' is not a directly measurable entity and there is considerable controversy among economists and philosophers as to whether it is a thing which could ever even in principle be measured either directly or indirectly. In the diagram, each indifference curve is supposed to represent a different level of satisfaction, and the curves are *ordered* in levels, but at first sight there is no way of saying *how much* more welfare is represented by any one given indifference curve of higher order than any given other of lower order. At first sight all we can say is that welfare is higher on the higher curve, and that is all. But suppose for the sake of argument we do assign numbers to the curves, numbering in order from bottom left to top right. Suppose we select arbitrarily one of the lower curves as a *reference curve* and assign to it the number 1. Suppose then we arbitrarily select a *reference point* on that curve and note the quantities of all commodities to be consumed as indicated at that point. Then let us arrange the numbers of the subsequent curves so that the curve (there can only be one such) which at some point in its path passes through the point on the diagram implying precisely double the consumption of each and every commodity taken at the reference point, is given the number 2; the curve which passes through a point implying treble the consumption of all the reference-point commodities, the number 3, and so on. Now these numbers would not measure welfare, but they would point towards welfare. They could not be compared between individuals (even if the reference point were made a standard bundle of commodities for all individuals) because one individual might claim he could derive much greater satisfaction out of a given quantity of commodities than another: i.e. one individual might claim that, say, indifference curve number 4 meant more to him than to anyone else. (This point should ring a bell with readers who have followed the controversy about the position of the middle classes in the post-war U.K.) Nor could the numbers be regarded as directly measuring differences in the welfare of a given individual in different situations, because of the likelihood of 'diminishing marginal utility' of income: if indifference curve number 2 yielded twice the satisfaction of indifference curve number 1, indifference curve number 4 would probably yield less than twice the satisfaction of indifference curve 2. Thus in proceeding from the system of numbers to deductions about welfare we proceed into an area of great difficulty and doubt, more in the realm of philosophy than social science. Nevertheless the numbering system itself, as an idea, is of considerable importance and interest. The numbers provide the foundations or starting point of welfare. In mathematical language we can say that the welfare of the individual is *some function* of the numbers, and it might be stated as a political objective of society that economic policy should aim to maximise some specified function of the numbers attained by its various citizens.† If this is so, the numbers themselves, or constructs analogous, are well worth trying to measure as such. In what follows we will describe the operations of measurement thus involved

† Such a function is known in the trade as a Social Welfare Function and represents an important and interesting idea which will be of value to us at several points later. In specifying the function, it would be necessary to take account of the nature and hours of the work required to produce the money income from which the level of welfare is ultimately deduced; alternatively 'leisure' might in some way be introduced as a form of consumer good in the conceptual system. Throughout the whole of this and the following chapter, it is for convenience implicitly assumed that the hours and nature of the work done by each and every individual in society are constant.

R

as measurements of changes in 'real income' or in 'real consumption'; we will regard changes in real income as more or less synony-
mous with changes in welfare and will therefore ignore all variations in the amount of welfare (considered as 'Utility') which the
individual may obtain from a given level of real income. A consumer who has been held on a constant indifference curve (see
above) will be referred to as having been kept at a constant real
income,† by definition, and vice versa. If a man's money income
doubles, while prices remain constant, his real income has doubled
(and the number assigned to the indifference curve which he is now
able to attain should be double the number attached to the earlier
curve). The 'index number problem' with which this chapter is
essentially concerned arises because (*a*) prices do not remain constant, either absolutely or relatively and (*b*) we do not know the
actual indifference curves of individuals. Thus there are considerable difficulties involved in measuring the indifference-curve
numbers, i.e. real income, let alone the more nebulous concepts of
Utility or Welfare derived from a given real income. But it is
essentially a measurement of the kind of measuring these numbers
which is being attempted when we ask how much extra money
income it is necessary to award the consumer in order to keep
him on the old indifference curve at the new prices. To this question we can now return.

The 'True' Index-Number Concept and the 'Bias' in Paasche and Laspeyres

We wish to put the consumer in a position where he is faced
with year 1 prices (i.e. 12s. per lb.) but remains on the year o in
difference curve, i.e. is kept at a constant level of real income. The
price of the commodity in the diagram, in terms of the prices of
other commodities, is given by the *slope* of the price-possibility line
(its *position* being fixed by his assumed money income) and since
all other prices are assumed constant, the change in the slope from

† 'Real Consumption' or 'Real Expenditure' would be better, since income
cannot strictly be evaluated in real terms until it is spent. However, real income
is an expression so widely used in this context that we have stuck to it, risking
such confusion as may be caused. In effect, we postulate a consumer who spends
all his income and saves nothing: this implication also underlies much of the
following chapter as well as the present one.

that of pp_0 to pp_1 unambiguously represents the absolute change in the commodity's price in this example. Suppose now therefore we start to shift pp_1 bodily to the right across the diagram, without altering its slope, we are in effect depicting successively a series of price-possibility situations all involving not only the new price of 12s. but also new and successively higher levels of the consumer's money income (since such lines must intercept the vertical axis at successively higher points above £1,000). And if we continue to shift the line until we find the point at which it is tangential to the old indifference curve ii_0, we shall find evidently, at *position 2*, the combination of purchases the consumer would choose under the conditions in question. Where the transferred line, which is labelled TT, cuts the vertical axis, we have the cost of this combination at the new prices, i.e. we have the amount of the money income which would just enable him to purchase it. In the diagram, TT cuts the vertical axis at an income of £1,280, and £1,280 is the income which would be necessary therefore to provide complete 'compensation' to the consumer for the price increase which has occurred. The excess of this new hypothetical income over his actual income in year o is £280, or 28 per cent. 28 per cent may then be taken as a measure of this consumer's personal experience of the rise in the cost of living (less than 75 per cent, the rise in the price of the single commodity, of course, because the commodity represents only a part of his total consumption). The 'value of money' to the consumer, that is the power of money to purchase real income for him, has fallen by the reciprocal amount, 22 per cent. For want of a better term we shall call the measure TT, or more precisely the index number 128, the 'true index' of the cost of living, although as we shall see it is not an index number proper in the sense of the definition given in the appendix to Chapter 8, nor is it the only concept of a 'true' index number which could reasonably be defined: in certain circumstances there are other possible definitions of the 'true' index, not necessarily giving the same answers. However, the point which more immediately concerns us is that the true index, whether defined as above or in some other way, will normally differ significantly from the measure provided both by Laspeyres' index and by Paasche's index.

For it is to be noticed that despite the fact that our imaginary consumer has hypothetically been maintained at his original level of real income by means of a compensating variation in money income, he has nevertheless been found to choose to reduce his consumption (in lbs.) of the subject commodity. This is because it is assumed implicitly in drawing up the shape of the indifference curve that, the relative price of the commodity having risen, he prefers to substitute some increased consumption of other commodities for the now more expensive subject commodity, as evinced by the movement round the indifference curve in response to the change in the slope of the price line. His chosen pattern of consumption is now therefore different from what it was, and the true index assesses the rise in his personal cost of living by comparing the cost of the new *desired* combination (on the assumption of constant real income) at the new prices with the cost of the old (then desired) combination at the old prices. If there was a large number of separate commodities under consideration, instead of as here in effect only two (the subject commodity and 'commodities' in general), the true index would most conveniently be expressed by an aggregation formula, say,

$$\mathbf{T}_0(P_{1/0}) = \frac{\Sigma\, Q_{i*}P_{i1}}{\Sigma\, Q_{i0}P_{i0}}$$

where Q_{i*} stands for the quantity of the ith commodity which would be *desired* in year 1, if, and only if, the consumer had somehow been maintained on the same indifference curve (level of real income) as in year 0 in face of year 1 prices: Q_{i*} is therefore the quantity taken at the position on ii_0 where ii_0 has the tangent-slope of pp_1 (i.e. at position 2).

(When the formula for the true index is set out in the above manner we see what is meant by saying that it is not an index number proper, since the quantities as well as the prices change from the bottom to the top line of the fraction. However, although the quantity weights are not themselves constant, both sets are of a level and pattern which represent, in principle, a constant level of real income. Real income, it will be remembered, is deemed to depend on the quantities of goods which are consumed: Q_0, which he consumes at position 1, and Q_*, which he consumes at position 2 are sets of quantities which represent the same real income, each basket containing more of some commodities but less of others, than the other.)

Now, the Laspeyres index, it will be remembered, is

$$\mathbf{I}_{Q0}(P_{1/0}) = \frac{\Sigma Q_{i0} P_{i1}}{\Sigma Q_{i0} P_{i0}}$$

and thus differs from the true index in substituting Q_{i0} for Q_{i*} in the top line. The Laspeyres index may therefore be depicted in the simplified diagrammatic example by drawing a straight line, labelled L, starting from the old position 1 but possessing the slope of the new prices, i.e. a line parallel to pp_1; and noting the point of intersection with the vertical axis. This point evidently indicates the new income which would be required in order to be able to go on buying the *old* actual combination, Q_0, (in contrast to the new desired combination, Q_*), but at the new prices. In the example, L intersects the axis at £1,400, hence indicating that if compensation were computed according to the Laspeyres formula, a 40 per cent increase in income would be required (i.e. the Laspeyres index is 140), which it will be noted is twelve points in excess of the 'true' amount. The discrepancy is inevitable from the fact that, as a result of the postulated substitution on the part of the consumer, the Q_{i*} are lower relatively to the Q_{i0} for just the commodities (in the simplified example, 'for just the commodity') whose P_{i1} are highest relatively to their P_{i0}.†

So long as the consumer's system of indifference curves remains unaltered (a state of affairs which is sometimes described as his

---

† The point can be seen on the diagram as follows. The Laspeyres index, L, is in effect obtained by swinging pp_0 on the pivot of position 1 until it is parallel with pp_1 although still passing through the pivot. The procedure for obtaining TT may be thought of as commencing in the same manner but then, when the correct angle has been obtained, transferring the line bodily so that it no longer passes through position 1 but does pass through position 2. Since the location of position 2 is governed by the condition that it is the point where TT is just tangential to ii_0, the transfer must be in a leftward direction (making the intersection of TT with the axis lower than that of L) so long as we accept that the indifference curves are convex to the origin, i.e. so long as we accept that consumers are less and less prepared to substitute other goods for the subject commodity the further the substitution itself proceeds.

'tastes' remaining unaltered) the Laspeyres index will always exceed the true index in the sense that the latter has just been defined. This is what is meant or implied when it is stated that the Laspeyres index, the commonest type of index in every-day use, is possessed of upward bias or 'flatters' the rise in prices. A layman's way of putting the point is to say that the Laspeyres index, in assuming a rigid quantitative pattern of consumption, makes no allowance for the fact that when prices rise unevenly the consumer can partly evade the effect by switching his or her purchases towards the things whose prices have risen least and away from the things whose prices have risen most. Of course, if all prices rose in the same proportion this possibility would not exist, but in that case there would be no need to construct an index number to measure the 'average' increase. Alternatively, if the consumer himself is possessed of a very rigid pattern of tastes, and regards most commodities as being possessed of few substitutes, the substitution behaviour assumed in the proposition that Laspeyres' index is upward biased could not and would not occur, (or could only occur in response to very violent changes in relative prices) and hence the bias would be non-existent or small. In terms of the formal theory, a very rigid pattern of tastes is indicated by indifference curves with a narrow range of very steep curvature, the extreme case being a 'curve' consisting of a right-angled triangle without hypotenuse, with the angle opening away from the origin. (There is only one point of equilibrium on such a curve, and no change in relative price will alter the quantity demanded of the subject commodity at a given level of real income.) It is easy to see that with curves of this type the excess of the L intersection over that of the TT will be negligible, since TT will only have had to be shifted very little or not at all in order to find the Q_{i*} combination.†

Paasche's index, by contrast, tends to exaggerate the effect of the savings available to the consumer by substitution behaviour. This is not quite so obvious as is the upward bias in Laspeyres, because Paasche's index, it will be remembered, in contrast to the true index and also in effect in contrast to Laspeyres', is weighted not

† The situation corresponds to one in which ϵ, in equation (10.3) in the appendix to Chapter 8, was zero or very small.

according to some hypothetical pattern of consumption, but according to the pattern which expresses what the consumer, in the event, actually does. And what the consumer actually does will depend on what actually happens to his tastes and what actually happens to his money income. Assuming for the moment that his tastes are unchanged, we must allow for the various possibilities that his money income remains constant (or even diminishes), or that as a result of vigorous action on the part of the Trade Union to which he belongs, increases by as much as (or even more than) the amount theoretically necessary to achieve 'true' compensation for the complex of price increases which has actually occurred. But it is not the case, as might be imagined, that if his income happened to increase by just the right amount to achieve precise compensation, Paasche's index would possess no bias. Furthermore, even should income have increased by the appropriate amount, the statistician will not know it, because 'the appropriate amount' is just the thing he is trying to find out. And if he uses either a Laspeyres index *or* a Paasche index he will get the wrong answer; he might well announce that precise compensation had not occurred (i.e. that real income had either risen or fallen) when in fact it had (i.e. real income had remained constant). For the Paasche index is,

$$\mathbf{I}_{Q1}(P_{1/0}) = \frac{\sum Q_{i1}P_{i1}}{\sum Q_{i1}P_{i0}}$$

and this, in the special case of precise compensation, is equivalent to

$$\mathbf{I}_{Q*}(P_{1/0}) = \frac{\sum Q_{i*}P_{i1}}{\sum Q_{i*}P_{i0}}$$

and thus differs from the true index in substituting Q_{i*} for Q_{i1} in the *bottom* line: Q_{i*} is a desired set of quantities appropriate to the year 1 pattern of relative prices, but it is not the set which was appropriate to the year 0 prices (these quantities were the Q_{i0}, *ex hypothesi*). Paasche will therefore be lower than the true index for a reason which is a mirror image of the reason which made Laspeyres higher: the commodity or commodities with the *lowest* P_{i0} relatively to their P_{i1} will also possess the *highest* Q_{i0} relatively to their Q_{i1}, thus producing the effect stated. In Diagram III the price increase indicated by Paasche is the difference between the cost of the new actual combination at the new prices and the cost of the same combination at the old. In the special case that precise compensation has occurred the new actual combination is the desired combination at Position 2 and its *cost* at the new prices is already indicated by TT. The cost at the old prices can be indicated by a line (labelled P) drawn from Position 2 parallel to the old price line pp_0. P intersects the vertical axis at £80 above the old £1,000 mark, and the index is the ratio of the TT intersection, £1,280, to this intersection £1,080, i.e. 118, which is ten percentage points less than the true index. Such understatement is inevitable if the indifference curves are of the shape required by the theory.†

'Abormal' influences on Paasche: Change in Real Income

If money income has changed by an amount which is different from that required for precise compensation, as will normally be the case in practice, it is evidently more difficult to generalise about the nature of the Paasche result, since the consequence must be that the actual Q_{i1}'s lie on some indifference curve other than ii_0; hence the *observed* result must depend in some rather complicated way on the pattern of the whole indifference-curve system. In addition, the ambiguity concerning the definition of the true index of which we have already been warned now arises, for it can effectively be argued that this index should as well be located by refer-

† The reader should not be alarmed at the magnitude of the error displayed in this example; it is deliberately exaggerated for purposes of exposition: the errors in empirical examples are typically considerably smaller. As will become apparent later, the magnitude of the bias either in Paasche or in Laspeyres varies directly with the magnitude of the spread between the Paasche and Laspeyres results themselves. This spread, as will be remembered from sections 9 and 10 of the appendix to Chapter 8, depends on the representative magnitude of the elasticity of substitution (which varies inversely with the rate of change of the curvature of the typical indifference curve) and the relative variance of the price changes. In the example, the relative variance of the price changes was unrealistically large, one commodity which in position 1 accounted for 50 per cent of the consumer's total expenditure (i.e. carrying a 'weight', c_{i0}, of precisely ·50) having risen in price by 75 per cent, the rest remaining constant. The reader may test his comprehension of the section in reference by verifying that these figures imply RV about ·08 and, since ϕ is ·16, ϵ about − 2. Both are high for real life. In real life price changes over time are usually more uniform than those assumed in Diagram III and indifference curves for major commodities display more curvature.

ence to the curvature of the new indifference curve as of that of the old—i.e. TT should be obtained by swinging round ii_1 in contrast to ii_0. However, let us leave that point for the moment and consider the problems which arise even when we stick to our original definition of the index. In Diagram III we could experiment with various alternative *types* of indifference curve patterns. Then suppose for instance we assumed that money income had remained constant we would note in each case where pp_1 was just tangential to an indifference curve and we could note this equilibrium as a *position* 3. Then from Position 3 we could draw a line parallel to pp_0 and note where it cut the vertical axis. The ratio of the old income (now representing ΣP_1Q_1 as well as ΣP_0Q_0) to this new intersection is Paasche's index under these conditions. This line is not shown on the diagram but the reader may verify by experiment the following propositions:

(1) It is possible for the Paasche index to bear much the same relation to the true index whatever the change in money income. (This will be the case if the indifference curves are well and evenly rounded and of a certain symmetrical pattern such that the 'income-elasticity' of demand is the same for all commodities throughout the system—in which case it can be said that the system is 'iso-income-elastic'.†)

† We deduce the 'income-effect' at any one point in the system (change in demand for a given commodity consequent upon a change in money income with all prices remaining constant, or more precisely, the change in demand consequent upon a shift from one indifference curve to another, all relative prices remaining constant) by considering the effects of bodily shifts in the price-possibility line with slope remaining constant in the manner already described in connection with the construction of the true index: the income elasticity is the income effect expressed as a ratio of initial consumption, divided by the proportionate change in money income postulated. However, unless the curves are symmetrical, it is possible that the income elasticity involved in a shift from ii_0 to ii_1 for example, may differ according to whether we took as a starting point, Position 1 (and hence relative prices of year 0) or Position 2, and hence relative prices of year 1. Strictly therefore the condition of iso-income elasticity throughout the system means that in the case of a shift from any point of equilibrium on any indifference curve to the corresponding point of equilibrium on any other curve, with a given set of relative prices, the equilibrium quantity purchased of the subject commodity will change in the *same proportion* as that of commodities in general: geometrically this involves that if points where the tangent-slope is the same on successive indifference curves are joined together by lines radiating from the origin, these lines will be straight lines.

(2) If the pattern of the indifference curves is not symmetrical it
appears possible for Paasche to come out *higher* than the true
index,† in contrast to what we will term its 'normal' behaviour in coming out lower; and in extreme cases Paasche
could come out as high as Laspeyres, or even higher. These
conditions could be accompanied by the conditions for
normal upward bias in Laspeyres (see above)‡ so that the
extremely deceptive result could arise that Paasche and Laspeyres came out rather close together, thus creating the presumption that average elasticities of substitution were rather
low and therefore the 'true' index was unlikely to be far
away,§ when in fact this invisible entity was lying a substantial distance below.

The Cancelling-Out Proposition

But the foregoing applies to the simplified case only. When we come
to consider the realistic case, where the relative prices of a large
number of commodities are all allowed to vary, things are different.
What is really happening in the second of the two simplified cases
described, where Paasche succeeds in exceeding the true index
defined along ii_0, is that the reduction in real income has tended to
increase the *relative* consumption of the subject commodity, in
opposition to the tendency to reduction in relative consumption
induced by the change in relative price. In the circumstances
envisaged, the former effect is so strong as to swamp the latter (in

† The curves should bunch at the top left-hand end and spread out at the
bottom right-hand end, so that consumption of the subject commodity is substantially less sensitive to changes in real income (shifts from one indifference
curve to another) than is that of commodities in general. The effect is that in
shifting from the higher indifference curve to the lower, the *relative* consumption
of the subject commodity tends to increase, e.g. it is a 'necessity' in contrast to a
'luxury'.

‡ This implies a subject commodity whose consumption is insensitive to
changes in real income but sensitive to changes in relative price. That at first
sight seems improbable, but could be applied to the case of say square (as
against round) loaves of bread, considered as a single commodity distinct from
bread in general. A small rise in relative price will cause many people to
switch to buying round loaves, but a fall in real income with relative price
unchanged would not reduce consumption of bread in general (and indeed might
well increase it) nor hence of either square loaves or round loaves.

§ See fn. p. 244 above.

the jargon, the income effect has swamped the substitution effect)
so that the commodity whose price has increased the most has
experienced the smallest reduction in its quantity weight. This pulls
the Paasche index in the opposite direction to the 'normal' bias.
However, when we consider a large number of commodities together it becomes apparent that for every commodity whose
sensitivity to real income changes is below average, there must be
another whose sensitivity is above average: 'abnormality' of indifference curves in a given direction for one commodity implies
the opposite kind of abnormality for others. Hence when we come
to think in more general terms we see that there must also be many
cases where the deviation has the opposite effect to that just discussed; and the latter occurrences will tend to drive Paasche down
even lower, in relation to the true index, than would be the case
with iso-income-elastic curves. The two types of occurrence must
therefore to some extent counteract one another and if the number
of commodities is sufficiently large the net effect should be much
the same as if the indifference curves were in fact iso-income-
elastic in pattern throughout. However, since the direction of the
bias imparted in the case of any particular commodity depends also
on the direction of the relative price change experienced by that
commodity, overall cancelling out would not materialise if there
were some systematic statistical association, commoditywise,
between the income-elasticity characteristics of the relevant
indifference curves and the relative price changes which happened
to occur over the period in question.

At first sight it would seem from the nature of the case that such
correlation between price changes and income elasticities could
only occur by chance, and that so long as a sufficiently large number of commodities was considered, would be most unlikely therefore to be substantial in magnitude.† There is however one consideration which has been put in opposition to this otherwise
rather comforting proposition. It often happens that although the
number of different economic commodities which the consumer
buys is legion, the prices within broad groups of commodities such

† It can be shewn that the error depends directly on the co-variance of price
changes and income elasticities. Again see Chapter 8, appendix, section 9.

as 'food', 'drink', 'furniture' and so on move rather closely together. That is to say, the overall dispersion in the price changes as a whole, which might itself be quite large, would consist mainly of variations as between broad groups rather than within such groups. If this happens, we are in effect, and so far as is relevant for the present discussion, faced not so much with a large number of homogeneous commodities, as with a relatively small number of 'composite' commodities, each more or less homogeneous however in respect of relative price change. The 'laws of large numbers'† then no longer apply and the likelihood of substantial co-variance between price changes and income elasticities arising by chance, or 'coincidence', if the word is preferred, may by no means be so small. Thus supposing that for some general economic reason the prices of agricultural products in general rose relatively to the prices of other goods in general, causing a corresponding rise in the retail prices of foodstuffs relatively to those of other consumer goods and services. Foodstuffs may generally be expected to possess below average income elasticities and the correlation in question might thus well arise in practice. The point is formally quite unimpeachable; its importance depends on our judgement of fact. It can be argued in reply that the dispersion of price movements and income elasticities within commodity groups is typically considerably greater, in modern industrial communities, than is sometimes imagined. Thus as food prices rose, for example, it would be likely that the major part of the movement occurred in narrower subgroups, such as cereals in contrast to dairy products and meat. Similarly, income elasticities for the superior sources of protein, such as meat and cheese, are often quite high. It might still be true that prices of foodstuffs in general had on average risen more than prices in general, and that a weighted average of the income elasticities for foodstuffs worked out at noticeably less than unity, but if prices within the group had also happened to rise most for just those food products with relatively high income-elasticities within the group, much of the effect under discussion would be lost. There is an even more important comment which must be

† This is a loose but convenient use of an expression which is used by mathematical statisticians somewhat more narrowly and precisely.

made in this connection. If there genuinely occurs a rather tight grouping of the price changes, with very little within-group dispersion, this is bound to have an effect on the bias of the Laspeyres' index. For in these circumsances there can be little or no within-group substitution, and from the nature of things, elasticities of substitution as between groups are likely to be small, because the needs which different broad groups of commodities satisfy are so very different: clothing is not much of a substitute for food (except at perhaps very low levels of living indeed where the conservation of bodily energy is all that counts) and is unlikely to receive a significant diversion of purchases in the event of its price falling relatively to that of foodstuffs. Hence in this type of circumstance the bias in the Laspeyres' index is likely to be unusually small. Thus in the particular combination of circumstances in which the Paasche index is likely to behave in an 'abnormal' fashion it may well be safe to employ the Laspeyres' index *simpliciter*, without adjustment for bias. The circumstances could be identified by means of what is known as an *analysis of variance* performed on the price changes: the commodities would be separated into broad groups and an assessment made as to what proportions of the total variance were attributable to inter-group variations on the one hand and intra-group variations on the other, respectively.† By a similar argument it can be shown that if in these circumstances the index T_1 is required (see below) rather than T_0, then Paasche should be employed, *simpliciter*, rather than Laspeyres.

Changes in Tastes

Up to the present point we have been assuming that throughout the period over which our comparison is to be made, the pattern of the consumer's indifference curves remain fixed, i.e. he has 'constant tastes'. In practice this assumption is most unlikely to be a valid one. What are the implications? In the first place there are evident philosophical difficulties, which will be reverted to later, in making any comparison of welfare for a person with non-constant tastes. *Inter alia* we have to decide whether the measurement should be made according to the old tastes or according to the new, and so

† See any standard textbook of general statistical methods.

on. However, it is nevertheless well worth while pointing out that the 'cancelling out' propositions which have just been described in connection with the effect of changes in real income have considerable application to the present question also. For it can be shewn that in practice, if tastes change, the values of Paasche, Laspeyres and the true index may come out much the same whether the measurement is made on the basis of the new tastes, of the old tastes or of a mixture of the two. For this not to be so it is necessary that there be some sort of statistical association, commoditywise, between the changes in tastes and the changes in prices,† and again

† The best way of precisely formulating this proposition is to imagine in theory that we knew the detailed features of the entire indifference system of some individual consumer in say, year 0. If then this consumer were subjected to a certain set of price changes coupled with a certain stated change in his money income (from year 0 to year 1) we could in principle predict with complete accuracy the adjustments he would make in his purchases of each and every commodity; in other words we could predict the value of every relevant $q_{i1/0}$. But, in practice, of course, his indifference system might change its shape between the two years and hence our predictions would turn out to be in error. The difference between the actually experienced $q_{i1/0}$'s and the original predicted values, say $dq_{i1/0}$ (which could of course be either positive or negative), would be taken as a quantitative measure of the 'change in taste' in respect of each commodity, and the whole set of such magnitudes, $dq_1, dq_2, \ldots, dq_i \ldots, dq_n$ as a general statement of the change in the system as a whole. The proposition is that the index number will remain unaffected unless these deviations are possessed of a substantial co-variance with the price changes, a requirement which means of course that they must be reasonably dispersed and must possess a significant correlation coefficient with the $p_{i1/0}$. One way of seeing this is to appreciate that the changes in taste are a form of autonomous disturbance to the system of quantity weights from which the price-index number is constructed, that is an outside disturbance additional to, and independent from, the systematic changes in the weights caused by substitution effects and income effects: we have already seen in the appendix to Chapter 8 that random disturbances to weights leave an index number unaffected. A more sophisticated line of reasoning (which amounts to the same thing in the end) is by analogy with the application of the analysis of the difference between the Paasche and Laspeyres' indexes given in the appendix to Chapter 8, section 10. There it is shown that this difference (if there be no changes in tastes or in real income) depends directly on the representative magnitude of the elasticity of substitution over the commodities as a whole as given by regression analysis. The scatter in such a regression would be caused by inter-commodity variation in actual substitution elasticities. In practical cases, changes in taste as just defined would be an additional cause of such scatter but should only influence the estimated regression coefficient if they were biased: we saw in Chapter 7 that the circumstances in which scatter-causing disturbances will bias the result are that the variations in their magnitudes be themselves statistically associated with variations in the determining variable. The same line of argument can of course equally be applied to the case of the income effects.

it is difficult to see how this can happen except through a break-down in the 'laws of large numbers' of the type already mentioned. It is quite wrong, of course, to argue that the consumer's tastes will tend to be influenced by changes in relative prices, because this kind of effect is already subsumed in the substitution system: such adjustments represent movement within the pattern of a given indifference system, whereas the consequences of changes in taste are the consequences of changes in the indifference system itself and thus by definition consist in all those, and only those, changes in the pattern of consumption which cannot in principle be explained by known changes in relative prices or in real income. However, the qualification about the laws of large numbers is considerably more serious here than it was in the case of the income effect. A change in taste might well consist of a large homogeneous switch in favour of some new heterogeneous group of commodities (and away from other older groups) and it would be more than likely that this group would display a rather homogeneous falling tendency in prices.

Influences of Effects from the Supply side

We have seen that if the 'disturbances' to the pattern of demand caused either by changes in real income, or by changes in tastes (for certain purposes the two may be regarded as similar) are uncorrelated, commoditywise, with the relative price changes which happen to occur, they will leave the Paasche index unaffected, i.e. leave it to bear its 'normal' relationship to the Laspeyres' and true indexes. Let us term such a set of changes 'neutral'. We have suggested that except in the 'small numbers' case just discussed, the neutral result is in fact normally the one to be expected from the operation of the laws of chance. But we must now discuss a major qualification to that proposition.

Suppose a commodity which experiences no change in relative price in the first instance, experiences nevertheless a substantial relative increase in demand on account of income effect or change in taste. Now suppose this happens to be a commodity which is produced and sold under conditions of sharply increasing or, alternatively sharply decreasing supply price; say for the sake of argument the latter. Then, in the event, its relative price would fall, the drop being *caused* by the rise in relative demand. If this sort of thing happened over the whole range of commodities, because commodities in general were not sold under conditions of constant supply price (infinite elasticity of supply), changes in relative prices would indeed be correlated with changes in relative quantities—the more so, *inter alia*, the greater in general the steepness of supply curves and the magnitude of the disturbances. The idea of 'probable neutrality' is therefore only valid if supply-elasticities are generally infinite or at least large.† In a number of cases this may be a reasonable assumption, but in others clearly it is not. Some of the theoretical consequences will become apparent in the sections which follow.

Alternative 'True' Index Numbers

If there occur changes in taste or real incomes which are not neutral, the existence of alternative possible definitions for the true index already referred to (p. 246) can no longer be ignored. In Diagram III, the situation of a consumer who is driven onto the lower indifference curve ii_1 is depicted as at Position 3. The point at issue is that instead of asking how much more money income he would have needed to have prevented this lamentable decline in his standard of living occurring, we might as well assume that the consumer is already at Position 3 and ask how much his money income would have had to be *reduced* to keep him at this level, had the price of the commodity *fallen* from 12s. to 6s. 8d. in contrast to the other way about. Computation of the amount in question would of course involve swinging pp_1 round ii_1 until tangential equilibrium was reached with a slope of pp_0 (at Position 4). At Position 4 the consumer purchases the combination Q_{**}, representing the desired quantities on ii_1, appropriate to pp_0 relative prices. The index

† In other words ϵ' as defined in the second part of section 10 of the appendix to Chapter 8 is zero. The difficulty cannot be overcome by postulating an even mixture of increasing and decreasing supply price commodities cancelling each other out, for it can be shewn that owing to the interaction of supply elasticities with substitution elasticities, bias would remain. Bias is eliminated only in a special case. For a fuller treatment see an article by the author in the *Review of Economic Studies*, Oct. 1957.

number definition is,

$$\mathbf{T}_1(P_{0/1}) = \frac{\Sigma\, Q_{**} P_0}{\Sigma\, Q_1 P_1}$$

and we could validly set up the reciprocal of this, $\mathbf{T}_1(P_{1/0})$ as a rival to $\mathbf{T}_0(P_{1/0})$.

The reader may well feel that the foregoing argument is unrealistic and that it is only the indifference curve on which the consumer was initially to be found that can have any relevance to the basic problem we are considering. The unrealism, however, lies not so much in the proposition itself as in the restricted aspect of the basic problem presented in the example we have so far been using for illustration (that of a consumer faced with the need to maintain his real income in face of rising prices). The moment is therefore ripe to discuss the matter in more general terms. What we are really trying to do is not just to draw up a 'cost of living' index *per se*, but to attack generally the problem of providing a numerical indicator of the change in real income associated with shifts in the consumer situation from one indifference curve to another. We are in effect searching for measures which correspond to the hypothetical numbering system for indifference curves which we discussed by way of introduction earlier. We certainly do not want to restrict ourselves to a system of numbering which is pegged to a particular point in the indifference system. Thus, if our consumer has been forced from ii_0 to ii_1 *or* vice versa, we should like a general measure of the monetary equivalent of his actual loss or gain. Start from say Position 2, and shift the price-possibility line bodily until it is tangential to ii_1, at Position 3: note the change in money income implied on the axis. In other words, compare TT with pp_1 and obtain a 'true' *volume* index of the change in real income:

$$\mathbf{T}_1(Q_{1/0}) = \frac{\Sigma\, P_1 Q_1}{\Sigma\, P_1 Q_*} = \mathbf{I}_{P1}(Q_{1/*})$$

This, as indicated, is an index number proper, comparing the desired quantities in year 1 with the desired quantities in year 0, on the assumption that real income has changed but that the quan-

s

tities taken are the quantities appropriate to year 1 prices in both cases—and employing these year 1 prices as weights. Thus we see that in order to define the measurement of the change in real income from one curve to another, we have to postulate a movement from equilibrium on the one to equilibrium on the other, i.e. we must *already* have postulated some specific pattern of relative prices. Clearly, however, the year 1 prices are not the only prices we might have specified. We might just as well have specified the prices of year 0, comparing pp_0 with the tangent line at position 4, in which case we get the index,

$$\mathbf{T}_0(Q_{1/0}) = \frac{\sum P_0 Q_{**}}{\sum P_0 Q_0} = \mathbf{I}_{P_0}(Q_{**/0})$$

Indeed, if we are discussing the question in full generality, we might have specified any prices.

The two alternative volume indexes cross-match with the two alternative price indexes in the usual way,

$$\frac{\sum P_1 Q_1}{\sum P_0 Q_0} = \mathbf{T}_1(P_{1/0}) \cdot \mathbf{T}_0(Q_{1/0}) = \mathbf{T}_0(P_{1/0}) \cdot \mathbf{T}_1(Q_{1/0})$$

(their relationship can also be seen quite clearly on the diagram), and we appear to be faced with an unresolvable ambiguity. To some extent the appearance is correct. The index we take must depend on the nature of the economic question we are asking in the particular circumstances of each interpretation. The ambiguity itself is inherent in the nature of the fundamental problem: if we knew, and could measure cardinally, the levels of welfare associated with each indifference curve the difficulty would not arise.

However, we must not be disheartened by necessary ambiguities. Furthermore we may take some comfort from the fact that in conditions of general neutrality it is likely that the alternative index numbers will lie very close to one another, if not be equal.† It also appears that departures from neutrality have to be rather severe for the difference between the alternative indexes to be of a magnitude that the reasonable man would consider significant. There are, as we shall see, much worse criticisms to be made of the theory than this.

† See article *op. cit.* (p. 254 above) and also section which follows.

Summary

We may summarise our findings up to this point in three tables, as below:

TABLE A. *Laspeyres, Paasche and 'True' Index Numbers, Real Income and Tastes assumed constant*

	Laspeyres		'True'		Paasche
Price Indexes	$\dfrac{\Sigma Q_0 P_1}{\Sigma Q_0 P_0}$	$>$	$\dfrac{\Sigma Q_* P_1}{\Sigma Q_0 P_0}$	$>$	$\dfrac{\Sigma Q_* P_1}{\Sigma Q_* P_0}$
Volume Indexes	$\dfrac{\Sigma P_0 Q_*}{\Sigma P_0 Q_0}$	$>$	1	$>$	$\dfrac{\Sigma P_1 Q_*}{\Sigma P_1 Q_0}$

N.B. The suffix 'i' has for simplicity been omitted throughout. Q_* is a 'desired' combination of quantities indicated by the tangential equilibrium requirements of indifference-curve theory on the assumptions that (i) prices are as in year 1, but (ii) the consumer has been able to keep on the same indifference curve as in year 0.

TABLE B. *Tastes and Real Income not Constant*

	Laspeyres		'True'			Paasche
			either	or		
Price Indexes	$\dfrac{\Sigma Q_0 P_1}{\Sigma Q_0 P_0}$	$>$	$\dfrac{\Sigma Q_* P_1}{\Sigma Q_0 P_0}$	$\dfrac{\Sigma Q_1 P_1}{\Sigma Q_{**} P_0}$	$>$	$\dfrac{\Sigma Q_1 P_1}{\Sigma Q_1 P_0}$
Volume Indexes	$\dfrac{\Sigma P_0 Q_1}{\Sigma P_0 Q_0}$	$>$	$\dfrac{\Sigma P_0 Q_{**}}{\Sigma P_0 Q_0}$	$\dfrac{\Sigma P_1 Q_1}{\Sigma P_1 Q_*}$	$>$	$\dfrac{\Sigma P_1 Q_1}{\Sigma P_1 Q_0}$

N.B. Q_{**} represents a desired combination of quantities on the new, year 1, indifference curve but appropriate to the year 0 prices. Thus Q_0 and Q_* are combinations lying on the *old* indifference curve; Q_1 and Q_{**} are on the new. But only Q_0 and Q_1 are observable.

TABLE C. *Tastes and Real Income not Constant but Neutral*

	Laspeyres		'True'			Paasche
			either	or		
Price Indexes	$\dfrac{\Sigma Q_0 P_1}{\Sigma Q_0 P_0}$	$>$	$\dfrac{\Sigma Q_* P_1}{\Sigma Q_0 P_0} =$	$\dfrac{\Sigma Q_1 P_1}{\Sigma Q_{**} P_0}$	$>$	$\dfrac{\Sigma Q_1 P_1}{\Sigma Q_1 P_0}$
Volume Indexes	$\dfrac{\Sigma P_0 Q_1}{\Sigma P_0 Q_0}$	$>$	$\dfrac{\Sigma P_0 Q_{**}}{\Sigma P_0 Q_0} =$	$\dfrac{\Sigma P_1 Q_1}{\Sigma P_1 Q_*}$	$>$	$\dfrac{\Sigma P_1 Q_1}{\Sigma P_1 Q_0}$

TABLE C in the other notation

Price	$\mathbf{I}_{Q_0}(P_{1/0}) > \mathbf{T}_0(P_{1/0}) = \mathbf{T}_1(P_{1/0}) > \mathbf{I}_{Q_1}(P_{1/0})$
Volume	$\mathbf{I}_{P_0}(Q_{1/0}) > \mathbf{T}_0(Q_{1/0}) = \mathbf{T}_1(Q_{1/0}) > \mathbf{I}_{P1}(Q_{1/0})$

In connection with the interpretation of the above summary the reader is asked to remember the following points:

(i) On the arguments as far as we have carried them, the 'true' indexes in the centre columns cannot be computed by direct statistical measurement, except in the unlikely circumstance that the actual details of a large part of the consumer in-difference system are objectively known to us. (But see 'An Ideal Index', below.)

(ii) The other indexes can be computed by simple operations of multiplication and division provided that the statistician can obtain data relating to the prices and quantities of all the commodities to be covered by the index both in year o and in year 1, or alternatively information which gives this data indirectly.

(iii) Although the theoretical specification of the index numbers is given separately for the case in which there is assumed no change in real income and the case in which real income is theoretically permitted to vary, it must be appreciated that the statistician has in practice no *independent* indication as to whether the consumer has remained on the same indifference curve or not.

With the above points in mind we now recapitulate the conclusions arrived at in the preceding sections, concerning the relationships of equality and inequality as depicted in the Tables A, B and C.

In the circumstances envisaged in Table A, the index numbers are theoretically bound to bear the relationships of inequality to one another there indicated. The most compressed proof is to note that if the consumer remains on a constant indifference curve the requirement of tangential equilibrium insists that Q_0, which is the equilibrium combination at P_0 prices, is the cheapest combination lying on the curve, obtainable at those prices, and hence $\Sigma Q_0 P_0$

must be less than $\Sigma Q_* P_0$. By analogous reasoning $\Sigma Q_* P_1$ must
be less than $\Sigma Q_0 P_1$. From these two propositions it will be seen
that all four inequalities indicated in Table A must follow. We call
this chain of relationships 'normal'. In the circumstances envisaged
in Table B, the normal chain is broken by the existence of the
alternative true indexes, which are not necessarily identical. But it
is still true that $\Sigma Q_0 P_1$ must always exceed $\Sigma Q_* P_1$ and also,
evidently, $\Sigma Q_1 P_0 > \Sigma Q_{**} P_0$; hence certain inequalities as indicated remain valid in all circumstances. In the circumstances
envisaged in Table C the normal chain of relationships is restored.
In the discussion earlier, 'neutrality' was seen as playing its role by
leaving Paasche unaffected by changes in real income or tastes, i.e.
fixing the index, both absolutely and in relation to Laspeyres and
one of the true indexes, T_0, at precisely the level which would have
been observed had no changes in tastes or real income occurred.
In the presentation adopted in Table C, where two alternative
definitions of T are admitted, neutrality achieves a similar effect by
bringing the two into approximate equality.

An 'Ideal' Index

It is evident that if the conditions postulated in Table C are met
in real life, any number which lies somewhere between the values
of the Laspeyres' and Paasche results obtained from the data of a
real example will normally come closer to the theoretical 'true'
index appropriate to the example than will either the Paasche or
Laspeyres' indexes taken alone. Indeed, the reader who wishes to
experiment with some simple geometric examples (assuming only
two commodities and constant real income, i.e. keeping the consumer on a constant indifference curve) will find that in a considerable number of cases the measured value of either true index
will differ little from the simple arithmetic average of the Paasche
and Laspeyres ratios: in Diagram III for instance, T_0, located by
TT, is 1·28 and the arithmetic average of Paasche and Laspeyres is
1·29. (The geometric average, see below, is actually 1·28.) However,
it is also obvious that the *exact* relationship between a 'true' index
on the one hand and Paasche and Laspeyres' on the other must in
any individual case depend on the curvature pattern of the system

of indifference curves in question. These, in our present state of knowledge, cannot normally be measured.

However, as long ago as 1923, *Prof. Irving Fisher* suggested that a particular kind of average of the Paasche and Laspeyres' indexes appeared to him to represent an 'ideal' measurement. This combination was the *geometric average*, i.e. the square root of the product of, Paasche and Laspeyres—either of the volume index or of the price index as the case might be, thus:

$$\text{'Ideal' price index} = \sqrt{\mathbf{I}_{Q_0}(P_{1/0}) \cdot \mathbf{I}_{Q_1}(P_{1/0})}$$

and

$$\text{'Ideal' volume index} = \sqrt{\mathbf{I}_{P_0}(Q_{1/0}) \cdot \mathbf{I}_{P_0}(Q_{1/0})}$$

This index, in either form, is sometimes referred to as 'Fisher's' index. Prof. Fisher recommended the formula because it successfully passed certain tests of mathematical consistency which he had devised for evaluating the merits of the many different types of index number formulae which had from time to time been proposed since the middle of the nineteenth century, but he could not base his case directly on the theory of consumer behaviour and welfare, as outlined in the present chapter, because this theory, in its modern form, was not then known in the English speaking world. Nevertheless, in the following year, Prof. Buscheguennce of Moscow University published in a Russian mathematical journal an important proof which in effect linked the Fisher index with indifference curve theory† as we now know it. The effect of Professor Buscheguennce's mathematical findings was that if the system of indifference curves takes on a certain general mathematical form, to wit that of a family of quadrics with centre at the origin, and if there is no change in real income, then the Fisher index will in fact be the true index; this would be so whatever the actual path of the individual indifference curves so long as they conformed to the required mathematical law. Now, of course, there

† The reference is S. S. Buscheguennce, 'Sur une Classe des Hypersurfaces', *Receuil Mathematiques de la Société Mathematique de Moscou*, XXXI, 1924, p. 625. This article attracted little or no attention in the English speaking world at the time and the proposition has never been widely appreciated. But the result has been rediscovered independently from time to time, although as yet never brought up to date and published.

is no obvious reason for supposing that the preference systems of individual people follow this or any other specifiable general law and some commentators have argued therefore, that the Fisher index is no more 'ideal' than any other. But these arguments overlook that the class of curves involved is a wide one, and when applied to a preference system which covers a reasonably large number of commodities, allows of a considerable amount of individual variation in the characteristics of the system as it relates to the individual's attitude to particular commodities (varying elasticities of substitution, varying income elasticities, varying rates of change of these elasticities with changes in relative price and/or income, etc.). Thus it seems likely that in the case of any given individual's preference system it will normally be possible to find some family of curves which possesses both the property of forming a set of the necessary quadrics and the property of providing a reasonably close 'fit' to the paths of the actual indifference curves of the system. It would then follow that Fisher's index computed from the observed data relating to this individual would approximate closely to the appropriate 'true' index.

The foregoing only applies strictly if there is no change in real income, i.e. if the consumer has somehow been kept on the same general level of welfare as in the manner of Table A. However, we have seen that if conditions are neutral as in Table C, the actual Paasche index obtained from the data will be the same whether real income has changed or no. Furthermore in neutral conditions the ambiguity as to the *definition* of the true index may also be ignored. In these conditions, therefore, any given combination of Paasche and Laspeyres will be unaffected by a change in real income, and the Fisher index therefore is valid to tell us whether and how much real income has changed, whether real income has in fact changed or no.

The Ideal or Fisher index has received the support of a number of distinguished economists but the grounds have not in general been such as the foregoing: typically, the argument has been that the usual theoretical considerations having suggested that the right index lies somewhere between Paasche and Laspeyres', some average of them is desirable; the indexes are ratios and the mathematically proper average to take of a pair of ratios is the geometric average. However, the Fisher index also possesses another property which was particularly emphasised by its author, i.e. that the price index multiplied by the volume index yields exactly the ratio of the new total expenditure to the old.

$$\sqrt{\frac{\Sigma Q_0 P_1}{\Sigma Q_0 P_0} \cdot \frac{\Sigma Q_1 P_1}{\Sigma Q_1 P_0}} \times \sqrt{\frac{\Sigma P_0 Q_1}{\Sigma P_0 Q_0} \cdot \frac{\Sigma P_1 Q_1}{\Sigma P_1 Q_0}}$$
$$= \sqrt{\frac{(\Sigma Q_1 P_1)^2}{(\Sigma Q_0 P_0)^2}} = \frac{\Sigma Q_1 P_1}{\Sigma Q_0 P_0}$$

Hence the index provides an unambiguous partitioning of the change in total expenditure as between that part which is due to a change in the real income itself and that part which is due to any change in the value of money in terms of real income. But we can now see this property of the index as a natural corollary of its more fundamental properties: Prof. Fisher's index thus appears as more ideal than has sometimes been realised.

Scepticism of Index-Number Theory

As indicated already, the theory which has been outlined in the foregoing sections is rejected by many economists, not so much on the ground that it contains internal logical fallacies, but more from objection to the basic premises on which it is founded and from consideration of the real nature of the world to which the theory is intended to apply. Thus the most fundamental objection, it seems, is that the conscious, complete and rational *preference system,* which the theory supposes to exist in the mind of the consumer, is an illusion: no one in practice is able to provide a complete ordering of his preferences as between the multitude of permutations and combinations of alternative bundles of commodities which might be offered to him; hence 'indifference' curves as an objective reality do not exist; they are no more than a theoretical construct. 'Certainly', this argument runs, 'the consumer as a matter of empirical fact is observed to consume more of things when their prices fall, and less of things when his income falls, but his reactions to such changes, particularly to changes in relative prices, are capricious and frequently demonstrably irrational (in the sense that the consumer himself would regard them as silly if he fully appreciated what he was doing). Thus the empirical occurrence of these reactions is quite incapable of supporting the construction of an elaborate theory to determine, e.g., how much the consumer would need to be compensated to keep his 'satisfactions' constant in face of a given set of price increases. He does not know what his satisfactions are.' An alternative formulation of the objection would be to argue that if the indifference curves are imagined to be discovered by actually asking the consumer questions about his preferences as between alternative bundles, there would be no simple connection between what he would *say* in reply to such questions and what in some sense he 'really felt' (as the latter might be tested by observation of his reactions to specified situations). Hence, in effect, to compensate the wage earner for a rise in the cost of living calculated from indifference curves drawn up in this manner amounts to little more, it would be argued, than defining the rise in the cost of living as being whatever the wage earner says he thinks it to be. We will discuss the pros and cons of this line of argument further below, but in the meantime it should be noted that the theory does not in fact require the objective existence of a preference system which is literally complete, it requires merely that it should exist with reasonable stability, completeness and rationality within certain limits, those limits depending on the extent and nature of the changes in prices and incomes which occur in a given case: or, to put it the other way about, the changes in prices and incomes must be sufficiently moderate to avoid 'going off the map' of the objectively conscious area of the preference system in the course of the imaginary computation of the 'true' index as in Diagram III above. The objection itself can therefore be formulated more precisely as a statement that in actual cases a sufficiently complete, rational and objective system will not in general exist in the mind of the typical consumer even within the necessary limits.

The second considerable objection arises in connection with the step from deductions, as in the foregoing, concerning the measurement of changes in the real income and welfare of the individual, to generalisations about changes in the economic welfare of the nation as a whole; a step which must be made in nearly all cases if the computation is to have much point. The index-number type of measurement is supposed to avoid the questionable practice of inter-personal comparison of utility by measuring the change in the overall economic welfare of the nation by reference to the change in aggregate *real income* on the assumption that the distribution of purchasing power as between consumers remains constant; alternatively, it regards any change in such distribution as may occur as an event apart, i.e. as something akin to 'other things' not being equal, and hence to be taken account of in some quite other manner, separately. The measurement also ignores of course any possibility of a *national* change in the marginal increment in welfare to be attributed to a given increment of real income such as might be consequent upon the rise or fall in national real income itself. Thus the theory seeks to preserve, on the national plane, the distinction between the measurement of real income on the one hand and the measurement, or attempted measurement, of welfare (or utility or satisfaction, whichever word is preferred) on the other which was first discussed at the beginning of this chapter. Now this intellectual procedure would be satisfactory if it were the case that the only way the distribution of real income as between consumers could change was by way of changes in the distribution between them of money income; but unfortunately that is not the case. Formally, the level of real income (i.e. the number of the indifference curve) reached by any individual evidently depends on three things, the pattern of his complete preference system, his money income, and the level and pattern of the prices of different commodities. The common-sense version of this proposition has several aspects: it is common-sense that if of two people with a given money income, one has a strong taste for wine and the other for beer, the higher the price of the former commodity relatively to that of the latter, the better off will be the beer drinker relatively to the wine drinker. These two people would be said to have different 'tastes' in the sense that even if both succeeded in attaining the same *numbered* indifference curve, the *shape* of the two curves would differ nevertheless; so with a given slope of the relative price line the two people would find equilibrium at different points on the same-numbered curve, the two points involving different consumptions of beer versus wine. But even if the consumers had identical shaped systems of indifference curves, i.e. were to be said to be possessed of the same tastes, relative prices would still be liable to affect their relative levels of attainable real income unless either they both did in fact have the same money income or both their systems of curves were iso-income elastic throughout. The common-sense version of this proposition is that those who are rich in money terms are even more rich in real terms in a country where luxuries are relatively cheap and necessities are relatively dear, and vice versa, because, merely from being rich they wish to consume greater proportions of luxuries.† In consequence we see that inherent in any change in relative prices, and hence inherent in any change in prices in general which poses any index-number 'problem' at all, there is a change in the distribution of real income and purchasing power as between consumers, except in special circumstances. Thus the clear analytical separation of distributive changes in real income from aggregate changes is usually impossible.

The third ground of scepticism follows closely from the second, but is nevertheless distinct. In any comparison of real income made over a long period of time, say over ten years, a significant proportion of the total population will have died and many new consumers will have graduated from infancy into economic independence. Comparisons over periods of such length are in fact frequently made and in many ways form one of the most interesting and attractive applications of the index number idea, since they attempt to provide a measure of the rate of economic development. (An example has already been seen in the time-series of Real Domestic Product given in Chapter 6.) But if over the period of comparison the inhabitants of the population have changed, we are not comparing like with like; we are comparing the consumptions of one group of people with that of another group, and apart

† In formal diagrammatic terms this can be 'proved' by drawing two identical sets of indifference curves which are not, however, iso-income elastic. Give one consumer a much larger real income than the other, but make the slope of the price-possibility line the same in both diagrams. Make the same price change in both diagrams and compute the 'true' cost of living index for them both: the index will not be found to be the same for the two consumers, hence, in the event that their relative money income had remained constant their relative *real income* must have changed as a result of the price change postulated.

from the general philosophical difficulties which this raises, it is obvious that the two groups may not have the same tastes. Thus even if we could somehow avoid being trapped into making implicit interpersonal comparisons of utility within a given population, as discussed in the previous paragraph, we shall be forced into interpersonal comparisons (as between the living and the dead) by the fact of a changing population. If we somehow avoid being bowled by the one difficulty we shall be caught in the slips off the other, or so the argument runs.

Finally we have a major difficulty which has a certain analogy to the one raised by the fact of the changing personal composition of the population of consumers; this is the difficulty raised by the fact of the changing composition of the list of commodities available. The index-number formulae which we have been discussing assume that the list of commodities $1 \ldots i \ldots n$ is identical in period 1 to what it was in period 0. Furthermore they measure the quantities $q_1 \ldots q_i \ldots q_n$ in standard units which are also identical in both periods. If that were not so, the comparisons would be mathematically meaningless since we should not be comparing like with like. But what is the standard unit of quantity when there are occurring constant changes in quality? We may of course define p_i, the price of coal, say, as the price of a standard grade of coal of standard calorific value, but as we have already seen, the procedure is quite impossible of application to commodities such as motor cars and television sets which are subject to regular improvements in appearance, and performance and design generally. And what is to be done about new commodities which were unheard of in year 0, but are now in regular production and consumption in year 1? These are no minor difficulties, for it may well be argued that the introduction of new products and of radical improvements in the design and number of variants available of existing products is in practice a more important factor in economic progress than is the normal secular increase in the consumption of existing products.

The Reality of the Preference System

The foregoing clearly represents a powerful array of sceptical arguments. What is their total implication? As arguments, each on ts own is clearly legitimate and effective, but nevertheless there is a considerable danger that in carrying their totality too far one arrives at a position where no quantitative measure of economic progress is possible whatsoever, either precise or imprecise. We may be left unable to say, for example, whether we think the rate of growth of output in the U.K. was faster or slower after 1947 as compared with the period before 1938. Or, in a comparison with the United States, we may find that although common observation suggests that the standard of living in that country is higher than in our own, we shall be unable to say whether we think the order of the difference is 25 per cent or 100 per cent, and so on. In actual fact, however, many of those who subscribe heavily to the full array of sceptical arguments as a matter of principle, nevertheless are happy to quote index-number comparisons in the course of their day-to-day economic, researches. The comparisons are usually based on a 'Laspeyres' type of formula, and there is usually some recognition that in a vague sense this type of index can be said to possess a certain bias, but it is regarded nevertheless as a useful 'rough and ready' measure of relatively unambiguous interpretation. What is not properly appreciated is that attractive as it may be to look on the matter in that fashion, the sceptical arguments upon which the fashion is based (as outlined above) logically carry one to a much more extreme position. If there exists no rational preference system in the mind of the consumer, there is no particular rationality in the bundle of commodities which the consumer happens to be buying in the base period; any set of weights for the index is as good as any other, and the Laspeyres' weights have no special standing whatsoever. Thus it seems to be the case that the half-way house position between the extreme of the sceptical argument on the one hand, and positive if qualified adherence to some form of formal theory of consumer preference (as a basis for the measurement of real income) on the other, is not really logically tenable. What then, can we do?

The issue is so important that it will be worth while further discussing the sceptical arguments in turn. The denial that a reasonably objective, rational and stable preference system exists in the mind of the consumer is clearly the most critical in the list and it is best examined by reference to the kind of experiment, imaginary or real, with which the contrary hypothesis might be tested. One possibility is that we attempt to draw up a real map of a real consumer's actual indifference curves by asking him an exhaustive series of questions about the ordering of his preferences as between a large number of alternative bundles of commodities. We arbitrarily specify one bundle (combination) which might be offered to him and treat this as the reference point on this consumer's reference curve (see above, page 238). We then specify some other bundle, which may contain more of all goods, less of all goods, or more of some and less of others, and we ask him whether quite irrespective of his money income and the prices of the goods, he would prefer to consume the first bundle to the second, or vice versa. We would repeat the process over and again with a very large number of different bundles, noting the answers by arrows indicating 'preferred to' or 'not preferred to' and in some cases also perhaps the answer 'indifferent between', on an indifference map. The dividing line between arrows indicating preference in one direction in relation to the reference-point bundle, and arrows pointing in the opposite direction, together with any two-way arrows indicating 'indifference', would give us the path of the reference indifference curve. We would then change the reference point to that of a bundle known to be preferred or not preferred to the original reference bundle and by a similar series of questions determine the path of the indifference curve passing through this second reference point; this curve would by definition represent a higher or lower level of real income (constant by implication all along its path) than the reference curve. In this way we could draw up a family of curves representing the contour map of this individual's preference system: we could then number off the curves in the manner which has been described previously. It is to be noted that the map has been constructed entirely by asking questions about preferences between quantitative bundles of commodities, with no reference to prices or income whatsoever; this therefore is a method which would be applicable in an economic system of any kind, including a system in which money was unknown and including the system of Robinson Crusoe.

If the results of the above-described experiment were to be taken as confirming the hypothesis of the existence of the preference system as required by our theory, they must satisfy at least the following minimum conditions:

(i) The subject should be able to give definite answers to the questions asked, over a wide enough range of alternative bundles to specify enough of the indifference map for the purpose in hand; the necessity of providing these answers should not drive him into a nervous breakdown nor alternatively into giving answers merely for the sake of saying something.

(ii) That if the same set of questions were repeated in a different order, he should give substantially the same answers, even though he had taken no written note of his original answers.

(iii) That if the same set of questions were repeated a few weeks afterwards (just long enough for him to have forgotten the first answers he gave) he should give substantially the same answers.

(iv) If within a short space of time after the experiment he were put into the position of having to make an actual choice between an alternative pair of bundles, the choice made should be consistent with the indifference map drawn up by the question and answer method, and similarly with other actual choices.

It seems sufficient merely to state these conditions in order to appreciate the hopelessness of the position if the problem is looked at in this way. If that is the only experiment to be considered, the sceptics must surely win hands down. No consumer would be remotely likely to conform.

But we can consider another type of experiment. Our theory assumes that the actual choice made by a consumer in any given circumstances of prices and income facing him is the choice which puts him on the highest level of preference possible in those circumstances. Hence by subjecting the consumer to a controlled series of variations in prices, his income and both, and by noting his choices in each situation we could, if the experiment were in practice possible, *deduce* the pattern of his indifference curves. The consumer having failed, in the first experiment, to be able to *tell* us the pattern, would instead have *revealed* it to us by his actions. However, the results plotted on our data sheet might not appear at all as do the indifference curves drawn in textbook diagrams; they would only so appear if the consumer's preference system was stable and rational in accordance with the theory. More specifically, if the results of the experiment were to be taken as confirming the hypothesis, the following minimum conditions would be required to correspond with those of page 269 above:

   (i) Indifference curves must not intersect and must in general be concave to the origin.

  (ii) The results must be independent of the order in which the various price and income changes are made.

 (iii) Repetitions of the experiment within a reasonably short space of time must yield reasonably similar results (if the results were very different, it could be said merely that 'tastes' had changed, but if 'tastes' are capricious and unstable to an extreme degree the fundamental theory is of little value).

 (iv) When faced with actual choices in actual, uncontrolled, price and income situations within a reasonably short time from the experiment, the consumer must choose consistently with the results (alternatively some way must be found of conducting the experiment so that the consumer does not know he is being experimented upon).

It is by no means so obvious that the results of this second kind of experiment, if one could be conducted, would be bound to be negative, i.e. that the conditions specified would not reasonably be met. But if the results of the second type of experiment are positive (to a reasonable extent) while the results of the first type are recognised to be certain to be negative, the implication is that although the preference system may be said to exist in some objective sense, it exists in the consumer's pre-conscious mind only. More precisely, we may imagine that the preference system is something implanted physiologically in the brain as a result of life's accumulated economic experience, much in the manner of the content of the 'memory' which is implanted in an electronic computing machine. However, it must be recognised that such a 'store' of preferences implanted in the consumer's brain cannot be brought up into his consciousness *in toto* at any one moment of time (any more than can the whole of his personal memory of past events), but can only be illuminated bit by bit as it were, in response to specific stimuli. These stimuli must be appropriate to the nature of the contents of the store, i.e. they must be the stimuli involved in the necessity of making an actual choice between alternative economic bundles: the preference system was built up by life's experience of continual confrontation with such decisions† and cannot therefore be illuminated by inappropriate stimuli, e.g. the asking of hypothetical questions involving no actual decisions, as in the first experiment.

However, even if the preference system is an entity of the nature just suggested and even if, when tested, it satisfies the minimum requirements for a positive conclusion from the second experiment, we are not of course freed from the proposition that some form of unconscious motivation in the psychological sense is involved in our theory. For, as experience feeds individual pairs of preferences into the store, some unconscious mechanism must be presumed to exist which sorts the totality into a consistent and rational pattern, such that the observed result in terms of actual consumer behaviour plots out a 'rational' family of indifference curves (concave, reasonably stable, non-intersecting, etc.). The argument between the sceptic and the positivist thus becomes a philosophical one, which may be summed up in the question 'Can a preference system which is partly or wholly unconsciously determined form a valid basis for deciding (e.g.) how much compensation ought to be paid a consumer in order to set off a rise in the cost of living? Is the welfare of the pre-conscious mind a matter of concern to the economist at all? These questions we shall not attempt to answer.

The philosophical questions apart, however, the reader may well

---

† A babe in arms has no preference system and a poor man who had never tasted either, would not be able to say whether he preferred a dozen oysters plus half a bottle of champagne or half a dozen oysters and a whole bottle of champagne.

T

argue that since neither of the experiments postulated could ever be carried out in practice, the whole discussion was entirely academic. But it is here that the conclusions we previously reached concerning the properties of the Fisher index assume their greatest significance. When there occurs a widespread change in prices, perhaps accompanied by a major change in money incomes, there has in effect occurred an incomplete and *un*controlled version of the second experiment.† In other words, consumers' reactions in terms of quantities purchased of the various commodities can be observed and measured, and a certain amount of information about particular points in the indifference system is thus thrown up. But, because prices were not held constant when income changed, nor income constant when prices changed,‡ and because in any case the total number of changes was probably only a small proportion of those which would be required to reveal a substantial part of a whole preference system, the information obtained in these circumstances represents no more than a fitful and possibly deceptive gleam of moonlight thrown on to an otherwise blacked-out landscape. But here is the crux. We have discovered in the preceding sections that on certain assumptions ('neutrality', reasonable approximation to the quadratic form, etc.) we do not need to know the details of the whole of our landscape in order to deduce the 'true' index of real income which the landscape embodies: if we can accept certain assumptions as to the general form of the landscape, we need only certain limited information—to wit the information involved in the computation of the Fisher index—to obtain our estimate. The gleam of moonlight is sufficient. To put the point in another way; in the circumstances envisaged, the partial experiment of computing the Fisher index, which is a practical experiment, yields all the required information. This is the real basis of the case for using the Fisher index: the case stands or falls, of course, on the validity of the assumptions made.

The Distribution Conundrum

We have now to consider the second main group of sceptical

† P. 269 above.
‡ 'Econometric' studies of demand curves attempt to overcome the difficulty by highly developed forms of the methods discussed in Chapter 7.

arguments, those based on the fact that changes in relative prices inevitably involve changes in the interpersonal (or better, inter-family) distribution of real income and hence entangle the theory in the problem of interpersonal comparisons. The difficulty, as far as we are here concerned, is more practical than theoretical. For we could validly argue that the narrow objective of the statistician, ideally, was solely that of measuring the changes which occur in the real income of each individual or family in society, real income being defined as previously. It would then be for society as a whole to decide what weight to ascribe to each family's experience when assessing the nation's general economic progress; whether or not, for example, to make the 'democratic' assumption that all are to be regarded in this sense as equal. The real income of each individual would be assessed on some standardised basis† and then the 'economic welfare' of society could be regarded as some function (in the mathematical sense)—known in the jargon of the subject as a Social Welfare Function‡—of the thus measured changes in the real incomes of all the individuals or families within the society. The actual form of the Social Welfare Function could of course change with the times and change also with the prevailing political sentiments: the Social Welfare Function implied by the existence of a Labour Government would give disproportionate weight to changes in the real incomes of families whose absolute level of real income was low; that implied by the existence of a Conservative Government, vice versa, and so on. The 'democratic' function where all are regarded as equal is thus a special case.

Therefore, as a statistical problem this is essentially a practical one: the statistician cannot possibly in the normal course of events compute a separate Fisher index for each of the 15 million families in say the U.K. Yet if he contents himself with compu-ting a single, general, index only, based on observed market prices and national aggregate consumption data, the result may

† It would be necessary in principle to identify some arbitrarily chosen *reference consumer* and define for this consumer a reference curve in the manner described on page 238. Then the reference curve of every other consumer would be identified in such a way that at some point in its path it passed through the identical bundle of commodities as the bundle indicated at the reference point on the reference curve of the reference consumer.

‡ See fn. p. 239.

be accurate only for a small section of families who happen to be 'representative' in all relevant respects, i.e. in all their tastes and real incomes. (This is another way of stating the proposition that changes in relative prices always embody changes in the distribution of real income; a general index is inaccurate, because real income distribution having changed, individual families' experienced changes do not conform to the average). Therefore, the statistician, official or unofficial, in providing one index only is concealing from the politician facts of considerable importance required for his, the politician's, proper assessment of the effect of his economic policies. What the statistician should do, although he very rarely does, is to divide the population of families into groups, each group being thought to be relatively homogeneous in regard to tastes and incomes, and he should then collect the data necessary to compute the Fisher index separately for each group. In this manner he may hope to reduce considerably the errors with which we are here concerned. It may be objected that no group can be completely homogeneous and that the summary indexes computed for the groups may conceal important and significant variations (in the change in real income) within them. However, it is to be remembered that the difficulty we are concerned with arises basically from two causes, the first that the preference systems of individual families are differently shaped and the second that individual families find themselves at different real-income positions within their own system, i.e. are possessed of different standards of living. And it seems plausible that the second cause is likely to be the dominating cause of the two; if so, the position is apparently less discouraging, for it is relatively easy, as a matter of practice, to divide families into fairly fine income groupings. It would also appear possible then to make some further subdivision within income groups according to observed (major) differences in taste patterns. But unfortunately variations in the shape of the preference system of families within groups may mean, of course, that families with the same *money* income will experience different real income, even in face of a common set of prices; this in turn may lead to differences in the observed consumption pattern over and above those attributable to the difference in tastes. Thus the observed difference in the consumption pattern of two families with the same money income in face of a common set of prices is partly the result of the basic difference in tastes and secondarily the result of a difference in real income itself caused by the difference in tastes. Hence there is bound to be a certain amount of ambiguity in any attempt further to subdivide the income groups according to differences in taste. The ambiguity would only disappear completely if we knew the entire preference system of each family; and if we knew this there would be no problem anyway. However, if families are divided into income groups and then into subdivisions according to leading objective sociological characteristics (size of family, part of the country, age and religion of parents, occupation and so on)—these being the factors which are probably responsible for a large proportion of the grossest of the differences in 'taste'—it seems likely that the errors theoretical and practical involved in the ambiguity referred to would be reduced to a relatively low level. There remain of course the errors attributable to purely individual idiosyncrasies, quite unconnected with objective social factors, of which much the most glaring examples are the differences in the desire for habit-forming commodities such as drink and tobacco. Simply because they are habit-forming, these commodities tend to break up the population into sharply divided groups of smokers and non-smokers, heavy drinkers and light drinkers, and so on. Examples of such sort are fairly readily identifiable and can be allowed for by obvious sub-groupings, but there will be many others less obvious. Furthermore, it will be seen that as a practical proposition in the organisational sense, even the sort of grouping we have been so far discussing would involve great labour, since the permutations and combinations of income group and social subgroup would be enormous. Indeed the several hundred separate Fisher indexes with which the politician would thus be provided would merely bemuse, rather than inform him. Hence in practice very much cruder groupings must be used. This is not to say, however, that the present practice of computing officially only one single index for the whole community is in any way to be condoned.

With only relatively broad groupings (e.g. simply, say, three or four ranges of money income, and two or three of family size) the danger of inaccuracy due to interfamily variation in experience within the group would appear to be more serious. Here however one of our now familiar cancelling-out propositions can provide some assistance. For the extent to which the precise index number appropriate to a given individual with given tastes differs from the index computed for some group of individuals of which he is a member must depend not only on the extent to which his tastes differ from those which are representative of the group, but also on the correlation, commoditywise, of the deviations in his tastes (from the group average) with the changes in prices which happen to have occurred: even if his tastes differ considerably from that of the group, his index will not be in error unless, in general, it is the things which he likes most, relatively to the group, that have risen most in price and those he likes least which have fallen relatively in price, or vice versa. Such correlation may of course arise by chance —particularly if his main taste deviations are concentrated on a relatively small number of commodities—but nevertheless the effect of this cancelling-out proposition is that the danger of error from individual idiosyncrasies of taste is less serious than might at first have appeared. The danger diminishes, of course, the finer the subdivision of the population into groups which is found possible.

The Chain Index

The remaining arguments from the sceptical list can be taken together as they are closely related in theory and the same statistical device may be used in the attempt to overcome them. It will be remembered that the arguments derive from the facts of a changing population of consumers, a changing list of the economic commodities known to consumers and a secular tendency to changing qualitative content of the standard units of existing commodities. The theoretical connection between these three problems is as follows. If, for example, new commodities appear on the market, the ordinary index number formula must ignore them, since the formula must in logic relate to the same list of commodities in its denominator as in its numerator. Thus the list of quantities $Q_{11} \ldots Q_{i1} \ldots Q_{n1}$ included in an aggregate such as $\Sigma Q_{i1} P_{i0}$ (the top line of the Laspeyres volume index) can obviously involve only quantities of commodities for which a P_{i0} exists, i.e. commodities which were known, priced and consumed in period o. The difficulty over changes in quality is analogous; index number formulae must employ the same standard units for measuring quantities of the specified commodities in numerator and denominator, and in many cases the distinction between describing the result of some specific economic innovation as the case of an appearance of a 'new commodity' and describing it as a major improvement of an existing commodity is inevitably somewhat arbitrary. (Television is a new commodity compared with sound radio but is colour television a new commodity or 'improvement in quality' of black and white television?) Thus for one reason or another, either in a price index or a quantity index, be it Laspeyres, Paasche† or Fisher, a significant part of the fruits of economic development is likely to be excluded from the calculation. However, at this point the reader may well ask whether there is not some cancelling-out proposition which might come to our assistance in the now familiar manner. The appearance of new commodities evidently involves change in the shape of the preference system, a change in tastes in effect, and hence would appear to be capable of causing bias only if the disturbances are correlated, commoditywise, with the changes in prices which occur. In other words there will be no bias if the changes in prices of the new commodities are on average much the same as those of commodities in general. But this proposition does not help us, for new commodities, almost by definition, are known to show an atypical price development; their prices will fall more, or rise less, than those of commodities in general. The point can be seen more graphically by consideration of the case of the quantity index, where it is required that for no bias to occur, the *quantities* produced and consumed of the new commodities must change in the same proportion and in the same direction as those of the old, which is obviously absurd. Hence the difficulty is elemental.

† It is a fallacy to imagine that the Paasche index avoids the problem. The formula for the volume index is $\Sigma P_{i1}Q_{i1}/\Sigma P_{i1}Q_{i0}$ and therefore the index cannot include any commodity for which no quantity figure exists in period o; or to see the matter more clearly, the price index is $\Sigma Q_{i1}P_{i1}/\Sigma Q_{i1}P_{i0}$, the bottom line of which is the same as the top line of the Laspeyres' volume index and therefore can only include commodities for which a P_{i0} existed and was known.

It is in fact the difficulty over new commodities that is the real cause of the difficulty over the changing population (although the point is not widely appreciated in the literature). If the list of commodities were fixed, the changing population 'problem' is no more and no less than the general difficulty over interpersonal comparisons of welfare and we have seen that so long as we confine ourselves to attempting to measure real income, in contrast to utility, or satisfaction, or what have you, the problem only arises to the extent that different individuals possess different tastes and the differences in tastes happen to be correlated commoditywise with the changes in prices which happen to occur. (The proposition is equally valid as regards the comparison of two time-separated populations of the same country as to comparisons between two space-separated populations of different countries.)† But, unfortunately, there is every reason to suppose that such correlation will in fact be the normal rule, because the most striking differences in taste between the old population and the new will obviously be those relating to the 'new' commodities and will therefore be biased in the manner just described. When our parents complain that 'everything' seems to have become more expensive relatively as well as absolutely since the days when they were young, they do not take account of what has happened to the prices of 'new fangled' commodities that in their parents' day hardly existed. Hence, any 'solution' of the problem of the changing population of consumers is closely bound up with the solution of that of the changing list of commodities. In fact we cannot completely solve either problem,

† Index number comparisons of real income can be, and frequently are, made between countries: 'Period o' becomes 'country A' and 'Period 1' becomes 'country B': see for example Gilbert and Kravis, 'An International Comparison of National Product and the Purchasing Power of Currencies', OEEC, Paris, 1954. (2nd ed. believed in preparation, 1957.)

In international comparisons, there is always available the choice of weighting systems in either the relative prices or the relative quantities of country A or of country B, exactly analogous to the difference between Laspeyres and Paasche in the intertemporal comparison and indeed it is in these international examples that some of the most startling differences in the results obtained with the two types of index number are in fact observed. Most of what has been said in this book about the theory of index numbers in relation to intertemporal comparisons can be taken over without substantial modification for the interspatial case. The major conceptual difficulties are those being discussed in connection with changing population, above.

but with the aid of a *Chain Index* we can considerably reduce the errors arising from both. In order to compute a Chain Index we divide our given period of comparison into a number of sub-periods. For each sub-period we compute a separate index number, with the first year of the period as 100 and using the list of all commodities available to the consumer in that year. New commodities, therefore, will not be included in the index for the sub-period during which they were introduced, but they will be included in the index for the immediately subsequent sub-period. Thus if we wished to make an index-number comparison over a period, say of 27 years, we would subdivide into three overlapping *ten*-year periods A, B, and C representing years 0 to 9 inclusive, 9 to 18 inclusive, and 18 to 27 inclusive, respectively; then any new commodities coming on to the market in period A would be included in the index for period B, but excluded of course from that for period A, and conversely for commodities which disappear from the market, and so on. These index numbers for sub-periods can then be linked together into a chain capable of providing an estimate of the total change over the whole period: the actual form of the sub-indices computed from the relevant price and quantity data would of course depend on the desired form, in principle, of the final index, Laspeyres', Paasche or Fisher. Evidently, from what has been said earlier, the ideal arrangement is a chain of Fisher indexes. The linking of the chain is done as follows:

Computation of Chain Index
Year 0 to Year 27, year 0 = 100

Index number for last year of A (= first year of B, = year 9)
with year 0 = 100, say   110

Index number for last year of B (= first year of C, = year 18)
with year 9 = 100, say   115

Index number for last year of C (= last year of whole period,
= year 27), year 18 = 100, say   105

Total Index $= 100 \times 1 \cdot 10 \times 1 \cdot 15 \times 1 \cdot 05 = 133$

More formally, supposing that the full list of commodities available to the consumer in each of the relevant years can be listed by number as follows:

commodities available

year 0	$1 \ldots i \ldots n$
year 9	$1 \ldots i \ldots n \ldots p$
year 18	$1 \ldots i \ldots n \ldots p \ldots q$
year 27	$1 \ldots i \ldots n \ldots p \ldots q \ldots s$

The new commodities introduced in period A, for example, are then those after commodity n up to and including commodity p, and so on, it being assumed for simplicity that no commodities disappear. Then suppose also for simplicity that it is desired to compute a *Laspeyres' chain index of prices* for the whole twenty-seven year period, that is to say it is desired to compute by how much in some sense the level of prices rose between year 0 and year 27. Using the above notation, the formula for the complete chain index, i.e. the index number for the year 27 with year 0 conceptually as 100 would be

$$\frac{\sum\limits_{1}^{n} Q_0 P_9}{\sum\limits_{1}^{n} Q_0 P_0} \times \frac{\sum\limits_{1}^{p} Q_9 P_{18}}{\sum\limits_{1}^{p} Q_9 P_9} \times \frac{\sum\limits_{1}^{q} Q_{18} P_{27}}{\sum\limits_{1}^{q} Q_{18} P_{18}} =, \text{ in the example, } 133.$$

It may seem evident intuitively that the above method must reduce the error with which we are concerned, but the formal argument is less obvious than might be supposed. For each sub-index will still contain error—not so bad as treating an Austin A35 as equivalent to an old pre-war Austin 7, perhaps, but nevertheless still treating an A35 as on a par with an A30 and ignoring the significant superiority of the former over the latter—and it would seem that these errors must accumulate, and bias the final index accordingly. The point, however, is that the likely error in an index from the cause under discussion will vary, *inter alia* with the unrepresentativeness of the list of commodities included; the error will be zero if the index included all commodities known both at the end and at the beginning of the period (which can only be the case if no new commodities are marketed) and will be likely to be large if at the end of the period consumer expenditure on new commodities not included in the index is a large proportion of total expenditure. Thus assuming for simplicity that all commodities have equal weights so that the proportion of excluded expenditure to total expenditure is the same as the proportion of the *number* of excluded commodities to the total number of commodities on the market, and assuming also for simplicity that new commodities are introduced at an even rate over time, then it can be seen that the error in the index for period A will vary directly with $\frac{1}{2}\left(\frac{p-n}{p}\right)$, in period B with $\frac{1}{2}\left(\frac{q-p}{q}\right)$ and in $C, \frac{1}{2}\left(\frac{s-q}{s}\right)$. The error in the total index will then depend approximately on the *average* of the errors in these three periods, i.e. on $\frac{1}{6}\left(\frac{p-n}{p}+\frac{q-p}{q}+\frac{s-q}{s}\right)$. But the error in the total index had not the chain method not been used would evidently have varied with $\frac{1}{2}\left(\frac{s-n}{s}\right)$ and the reader does not need to have it explained why the latter ratio is much larger than the former. An index computed over a long period, without chaining, can only relate to commodities which were known at the beginning of the period and in some cases these may by the end of the period account for no more than perhaps 50 per cent of total actual consumers' expenditure; hence such an index may well be grossly biased.

Nevertheless the foregoing algebra demonstrates only too clearly that no chain index can completely eliminate the error. The residual error will be smaller the greater the number of sub-periods into which the main period is divided, but could only be eliminated completely if the sub-periods were infinite in number, i.e. zero in length, in which case no changes of price or quantity could occur in them whatsoever, the *reductio ad absurdum* in this matter. Thus any index number, even if 'chained', will tend to possess some bias from the group of causes we are here considering. The magnitude of the bias is not easy to estimate and may vary from country to country or from time to time. One might imagine that it would be greater in countries or periods in which economic innovation and technical progress are notoriously rapid, as for instance in the United States in the early part of the twentieth century, and less in countries and times which are more conservative. The last proposition however may be true in an absolute sense but not perhaps in a relative sense, and hence less disturbing if only comparative measurements are required. For the rapidly innovating economies will also be rapidly growing economically generally, and hence will also tend to demonstrate a faster rate of growth of production of existing commodities (as well as of new commodities) than the more conservative economies. The real difficulty arises if, of two countries with the same underlying rate of economic growth, one shows a preference for growing by expansion of existing commodities, the other mainly by the development of new ones.

The time series of U.K. Real Domestic product, given in Table 8 of Chapter 6, was constructed so as to possess the essential properties of a chain index, although, as already explained, the methods of estimation employed were somewhat rough and ready.

Conclusions

We have seen that index numbers are essential for the measurement of changes in real income of an individual or a society, and we have seen that real income is something whose changes may be measurable independently of any belief in the existence and measurability of Utility, Satisfaction or Economic Welfare. But we have seen that the use of index numbers for the purpose involves intellectual acceptance, explicit or implicit, of a rational theory of consumers' preference. And we have seen that such a theory leads inevitably to the conclusion that either the Laspeyres' type of index or the Paasche type of index employed alone, will yield biased estimates of the change in real income as the theory has defined it. The bias will vary from time to time according to several factors, of which the most important is the dispersion of the changes in relative prices. We can take account of the bias by feeding in to our calculation the combined information yielded by computation of both indexes, i.e. by computing the Fisher index. Consistent bias also arises from the introduction of new commodities and from the changing quality of existing commodities; this can partly, but not entirely, be reduced by the method of chaining. The reader must decide for himself where he stands in the debate between sceptic and positivist which has been outlined, i.e. he must decide for himself whether he accepts the positivist theory sufficiently to accept these summary conclusions. But it is safe to wager that if he continues to maintain interest in economic affairs at all, he will continue regularly to make use in one way or another of economic measurements in index-number form and it is hoped that the two chapters which are here concluded will have helped a little to clear his mind as to the nature of the intellectual process involved in so doing. He may, if he wishes, suppress in his mind the logical conclusion that there is no satisfactory compromise between, on the one hand, the acceptance of at least the substance of the theory which has been outlined and on the other, root and branch scepticism; but he should never forget that essentially the whole of, or nearly the whole of the index number 'problem' arises from the Achilles heel of positive economics itself, that is from the fact that the thing which it is the objective of Political Economy to improve —Economic Welfare—is a thing which cannot directly be measured.

CHAPTER TEN

MEASUREMENT OF CHANGES IN THE REAL NATIONAL PRODUCT

WHAT we have learned in Chapter 9 is a method of measuring the change in the real income of a single consumer or group of consumers, associated with a specified set of changes in the quantities of commodities which he or they consume, personal savings being ignored. In the present chapter we shall consider to what extent it is possible to extend the analysis over the whole range of the national production, the latter including, as we know, not only consumer goods but also investment goods and the products of the Government Sector. What meaning, if any, can we attach to a concept of real *national* income, or real national product, and how, given such meaning, may the measurement be made? An obvious difficulty is one which we have already fairly extensively discussed —the inevitability of changes in the interpersonal distribution of income during the course of almost any economic change†, but apart from this it would appear at first sight that our present task is merely to compute an ordinary volume index—Laspeyres, Paasche or Fisher as the case may be—covering all the economic goods and services which the Gross National Product comprises. We could work either from the expenditure side or from the production side in the former case we would construct a volume index of the production and consumption of all final goods, in the latter case a volume index of total industrial, agricultural, commercial and government production. However, we shall soon see how deceptively facile is this specification, and we shall discover that the poser connected with distribution‡ is by no means the most formidable

† See Chapter 9, pp. 264 *et seq*.
‡ It would be convenient if we could in some way distinguish a change in the capacity of the economy to produce commodities, before distribution, from the consequent change in distributed real income itself. But except in special

of the many difficulties both theoretical and practical which in fact are involved. In this chapter therefore we shall ignore the distribution question entirely and concentrate on difficulties as yet undiscussed: in effect, we shall assume conditions where all consumers' tastes are identical, or alternatively where price changes are always neutral in respect of distribution.

The National Income Blue Book presents estimates of Real Product and Expenditure in two tables, which have briefly been referred to in Chapter 4, under the general heading of 'output and expenditure at constant prices'. The first Blue Book table in reference gives data relating to the main constituent items of Total Domestic Expenditure† valued at constant base-year prices; the table then proceeds by adding data concerning exports and deducting for imports to an estimate of Real Gross Domestic Product measured from the expenditure side. The figures in this table are not presented as index numbers in ratio form but as a collection of series such as,

Year 0	Year 1	Year 2	Year 3	Year n
$\Sigma P_0 Q_0$	$\Sigma P_0 Q_1$	$\Sigma P_0 Q_2$	$\Sigma P_0 Q_3$	$\Sigma P_0 Q_n$

one series for each of the main components of Final Expenditure, one for exports, one for imports and one each for the two aggregates. The presentation thus provides the material from which any desired volume-index number of any one of the components or of the aggregates can be computed as desired, and at the same time indicates clearly how the figure for total Real Domestic Product at the bottom of the table is arrived at.

The second table provides a measurement of Real Domestic Product taken from the production side, and consists of a set of volume index numbers of the changes in output of the various productive industries and sectors of which the economy is composed, together with a weighted average of same—the index of Domestic Product itself. The latter, as printed, displays a slightly different

circumstances we cannot. Changes in productive efficiency rarely occur equally for all industries, and differential changes will benefit different families differentially unless all families posses the same tastes: thus improvements in the technique of pram production are of little benefit to the childless.

† The reader is advised to refer again to Diagram II of Chapter 3, to be found at the end of the book.

movement from that of the index taken from the expenditure side
on account of statistical discrepancies: in principle, of course, both
movements should be numerically identical. We shall discuss first
the measurement from the expenditure side and then shall pass to
the production side. We shall find that most of the fundamental
conceptual problems can be covered in the former discussion:
difficulties which are specific to the measurement from the production side tend to be more of a technical nature.

Conceptual Problems in the Measurement of Total Domestic Expenditure

The centre of the difficulty we are up against is that the theory of
economic index numbers which we worked out in the previous
chapter is only directly applicable to about 60 per cent† of our
aggregate. The theory was based on a specific conception of consumers' behaviour, postulating families freely determining the
amounts of the various commodities they would buy given the
prices asked: these postulates are hardly relevant to the circumstances of a business man ordering a piece of new machinery, and
still less to those involved in the production and consumption of
'government' commodities such as education. Therefore our most
immediate task is to answer some fundamental questions:

(1) What do we really mean by saying we desire to include, for
example, investment expenditure, since investment, by
definition, contributes nothing to the current standard of
living?

(2) Government expenditure consists of Defence, Health services, Education services, Basic services (e.g. Roads) and
general administration:

(a) Should these things be regarded as contributing directly
to the current standard of living or should they rather be
regarded as types of expenditure necessary for the standard
of living to be maintained, i.e. should they be regarded
not as final output, but, in effect, as a form of input?

† This is the proportion of consumers' expenditure in Total Domestic
Expenditure at market prices.

(*b*) How can we determine proper units in which to measure the 'quantity' of the output (or input) of these things? (What is a 'unit' of education?)

(3) What principles of weighting should we employ?

The answers to the questions are of course considerably inter-related, thus the principles of weighting will follow logically from the principles of inclusion. Also notice that question 2(*b*) is part of a wider problem which concerns many similar 'services' items in ordinary family consumption expenditure (services of professional men such as lawyers, or services of the entertainment industry). We will consider the questions in order.

Investment Expenditure and the Capacity Concept of Real Product

Obviously investment expenditure cannot be included in Domestic Expenditure as expenditure contributing directly to the current standard of living; should it then be ignored altogether? But to do so would yield an extremely deceptive picture of the real situation of a nation, say, which deliberately chose to increase the proportion of productive resources devoted to investment: we would observe an apparent fall in real income as defined in Chapter 9, but we should have no indication as to whether the change were due to a reduction in economic efficiency or to the real cause. We are led inevitably therefore into an attempt to include investment and other similar items on some principle which aims at measuring rather the *capacity* of the economy to produce real income, in contrast to the level of current real income actually obtaining. Hence, before considering our specific problem we must examine the groundwork for a 'capacity' concept as such.

Postulate an entirely imaginary economy in which there exist the classical conditions for the optimum distribution of economic resources between uses to be brought about entirely by the automatic functioning of market mechanisms—the 'optimum' distribution being that which maximises real income with given aggregate resources. (The familiar conditions are that there should be perfect competition in all markets for commodities and for factors of pro-

u

duction, perfect mobility of factors between employments and constant returns to scale in all industries; together with such institutional arrangements as may be necessary to avoid all other possible causes of discrepancy between marginal social and marginal private cost.) Also assume that consumers have identical tastes as depicted by the indifference curves of the usual simplified two-commodity example (Diagram IV below) in which one important commodity is plotted on the x-axis against money spent on

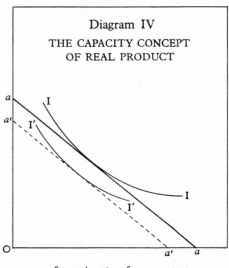

For explanation of axes, see text

all other commodities plotted on the y-axis, the diagram symbolising a general multi-commodity preference system. For the moment assume no investment. In the conditions assumed, the selling price of every commodity will be equal to the marginal cost of its production so that the price-possibility line, *aa*, with which consumers are actually faced, also represents the relation between the marginal costs of production of the commodities, given the current rates of reward of factors of production required to produce them. Conversely all the factors of production are paid rewards which represent the value of their marginal products according to these prices. Thus the line not only indicates the actual alternatives

available to the consumers as individuals, but—if the diagram be
'blown up' to the national scale—it also indicates all the alternative
commodity-patterns of production open to the nation with given
total resources of labour, capital, enterprise and land: as resources
are transferred from producing commodities in general to the production of the commodity depicted on the *x*-axis, the production
of this commodity will increase slowly or rapidly according to the
relative efficiency (marginal productivity) of resources when employed in the one use than in the other; if it is easy to increase the
output of the commodity, relatively to that of commodities in
general, *Oa* on the *x*-axis will be large relatively to *Oa* on the *y*-
axis, and vice versa. So the price-possibility line is also a representation of the production-transformation curve of the economy
(it is straight only because we have assumed constant returns). Thus
the consumer, in exercising his demands in the market so as to
place himself on the line and on the highest possible indifference
curve, is also bringing about a distribution of productive resources
which provides him with the maximum real income of which the
economy is capable at any moment of time. This maximum is the
capacity of the economy. Where *aa* cuts the *y*-axis, the line *Oa*
measures the total cost of the factors of production required to produce the capacity output, which is the total income of the factors
of production of the nation under the conditions when they are
fully and optimally employed (National Expenditure = National
Product = National Income; *Oa* is the Gross National Product).

How may the capacity be measured, or, at least how may changes
in capacity be measured? Capacity real income is the real income
associated with the indifference curve reached when the economy
is working at capacity in the sense defined; in the diagram this is
the real income associated with the indifference curve *II*. In principle therefore changes may be measured by means of the index-
number technique developed in Chapter 9. Thus, suppose capacity
expands, for example on account of a general improvement of
technical knowledge, *aa* would shift outwards and the consumer
would find a new equilibrium on a higher indifference curve:
the alternative 'true' index numbers† of the consequent improve-

† See pp. 254 *et seq.*, Chapter 9.

ment in real income would be either $\mathbf{T}_0$, the ratio to Oa of the intercept on the y-axis of a line parallel to aa but tangential to the new indifference curve, or $\mathbf{T}_1$, the corresponding ratio between the intercept of the new price-possibility line and the intercept of a line parallel to it, tangential to the old indifference curve. If aa happened to advance without changing its slope (i.e. technical improvements were uniform in all industries) both true measures would be identical and the index number measurement of the improvement would be the ratio of the new price-possibility line's intercept to Oa itself. This index number would also measure the change in real national product considered as capacity. In this special case the extent of the improvement in real income-producing capacity would depend entirely on the extent of the improvement in technical efficiency, but in all other cases the position is more complicated. Suppose aa twisted as it advanced, e.g. because the improvement was heavily concentrated on the industry producing the commodity depicted on the x-axis, then the level of the new indifference curve reached, and the index number measure of real income improvement, would depend also on the shape of the preference system: if the commodity in question were a popular commodity so that the indifference curves ran steeply down from left to right, the improvement in real income would be large, and if to the contrary, small. (An improvement in efficiency is valueless if it occurs in an industry for whose products there is no demand.) Thus economic capacity is not something which is exclusively determined by purely technical factors and its rate of improvement can be broken down into the following four distinct elements (1) the rate of increase of total resources available (population, stock of capital, etc.), (2) the average rate of improvement of the technical productive efficiency of these resources, and (3) the industrial pattern of the technical improvements in relation to (4) the commodity pattern of the consumer preference system. In the general case, where a large number of commodities is considered, there may be come cancelling out, so that cases where large relative improvements occur in industries producing strongly preferred commodities may be offset by cases where the reverse occurs. If the cancelling out is perfect, the effect on the index-number measurement is to produce a result much as if the price-possibility line had in fact shifted without twisting, a case which we will term that of a neutral advance. In the analysis which follows we shall for the time being work on the assumption that all advances are indeed neutral; an assumption which may be less unrealistic than it seems so long as we are considering relatively long analytical periods, long enough for resources of capital as well as labour to move into any use.

From the above groundwork we may now return to the problem of investment. If economic resources are pre-empted for investment purposes, the current level of consumption is reduced from the level indicated by capacity. Capacity remains as depicted by aa in Diagram IV (until such time as it is increased by the additions to capital stock from the investment), but the consumption-possibility alternatives are now reduced to those depicted by a line say, $a'a'$, (parallel to aa unless the resources diverted to investment are highly specific to the production of certain types of consumer goods) and the sacrifice involved may be measured by the index number of the consequent reduction of real income on to the indifference curve $I'I'$. On the assumptions made, this is indicated by the ratio of Oa' to Oa (on the y-axis). The *difference* between Oa' and Oa is the value, in £'s at constant prices, of the consumer goods given up for the present in order to provide for the future.

Here is a critical point. Suppose capacity increases, shifting aa uniformly. Some shift in $a'a'$ will also probably occur, depending on how much of the improvement is devoted to investment and how much to consumption: if the ratio of investment in the national product is in some sense kept constant, the proportionate increase in the intercept of $a'a'$ will be the same as that of aa, but otherwise not, and here is our problem. For we wish to measure the increase of capacity real income, i.e. of aa, and not of actual real income, $a'a'$. But it is in fact the increase of $a'a'$, in terms of consumer expenditure, which we can straightforwardly observe and measure. What we need to do therefore is to find some method of adjusting the movement of $a'a'$ so as to provide an estimate of the movement of aa, in other words to allow for the change in the volume of consumer goods sacrificed for investment. The change in question is the change in the quantity of consumer goods which could be produced with the economic resources devoted to investment, which is not necessarily the same thing as the change in the volume of investment goods themselves produced. However, on the highly rarefied assumptions with which we are for the moment operating, all is well. Resources are assumed to be paid exactly the value of their marginal products, whether in investment goods or consumption goods and, in a perfect market for resources (factors), like resources must be paid everywhere the same, so that the value of the marginal product of the marginal unit of resources in the investment goods industries must equal the value of the marginal product of the same unit if transferable to consumption goods, and vice versa. Hence, for marginal changes, the market prices of the investment goods can be used to weight investment goods in a general index of change in productive capacity just as if they were consumption goods; by including investment goods in real domestic expenditure weighted by the prices business men are prepared to pay for them (which is exactly what is done in the Blue Book), we include them, in effect, as an identity with the potential consumer goods sacrificed in producing them. The same principle can be applied to any other item of expenditure which pre-empts economic resources but cannot be described as a consumer good contributing to current real income.

The weakness of the foregoing argument lies obviously in the assumptions on which it is based. Perfect competition does not exist, and the degree of imperfection varies from industry to industry. Prices are neither equal nor proportional to marginal costs, factors are immobile and the markets for them also highly imperfect. Furthermore, the argument only relates to marginal changes and can hardly be valid if applied for example to the circumstances in which the level of investment were, say, doubled: there is no reason whatsoever to believe that £3,000 millions of investment goods production as a whole could facilely be converted into precisely £3,000 millions worth of consumer goods, or vice versa, even in the long run. Fortunately, however, rapid changes of such magnitude are rare, and the changes in the proportion of investment to the national product which typically occur within the period of a statistical index-number measurement are more of the type which could reasonably be described as marginal. And over longer periods some relief may be obtained by chaining. Very large *differences* in the degree of monopoly as between industries may be less common than is sometimes supposed (if the degree of monopoly is everywhere the same the effect is much akin to that of perfect competition) and many of the industries which produce investment goods also make consumer goods, and vice versa, so that resources may be less specific to the two types of production than at first sight would appear.†

Our conclusion then is that in including investment in our assessment of Real National Product and Expenditure we are (deliberately) moving towards a 'capacity' concept of the measurement: we are measuring changes not in consumer real income‡ itself, but in potential consumer real income—the standard of living which would be attained if all the economic resources of the community were devoted to current consumption. On this basis we find that it is not unreasonable to include investment goods in the aggregate volume index of Total Domestic Expenditure, weighted according to the market prices business men are observed to pay for them.

Government Expenditure: Output or Input?

There are, it will be remembered, two questions, the first concerned with the principles on which these items should be included, the second with problems of actual measurement. In the U.K.,

† The most serious case is probably that of the building and construction industries, which usually supply about half the annual output of investment goods, make no consumer goods and are atypical in economic development. Residents of the U.K. in particular would be extremely sceptical of any suggestion that the annual earnings of the labour and management employed in the nation's construction industries bears much relation to what these factors would be able to obtain if transferred elsewhere. However, even the sharp economic changes which occurred between 1948 and 1955, more than doubling the volume of 'real' net domestic investment, did no more than raise the proportion of constructional investment in the Domestic Product (at constant prices) from 6 per cent to 8 per cent.

‡ It should be remembered that we are using the expression 'real income' in a rather special sense (see Chapter 9). Strictly we mean 'real consumption', or alternatively we assume that consumer savings are zero. The latter would be reconcilable with the existence of positive net investment if we assumed that all the net saving of the community was done from undistributed profits.

at the present time, government consumption is presented in the Blue Book tables as accounting for about 16 per cent of total final Domestic Expenditure; about half is expenditure on Defence, about one third is the cost of social services (divided between the Health Service on the one hand and Education and miscellaneous services on the other in about equal proportions) and the remainder is the expenses of 'general administration', maintenance of basic services and etc. Each of these groups presents its own special problems. The pattern is not typical: in other countries or at other times in the history of the U.K., the share of defence would normally be considerably smaller and so also that of the social services; (relatively few western capitalist countries possess a general state health service, although most provide general state education.)

Fairly obviously, there are strong arguments for regarding the value of the services of Health, Education and to some extent social insurance, as exactly on a par with private consumer expenditure, contributing directly to the standard of living of the citizens in the sense that if the services were not provided by the state, many citizens would be prepared to purchase them privately. If these services are commodities which in certain circumstances the private citizen would purchase in the ordinary way, their consumption, even if organised by the state, must be regarded as a direct contribution to consumer real income. If not, we would reach the absurd position that expenditure on the fees of private schools would be treated as part of Final Expenditure, while the cost of running the state schools was not; and when the U.K. 'nationalised' the country's health services, the national standard of living would have appeared to fall by the whole amount of the value of the services taken over.† Nevertheless, despite the evident power of these arguments, quite a good case can be made for regarding items such as Education, in particular, not as components to the current standard of living but rather as 'investment'

† The Act was passed in 1948 and between that year and the next the Blue Book indicates a considerable increase in government expenditure on Current Goods and Services while the item in Consumer's Personal Expenditure which previously contained payments to doctors, hospitals and, etc., instead of rising with the general trend, actually fell.

for the future. Education, by and large, is (or should be) under-taken to benefit children rather than to gratify parents and it is certainly noticeable that in countries where the state does not pro-vide free education, relatively little is spent. Health services, on the other hand, do not provide pleasure but ward off pain. They do not contribute to the standard of living, they keep us sufficiently healthy to earn it and to enjoy it. When there is an epidemic of influenza in the middle of the winter which sets doctors and hos-pitals working intensive overtime, is this extra work to be regarded as increasing the total of real National Product and, therefore, *ceteris paribus* 'raising the standard of living' or should it not better be regarded as a necessary cost of maintaining the national product, i.e. of preventing the standard of living from falling? On these arguments, Education should be treated as investment, i.e. should be included in Final Expenditure but on a 'capacity' basis only, and health services should be treated as a form of input, to be excluded from final 'product' altogether.

The paradoxes just outlined have aroused considerable contro-versy and there can be no unique solutions of them. The case for treating Education as a form of investment is particularly arguable and is less disturbing in implication because its acceptance would not exclude the item from Final Expenditure altogether but merely modify the basis of inclusion; and, as will be seen below, if all factors of production, including schoolteachers, were always paid a wage or salary approximately equal to the value of their marginal product in alternative occupations, the appropriate methods of measurement and of weighting are the same whichever of the prin-ciples lie behind the item's inclusion. The Health paradox is more serious. 'Would it be right' one side would say, 'to regard a country which produced £X millions of ordinary consumer goods and in addition spent £Y millions (in consumer goods sacrificed) on health services, as possessing no higher standard of living than a country which produced only the £X millions of consumer goods and spent nothing on health services?'. The correct reply to the (rhetorical) question is that such a comparative problem would never arise; the first country, given the same resources of total population and etc., would almost certainly be able to produce more of other goods than the second because its population, being more healthy, would be more efficient. Health, whether state organised or privately organised, goes hand in hand with economic development. But however that may be, no official statistical publication in a western capitalist country has yet appeared in which expenditure on health and other social services has been excluded from final output, although sometimes the method of measurement of *changes* in health services 'output' is such as to appear to avoid the above-mentioned 'epidemic' paradox. The author's own view, for what it is worth, is that health services should be regarded as contributing directly to the real income of the beneficiaries, but not necessarily to their welfare. The latter, it will be remembered, is to be regarded as a function of real income, and a function which may change with circumstances, such as the current prevalence of the influenza virus.† Hence the value of the health services, measured and weighted in some appropriate manner to be discussed, can properly be included in the measurement of real Total Domestic Expenditure.

As soon as we move away from the type of government services which possess at least some form of direct analogy with ordinary consumer's expenditure, into the realm of items which never have been, and never will be, privately purchased and organised, the conceptual difficulties increase *pari passu* in severity. But there is one class of item, a small proportion of the total in the contemporary U.K. but more important (relatively) in some countries, which forms a part of 'General Administration and, etc.' and which, although possessing no direct analogy with private consumer's expenditure, is not necessarily a type of activity which can only be undertaken by the government. These are services which the Blue Book, in the table which analyses government expenditure in detail, classifies as 'Agricultural Services' or 'Regulation of Industry and Trade'. When the government provides an agricultural advisory service, or organises employment exchanges, it could be argued that these are services which private industry

† Other circumstances (see fn. p. 239), on the national plane, are the aggregate man hours which it was necessary for the population to work in order to produce the real income, the proportion of dependents in the population, the climate, and so on.

could easily organise for itself, paying an appropriate fee to the professional persons undertaking the service, just as are paid to private employment agencies or to firms of industrial consultants: the cost of the service is then clearly 'input' and not net output, i.e. the service is an intermediate commodity not to be included in final product. However, it is not entirely irrelevant to note that in the absence of government intervention relatively few of the services in question are in practice produced and consumed commercially: farmers, by and large, do not employ consultants and employment exchanges were originally provided mainly to benefit the employee, rather than the employer, the idea being to create a more perfect market for labour and thus reduce the degree of monopolistic exploitation. Furthermore, it has been forcibly argued that agricultural advisory services of the state-organised type have little effect on current (i.e. this year's) agricultural output, and hence should not be treated as the current input or cost of producing that output. Rather (again) they should be conceived as a form of investment contributing to the long term growth of agricultural output in exactly the same way as, say, the schemes of land-drainage which they may help and encourage the farmer himself to carry out. The debate, at the time of writing, continues: in the U.K. the total value of the items in question is relatively small, but this might not always be the case in other countries.

Roads, Sewers, Police Forces, Fire Services, the administration of justice and the like, have rarely been privately organised, with the major exception perhaps of the roads provided by the turnpike trusts in eighteenth-century England. General government administration, almost by definition, is a public rather than a private affair, but forms a relatively small proportion of the total. Much of the expenditure on roads, sewers and the like, by permitting faster personal travel and more salubrious domestic living would seem to constitute a fairly direct contribution to personal real income, but by contrast that part of the expenditure on roads and sewers which is attributable to commercial use (even factories have drains) is as clearly a form of 'input' expenditure as any of the items so far discussed. A strict treatment would carefully distinguish between these various cases, separating out the group which are obviously inputs and therefore to be excluded from final expenditure, and treating the rest as either direct contributors to current real income or alternatively on some 'capacity' basis. However, the combined group of items amounts in the U.K. at the present time to only two and one half per cent of the total Domestic Expenditure, and is treated by the Blue Book as wholly Final. But we shall from here on regard them all (i.e. all of 'general administration, etc.') as part of the basic overheads necessary for the efficient running of the national economy and society, to be put in much the same category with the next and final item, Defence—the item which is conceptually the most thorny and, because of its magnitude on the contemporary British scene, probably the most intellectually disturbing.

Since 1950, defence expenditure in this country, as measured by the bare cost of the Armed Forces' pay, their food, clothing and housing and the cost at market prices of the armaments with which they have been provided (including atom bombs, rockets and the cost of research on same) has generally been larger and in some years substantially larger than the whole of the amount now estimated to have been devoted to *net* investment (i.e. gross investment less the estimated cost of real capital consumed) for the purpose of expanding the nation's stock of industrial and social capital.† Many people have argued that military expenditure should in no circumstances be regarded as Final Product and that together with general administration, etc., it should be treated instead (yet again) as a form of 'input'—part of the necessary cost of maintaining the national economy in a fit condition to produce the national output. Others have treated these items in a compromise fashion—as a form of final expenditure, but a special form—i.e. as 'regrettable necessities'‡ which do not contribute to welfare, but may yet perhaps be regarded as a part of real income in the manner of the extra work of doctors (see above) during an epidemic. (The 'epidemic' here would be the deplorable state of world affairs which made the ex-

† Written in January 1957: since then some reductions in defence expenditure have been announced, which should eventually permit an increase in investment.

‡ See W. B. Reddaway, 'Some Problems in the Measurement of Changes in the Real Geographical Product'. *Income and Wealth, Series I,* (Cambridge, Bowes and Bowes, 1951) p. 278.

penditure necessary.) The 'total exclusion' view is strongly held by a distinguished pioneer of real-product measurements, Prof. Kuznets of the University of Pennsylvania, and also, strangely enough, by the official statisticians in Communist countries. At the other extreme are those who hold that the decision to devote substantial economic resources to armaments is a deliberate (collective) social choice, designed to create additional collective happiness through increased sense of national security. Bizarre results are obtained whichever philosophy is followed: if Defence is treated as an input, and excluded therefore from all mention in final output, a nation which decides on re-armament programme as a necessary security against hostile neighbours will appear to display a sudden reduction in production: conversely, as we have seen, it is difficult seriously to regard armaments as a form of real income.

The importance of the controversy lies in the fact of its existence. The very ambiguity of the economic significance of expenditures on defence and general administration makes the case for some form of special treatment. In short, the only question which can validly be posed and answered is again the question relating to the productive capacity involved. We may inform ourselves, (or at least may attempt to do so) as to the sacrifice of potential consumer goods production involved in various defence and administrative expenditures and we can then draw our own conclusions from the figures according to our own views about the nature of the circumstances. However, the estimate, in real terms, of the potential sacrifice of consumer-goods production is more difficult than in the case of investment goods. The prices paid to private-enterprise armaments manufacturers for the goods they supply may reasonably be taken to indicate the value of the marginal product in alternative uses of the factors of production concerned, but the same can hardly be said of the pay and allowances of conscripts. If the 'factors', i.e. the men conscripted, were paid rates as high as they could earn in alternative occupations, (such as the production of consumer goods), conscription would not be necessary. Peacetime conscription is essentially a fiscal device, designed to save the taxpayer from the consequences of paying soldiers wages which are large enough to attract a sufficient number of volunteers.† This raises two problems, first that the 'factor-price' weight which would otherwise be applied is too low in relation to the principle here being considered and second that there is a considerable difficulty in assessing the *change* in potential consumer-goods production sacrificed in the maintenance of an army of a given size, since we do not know what change in output per man would have been displayed by the soldiers, sailors and airmen had they been employed in civilian occupations; yet without some estimate of that change we cannot estimate the change in the nation's productive capacity for consumer goods. We shall revert to these problems below.

To recapitulate. Health and education services and a proportion of other non-military government services can reasonably be regarded as forms of final output contributing directly to the current standard of living, although there are perfectly valid arguments for regarding them as contributing rather to the future standard of living and hence to be treated on a 'capacity' basis as investment. All other forms of government expenditure (except those which are clearly substitutes for industrial input) are far too ambiguous of interpretation to be treated on anything but a capacity basis, leaving the individual to draw his own conclusions at will.

What Units of Quantity?

This problem may best be defined in terms of changes. Normally we know the change in the amount of money spent, but in order to incorporate the information into any kind of a volume index we must be able to decide how much is to be regarded as change in 'quantity' and how much change in 'price'. In the case of items which are to be included on a 'capacity' principle, the problem in

† There is an interesting reversal of this proposition which bears some consideration: the conditions of life in a military organisation are so utterly different from those of industrial employment, involving as they do a major sacrifice of individual privacy and freedom, that perhaps they are sufficiently repugnant that the terms of service offered to voluntary recruits represent a distinct improvement on the man's earning power in civilian employment. If so, the weighting bias in the case of volunteers is in the opposite direction to that suggested above for the case of conscripts and, in the case of the conscripts, the two considerations vie in opposite directions, so that the bias may be smaller than at first appears.

this form does not arise, since the task there is to measure the change in quantity of consumer goods which could have been produced with the factors of production employed: we must assess the change in the potential rather than the actual quantitative output of the factors (see the end of this section). But with Health and Education, if they are not being included on the capacity principle, the problem is serious. Do we measure the change in the output of education by the change in the number of teachers employed, the number of children in school, the number of examinations passed, or of what? Do we measure the change in the output of Health by the change in the number of doctors employed (together with other medical staff in hospitals and clinics), in the number of doctors' visits (together with the number of hospital beds occupied) or in the number of illnesses cured? The difficulties illustrated in these two examples are in fact an acute version of a problem which arises generally over a significant field of private consumer expenditure as well, and also importantly in the field of intermediate production. Thus in private consumer expenditure we have to consider how to measure quantitative changes in the 'consumption' of the services of cinemas, theatres and of sporting events, of passenger travel by rail, road, and sea, of the services rendered by the Post Office, by insurance companies, by hotels, restaurants and public houses, by laundries and dry cleaning establishments, by hairdressers, by domestic servants and by the gambling industry. Among intermediate services, we must consider Goods Transport by rail, road, sea and air, Wholesale and Retail Distribution, Insurance, Banking and Finance, and a host of minor professional commercial services such as Accountancy, Advertising and Publishing. In all, final services of one kind or another (excluding housing) make up about 15 per cent of Total Domestic Expenditure, of which rather over one third is represented by Education, Health and other publicly provided social services and the rest consists of items such as we have just mentioned. And the intermediate services in question (looking at the matter from the production side) would appear to contribute slightly under 10 per cent of total Domestic Product. However, there is an important sense in which the intermediate services can be said to present a rather less serious intellectual problem than do the final services. We are only concerned to take account of the change in real output of intermediate services when we come to attempt a measurement of Real Product from the production side: and any measurement from the production side, as we shall see, must consist of an aggregate of changes in the 'real' *net* output† of industries, i.e. of changes in real gross output minus the corresponding changes in real input: but the whole of the 'output' of an intermediate good or service is by definition consumed as input in some other industry, so that if we underestimate the quantitative change in production of an intermediate commodity we shall inevitably create an error in the opposite direction in the estimate of change in net output of the industries which use the commodity as input. Therefore, unlike the case of final services, ambiguities involved in defining the unit of quantity for change in output of intermediate services cannot involve ambiguity in the estimate of change in real national product as a whole; they create instead the possibility of misattribution of the total change in net output as between industries.

As far as concerns the final services, the 'hard core' of cases lies essentially in Health, Education and miscellaneous government-provided social services. One may measure the change in output of cinemas by the change in the number of seats sold, of hairdressers by the number of heads dressed, of trains and buses by the aggregate number of passenger-miles travelled, of laundries by the quantities of garments washed, and so on. There will be difficulties and ambiguities in such cases—do overcrowded trains carrying more passengers necessarily increase real income? is the speed of the journey to be taken into consideration? should the more expensive seats in the cinema be given extra weight?—and one or two items in private expenditure, such as expenditure on gambling, in public houses and on domestic service, present peculiar difficulties. But, by and large, the difficulties with service items which are outside the hard core are no greater, for example, than the difficulties involved when there occur significant changes in the quality of privately purchased consumer goods (in contrast to services) as discussed at the end of Chapter 9.

† See Chapter 3, pp. 43–4.

With the hard core and with gambling, catering and domestic services, the central problem is to avoid falling back on indicators which either overtly or implicitly have the effect of ascribing to the factors of production involved a never-changing level of productivity.† There is a tendency to argue that since the 'output' of the services of schoolteachers and doctors is so elusive of measurement, the only course available is to assume that the output moves in proportion to the input, that is in proportion to the number of schoolteachers or doctors employed. Any improvement in the efficiency of these worthy persons, as standards of medicine and of teaching technique gradually rise over the years, is thus completely lost to the data, and a country which deliberately devotes an unusually large proportion of resources to education will, *ceteris paribus*, appear to be developing more slowly economically than a country which does the opposite. The alternative is to measure output according to number of patients visited or number of children in school. But then we come up against the 'epidemic' paradox in the case of the health services, and in the case of education against the paradox that a sharp rise in the average size of classes which is universally regarded as a symptom of decline in educational standards must, by

---

† The treatment of Gambling in the Blue Book provides an interesting example of implicit constant-productivity measure. The 'service' provided by the Gambling industry is that of transferring money from losers to winners, and 'money' should here be interpreted as purchasing power over consumer goods. Hence gross turnover deflated by a retail price index might be suggested as an indicator. However it could as well be argued that the proper indicator was the number of bets placed, since a branch of the gambling industry such as the football pools which transfers a large number of small sums between a large number of participants is probably rendering a greater service than a branch, such as the bookmakers' Ring at a large racecourse, which transfers large sums between a small number of rich participants. Certainly more labour is required by the first type of operation than the second. Be that as it may, the Blue Book at the time of writing employs a series described as 'net losses deflated by the consumer price index'. This is based on neither of the two conceptions above and in fact ascribes constant productivity to the factors employed in the gambling industry. For suppose neither the consumer price index nor the gross turnover of the industry altered, but that an improvement in clerical technique enabled the football pools to dismiss a proportion of their labour force, the productivity of the remainder having been raised. Then suppose that the pools benevolently decided to pass on the entire benefits of the improvement to the punters, through adjustment of the odds: 'net losses' would decline, indicating a *fall* in the industry's output, when consumer real income associated with gambling had if anything *increased!*

x

this method, appear as an improvement in the 'productivity' of teachers. Ideally, it seems, we should measure the output of the health services by the number of patients cured (although what of patients who die, what of preventive medicine generally?) and of the education services by the average marks obtained in examinations of given standard. The Blue Book however regards such solutions as impracticable and instead employs indicators which represent a mixture of the 'crude-input' and 'crude-output' principles: for Education the indicator is a simple unweighted average of the proportionate change in numbers of teachers employed and the proportionate change in numbers of children taught; for hospitals it is a similar average of the proportionate changes in doctors and hospital staffs employed on the one hand and of patients treated on the other. This solution has to recommend it that it will tend to reduce the extreme errors of either of the two methods mixed, but otherwise appears somewhat arbitrary. The Blue Book does, however, employ a number of separate series for primary, secondary and university education, and for different types of health-service patient, so that an increase in teachers or pupils in secondary schools, for example, is given a larger weight than a corresponding increase in primary schools. Nevertheless, we are left in the situation that if the number of teachers, doctors, pupils and patients were to remain constant, while the health and educational standards of the nation steadily improved (as would be perfectly possible) no increase in the real national product would on this account be indicated.

At a rough calculation it would appear that despite the exercise of considerable ingenuity by the official statisticians, over ten per cent of the total of Final Domestic Expenditure (other than expenditure on Defence and general administration, which is discussed below) is measured in the U.K. Blue Book by the constant-productivity type of measure or measures coming near to having that effect. In Communist countries at the time of writing, following the 'Marxist' definition of National Product—a large proportion of the items we are discussing is excluded altogether and payments to the factors of production concerned are treated as transfer income. But this appears an unduly if characteristically drastic solution: to treat the earnings of doctors and schoolteachers as similar in character to the payments received by Old Age Pensioners and the unemployed seems even less intellectually satisfying than the more adventurous, if rough and ready solutions which have just been described as typical of the practice in capitalist countries. But nevertheless, in capitalist countries, we seem to be caught in something of a dilemma. If we include the items we are in grave danger of imparting significant downward bias into our estimates of the rise in real national product, because we underestimate the average increase in national productivity. If we exclude the items we provide a distorted and unrealistic picture of economic structure and economic growth. On reflection however, we see that we must not exaggerate these points. It is not unreasonable to assume that the 'true' productivity of the service industries does in fact rise rather more slowly than the productivity of other industries, if only because many of the service trades are by nature labour intensive and offer little opportunity for mechanisation. If so, the error involved in the estimate of overall change in real national product when ten per cent of service industries are included on a constant-productivity basis may be fairly modest, although not, it must be insisted, negligible.

Finally we must consider further the precise treatment of Defence and General Administration. The 'factors of production' whose change in potential consumer-goods output we have to assess are, of course, all various forms of labour:—Generals and Treasury Knights at one end of the scale, privates and typists at the other. We know the change in their numbers, but we have to decide how their consumer-goods potential productivity might be expected to change while they are not in fact themselves engaged in consumer-goods production (neither directly in consumer goods industries nor making intermediate goods for consumer goods). To put the problem in a simplified form, suppose at a certain moment there were no employment in Defence or General Administration (a happy country?) and the whole population were engaged in manufacturing consumer or investment goods. Then suppose force of circumstances caused the government to take a certain number of people—say Z hundred thousand—into the baleful military and administrative employments, and suppose that these people happened to be a fair cross section of the working population, so that production of consumer and investment goods declined *pro rata*. We have to decide how great would be the *increase* in the production of consumer and investment goods if and when some years later the Z hundred thousand people were sent back to civilian life.

One's initial reaction is to assume as a first approximation that the *proportionate* recovery of production (assuming the total population has not changed) is the same as the original proportionate reduction, i.e. that the consumer-goods-productivity of the ex-soldiers will be found to have increased by the same proportion as those who remained in industry. But unfortunately there may be reasons for doubting that assumption. In the first place, the men will have been acquring different and inappropriate skills; in the second, the stock of capital which will have been built up in the country in the meantime will be a stock appropriate to the industrial population only (assuming that a long enough time has passed for the capital made redundant by the original debacle to have disappeared). The initial impact of the new development will therefore be the application of an enlarged industrial labour force to an inappropriately small stock of industrial capital: on this argument the losses attributable to the need for the 'regrettable necessities' would be not only the direct loss of the services of the men and women concerned, but also the loss from the retarding of economic development generally, from the retarding of the growth of the national stock of capital and skill. On the whole, we probably do not need to take this point too seriously: we may describe the process of economic development as a process of secular improvement in techniques of production—in which new ways of doing old jobs, or new jobs to substitute for old ways are perpetually sought and regularly found —each new technique nearly always involving the use of more capital relatively to labour. If the soldiers and civil servants were re-employed in industry they would be re-employed to use the prevailing techniques of production, in collaboration with whatever capital was required by those techniques: it is true that if the change were sudden and violent a little time might be required for the necessary additional capital to be accumulated and installed, but that is another matter. Therefore, the assumption that potential productivity of factors employed in defence and general administration increases at the same rate as the actual productivity of the industrially employed population as a whole can, by and large, be recommended.

It may be argued that the section of the population employed in administration and defence is not, for one reason or another, a typical cross-section in respect of productivity. This is a reasonable criticism but it appears less serious when we remember that our task is only to estimate changes: for the criticism to apply it is necessary to show that the workers concerned are atypical in the sense that the average *change* in their potential consumer-goods productivity is likely to differ from that of the working population as a whole, which is not the same thing as showing that their average absolute level of output *per capita* is likely to differ (a matter which can be taken care of in the weighting system, see below). However, there is one possibility which must indeed be watched, that is that of an atypical development in potential real-product *per capita* due to a change in the internal composition of the sector: if the proportion of civil servants to soldiers (or less likely, within the military branch itself, the proportion of Generals to Privates) changed sharply during the period of measurement, the average potential real product of the group as a whole would clearly change in some way, although the direction in which the effect would go is a question which might invite ribald controversy. If we assume that the differences in level of potential real product are roughly measured by differences in pay (i.e. that the difference between an officer's pay and a private's represents a real difference in the potential earnings in civilian life, etc.) an assumption which is clearly false in the case of conscripts *versus*, say, civil service clerks, we may roughly take account of the point by measuring the change in 'quantity' of factors of production employed in the sector as the change in the total wage, pay and salary bill, deflated by an index of change in wage, pay and salary rates. The change in the capacity of the sector, i.e. of capacity to produce consumer goods, is then to be taken as the index just defined, multiplied by an index of change in average real product per head in the rest of the economy: the Blue Book follows the first part of this procedure (in principle), but not the second. The Blue Book assumes that the productivity of soldiers and civil servants is never changing.

What Weights?

The position we have now reached is that we are looking for an estimate of the change in real Domestic Expenditure—intended to lead to an estimate of change in Real Domestic Product considered as a capacity concept—comprising the following items:

I   The change, between year 0 and year 1, in the volume of consumers' personal expenditure on current goods and services, as measured by the methods discussed in Chapter 9, adopting the best solutions as can be found for the problems of measurement of quantity for the difficult 'services' items.

II   The least biased of the possible quantitative indicators of the change in the volume of output and consumption of the collectively provided final services, in this country mainly Health and Education;

III   The change in the volume of expenditure on investment goods, employing the same type of index number as is used for I above (Laspeyres, Paasche or Fisher), with the observed market prices of investment goods as weights; this index being intended to represent the change in the capacity to produce *consumer goods* of the factors of production actually engaged in producing investment goods;

IV   An index of change in the quantity of factors of production employed in general administration, defence and all other government services (as measured by an index of wages, pay and salaries deflated by an index of wage-, pay- and salary-rates)† multiplied by an index of change in average real product *per capita* in the rest of the economy; this index being intended to represent the change in potential consumer-goods production capacity sacrificed to the demands of so-called 'regrettable necessities'.

† The reader will recognise that if the volume index is to be Laspeyres this index must be Paasche.

Our task now is to decide on the weighting system by which the above four elements should be combined: evidently, the system will largely follow logically from the principles of inclusion and measurement already developed. We can usefully conduct the discussion by first analysing the methods followed in the Blue Book (the Blue Book broadly accepts the above list of components to be combined, with the single exception already noted in the case of IV) and then considering how the Blue Book theory and practice matches up to consistency with the theory developed here. The weighting system in the Blue Book, at the time of writing, in general follows the principles of a Laspeyres volume index with 1948 as the year of base, i.e. year o is 1948. In effect, if we think in terms of the 'contracted' formula for an index number,† the Blue Book method consists in 'weighting' each series in accordance with the total value of expenditure on the item in the base year. In other words, I above is given a weight proportionate to total consumers' expenditure at market prices in 1948, II a weight proportionate to the total cost of the services concerned as indicated in the government accounts and III a weight proportionate to the market value of expenditure on investment goods while the weight for IV is based on the total cost of the Forces' Pay and Allowances, of their food, clothing and accommodation, armaments and other material plus the total wage and salary bill for civil servants and the value of rents imputed to government buildings. A moment's thought, aided if necessary by a little revision in the appendix to Chapter 8 will confirm that if the system described is expressed in terms of the 'open' formula for an index number—that is as $\Sigma P_0 Q_1 / \Sigma P_0 Q_0$—the P's or 'prices' which are effectively functioning as weights must be as follows:

for I ... the market prices of the consumer goods in 1948;

for II ... the average wage- and salary-cost, plus some element of capital and ancillary cost, per 'quantity' unit in the base year (thus where the indicator of quantity change is the number of doctors employed, the weight is the

† $\mathbf{W}c_0(q_1/_0) = \Sigma c_{i0} q_i$, where c_{i0} is the value of purchases of the ith commodity in year o, expressed as a ratio of total expenditure in that year, $\Sigma P_0 Q_0$; and q_{i0} is the ratio of quantity bought in year 1 to quantity bought in year o. We know that the formula is just another way of expressing $\Sigma P_0 Q_1 / \Sigma P_0 Q_0$, see Appendix to Chapter 8.

average annual earnings per doctor in 1948; where the
indicator is the number of children in school, the
weight is the average cost of educating each child, per
annum, in 1948);

for III ... the market prices of the investment goods in 1948;

for IV ... the market prices of armaments; pay (in cash and
kind) per soldier or per civil servant, per annum, as
the case may be, in 1948.

In short, for I and III the weighting is straightforwardly by the
selling prices of the outputs; in II it is by the *cost* per unit of output
in some cases, by the cost per unit of *input* in others; in IV the
weighting is by cost per unit of input exclusively.

The Blue Book system of weighting for I is clearly in accordance
with our principles derived from the theory of consumer preference.
The Blue Book system is also consistent with the principles appropriate to our capacity concept of real domestic product in the
application to III (investment) provided we have swallowed and
kept down the assumption that the value of the marginal product
of a unit of economic resources devoted to production of investment goods is roughly the same as the value of its marginal product
if transferred to consumer goods. The capacity concept would also
be supported by the Blue Book treatment of IV if all the people
employed by the government were paid at rates equivalent to those
they would be able to obtain in other occupations. However, we
have seen that where there is conscription the official system must
involve some underweighting at this point: fortunately the effect
is to underweight an item whose rise in volume of output is also
according to our lights understated (see above) so that the two errors
vie in opposite directions.

We have not mentioned the case of item II, Health and Education. If these services are not to be included on a capacity basis, but
treated as direct constituents of current real income (see above)
weighting by factor-of-production cost seems hardly appropriate.
On the other hand we cannot determine a system which should be
used instead by analogy from the case of ordinary consumer goods
since the essential distinguishing feature of services provided by

the government is that they very definitely do not possess any kind of market price. They are not sold to the consumer on a free market, in which given the prices asked the consumer may choose what quantities to buy; they are provided for the consumer in quantities pre-determined by the government and allocated between individuals according to social criteria of need. Consumers as a whole in effect are compelled to 'buy' these quantities (payment being made through taxation) whether at the time they want them or not: if they *wish* the quantities changed their remedy is through the ballot box, not the market. Obviously, therefore, the theory of individual consumer preference and choice such as was applied to item I cannot be applied here. But as we shall see, this by no means implies that society is unable to decide rationally how much should be spent on these items.

A Collectivist Index Number Theory

We may consider the problem more effectively by imagining a society in which all goods and services, of all kinds, were in fact collectively provided. The government might simply provide everybody with a ration book in which there was a fixed number of tickets of different types, entitling the holder to purchase given quantities of each and every consumer good that was available on the market. (We can ignore distribution questions by allowing some people, Commissars and such, legally to hold more than one book, according to government fiat.) Given the total number of books issued, the relative proportions of different tickets would have to depend on the relative productions of different commodities decided on in a central production plan: but the question is, how would the plan be determined? If we can answer that question we can define the appropriate weighting system for an index of real product in such a country, and this will lead in turn to the theory of a weighting system for collective consumptions in mixed economies.

We must assume that in our wholly collectivist country the government, whether it take the form of dictatorship, one-party oligarchy or Cabinet appointed by a democratic parliament, considers that it knows best what is good for the economy, and what is good for the consumers who form it. The government must therefore possess, either explicitly or implicitly, some form of scale of social preference as between the alternative possible patterns of production which are possible with the given resources. In effect, the government should be able to lay down what it believes to be the marginal *social* utility of increments of production and consumption of the different commodities; such social utilities or 'marks' could validly be thought of as cardinal numbers since, at least in principle, they could be communicated to the production planning Ministry as a list of such numbers. It is to be assumed that unless the government were unusually wrongheaded, the marginal social utility awarded would in general diminish with increasing postulated relative production of a commodity. Hence, given the complete schedule of utilities for successive postulated increments of each commodity, the 'best' production plan would evidently be the one which set the aggregate amount of social utility at a maximum: each hypothetical plan would be 'marked' according to the total number of social utility points which would be scored if it were successfully fulfilled; the best plan would be the plan showing the largest aggregate score in that sense. The operational determination of the best plan which is possible with given resources of labour and capital would therefore proceed as follows:

(a) If the government valued all labour equally, then the production of all commodities should be determined at the point where the marginal social utility bore the same ratio to marginal cost in required manhours (direct and indirect) as in the case of every other commodity.

(b) If the government ascribed different social marginal costs to different types of labour, (either on account of varying scarcity, or on some view about varying social disutility), substitute in (a) above 'social marginal cost of the required manhours' for 'marginal cost in required manhours'.

To put the proposition in less rarefied terms, a sensible production plan in a wholly collectivist society will be balanced so as not to push the relative production of any one commodity beyond the point at which commonsense suggests that the social cost is grossly disproportionate to the social gain.

We now have to ask how we should measure changes in *realised* 'real' national product in a hypothetical society such as described. Clearly the measure must relate to the realised change in aggregate social utility, since the most rapid growth of social utility is the society's collective objective. If the production plan were to succeed as exactly laid down, each 'target' for an individual commodity being just reached but never overreached, the measure of the realised change in real product is the original 'planned' increment of social utility itself, as computed for the purpose of deciding between this plan and alternative plans (see above). But if the plan for any reason is not exactly followed, production of some commodities falling short of target and of others perhaps exceeding same, then the under-productions and over-productions can be set against one another—in computing the 'realised' in contrast to the 'planned' increment in aggregate social utility—in accordance with the schedules of marginal social utility for the commodities concerned as originally laid down.† In other words the measure of realised real product would be drawn up exactly as a volume index for a free market economy, except that for weights, instead of market prices, we would use the specified social marginal utilities. An index so computed would represent a collective social valuation of the benefits of the production changes which had occurred, in contrast to the more usual subjective individualistic valuation; the index would represent the society's own assessment of success or failure in the realisation of its collective economic ambitions.

If we add to the foregoing the assumption that the government so arranged things that the factor rewards which individual citizens were actually paid (rewards paid in ration books, perhaps) corresponded exactly with the social valuation of each citizen's services —which means of course assuming that the government 'approves' the distribution of income which thus eventuates—and if the plan were executed in such a way that even when technical failures occurred the subsequent adjustments and redeployment of resources maintained the marginal social utility of production in-

† Actually it is not quite as simple as that since the course of events may have affected the governments' assessment of these schedules; Paasche and Laspeyres haunt collectivist economies no less than capitalist ones.

crements in every case in the same ratio to social marginal cost, and hence in the same ratio to factor rewards or earnings; if all this, then the weighting system for the index number could as well be based on unit factor costs (as is actually done for much of the collective sector in the British index) as on the actual social marginal utilities.

Self evidently, the foregoing represents an extremely rarefied model. The object essentially was to provide what might be thought of as a rationalisation of the process of decision and assessment in a country such as the Soviet Union—a rationalisation but hardly a description.† Can we, nevertheless in any way apply such ideas to the position in a 'mixed' economy, the latter being defined for the present purpose as any economy where some, but not all, of the commodities which are properly definable as constituents of *final* expenditure, are organised by the State, financed by taxation and provided to individuals in predetermined quantities largely free of charge? The answer is that *in principle* we can, but only if we are prepared to make a further and difficult assumption; that the government is able consciously to ascribe relative marginal social utilities to increments of collective sector output as a whole versus increments of private sector output as a whole. The assumption would be sufficient to provide a principle for weighting together the index numbers of the two types of output, provided only of course that we knew what the relative marginal utilities assigned by the government were. If however we wish to justify the actual Blue Book system of weighting we must further assume that the government (representing society) continues to believe that actual factor rewards currently being earned do represent social marginal costs —despite the fact that in a mixed economy the government possesses only a limited control over personal incomes—and still further we must assume that the government has consciously organised the level of production of collective services just up to the point where the actual marginal cost in terms of wages and salaries bears the same ratio to social marginal utility as is judged to be the case in the private sector.

† But some would argue that it is no more tenuous a rationalisation than the preference hypothesis on which we have based our theory of capitalist index numbers.

Most people would argue that the political and administrative processes by which a typical Parliamentary democracy determines the amounts to be spent on such things as education and health services is as different from the model just described as Earth from Mars. All one can reasonably say, perhaps, is that if collective expenditure is carried too far the electorate may indicate displeasure in the ballot box. That is assuming, of course, that the redistributive element in the taxation system does not confuse the issue beyond all possibility of resolution and that the electorate is sufficiently educated fully to appreciate the connection between government taxation and expenditure. But deep down, perhaps, in the democratic process there is a sufficient element of collective good sense that the relative quantities of economic resources devoted to collective services do bear some relation, however rough and vague, both to the community gains and to the community sacrifices involved. Needless to say the reader is not asked to accept what he has just read; he is only asked to accept the logic of what would properly be involved in a rationalisation of the present Blue Book system of weights for Education and Health. There is no alternative but to fall back on the 'capacity' principle for the inclusion of these items, in which case, as we have seen, the Blue Book system is not unreasonable. The only difficulty then, of course, is that as with General Administration and Defence, the Blue Book method of measuring change in quantity understates, although to a less extent, the change in potential consumer-goods productivity of the factors employed. However, subject to that qualification, we have now reached the position that unless we can swallow the assumptions of the theory of social choice outlined, we should regard the Blue Book's index of Real Domestic Expenditure as representing for a closed economy (1) an index of change in the volume of ordinary (i.e. non-collectively provided) consumer goods actually produced and consumed, combined with (2) an index of the change in capacity to produce (ordinary) consumer goods of the factors of production actually employed in doing other things, i.e. engaged in government general administration, defence, the health and education services or in the production of investment goods.

The Blue Book Adjusted

The official statisticians cannot be criticised for the principles they follow. Few alternatives are open to them. As officials they cannot possibly assign 'social marginal utilities' to particular services or engage in political speculation as to the relative merits of additional government expenditure versus additional private production. Nor can they be expected to estimate imaginary changes in the potential productivity of soldiers and civil servants or speculate as to how much it would be necessary to increase the rates of pay in the armed services in order to permit the abolition of conscription without reduction in the services' size.† The official presentation has indeed the merit of being clear and explicit. More subjective, if economically more meaningful interpretation can be left to the individual. A roughly worked example, intended for purposes of illustration only, follows.

Defence, General Administration, Education and the Health services (that is the whole of public authorities' current expenditure on goods and services) accounted in 1948 for about 15 per cent of Total Domestic Expenditure at current market prices. Suppose, to put the error in weighting at its highest, this figure should on our principles (i.e. the principles required for the capacity index) be raised to 20 per cent. Well over a half of the output of the sector is in fact measured in the Blue Book by constant-productivity type indicators, and much of the rest by indicators which imply productivity rising significantly more slowly than would be typical in the Market Sector: one might guess that overall the potential productivity gain of the factors in the Government Sector is understated by about one percentage point per annum; thus between 1948 and 1955 'output' instead of increasing by 27 per cent as shown, should be adjusted to increase by 40 per cent. The implications are worked out in Table 19 below, the 'adjusted' column representing the index of Total Domestic Expenditure according to the principles outlined in the preceding pages.

† But it is nevertheless worth emphasising that the contemporary method of assessing the Defence 'burden' as the ratio of actual expenditure to Gross National Product must significantly understate the real burden, the error increasing with the size of the real burden itself; hence comparisons between countries may require special interpretation.

TABLE 19. *Changes in the Components of Real Domestic Expenditure*
(Percentages of Total in 1948)

	1948		1955	
	Blue Book	Adjusted	Blue Book	Adjusted
Government Sector services	15	20	19	28
Investment	13½	13	20	19
'Ordinary' Consumer goods and services	71½	67	85	80
Total Domestic Expenditure at 1948 Prices	100	100	124	127

Note: This is a table of the type described in Chapter 5, p. 110.

Thus the effect of the adjustment is to raise the apparent rate of increase in real national expenditure by something of the order of one third of one percentage point per annum above the figure indicated by the Blue Book. This discrepancy, though small, is not insignificant, especially if viewed in relation to comparisons over longer periods of time. Nevertheless the example demonstrates that even on fairly extreme assumptions concerning the weighting and productivity biases in the Government Sector, real national product estimated on the Blue Book principles comes remarkably close to our 'guesstimate' of the result which would be obtained employing the consumer-goods-capacity principle. The difference will vary of course at different times or in different countries according to the general proportion of the national resources devoted to collective items.

From Real Domestic Expenditure to Real Domestic Product

We have now discussed problems of concept, of measurement and of weighting for the component items of an index of Real Total Domestic Expenditure, but in an open economy this is not necessarily the same thing as measuring the change in real National Product. Evidently, for the latter purpose, we should add, appropriately weighted, any change in the volume of exports and subtract any change in the volume of imports; and so long as we use the same type of basic weighting system for the volume indexes of external trade thus inserted into the calculation, as was applied to domestic expenditure, there would appear to be little conceptual difficulty: the observed market prices at which the exports are sold to foreigners and the observed prices which British business men are prepared to pay for the imports should as well represent the sacrifice of consumer-goods capacity embodied in the exports on the one hand and the corresponding gain from imports on the other, as would, for example, the market prices of investment goods in their case: if we can swallow the assumptions made in regard to investment goods, we can certainly swallow the necessary assumptions here.

But in fact it is by no means the case that all is conceptually plain sailing onwards. We are aiming at a concept of real domestic product which represents consumer-goods production capacity. We have seen that in any case such capacity depends on more than the total economic resources of the community and the average level of technical knowledge, it depends also on the pattern of relative efficiencies of the resources in relation to the community's pattern of tastes. In a closed economy, that would be the end of the matter; the actual standard of living of the community would depend solely on the factors mentioned, together with the current choice as to how much potential consumer production should be sacrificed to investment and collective expenditure. But in any open economy, which engages in the exchange of goods abroad, which may be in receipt of a substantial net income from abroad and which may on occasion borrow or lend abroad, i.e. run a deficit or surplus in overseas balance of payments on current account; in this more realistic economy there are considerable further complications.

Apart from the possibility of 'living beyond' the national real income, in the sense of running a balance-of-payments deficit, it is by no means the case that national capacity to provide real income (consumer goods or equivalent investment goods) for the citizens will exactly follow the proportionate changes in real domestic production. In the first place, for example, an unfavourable movement in the overseas terms of trade (the ratio of the average price of exports to that of imports) must obviously reduce the nation's consumption capacity without any change in domestic production whatsoever, and if the terms of trade improve, consumption capacity can increase without any increase in production. Thus, for example, in the case of the unfavourable movement, in order to keep the balance of payments constant, more exports in volume must be sent out without any compensating increase in imports. In the second place, the real purchasing value of the income from abroad may suffer changes, either of money value or from the effect of changed price levels: the effect of a reduction in 'real' income from abroad is similar to that of a change in the terms of trade; the portion of imports which is obtained 'free' (that is without the need for real payment in current exports) is reduced, so that if the balance of payments is to be maintained, more exports must be exported. We may summarise the position as follows:

Total Economic Resources,
Average Technical Efficiency,
Pattern of Technical Efficiency,

together determine

Real Domestic Product

which, modified by the Terms of Trade,

determines

Real Domestic National Income
(i.e. capacity of Domestic Product to provide consumer goods)

which, plus Real Income from Abroad (net)

gives

Real National Income

which, plus real value of the Balance of Payments Deficit

gives

Real Domestic Expenditure

Y

Since all the above are 'real' the conception can only be applied with some form of index number formula, and only of course in terms of changes. Suppose, for simplicity, we assume we wish to derive a Laspeyres' index of Domestic Product. Domestic Product is Domestic Expenditure plus exports minus imports. The change in Domestic Product at year o prices is the change in the value of Domestic Expenditure at year o prices, plus the change in exports at year o export prices, less the change in imports at year o import prices. Essentially therefore, the various stages of the progression from change in Real Domestic Product to change in Real Domestic Expenditure described in the formal presentation above amount to no more than a partitioning of the difference between the change in the volume of imports and that of exports: the change in the terms of trade, in real income from abroad and in the real value of the balance of payments are together sufficient to explain the differential movement in the volume of imports and exports completely. And fairly obviously, given the initial values of the various components of the problem, in year o at year o prices, we can obtain the complete picture in terms of changes if we can effectively partition simply the absolute difference between the quantity of exports exported in year 1, valued at year o export prices, and the quantity of imports in year 1, valued at year o import prices. Hence the algebra follows:

$\Sigma P_0 Q_1^P$ = Total Domestic Expenditure in year 1, at year o prices.

$\Sigma P_0 Q_1^P$ = Real Domestic Product in year 1, at year o prices.

$\Sigma P_0 Q_1^E$ = Exports, similarly valued.

$\Sigma P_0 Q_1^I$ = Imports, ditto.

(Also write e.g. $\Sigma P_1 Q_1^I$ for the current value of imports, i.e. year 1 imports at year 1 prices, etc.)

A_1 = Income from abroad (net) in current money value, in year 1.

B_1 = Balance-of-payments deficit in current money value, in year 1.

There are two rather obvious fundamental equations:

$$\Sigma P_0 Q_1^P - \Sigma P_0 Q_1^D = \Sigma P_0 Q_1^E - \Sigma P_0 Q_1^I \qquad (1)$$
$$\Sigma P_1 Q_1^I - \Sigma P_1 Q_1^E = A_1 + B_1 \qquad (2)$$

It should also be noted that:

$$\Sigma P_0 Q_1^E = \frac{\Sigma P_1 Q_1^E}{I_{Q_1}(P_{1/0}^E)} \tag{3.1}$$

and

$$\Sigma P_0 Q_1^I = \frac{\Sigma P_1 Q_1^I}{I_{Q_1}(P_{1/0}^I)} \tag{3.2}$$

that is that $\Sigma P_0 Q_1^E$ is equivalent to the money value of exports in year 1 at year 1 prices, divided by a Paasche index of export prices; and similarly for imports (the snag disappears, of course, if Fisher indexes are used).

By a simple re-arrangement of the above equations we obtain:

$$\Sigma P_0 Q_1^P - \Sigma P_0 Q_1^D = \Sigma P_1 Q_1^E \left(\frac{1}{I_{Q_1}(P_{1/0}^E)} - \frac{1}{I_{Q_1}(P_{1/0}^I)} \right) - \frac{A_1 + B_1}{I_{Q_1}(P_{1/0}^I)} \tag{4.1}$$

or

$$\Sigma P_0 Q_1^P - \Sigma P_0 Q_1^D = \Sigma P_1 Q_1^I \left(\frac{1}{I_{Q_1}(P_{1/0}^E)} - \frac{1}{I_{Q_1}(P_{1/0}^I)} \right) - \frac{A_1 + B_1}{I_{Q_1}(P_{1/0}^E)} \tag{4.2}$$

Either (4.1) or (4.2) (for discussion of the difference, see below) are the best formulae to employ in practical statistical application, but the following further slight re-arrangement is easier for economic interpretation:

$$(4.1) \text{ becomes} = \Sigma P_0 Q_1^E \left(1 - \frac{I_{Q_1}(P_{1/0}^E)}{I_{Q_1}(P_{1/0}^I)} \right) - \text{etc.} \tag{5.1}$$

$$(4.2) \text{ becomes} = \Sigma P_0 Q_1^I \left(\frac{I_{Q_1}(P_{1/0}^I)}{I_{Q_1}(P_{1/0}^E)} - 1 \right) - \text{etc.} \tag{5.2}$$

$I_{Q_1}(P_{1/0}^E)/I_{Q_1}(P_{1/0}^I)$ is, in effect, an index number of the terms of trade (Paasche) expressed in such a way that a rise in the index indicates a favourable movement (an arrangement which in some publications is reversed). Thus the formulae partition the difference between domestic product and expenditure—that is between imports at constant prices and exports at constant prices—into three parts, I, II and III, alternatively, as follows:

I. The percentage change since the base year in the terms of trade—defined as the proportionate decrease in the power of a given volume of exports to purchase imports—weighted in accordance with the *current volume* of exports in year 1.

II. Net overseas income deflated into real terms by the index of

TABLE 20. *Data taken from the Blue Book*

£ millions at '48 market prices

	1948	*1951*	*1955*
Total Domestic Expenditure	*11,800*	*12,900*	*14,400*
plus Exports of Goods & Services	2,000	2,700	3,000
less Imports of Goods & Services	2,200	2,700	3,000
Real Gross Domestic Product	*11,600*	*12,900*	*14,400*

Note: The figures differ from those actually published in that they have been severely rounded and also that the value of import duties which in the Blue Book are included in imports (and hence deducted from Real Product) are here for convenience omitted. The basis is the data published in the Blue Book current at the time of writing (1957).

> import prices, i.e. expressed in terms of the income's power to purchase imports.
>
> III. Balance-of-payments deficit deflated in the same way as overseas income.

or (formula 5.2)

> I. The proportionate change in the terms of trade—defined as the proportionate *increase* in the export cost of a given volume of imports—weighted in accordance with the current volume of *imports*.
>
> II. Overseas income deflated by export prices, i.e. measuring the quantity of potential export resources freed for domestic production by virtue of income from overseas.
>
> III. Balance-of-payments deficit similarly deflated.

Both methods of partitioning exhaust precisely the difference between real imports and real exports, but they will not normally yield precisely the same allocation between the different elements I, II and III, so that the partitioning is not unambiguous. Fortunately, however, in typical cases the differences are not likely to be serious; for example, the estimate of I varies between the two methods in proportion to the ratio of the value of imports to the value of exports, or $1 + \dfrac{A_1 + B_1}{\Sigma P_1 Q_1^{\mathrm{E}}}$.

For obvious financial reasons this ratio will not normally be very large, except perhaps in rapidly developing countries or in extreme circumstances such as those of the U.K. in 1951 (when the ratio reached 1·17). In the example below we shall for convenience employ formula (5.1) only.

With the aid of algebraical development we can now express the definitions of the terms introduced above more precisely:

Real Domestic Product
less I
gives
Real Domestic National Income
plus II
gives
Real National Income
plus III
gives
Real Domestic Expenditure

The index numbers in Table 21 below, (which are taken from a supplementary table in the Blue Book, 'Index Numbers of Prices and Costs'—third chapter) may be applied to the data of Table 20 on the opposite page in order to provide our example.

TABLE 21. *Price Index Numbers* (Paasche)[1]

	1948	*1951*	*1955*
Exports of Goods and Services	100	129	130
Imports of Goods and Services	100	150	136
Terms of Trade[2]	100	86	95

[1] Strictly, the series are of the 'improper' type described in the appendix to Chapter 8, p. 215.

[2] Note that this index differs from indexes commonly published in that it includes the terms of 'invisible' as well as of visible trade.

Our task is to explain such differences as the data display between the movements of exports and of imports and thus between the movements of Domestic Expenditure and Product (we shall see that the absence of differential after 1951 is economically deceptive).

If we recollect formula (5.1) for the partitioning it is easy to see that the above price-index numbers, together with the following rough figures of income from abroad and balance of payments deficit (the latter being here for convenience defined as the whole of the difference between the current money value of imports and of exports left unexplained by income from abroad) are all we need;

TABLE 22. *Income from Abroad and Balance of Payments*

£ *millions, current values*

	1948	*1951*	*1955*
Income from abroad (net) (A_1)	200	200	150
Balance of Payments Deficit (B_1)	—	400	50

Making our adjustments very roughly, rounding each figure to the nearest £25 millions (which means that the £50 millions balance-of-payments deficit in 1955 deflated by the import-price index still remains shown as £50 millions) we obtain:

TABLE 23. *Domestic Expenditure and Domestic Product at* 1948 *Market Prices*

	1948	*1951*	*1955*
(a) *in £ millions:*			
1. *Domestic Expenditure*	*11,800*	*12,900*	*14,400*
less Balance of Payments	—	275	50
2. *Real National Income*	*11,800*	*12,625*	*14,350*
less Income from Abroad	200	125	100
3. *Real Domestic National In-*			
come	*11,600*	*12,500*	*14,250*
plus Terms of Trade		400	150
4. *Real Domestic Product*	*11,600*	*12,900*	*14,400*
(b) *in index numbers:*			
1. *Domestic Expenditure*	100	109	122
2. *Real National Income*	100	107	$121\frac{1}{2}$
3. *Real Domestic Income*	100	108	123
4. *Real Domestic Product*	100	111	124

Thus the total real production of the U.K. (as measured in the official manner)† rose by about $3\frac{1}{2}$ per cent per annum in the first period but a little less—3 per cent per annum—in the second, the

† See p. 316 above.

difference in fact being largely due to the effects of an economic recession in 1952. But the Domestic Expenditure which the nation was able to enjoy, either literally in the form of consumer goods (current and prospective), or regrettably in the form of armaments showed a significantly different development. During 1950 and 1951 there occurred a sharp deterioration in the terms of trade, on account of the historic world wide inflation of raw material prices engendered by war in Korea and rumours of war elsewhere: this cost the U.K. in 1951 the equivalent of £400 millions of real product at 1948 prices, or about 3 per cent of the product itself. Therefore the index of Real Domestic National Income—the capacity of domestic production to provide real income—stood in 1951 at 108, in contrast to the real product index of 111. In addition, the same factors attrited the purchasing power of our overseas income, which latter, remaining in money terms at about the same value as in 1948, was therefore reduced in purchasing power by about one third: Real *National* Income, the total amount of real income available to the nation without borrowing from abroad, stood at an index of 107 only; the difference between the product index of 111 and the last mentioned figure representing the measure of the cost to the U.K. of the external events of the year. In the event, the Domestic Expenditure was not restrained to the necessary level, and considerably exceeded real national income; for the balance of payments could not stand the strain of such violent adjustment and there occurred a deficit of about £400 millions, with consequences for the national gold and foreign exchange reserves which are now a matter of history. This deficit however was only 'worth' about £275 millions at 1948 purchasing power because it was necessarily expended on imports bought at the inflated level of world prices.

After 1951 import prices fell back while export prices continued to creep upwards; the terms-of-trade adjustment in 1955 cost barely one per cent of the total product, so that the Real Domestic National Income and Product were both standing at much the same level. But by this time it had become necessary to commence substantial payments of interest on the North American loans which the country had received in the early post war years, so that the money value of *net* income from abroad was somewhat reduced; in addition import prices though now lower than in 1951, were nevertheless over a third higher than in 1948, and the combined effect of these two factors was to cut real income from abroad to as little as a half of the 1948 figure. Real National Income therefore was some one and a half percentage points below Real Domestic National Income. Within this reduced real income, the nation almost managed to live; the balance of payments, favoured by the easier terms of trade, being almost in balance.

The little history illustrates a general point of some interest. In the short run, when the terms of trade of a country move unfavourably, the balance of payments is for obvious reasons likely to move into deficit (so long as either adequate international reserves or adequate overseas borrowing power are available) and vice versa in the opposite event. From the point of view of our analysis of the relation between Domestic Expenditure and Domestic Product, the two movements evidently are offsetting; so that in practice divergence between movements of product and expenditure are less than might be expected from observation of the movement of the terms of trade alone: when the terms of trade are favourable, the nation lives within its income, that income being enhanced by the favourable terms of trade themselves; when the terms of trade are unfavourable, the nation lives beyond its (now somewhat eroded) income, borrowing against the hope of better times. But the point to appreciate is that the observation of a relatively close correspondence between the movements of Real Domestic Expenditure and Real National Product, as for example in the comparison of lines 1 and 4 in the table of index numbers above, may well deceive us as to the development of the nation's real situation. The latter is much more realistically indicated by the index of Real National Income; Real Expenditure may be being, and in the example certainly was being sustained by drawing down the national wealth, borrowing money which will have to be repaid, or selling liquid assets.† Thus the computation of Real National Income,

† Actually, as it happened in 1951 the greater part of the excess Domestic Expenditure was used for investment, and that investment was in the form of increasing stocks and work in progress ('Expenditure' here is perhaps a little

although beset with ambiguities which we have examined, is nevertheless as significant as the computations of Real Domestic Product and Expenditure themselves. It is not given in the Blue Book, and is not very often seen elsewhere,† because many people hold philosophical objections to the presentation of any concept of 'real' income, in contrast to real expenditure or real product. It is argued, not unreasonably, that Income is a flow of current money received by an individual or a nation, which cannot be converted into real terms until we know on what it is to be spent (and so can determine the price index to be employed for the conversion). But once the income is spent it has become Expenditure, and hence no independent concept of real income can be said validly to exist.‡ Now this argument is of some power in relation to any suggestion for, for example, 'deflating' the total of Gross National Income and Depreciation in order to obtain yet another 'real' aggregate, but it appears purist to the extent of sterility if it is carried so far as to deny the validity of the concept of Real National Income, largely estimated from the expenditure side, as presented above.

Domestic Product at Market Prices and at Factor Cost

So far we have been considering measurements of Domestic Expenditure (and Domestic Product taken from the expenditure side) weighted by market prices, that is by the selling prices of the commodities involved including any indirect taxes which they may have to bear. Implicitly therefore we have included indirect taxes even where the rationale of the weighting principle was derived from the capacity concept of measurement (some indirect taxes even fall on government expenditure). In other words, the weight-

confusing). Thus the national wealth was not so much reduced as at first would appear and it was possible in the subsequent years to some extent to live off the inventories accumulated in 1951. But the stockpiling movement was much of it speculative and uncontrolled (although some was organised by the government as a military precaution) and precious gold and dollars were expended to buy at inflated prices raw materials which could have been bought as they were needed in the subsequent years at prices substantially lower.

† But see an article by the late Arthur Adams in the *London and Cambridge Economic Bulletin* published in the *Times Review of Industry*, September, 1953.

‡ Cf. for example the ambiguity which we encountered in the deflation of income from abroad; the job can as validly be done with import prices as with export prices.

328 ECONOMIC ARITHMETIC

ing of the 'capacity' elements was not in fact strictly according to 'Factor Cost' and furthermore, by ignoring the influence of indirect taxes generally we have ignored one obvious and powerful reason tending to invalidate a fundamental assumption on which our 'capacity' concept was based, to wit that the prices employed as weights bore everywhere much the same proportion to marginal factor cost.

The problem may usefully be considered by reference back to Diagram IV (p. 288). Our concept of Gross Domestic Product as a capacity measure depended on the assumption that the slope of the price line in the diagram, as well as representing relative prices facing consumers, also roughly represented the relativity of marginal costs of production. Now suppose that apart from the distortions introduced by varying degrees of monopoly in different industries (which we ignore), we introduce the further and often very violent distortion caused by varying incidence of the taxes which are levied on the sale of particular commodities, and let us imagine such a case on the diagram. Suppose the commodity depicted on the x-axis were beer. The effect of taxation on beer sales at contemporary British rates would be that a line which would represent the actual market price of beer would slope downwards from left to right just about twice as steeply as the line actually shown, for the tax causes the price of a pint paid over the bar to be just about double the cost of production plus profit earned by brewer and publican. The equilibrium position for the consumer would therefore be a position somewhere on this distorted price line and on a lower indifference curve (the difference between the real income level of the new curve and the old representing the real income taken by the government). The capacity equilibrium would however remain as indicated. Now if capacity expands in the manner discussed in the analysis following the original introduction of the diagram (page 289) and if the rate of the tax *ad valorem*† is kept by the government constant, the *market* price line would be carried outwards bodily, *pari passu* with the capacity line, maintaining the same original angle of divergence. Two new equilibria would then exist, the one indicating the new level of

† The beer tax, as a matter of fact, is not *ad valorem* but specific.

actual consumer situation and choice, the other the new level of
hypothetical capacity, i.e. equilibrium position which the consumer would choose if he were able to consume the whole of the
maximum potential product. If the preference system of the consumer were iso-income elastic and tastes were constant, the index
number measure of the shift in capacity would be the same as that
of actual consumer real income; the government would take a constant proportion of an increased total. But if any of the assumptions
mentioned is relaxed we have to consider the possibility, for example, that the income elasticity for the heavily taxed articles was
greater than that for the lightly taxed articles, so that in face of an
advance in real income the commodities whose production and
consumption increased most were commodities whose prices
(i.e. weights) were higher in the market-price index than in the
capacity index: hence the market-price index, i.e. index of actual
real income, would show a greater rise than the capacity index, and
similarly for a change in tastes; vice versa for the opposite cases.
To generalise, we have to define a form of 'neutral' preference
system and/or a neutral set of taste-changes in a special manner if
we want to define conditions for the two indexes not to diverge;
that is, there must be no correlation, commoditywise, between
rates of tax and either income-elasticities or taste-changes. (The
argument can be extended appropriately to the case where tax rates
change during the period of measurement.)

Since taxes are often heavily concentrated on a relatively small
number of commodities—for example two fifths of the total
revenue from indirect taxes in the U.K. is accounted for by taxes
on tobacco and strong drink—we cannot necessarily rely on finding
'neutrality' in the above sense through the operation of the laws of
probability. (This point will be reverted to in a moment.) We must
therefore accept that an index based on observed market prices,
such as we have been assuming to date, may not in fact represent
an unbiased estimate of our capacity concept of change in real product. Interest therefore attaches to the possibility of a more direct
measure, i.e. an index in which market prices are adjusted to
eliminate taxes before being inserted into the weighting system.
The Blue Book in fact provides such an index and the price-weights

involved, as we have already noted, are referred to as 'factor costs'†
and this second Blue-Book index number might be regarded
as approaching our true capacity measure. However, there is a
considerable theoretical difficulty about the idea: the index so computed does not in fact represent an index of the quantities of commodities which could and would be produced and consumed if
there were no taxes, but instead is an index of the quantities which
are consumed and produced in face of the distorting influence of
taxation, although weighted with the prices at which it is conceived
they would be sold were there no taxation, i.e. at so-called factor
costs. In fact, of course, if there were no taxes commodities would
be consumed in entirely different proportions and as likely as not
sold at prices significantly higher than present market-prices-less-
tax. In other words the factor-cost index presented in the Blue
Book is, necessarily, a cross-breed and indeed could reasonably
be described as bastard. But on investigation, the relationship
between the bastard and its legitimate brother proves to be closer
than might have been expected: the two indexes are unlikely
seriously to diverge unless *ad valorem* tax rates change sharply
during the period of measurement; so long as they do not, the distortion in the consumption pattern caused by taxation can be expected to be similar in character in year 1 as in year 0 and hence as
far as the index number is concerned, the effects should cancel out.

It is interesting to note that between 1948 and 1955 the index of
Domestic Product measured from the expenditure side as given in
the Blue Book current at the time of writing rose 24 per cent at
market prices but 26 per cent at factor cost. This is not a great discrepancy over a period of such length, because unlike some other
types of bias we have discussed, this type should not be expected to
continue systematically year after year. In fact the discrepancy
mentioned was entirely due to the abnormally puritanical characteristic of the British tax system already mentioned: if the consumption and production of alcoholic drink and tobacco be entirely
eliminated from the computation (i.e. for the purposes of measuring

† It has been not unreasonably argued that since even after adjustment for
taxes these prices may contain substantial elements of monopoly profits, a better
expression would be 'factor rewards'. See Nicholson, *op. cit.*, above (in Fore-
word).

national income and product, simply treated as if they did not exist) the whole of the discrepancy vanishes and Domestic Product then appears as rising by 27 per cent according to market prices and factor cost both. It so happens that since the end of the war the British had been increasing their indulgence in tobacco and alcohol at a slower rate than that of the rise in national product generally, with the statistical consequences described. The result is rather encouraging not only for advocates of temperance but also for those who hope that neutrality—leading to relatively small divergence between the true capacity index and the observed index—would be expected from a more typical tax system. For the remaining British taxes and subsidies are by no means evenly spread over commodities in general; nevertheless, working on a relatively small number of commodities and taxes it so happened that throughout the period (including intermediate years) the cases where commodities whose consumption increased relatively to the average and whose rates of tax were above average, were always just offset by the cases of commodities where the reverse was true. It may well be that this situation in the field outside drink and tobacco is the more typical, in which case we need not in practical situations worry unduly which of the two weighting systems—market prices or factor cost— is employed. But in application to the statistics of any country where the fiscal system discriminates severely against certain specific forms of consumption, (as against those of a country, say, where most of the revenue is raised by a general sales tax), both indexes for safety should always be computed.

The foregoing arguments apply essentially to indirect taxes levied on the sales of final commodities, of which the British taxes on drink and tobacco are, as we have seen, leading examples. Where taxes are levied on intermediate commodities, for example in the case of the tax levied on petrol when sold for commercial use, or of negative taxes, i.e. subsidies, on marginal agricultural acreage, the position is more complicated. It can be argued then that the taxes properly enter into the marginal costs of employing the factors of production on which they are levied, and should not therefore be deducted in any 'capacity' calculation.† If this argument is correct,

† See Nicholson, *op. cit.*

the main problem of adjustment relates to final consumer goods, as above; investment and government goods can continue to be included at the market prices.

Measurement of the Real National Product from the Production Side

We have completed our discussion of methods of measurement of real product from the expenditure side. We shall here consider the possibility of a measurement from the production side, with the idea of obtaining an index which should in principle move identically with the index we have already derived, which means to say that *conceptually* we shall be making no changes of principle: the final result will still therefore be a 'capacity' measure, employing factor cost weights. The operation will be undertaken partly to provide a statistical check on the measure taken from the expenditure side and partly in order to illuminate the industrial origins of the changes in real product which are thus observed. An index taken from the expenditure side provides only an incomplete picture of the rôle played by individual industries in raising the nation's production, since industries which provide intermediate commodities only—vitally important nevertheless—are entirely excluded, and industries which provide both final and intermediate commodities are included only to the extent of their final production.

Looking again at Diagram II at the end of the book, we will remember that in order to construct an estimate of the National Product, in ordinary current prices, from the production side, it was necessary to take special steps to avoid double-counting of the value of intermediate output (input) as it passed through the industrial system: we found we must assess only the net output of the industries, that is the total value of their output less the cost of intermediate goods and services required from other industries in order to produce that output, i.e. the value of their current output less the value of their current input. The question is, can we obtain a *volume* measure of each industry's net output, then aggregate all such measures and thus obtain a volume measure of the change in *national* net output—that is to say of the change in Real National

Product? To put the matter in another way, we want to measure national product by measuring the output of individual industries. But part of the output of the typical industry consists of intermediate goods as well as final goods, and hence there is danger of overlapping. If we merely exclude from our measurements that part of each industry's output which is not Final, we shall not only provide a distorted picture of individual industrial contributions for the reasons already mentioned, but we shall also find that we have an index which is no more and no less than the index taken from the expenditure side, i.e. nothing new. Therefore we must approach the problem differently.

The usual approach adopted by most modern textbooks is by reference to an imaginary Input-Output table, a simplified version of the table of inter-industry relations in the Blue Book.†

TABLE 24. *Imaginary Input-Output Table, Year* o
Quantities in millions of conventional units[1]

Sales TO	Industry A	Industry B	Industry C	Final Consumption or Investment	Total Output
Sales FROM:					
Industry A	—	15	5	10	30
Industry B	5	—	10	10	25
Industry C	—	—	—	20	20

[1] Thus the figures for Industries A and B might relate to millions of tons, while those for industry C might relate to millions of, say, washing machines.

Industry A is a 'primary' industry, for example a fuel industry, producing 30 million tons of stuff per annum in year o, ten millions of which are sold to the final consumer for warming domestic hearths while the rest is divided in the ratio of 15 : 5 between the needs of Industries B and C respectively. Industry B is some intermediate industry such as Iron and Steel, requiring large amounts of fuel for the production process. Industry B sells more than half its output to other industries (5 million tons going back to Industry A for pit props) but also sells a substantial tonnage to the Final column for direct investment (rails, girders and the like). Industry C is solely a consumer-goods industry, with a total output of 20

† See p. 71 above.

million units per annum produced with the aid of 5 million tons of fuel and 10 million tons of steel. Thus the row totals indicate each industry's aggregate 'gross' output; the columns indicate the industries' various inputs but cannot at this stage be added up because their content is not homogeneous. The penultimate column indicates each industry's total Final Sales, so that it would be possible to insert a further column showing each industry's total intermediate output as the difference between Gross Output and Final Output.

Now suppose each industry sells its output at the following prices, the same to all comers, (chosen for arithmetical convenience rather than realism):

Selling Prices (£'s per conventional unit)

	Year 0	Year 1
Industry A	·8	1·0
Industry B	1·2	1·4
Industry C	1·5	1·6

The money flows, corresponding to the quantity flows depicted in Table 24 must have been, (by simple multiplication)

TABLE 25. Imaginary Input-Output Table, Year 0

£ millions, current prices

Sales TO	Industry A	Industry B	Industry C	Final	Gross Output	Input	Net Output
Sales FROM:							
Industry A	—	12	4	8	24	6	18
Industry B	6	—	12	12	30	12	18
Industry C	—	—	—	30	30	16	14
Total	6	12	16	50	84	34	50

[*Example*: The first row is obtained by multiplying each of the entries in the first row of Table 24 by ·8, the price of A, up to the Total Output entry, (·8 × 30 = 24), then carrying the column total £6 m. (i.e. the total value of the industry's inputs from all sources) into the input column and obtaining Net Output by subtraction.]

We can now with the aid of the measuring rod of money aggregate the total of the heterogeneous collection of inputs into each industry in a single figure (thus the 5 million tons of coal and 10 million tons of steel cost Industry C a total of £16 millions), which can be carried into an 'input' column and subtracted from the value of Gross Output to obtain Net Output. The Net Output column and the Input column can also each then be summed (£50 millions and £34 millions respectively) so that the table as a whole provides us with the following information about our imaginary economy in year o, (assuming for the time being that it is a closed economy):

Total Final Output (= Total Domestic Expenditure) =
Total Net Output (= Gross Domestic Product) =
£50 millions =
Total Gross Output (£84 millions) – Total Input
(£34 millions)

Total Input, clearly, is the same thing as Total Output of intermediate goods. Thus we have here the usual national accounting identities as they appear in a table of this type. Following the previous notation we will write,

$\Sigma P_0 Q_0^D$ for Total Final Output
$\Sigma P_0 Q_0^P$ for Total Net Output

(the two are in aggregate identical, but are differently composed)

$\Sigma P_0 Q_0^G$ for Total Gross Output
$\Sigma P_0 Q_0^{In}$ for Total Input

Then $\Sigma P_0 Q_0^D \equiv \Sigma P_0 Q_0^P \equiv \Sigma P_0 Q_0^G - \Sigma P_0 Q_0^{In}$ (6.0)

Thus the table brings out clearly the general point already emphasised, that an industry's contribution to final output is a very different thing from its contribution to net output, i.e. to national product. Total Final Output and Total Net Output, although identical aggregates, are quite differently industrially composed. Thus when we talked earlier of factors of production engaged in producing investment goods or non-final services as possessing a certain potential capacity for the production of consumer goods,

z

we did not need to imagine the possibility of these factors being literally transferred to industries specialising in the production of final consumer goods; they might transfer to any activity which contributes directly or indirectly to consumer-goods production. Thus factors producing steel for armaments might now produce the steel instead for private motor cars. In this light the theory of the 'consumer-goods capacity' index (of Real Product) perhaps seems more realistic.

Suppose now that the quantities produced and consumed change between year o and year 1 to the following:

TABLE 26. *Imaginary Input-Output Table, Year* 1
Quantities in conventional units

Sales TO	A	B	C	F	Total
Sales FROM:					
Industry A	—	16	5	11	32
Industry B	6	—	12	11	29
Industry C	—	—	—	25	25

The total quantity output of Industry C has increased by 25 per cent to 25 million units thus contributing to a general rise in the standard of living; but in order to achieve this the industry has required 20 per cent more steel (thereby displaying a slightly increased economy in the steel content of its output) but, owing to considerable improvements in fuel conversion efficiency, has managed to do with the same amount of fuel as before. Industry B has increased its intermediate output in response to the demands of Industry C and has also increased its final output, yielding a 16 per cent increase overall. But Industry B has also achieved fuel economies, so that it has increased its purchases from A by 7 per cent only. The rise in the standard of living has led to an increased demand (by 10 per cent) for fuel in the home, so that Industry A experienced a modest but significant increase in total demand (and output) of about 2 million tons or 7 per cent; and so on. We do not ask what has happened to the wages bill and labour force of the various industries; some of the increases will have been brought about by increased employment, some by increased labour productivity, most by both. It has merely to be assumed that for one reason or another—increased wage rates, increased employment or increased profits—the income and expenditure of factors of production (the Gross National Income and Depreciation) has risen sufficiently to purchase the Total Final Output indicated: indeed this is more than an assumption, it is an identity.

Suppose we now multiply the whole of the year 1 set of quantities by the corresponding *year* 0 prices, as follows:

TABLE 27. *Imaginary Input-Output Table, Year 1*

£ *millions, year 0 prices*

Sales TO	A	B	C	F	G	In	N
Sales FROM:							
A	—	13	4	9	26	7	19
B	7	—	$14\frac{1}{2}$	13	$34\frac{1}{2}$	13	$21\frac{1}{2}$
C	—	—	—	$37\frac{1}{2}$	$37\frac{1}{2}$	$18\frac{1}{2}$	19
Total	7	13	$18\frac{1}{2}$	$59\frac{1}{2}$	98	$38\frac{1}{2}$	$59\frac{1}{2}$

In the above system the net output of an individual industry, say the ith, that is, its contribution to Total Net Output in year 1 at year 0 prices, is:

$$P_{i0}Q_{i1} - \sum_j P_{j0}Q_{ji1}$$

In words: the industry's gross output in year 1, valued at year 0 selling prices of the industry, less the total value, at year 0 prices of the vending industries, of all the industry's inputs in year 1; P_i and Q_i representing the prices and quantities of the ith industry's gross output and Q_{ji} representing the input into the ith industry from some other industry j; P_j is the selling price of such other industry and $\sum_j$ means 'the sum over all such industries, i.e. the sum over all i's suppliers, such as j'. The aggregate Net Output of the system, in year 1 at year 0 prices, that is, Real Domestic Product in year 1 at year 0 prices, is:

$$\sum P_0 Q_1^p = \sum_i (P_{i0}Q_{i1} - \sum_j P_{j0}Q_{ji1}) = £59\frac{1}{2} \text{ millions.}$$

Now evidently, this can also be written:

$$= \sum_i P_{i0}Q_{i1} - \sum_i \sum_j P_{j0}Q_{ji}$$

in other words:

$$= \sum P_0 Q_1^G - \sum P_0 Q_1^{In} = £98 - £38\tfrac{1}{2} = £59\tfrac{1}{2} \text{ millions.}$$

(C.f. Table 27.)

Thus the system of values aggregating year 1 quantities at year 0 prices follows the same consistent set of relationships and identities as the original social accounting of the system of year 0 quantities at year 0 prices. We have laboured the argument because the results are not entirely obvious and it is often stated that there cannot exist a valid concept of the 'real' net output of an industry.† But we can now see that in the sense in which we have defined it, Real Net Output is a concept both valid and useful and paves the way to a direct measurement of changes in Real Product from the production side consisting of the aggregate of a set of changes in individual industry contributions; and these contributions genuinely reflect changes in the effective volume of work done by the factors of production in the industries concerned, changes which may be due either to changes in the quantities of factors employed or to changes in the efficiency of existing factors. But—and here is the key point —'changes in efficiency' include not only changes which affect gross output per unit of factor employed but also changes which affect the quantity of input per unit of gross output, such as for example the fuel economies depicted in the example. The difficulty is however, that for reasons originally noted in Chapter 1,‡ although there exists a wealth of statistical information about gross outputs, and also about the total production of various types of intermediate commodities, (e.g. of the total gross output of a commodity such as produced by Industry A) information about changes in the flow of these inputs into the individual industries

† What this really means is that there can be no such concept if net output is still to be considered as an identity with the income of the industry's factors of production: that particular identity certainly breaks down; the change in real net output as defined above is by no means identical, as we shall later see, with the change in the command over commodities earned by an industry's factors of production.

‡ See pp. 13–14.

tends to be considerably more sparse: in other words we know the changes in column- and row-totals of the Input-Output table, but not the changes in the intermediate entries. (The Input-Output table given in the Blue Book, although of very considerable general economic interest, is insufficiently detailed for the purpose under discussion.) This being so, it is necessary to approach the problem by approximation. Write the index number of real Domestic Expenditure in the general index number notation developed in the previous chapter, i.e. as $I_{P_0}(Q_{1/0}^D)$. Now evidently, as:

$$I_{P_0}(Q_{1/0}^D) = \Sigma P_0 Q_1^D / \Sigma P_0 Q_0^D$$

so

$$I_{P_0}(Q_{1/0}^P) = \frac{\Sigma P_0 Q_1^G - \Sigma P_0 Q_1^{In}}{\Sigma P_0 Q_0^D}$$

$$= \frac{\Sigma P_0 Q_1^G}{\Sigma P_0 Q_0^G} \cdot \frac{\Sigma P_0 Q_0^G}{\Sigma P_0 Q_0^D} - \frac{\Sigma P_0 Q_1^{In}}{\Sigma P_0 Q_0^{In}} \cdot \frac{\Sigma P_0 Q_0^{In}}{\Sigma P_0 Q_0^D}$$

$$= I_{P_0}(Q_{1/0}^G) \cdot (1 + R_0) - I_{P_0}(Q_{1/0}^{In}) \cdot R_0 \qquad (7.0)$$

where R_0 is $\Sigma P_0 Q_0^{In} / \Sigma P_0 Q_0^D$—the ratio of total intermediate output to total final output in the base year. The equation states the obvious, that the index number of Domestic Product is the index number of Gross Output (i.e. the ratio of 98/84 in the example) appropriately weighted, less an index of production of intermediate goods only, appropriately weighted. This leads to the most elementary type of approximation. For in the above equations, if $I_{P_0}(Q_{1/0}^G) = I_{P_0}(Q_{1/0}^{In})$, then $I_{P_0}(Q_{1/0}^D) = I_{P_0}(Q_{1/0}^G)$; so if the volume of intermediate production rises in exact proportion to the volume of gross production, the direct index of Domestic Product is identical with the index of Gross Output, which latter is relatively easy to compute. In Communist countries this method is followed very frequently, the distinction between gross output and net output being somewhat glossed over. And it might seem reasonable to argue that since the requirements of intermediate output are entirely derived from the requirements for final output, the two index numbers ought, by and large, to move together. However, in the not unreasonable example which we constructed, the assumption will be found to fail:

$$\mathbf{I}_{P_0}(Q_{1/0}^{\mathrm{P}}) = 59\tfrac{1}{2}/50 = 119$$
$$\mathbf{I}_{P_0}(Q_{1/0}^{\mathrm{G}}) = 98/84 = 117$$
$$\mathbf{I}_{P_0}(Q_{1/0}^{\mathrm{In}}) = 113$$

Basically, there are two distinct causes of these discrepancies. First, there is the tendency of individual industries, in the course of the years to vary the input content of their gross output, so that proportionate changes in physical input into individual industries do not necessarily exactly follow the proportionate change in output, (in the imaginary table economies in the use of fuel were the main example). Second, it may happen that those industries which increase their output most are industries which are heavy users of raw materials in the first place (i.e. their base-year ratio of value of input to output is above average), or vice versa. Such an association, if it occurs, can evidently influence the aggregative index of intermediate output, even if the input-output ratio in no single industry has altered.

If the reader is prepared to tolerate one last helping of algebra we can put the position more precisely.

$$q_i = \frac{Q_{i1}^{\mathrm{G}}}{Q_i^{\mathrm{G}}}$$

Change in gross output, expressed as a ratio.

$$d_i = q_i - \frac{\sum\limits_j P_{j0} Q_{ji1}}{\sum\limits_j P_{j0} Q_{ji0}}$$

The difference between the proportionate change in the gross output volume of industry i, and the proportionate change in the volume of its various non-labour inputs, the latter expressed as an index with year 0 input-prices as weights.

$$r_{i0} = \frac{\sum\limits_j P_{i0} Q_{ji0}}{P_{i0} Q_{i0}}$$

The ratio, in industry i, of the value of input to the value of gross output, in the base-year.

$$v_{i0} = \frac{\sum\limits_j P_{i0} Q_{ji0}}{\sum P_0 Q_0^{\mathrm{In}}}$$

The proportion of total national intermediate production in the base-year which was accounted for by input into industry i.

$$n_{i0} = \frac{P_{i0}Q_{i0} - \sum_j P_{i0}Q_{ji0}}{\sum P_0 Q_0^N}$$

The top line is the base-year net output of industry i, therefore n_{i0} represents the relative net output of the industry, i.e. its net output as a proportion of national net output (national product).

$$R_0 = \sum P_0 Q_0^{IN} / \sum P_0 Q_0^D$$

As already defined.

It will be seen that d_i measures the extent to which the industry has achieved economies in the use of inputs during the period of measurement. Thus in the example, Industry C achieved economies both in the use of coal and in the use of steel; d_i in effect is a weighted average of such economies.

Then it can be shewn that:

$$\mathbf{I}_{P_0}(Q^P_{1/0}) = \mathbf{I}_{P_0}(Q^G_{1/0}) - \text{cov}_{rq}.(1 + R_0) + \mathbf{W}_{v_0}(d).R_0 \qquad (9.0)$$

Equation (9.0) states that the difference between an index of national Net Output and the crude index based on changes in the gross outputs of the individual industries is made up in part of a weighted average of the d's, (in other words a measure of the extent to which industry in general has achieved economies in the use of inputs), and in part of the covariance of the gross output changes with the r's, which latter characterise the extent to which individual industries depend on inputs for the manufacture of output. Such co-variance may easily arise in the normal course of economic development: thus for example in Communist countries, the output of 'heavy' industries, which are substantial users of raw materials, usually runs ahead of that of 'light' industry where the most important input is labour. The effect could be to produce upward bias in the Gross Output index in relation to the correct index of national product.

In capitalist countries the point is usually taken care of by what amounts to a re-arrangement of equation (9.0). For it can be shown that we may alternatively write:

$$\mathbf{I}_{P_0}(Q^P_{1/0}) = \mathbf{W}_{n_0}(q) + \mathbf{W}_{v_0}(d).R_0 \qquad (9.1)$$

where $\mathbf{W}_{n_0}(q) = \sum n_{i0} q_i = \dfrac{\sum P_{i0}^n Q_{i1}}{\sum P_{i0}^n Q_{i0}} = \mathbf{I}_{P_0^n}(Q_{1/0})$

$\mathbf{W}_{n_0}(q)$ is an index number in which the changes in the gross outputs are weighted according to the base-year values of *net outputs*, (in the language of the contracted formula for an index number) that is to say an index of the Gross Output quantities weighted by base-year *net prices* in the language of the open formula. The net price of a commodity is that part of the price which is available for rewarding factors of production in the industry making it; it is the actual selling price per unit less the cost of raw materials and other non-labour inputs purchased from other industries, per unit.† Thus equation (9.1) states that an index of Gross Output quantities weighted in this way eliminates the possibility of error on account of cov_{rq}; the only error remaining is therefore that due to $\mathbf{W}_{v_0}(d)$. In the example, $\mathbf{I}_{n_0}(q)$ works out at 115·5, whereas it will be remembered that $\mathbf{I}_{P0}(Q^p_{1/0})$ was 119. Since R_0 was 68 per cent, the two results together imply that $\mathbf{W}(d)$ was 5 per cent, and that the value of cov_{rq} was ·009. This value of cov_{rq} is not unrealistic and is attributable mainly to the fact that industry C, which possessed a high initial input/output ratio, displayed a very much above average increase in gross output. The example value of $\mathbf{W}(d)$ on the other hand is unrealistically large, since in practice unless the period of measurement is a long one, economies in the use of non-labour inputs of such magnitude are unusual.

The Blue Book employs the method of equation (9.1)‡§ largely ignoring the influence of $\mathbf{W}(d)$, with the single exception in the case of Agriculture where the necessary information happens to be available and where it is known that changes in net output are as often the result of changes in input (mainly feedingstuffs and fertilisers) as of changes in gross output itself.‖ Curiously enough the Blue Book index of Domestic Product taken from the production side by

† Also less any indirect taxes levied on the commodity, per unit.

‡ A full account of the series employed will be found in 'Sources and Methods' *op. cit.* (p. 29 above). It should be noted that one effect of the use of this method is to qualify what was said on pages 301–2 about the significance of errors in the estimates of changes in the outputs of intermediate industries.

§ The official monthly Index of Industrial Production, published in the *Monthly Digest*, also, of course, follows this principle.

‖ The large increase in the net output of British Agriculture during World War II mainly represented the effect of a substantial reduction in feedingstuffs imports while gross output was sustained by increased arable production and the effects of a vigorous policy of grassland improvement.

this method shows a tendency to increase if anything slightly faster than the index taken from the expenditure side, a fact which would strictly imply a negative value to $\mathbf{W}(d)$. A more likely explanation is that $\mathbf{W}(d)$ is in any case fairly small and that the discrepancy between the two indexes is due to minor statistical errors of a more practical origin: indeed, given the methods employed, the closeness with which the two index numbers follow one another is rather surprising.

Real Net Output, Real Income of Factors of Production and the Terms of Trade

As we have already indicated, the concept of real Net Output which we have been using in the previous section is not identical with the real income of the factors of production employed in the industry in question. The change in the purchasing power of factors of production in an industry depends not only on what happens to the industry's net output as it has been defined, but also on what happens to the relative prices of the industry's products *vis a vis* those of goods in general, and also on the relative movements of the industry's *input prices* relatively to its output prices. Suppose the industry's selling prices have remained constant, and also the prices of final goods in general, but suppose that some readjustment of relative prices within the economy has meant that nevertheless there has been an increase in the average prices which the industry pays for its raw materials and components. Unless the industry has increased the volume of its real net output as defined above, the factors of production must have experienced a decline in their real income; the decline will be greater the greater the rise in input prices and the greater the proportion of the value of input to gross output in the base year (i.e. the greater r_{i0}). In other words the industry has experienced a deterioration in its 'terms of trade' *vis a vis* other industries in the economy.

This point may be generalised to show how in an open economy, the measurement of Domestic Product from the production side may be converted into a measurement of Real Domestic National Income. For what applies to one industry also applies to a group.

The change in the real income of a group of industries depends on the change in their real net output, increased by the effect of any rise in the prices of goods they sell to industries outside the group, diminished by any rise in the prices they pay for inputs from industries outside the group. (Real income is purchasing power over final goods.) Thus in the example we might imagine that Industry *A* was entirely located in an overseas colony of the country in question, and that this colony then became politically and economically independent so that transactions with Industry *A* now counted as foreign trade. Then the change in the real income of factors employed in Industries *A* and *B* (that is the real income of the population of the metropolitan territory) will now depend not only on the change in these industries' real Net Output, but also on the change in the terms of trade with Industry *C*, i.e. with the ex-colony. The quantitative effect of the adjustment of course, will in principle be exactly the same as the adjustment to Domestic Product measured from the expenditure side described in a previous section.†

† Page 320 et seq.

INDEX

PRINTED IN GREAT BRITAIN BY ROBERT MACLEHOSE AND CO. LTD
THE UNIVERSITY PRESS, GLASGOW